Fourteenth Edition

McKeachie's Teaching Tips

Strategies, Research, and Theory for College and University Teachers

Marilla D. Svinicki & Wilbert J. McKeachie

with chapters by

David Nicol

Barbara Hofer

Richard M. Suinn

Peter Elbow and Mary Deane Sorcinelli

Erping Zhu and Matthew Kaplan

Brian Coppola

Claire Ellen Weinstein

Jane Halonen

Australia • Brazil • Japan • Korea • Mexico • Singapore • Spain • United Kingdom • United States

McKeachie's Teaching Tips: Strategies, Research, and Theory for College and University Teachers,
Fourteenth Edition
Marilla D. Svinicki, Wilbert J. Mckeachie

Editor-in-Chief: Linda Ganster

Executive Editor: Mark Kerr

Developmental Editor: Joshua Taylor

Freelance Project Manager: Marlene Veach

Media Editor: Renee Schaaf

Executive Brand Manager: Melissa Larmon

Senior Market Development Manager: Kara Kindstrom

Manufacturing Planner: Doug Bertke

Rights Acquisitions Specialist: Roberta Broyer

Art and Cover Direction, Design, Production Services, and Composition: PreMediaGlobal

Library of Congress Control Number: 2012945451

ISBN-13: 978-1-133-93679-4

ISBN-10: 1-133-93679-2

Wadsworth
20 Davis Drive
Belmont, CA 94002
USA

Cengage Learning is a leading provider of customized learning solutions with office locations around the globe, including Singapore, the United Kingdom, Australia, Mexico, Brazil, and Japan. Locate your local office at **www.cengage.com/global.**

Cengage Learning products are represented in Canada by Nelson Education, Ltd.

To learn more about Wadsworth, visit **www.cengage.com/wadsworth**

Purchase any of our products at your local college store or at our preferred online store **www.cengagebrain.com**

Printed in the United States of America
5 6 7   19 18 17

We dedicate this edition to all the teachers all over the world who are working to move college teaching and learning toward a collaborative process between teacher and student. We applaud your efforts and thank you on behalf of your students.

CONTENTS

PREFACE

TEACHING TIPS was originally written to answer the questions posed by new college teachers, to place them at ease in their jobs, and to get them started effectively in the classroom. It also has proven useful to experienced instructors, to teachers in community colleges, to distance educators, adult educators, adjunct faculty, and faculty members in many other countries.

The organization of the book begins with the issues involved in getting started, then moves on to the basic skills needed by all teachers—getting student participation, lecturing, assessing learning, and assigning grades (Parts 1 and 2). Equally important are awareness of, respect for, and ability to adapt to differences among students (Part 3). Parts 4 and 5 deal with additional skills and strategies important for other aspects of teaching. In Part 6 we discuss goals of education going beyond simple memorization of facts, concepts, and theories, and Part 7 points toward your continued development as a teacher.

Effective teaching demands more than the acquisition of skills. To adapt to the educational needs of a particular class at a particular time, the teacher needs to understand the underlying theory of learning and teaching so that each teacher can develop his or her own methods. Thus, the "teaching tips" are supported by discussion of relevant research and theory. Skill in teaching is not something to be learned and simply repeated; what makes it exciting is that there is always room to grow. As you reflect on your classes, you will get new insights and will continue to develop your own theory of teaching and learning. Today, teaching has been recognized as an area of scholarship in itself.

Teaching as Scholarship

In 1990, Ernest Boyer's book *Scholarship Reconsidered* stimulated discussion throughout higher education about the nature of scholarship. In most American universities scholarship has been evaluated in terms of published research. Boyer suggested that teachers who keep up with current developments, who devise and assess better ways to help students learn, or who do research on methods of teaching are also scholars.

As a result of the debates about Boyer's proposal, there is increasing acceptance of the idea that good teaching involves much scholarly activity.

Most faculty choose the balance between teaching and research that suits their own talents and interests with an informed awareness of the likelihood of support by their institution. Although time is not infinitely elastic, most of us find that a 50- to 60-hour work week is satisfying because we enjoy both teaching and research.

Whatever your chosen balance, it is likely that teaching will always be a part of your role. Whenever you work with students, in a class or in a research lab, you are teaching. *Teaching skillfully may be less time consuming than teaching badly*. Teaching well is more fun than teaching poorly. Moreover, you will be better able to focus on your research if you are not worrying about teaching. Thus, some investment of time and attention to developing skill in teaching is likely to have substantial payoff in self-satisfaction and effectiveness in your career.

One of the best aspects of teaching is that we, too, are learners. Each time we teach, we not only learn more about the subject matter, but are also learning more about teaching.

NEW TO THIS EDITION

For this edition, I (Marilla Svinicki) have been serving as the main editor with Bill as my guide and model. Throughout the text I vary between saying "we" and "I" because Bill and I are so similar in our perspectives on learning and teaching that it was impossible to separate us. Nevertheless, I've attempted to stay true to Bill's original vision of the book in its mix of practice and theory. I hope this meets with your approval. If you find something I've taken out that you think is crucial, or if I've missed some new developments that are important to the field, please let me know at msvinicki@austin.utexas.edu. *Teaching Tips* will never stop changing with the times and I count on you, the readers, to keep Bill and me on our toes!

In this edition, I've listened to our wonderful reviewers and expanded the treatment of teaching thinking with a much longer discussion from Jane Halonen. In addition, they asked for more about reading as active learning, so I've added quite a bit to that chapter, elaborating on how teachers can help their students be better active readers. Our reviewers also asked for some information about the new generation of students called "Millennials" because they seem to have some unique abilities and qualities that we need to consider, so I've added that perspective to the chapter on student problems. As always, I've added new research and practice, for the use of technology, for ways of thinking about discussion and lecture, and I've tried to reflect changes in some of the forces that are influencing our world of higher education, such as the push for accountability for student outcomes. Of course, I've had to take out some things to make room for the new, but I think we've hit a good balance because our reviewers also said they like the book as it is. My thanks to them and to you for your continued use of *Teaching Tips*.

On behalf of Bill McKeachie and everyone who works to make this a good text for teachers, thank you and good journey!

MARILLA SVINICKI

ACKNOWLEDGMENTS

Our thanks to all the reviewers, who will see evidence of the impact of their comments:

Ngoc Bui, *University of La Verne*
Lorinda Coan, *Indiana University School of Dentistry*
Joan Glacken, *Florida Gulf Coast University*
Christine Martin, *Renton Technical College*
Laura Mayhall, *The Catholic University of America*
Jessica McCall, *The University of North Carolina, Greensboro*
Chandra Mehrotra, *The College of Saint Scholastica*
Steve Price, *Mississippi College*
Stephanie Riger, *University of Illinois, Chicago*
Richard Shingles, *Johns Hopkins University*

ABOUT THE AUTHORS

Marilla Svinicki is a professor in the Department of Educational Psychology and Chair of Human Development, Culture, and Learning Sciences at the University of Texas at Austin. She served for 30 years in the Center for Teaching Effectiveness at UT. She earned both her BA and MA at Western Michigan University and her PhD at the University of Colorado. Her research interests include application of principles of learning to instruction in higher education and development of faculty and graduate students as teachers. She regularly teaches courses in the psychology of human learning, instructional psychology, and the preparation and psychology of teachers. She was the editor of *New Directions for Teaching and Learning*, an influential journal on instructional issues for faculty, for 20 years. Her proudest accomplishments were receiving the Wilbert J. McKeachie Career Achievement Award from the American Educational Research Association and being asked to edit this book.

Wilbert J. McKeachie is professor Emeritus of Psychology and former Director of the Center for Research on Learning and Teaching at the University of Michigan, where he has spent his entire professional career since taking his doctorate in 1949. His primary activities have been college teaching, research on college teaching, and training college teachers. He is a past president of the American Psychological Association; the American Association of Higher Education; the American Psychological Foundation; the Division of Educational, Instructional, and School Psychology of the International Association of Applied Psychology; and the Center for Social Gerontology. He is also a past chairman of the Committee on Teaching, Research, and Publication of the American Association of University Professors, and of Division J (Psychology) of the American Association for the Advancement of Science. He has been a member of the National Institute of Mental Health Council, the Veteran's Association Special Medical Advisory Group, and various other government advisory committees on mental health, behavioral and biological research, and graduate training. Among other honors, he has received eight honorary degrees and the American Psychological Foundation Gold Medal for Lifetime Contributions to Psychology.

Part 1

Getting Started

Chapter 1

Introduction

The first few years of teaching are all-important. Experiences during this period can either blight a promising teaching career or start one on a path of continued growth and development.

Most of us go into our first classes as teachers with a good deal of fear and trembling. We don't want to appear to be fools, and so we have prepared well, but we dread the embarrassment of not being able to answer students' questions. We want to be liked and respected by our students, and yet we know that we have to achieve liking and respect in a new role that carries expectations, such as evaluation, that make our relationship with students edgy and uneasy. We want to get through the first class with éclat, but we don't know how much material we can cover in a class period.

In most cases, anxiety passes as one finds that students do respond positively, that one does have some expertise in the subject, and that class periods can be exciting. But for some teachers the first days are not happy experiences. What makes the difference in these first few days?

It's probably not the subject matter. More often than not, the key to a good start is not the choice of interesting content (important as that may be) but rather the ability to manage the activities of the class effectively—simple teaching techniques get the students involved so that they can get to work and learn.

The new teacher who has techniques for breaking the ice, for encouraging class participation, and for getting the course organized is more likely to get off to a good start. Once you find that teaching can be fun, you will enjoy devoting time to it, you will think about it, and you will develop into a competent teacher.

When you are just starting, discussions of philosophy of education and theories of learning and teaching are probably not as important as learning enough simple skills to get through the first few weeks without great stress and with some satisfaction. Once some comfort has been achieved, you can think more deeply about the larger issues discussed in later chapters, and you can have more fun, too.

THE COLLEGE OR UNIVERSITY CULTURE

A course cannot be divorced from the total college or university culture.

First of all, the institution makes certain requirements of instructors. In most institutions, you must submit grades for the students' work. You probably must give a final course examination. A specific time and room are assigned to the class, so that it meets at regularly scheduled periods in the same place.

There are, however, areas not covered by the formal rules or routine practices of the college, and it is within these areas that instructors must tread lightly. For example, in most college cultures, instructors who become intimately involved with their students are overstepping the bounds of propriety. Certain limits on class discussion of religion, sex, or politics may exist. Instructors must learn not only to operate within the fences of college regulations but also to skirt the pitfalls of the college mores. In addition, each department or discipline has its own culture with customs related to teaching methods, testing, standards, and styles of communication and instruction.

Each reader will need to adapt our suggestions to the college culture of which he or she is a part. In a new teaching position, talk to other faculty members about their perceptions of the students, about how these instructors teach and perceive others as teaching. Ask for examples of syllabi, tests, and other course materials.

In many institutions, students have had experience in previous classes with instructors who, in a more or less parental way, gave information and rewarded those students who could best give it back. The type of tests, frequency of tests, and methods of grading also have conformed closely to certain norms. As a result, instructors who attempt to teach with new methods may find they are frustrating the expectations their students have developed in the culture of the college. So, if you are trying something new, be sure that students understand why the new method is likely to be valuable.

Although there are many norms and folkways that characterize an entire campus, you need to recognize that there are many subcultures. Some of them are subcultures of faculty in different disciplines, but it is important to recognize that there are student subcultures that have their own norms and expectations. And within the student cultures there are important individual differences among students. Taking account of the diversity of students is so important in teaching that "Understanding Students" is a separate part (part 3) of this book.

IN CONCLUSION

Because the suggestions we make throughout this book are based not only on successful practices but also on our own philosophies of teaching, you should be forewarned of our biases or hypotheses, listed below.

1. What is important is learning, not teaching.

2. Teachers can occasionally be wrong. If they are wrong too often, they should not be teaching. If they are never wrong, they belong in heaven, not a college classroom.

3. Classes are as unique as the students in them, so they can be unpredictable.

4. An important goal of college and university teaching is that of increasing the student's motivation and ability to *continue* learning after leaving college.

5. Most student learning occurs outside the classroom. This is both humbling and reassuring for the beginning teacher.

6. Students can learn more in talking to one another than in listening to us, if we prepare them for such interaction.

7. One key to improvement is reflection—thinking about what you want to accomplish, and what you and the students need to do to achieve these goals.

This book will not make you a "great teacher." It may be that great teachers are born and not made, but anyone with the ability to get a job as a college teacher can be a *good* teacher. Every teacher is a work in progress, no matter how long they've been at it. At the end of the chapter, "Vitality and Growth Throughout Your Teaching Career," we've compiled an array of resources to help you continue toward your goal. It will never be boring.

Chapter 2

Countdown for Course Preparation[1]

For teachers, courses do not start on the first day of classes. Rather, a course begins long before you meet your students. The components of course planning, are shown in Figure 2.1, but you can see that they don't follow an orderly, linear pattern. Instead, all of the pieces are interconnected to student learning, so you move back and forth as you progress. The main idea is to get started!

TIME: THREE MONTHS BEFORE THE FIRST CLASS

Identify the Student Learning Goals, or Outcomes

The first step in preparing for a course is working out the student learning goals as expressed by the course objectives, because all the other decisions involved in course planning should derive from those objectives. What do you want your students to be able to do as a result of their learning in the course? What outcomes do you expect them to achieve? What goals might the students themselves have? What does the department expect of them as well? At this point, your list of goals or objectives should only be used as a rough reminder to be revised as you develop other aspects of the course plan, and further revised in interaction with

[1] This chapter incorporates material from Graham Gibbs's chapter in the tenth edition, "Planning Your Students' Learning Activities."

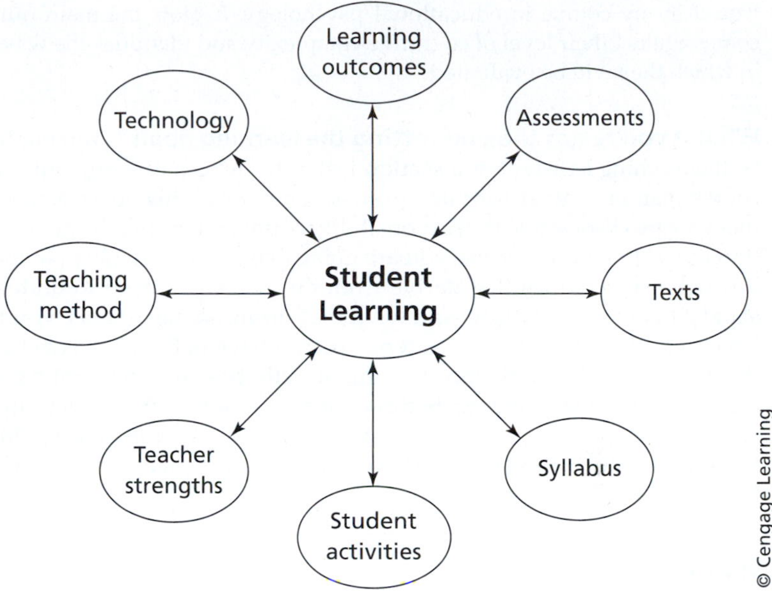

FIGURE 2.1 Components of Course Design

students. Writing out your goals now helps clarify and direct your thinking about the other components of the course plan.

Because they describe learning outcomes, your course objectives have the great advantage of pointing clearly to what you can look for as evidence that the objective has been achieved. Your students will see your methods of assessing their achievement of the objectives as the most important operational definition of your goals; hence, goals and testing are inseparable teaching tasks. This does not mean that all of your goals should be assessed and count toward a grade. Some of your goals will involve motivational, attitudinal, and value outcomes, as discussed in the chapters "Motivation in the College Classroom," "Teaching Students How to Become More Strategic and Self-Regulated Learners," and "The Ethics of Teaching and the Teaching of Ethics." Despite the importance of goals related to motivation and attitude, most course grades are based only on cognitive and skill outcomes.

The goals you select eventually determine a lot of what you do in the course, especially in terms of assessment choices. Blumberg, P. (2009), illustrates how creating a chart of objectives and course content helps you see how to tie together these two important decision variables and add the assessment type as well. Figure 2.2 shows an example of a chart

I used in my course in educational psychology. It plots the main outcomes against their level of cognitive complexity and identifies the ways in which they will be evaluated.

What if you're not the one setting the learning goals? You might be the teaching assistant or a section instructor who is carrying out the course plan of a supervisor or a course committee. This doesn't mean that you are absolved of the responsibility of understanding the goals of the course. Precisely because you are going to be deeply involved in the instructional activities that derive from the goals, you need to understand where they came from and what they mean. Sooner or later, you'll have to explain them to the students, so you have to be well-versed in them and how they influence the course activities. You may not have access to all the learning goals three months in advance (the way the course developer has), but as soon as you can, ask for a conference with the instructor to help you get control over the entire plan and how you fit into it.

What Goals?

This answer obviously depends on the course and discipline, but it is important to note that the overall course objectives involve *educating students*; the objective of a course is not just to cover a certain set of topics, but rather *to facilitate student learning and thinking in general*. Ordinarily we are concerned not simply with learning a set of facts, but rather with learning that can be applied and used in situations outside course assignments. In fact, *in most courses we are concerned about helping our students in a lifelong learning process; we want them to develop interest in further learning and have a base of concepts and skills that will facilitate further learning, thinking, and appreciation*. Thus, in framing your goals, think about what will be meaningful to your students both now and in the future.

In thinking about your goals, remember that each course contributes to other general goals of a university education that transcend specific subject matter, such as critical thinking, being willing to explore ideas contrary to one's own beliefs, knowing when information or data are relevant to an issue and how to find that information, and developing skills for learning and self-regulation. (See the chapters "Teaching Students How to Become More Strategic and Self-Regulated Learners" and "Teaching Thinking.")

Another source of goals that most, if not all, institutions are paying close attention to is the accrediting society that evaluates them on a periodic basis. For professional schools, there are additional evaluations

Learning Outcomes	Understanding of theory basics	Recognize examples of theories in real life	Use theories in designing instruction	Choose instructional design appropriate for situation
Knowledge	X (exams)			
Comprehension	X (exams and in-class activities)	X (exams and in-class activities)		
Application			X (in-class design activities)	
Analysis				X (case analysis)
Synthesis			X (design project)	
Evaluation				X (case critique)

FIGURE 2.2 A Planning Chart for Use in Setting Up a Course

to make sure that a department or college is meeting the professional standards. Even if you feel far removed from the connection of your department to these external goals, it is a great help to see if you can align the goals of your course to the goals of the external reviewers. In reality, those bodies have very good people working on strong learning outcomes that fit the purpose of the institutions or disciplines they serve. For example, the move to more active learning strategies, student-centered design, and clearer objectives was championed by most of the regional and disciplinary accrediting units long before those practices became standard. In fact I would say that the progress we've made came in no small part from those groups holding the institutions' collective feet to the fire. So while it may seem like unnecessary detail work, it is valuable to see if your class outcomes can be used to support those larger institutional goals.

In addition to this general perspective, you need to keep in mind characteristics of the setting in which you teach. What is the role of this course in the curriculum? Are other instructors depending on this course to provide specific kinds of background knowledge or skill? What are your students like? How do they differ? (See part 3 of this book, "Understanding Students.") What are their current concerns? Self-discovery?

Level of Objective in Bloom's Taxonomy	Example (These are stated fairly generically, so the instructor should adapt them to the specific course ideas and language.)
Knowledge	Students will be able to match key terms to the appropriate definition.
Comprehension	Students will be able to define key terms in their own words.
Application	Students will be able to recognize and use concepts and procedures correctly in new situations appropriate to the discipline.
Analysis	Students will be able to break larger issues and/or problems in the course into their component parts to facilitate problem solving and deeper understanding.
Synthesis	Students will be able to combine concepts and procedures from the course in new ways to solve problems or create new ways of seeing the course content.
Evaluation	Students will be able to compare data in ways that will allow them to choose among the data to solve problems or accomplish goals.

TABLE 2.1 Sample Objectives at Different Levels

Social action? Getting a job? How can their goals be integrated with other goals of the course?

Learning goals can be pitched at several different depths of complexity depending on the level of the course. I've provided some examples in Table 2.1.

The most well-known description of different depths is the *Taxonomy of Educational Objectives, Handbook I: Cognitive Domain* (Bloom, 1956). Although this was crafted in the 1950s, it has retained its usefulness. A significant revision by Anderson and Krathwohl (2001), which added a second dimension separating the types of knowledge being learned, made it even better. These taxonomies are widely used for course planning as well as assessment standards, so it's good to think about where your course goals fall or even to build your course around them. Another good goal framework is the SOLO (Structure of the Observed Learning Outcomes) taxonomy (see Biggs, 1999). A recent expansion of these taxonomies was provided by Fink (2003), which he characterizes as "significant learning experiences." Fink's expansion includes three of Bloom's lists, and adds three dealing more with motivation, self-understanding, and learning how to learn, along with suggestions about how to achieve them. The book by Wiggins and McTighe (2001) listed at the end of this chapter is a practical guide to creating key learning objectives regardless of content.

Having explained the importance of starting with clear goals, it's okay if you started on your syllabus with only vague notions about goals. Although it seems logical to start with goals, in reality, content, teaching methods, and the nature of the students all interact in dynamic ways. So if you find it easier to start by outlining the content of the course, do so. Ideally you would then tie the content to goals. But many effective teachers never state their goals very explicitly, yet their students achieve the kinds of motivational and cognitive outcomes that we all desire.

Order Textbooks, Lab Supplies, or Other Resources Students May Need

Should You Use a Textbook? You can skip this section if your department has already chosen the textbook, although it won't hurt to think about these issues anyway. With paperback books, reprint series, photocopiers, and the World Wide Web, young instructors are immediately beguiled by the thought that they can do a much better job of compiling a set of required readings than any previous author or editor. "Coursepacks"—compilations of relevant articles and book chapters—may be used in place of a textbook or as supplementary reading.

There is much to be said for such a procedure. It provides flexibility, a variety of points of view, and an opportunity to maintain maximum interest. It's particularly useful if you are teaching a more advanced course that's based on recent topics that might not be out in textbooks yet. Moreover, since no single text covers every topic equally well, the use of a variety of sources enables the teacher to provide a more well-rounded collection of the information, offering the best material, ranging from theoretical papers and research reports to applications. Some publishers offer to help you customize their textbooks for your course.

The disadvantages of not using a textbook are apparent. Without a textbook the task of integration may be so overwhelming for students that great pressure is placed on instructors to provide integration. This may limit your freedom to use the class period for active learning. With a well-chosen textbook, you want to rely on the students to obtain the basic content and structure of the subject matter through reading. However, recent research on how students use textbooks (Berry, et al., 2011) indicates that students are less and less likely to read the textbook (see the chapter "Reading as Active Learning" in this book for ideas about how to affect this) or even buy it; the former because they're not clear on how it supports their learning, and the latter because textbooks are so expensive. It might also be possible for students to access sufficient information about basic topics on the Internet. I recently allowed a class of advanced students to tap the vast resources of our online library to get the basics about theories, rather than requiring them all to read the same textbook. There are only so many ways to describe the major theories in the field and they are all covered very adequately in the various discipline-based encyclopedias. In fact, researching and comparing different approaches to a theory is a good learning task. That activity represents one of the skills a professional needs anyway—to find and assess general information on a topic. After understanding the basics of a topic, everyone read the more advanced research articles that were the true texts of the course. It worked well, and those students who felt the need for a real text had several recommended texts to choose from those listed in the syllabus. Not everyone learns the same way, and having choices about the way you receive information is a great help to students. However, this probably would not be the most effective method in a lower division undergraduate course.

Choosing a Textbook or Other Reading Materials[2] In choosing reading materials, the most important thing is that they fit your objectives. One of the most annoying and confusing practices for students is instructor disagreement with the textbook. So if you use a textbook, choose one that is as much in line with your view as possible.

Students prefer going through a book as it was written. If the author wrote the book in a systematic way, building one concept on another, there may be good pedagogical reasons for following the author's order. I know of no text that completely suits every teacher, however, so I can only recommend that you keep the skipping around to a minimum and you make sure the students understand why your order of teaching the material may not mirror the textbook exactly.

There is no substitute for a detailed review of the competing texts for the course you are teaching. As textbooks multiply, it becomes increasingly tempting to throw up your hands in frustration over the time required for a conscientious review, and to simply choose the book primarily on the basis of appearance, the personality of the sales representative, or the inclusion of your name as author of one of the studies cited. Yet research on teaching suggests that the major influence on what students learn is not the teaching method, but the textbook. This is probably because the book is always available when the students are ready to learn, and they can control the pace of exposure, something they can't do

[2] Some of these ideas were stimulated by Russell Dewey's article, "Finding the right introductory psychology textbook," *APS Observer*, March 1995, 32–35.

with a real live teacher. Despite this fact, the recent study on textbooks cited above (Berry, et al., 2011) found that it wasn't so much *which* textbook the students had, but whether or not they *read* it. Therefore, you should spend an equal amount of time on encouraging the students to read the textbook, as you do on picking one. (See the chapter on "Reading as Active Learning" for ideas.)

To help make your choice a little easier, here are some strategies for selecting a textbook:

1. Winnow the possibilities down to two to five. You may be able to do some winnowing on the basis of the table of contents and preface, by checking with colleagues who have taught the course, or by reading reviews.

2. Read a couple of chapters. It is tempting to simply leaf through each book, reading bits here and there. But reading a couple of complete chapters will give you a better idea of the difficulty and interest level of each book. Try picking one chapter on a topic you know well and one that is not in your area of expertise.

3. Pick three or four key concepts. See how each text explains them. Will the explanations be clear to students? Will they be interesting?

4. Beware of seductive details or pictures that were included to make the book more attractive but may distract from the basic concepts.

5. Also beware of picking a textbook because it comes with a lot of extra resources for students. One study (Berry, et al., 2011) found that students tend not to use these extra resources unless they are required. Students are very busy, and they have to be strategic about their time. As a result, they tend to stick with things that they know will be key to their learning. Gurung (2003) did a study on pedagogical aids like boldface and italics, practice test questions, and other features that are used in texts. He found that students' use of the aids did not predict performance, so they, too, might not be as important as we think.

6. On a final and somewhat distressing note, instructors rarely think about the cost of textbooks, and yet they are a significant part of the students' financial burden in college. I was quite taken aback recently when I checked on the cost of the new edition of the textbook I use. It was twice the cost of when I first selected it! Fortunately there is a movement afoot to find less expensive alternatives, such as used textbook exchanges on campus, open source books, textbook rental, e-book versions, and even shared textbook coops (Lyman, 2008; Shelfstad, 2011). This is a reason to pick a good book and stick with it as long as possible; students are more able to find used copies to lower their costs.

TIME: TWO MONTHS BEFORE THE FIRST CLASS

Create a Syllabus for the Course

When we think about teaching, we usually think about what goes on in the classroom, but most student learning occurs outside the classroom. Planning assignments and out-of-class activities (and expectations) is even more important than planning for class meetings. A syllabus typically contains such a plan, with assignments correlated with topics to be discussed in class. If you are teaching a distance-learning course, a syllabus is indispensable. Like a contract, a syllabus should help students understand both their responsibilities and yours.

Constructing your syllabus will force you to begin thinking about the practicalities of what you must give up in order to achieve the most important objectives within the limitations of time, place, students, and resources. If you have taught the course before, you should consider what worked in the past, and what did not.

A new wrinkle to the design of the syllabus is to create a graphic syllabus (Nilson, 2007), which is built like a flow chart or concept map of the course rather than a listing of activities. It helps the students see how things fit together more effectively and shows them how you think about the course activities as integrated into a whole system. It might do the same thing for you as well.

How Much Student Time Does Your Course Involve? It is easy to forget that your course is not the only one your students are taking. After all, it is the only one you see. However, your students may be taking three, four, or five other courses in conjunction with yours. Thus, when planning your course and drafting the syllabus, it's important to calculate how much time your students have to devote to your course, both in and out of the classroom. Given a realistic studying week of about 40 hours, you have between about six and ten hours a week of your students' time available to allocate to learning on your course, including in-class time. If your students spend three hours a week in class with you, then you have between three and six hours a week of out-of-class learning activity to plan. You should expect to use all of this time, and you should be quite explicit with your students about what you expect them to do with it. The 2007 Your First College Year (YFCY) survey of freshmen across the nation reported that 37.5% of the students say they studied fewer than six hours per week (Berry, et al., 2011). Students experience wide variations in demands among courses because teachers often do not estimate or plan this time carefully. It can be helpful to calculate the total number of study hours available to your course and to plan what all of those hours would ideally be used for. Being explicit will help you to make realistic demands and will help students to see what is expected of them.

What Should Be in the Syllabus? There is no one perfect model, although there are lots of examples on the Internet. You can probably find some for your own discipline or even course title. Fairly complete lists of components of a syllabus can be found in the IDEA Paper #27, "Writing a Syllabus," by Altman and Cashin (1992), or in Slattery and Carlson (2005), which gives descriptions of the parts.

Parkes, Fix, and Harris (2003) suggest that you think about a syllabus serving multiple purposes. First, the syllabus is like a contract between the students and the instructor. It lays out what each party to the contract expects of the other and the agreed-upon activities of each. This is embodied in the list of learning goals and the general topic schedule.

Under the topic headings, you list readings and assignments for that topic and their due dates. I make a calendar of the semester showing the important dates and topics. As you lay out your schedule, consider alternate ways students might achieve the goals of a particular day or week of class. Be sure also to consider the diversity of your students. Alternative assignments can help. Students who have options and a sense of personal control are likely to be more highly motivated for learning.

Be clear about when and how learning will be assessed and grades determined. What students do is strongly influenced by their anticipation of the ways learning will be evaluated.

Finally, you may include any special rules you want to emphasize, such as a statement explaining that assignments for the course are to be completed by the dates indicated in the course outline, and your policies on make-up exams, attendance, and academic dishonesty. Most institutions also require legal statements about accommodating disabilities and religious observations. My own university even has us include a statement about e-mail being an official means of correspondence of the University.

But you might be thinking, "Isn't a syllabus that is printed or on a website a clue that the course is really instructor centered and that student needs are not going to be considered?" Not necessarily so. An experimental study by Saville, Zinn, Brown, and Marchuk (2010) had students rate teachers of a fictitious course based on the syllabus. The instructor with the more informative syllabus got higher ratings. The researchers speculated that the detailed syllabus convinced the students that the instructor was interested in their learning. The syllabus helps students discover at the outset what is expected of them and gives them the security of knowing where they are going. At the same time, your wording of assignment topics can convey excitement and stimulate curiosity.

That brings us to another of the purposes of a syllabus suggested by Parkes, Fix, and Harris: The syllabus as a learning tool. Students really benefit by understanding *how* to learn in a class as well as *what* to learn. The syllabus can communicate your perspective on both. Although learning your subject may seem simple and straightforward to you, it might seem very formidable and foreign to students, especially if they have no background in the content. You may include items that will be helpful for student learning, such as sites on the World Wide Web, strategies for maximizing learning, and what to do when having difficulty. Providing the students with the ways they can be successful in the class goes a long way to making the syllabus a living document and guide.

TIME: ONE MONTH BEFORE THE FIRST CLASS

Begin Preparing Class Session Plans

If you are planning to lecture, outline the content of the first few lectures and, more important, the ways you will get student involvement. Planning several classes at a time will make them more integrated and allow you some wiggle room if you get off schedule. You can reduce later sessions or expand them if you're not tied to the exact class period. If you are planning to teach by discussion, cooperative learning, or other methods, don't assume that they will take less preparation. Work out your plans. (See the chapters "Meeting a Class for the First Time," "Facilitating Discussion," "Active Learning: Group-Based Learning," and "Experiential Learning" for ideas.) If you spend a little time on your plans each day and let them percolate in your mind, ideas will come to you while driving, jogging, or walking to your office.

Choose Appropriate Teaching Methods

A key point for preparation that derives from your objectives is the type of instruction you use. For some goals and materials, a lecture presentation is as good as—or better than—any other method. For others, discussion may be preferable; or, cooperative learning or role-playing techniques may be useful. The most successful teachers vary their methods to suit their objectives. Thus, one day you may wish to present some new material in a lecture. You may then follow this with a class discussion on implications of this material, or with a laboratory or field exercise. This kind of dynamic course design has been shown to increase student satisfaction even when the material is difficult (Liu and Maddux, 2005). From the description of these techniques in later sections of the book, you may be able to decide which techniques are suited to your philosophy of teaching, your abilities, the class you are teaching, and the particular goals you are emphasizing at a particular time. Recent syntheses of the research on the relationship between teaching and learning have been provided by Pascarella and Terenzini (1991, 2005) in *How College Affects Students*. They make fascinating reading and can give you some good guidelines about what to choose.

Select Appropriate Technology

It is quite possible to teach an effective course without technology, but advances have increased its usefulness to outside the classroom (as in class management systems) as well as inside (as in bringing things into the classroom that couldn't have been accessed before). The chapter "Technology and Teaching" gives you a good overview of some of the possibilities. When used appropriately, technology can provide opportunities for students to interact with the content and with one another. It is an important instructional resource. But just as in considering other resources, ask yourself, "Will this help my students learn more effectively?" or "Will this save me and the students time and effort by enhancing communication?" before you decide.

TIME: TWO WEEKS BEFORE THE FIRST CLASS

Check Resources

Preparation and planning are still not done even after you've firmed up the syllabus. Look back over the syllabus to see what resources are required. Presumably your check with a colleague (as suggested in the "Introduction") has turned up any gross problems—such as assuming an unlimited budget for materials. This is a good time for another check. What are the library policies relevant to reserving any books you may want? What computer resources are available? Can you assume unlimited photocopying of exams and course materials to give to students? What do you do if you want to show a video from YouTube? What about going on a field trip, real or virtual?

Visit the classroom you've been assigned. Will the seating be conducive to discussion? Does it have the technology you need, and do you know how to use it? Do you have the right connectors and access to an electrical outlet, for example? Is there wireless Internet access in the room? Can you see all of the students and can they see and hear you? If the room is unsuitable, ask for another or modify your plans accordingly. This little trip to the classroom can prevent the first day of class from being chaotic and nerve-racking because there will be fewer surprises to deal with. Familiar settings make for less anxiety.

Start a Portfolio or Teaching Journal

A teaching portfolio not only will be useful when you discuss your teaching with your department head or supervisor, it will also be useful in your thinking and development in teaching. Plan on adding to it throughout the semester as you assess how well different approaches, discussions, and lectures were received. The same is true for a journal, which is more informal and relevant for the immediate course management. It always helps to remember why you made a particular decision in case the students ask later.

TIME: ONE WEEK BEFORE THE FIRST CLASS

If you teach first-year students and have their e-mail addresses, send an e-mail welcoming the students to your class. (It's also not a bad idea to do this with more advanced students.) Some instructors are beginning to invite students to introduce themselves online.

At this point, you're ready to prepare for the first class. For ideas about what to do and how to handle this meeting, enjoy the next chapter.

Supplementary Reading

- Robert Diamond's *Designing and Assessing Courses and Curricula: A Practical Guide* (San Francisco: Jossey-Bass, 1998) has a good chapter, "Developing a Learning-Centered Syllabus."
- Barbara Davis's book *Tools for Teaching*, 2nd ed. (San Francisco: Jossey-Bass, 1993) has a fine chapter on the syllabus (pp. 14–28).
- *Teaching Within the Rhythms of the Semester* by Donna K. Duffy and Janet W. Jones (San Francisco: Jossey-Bass, 1995) is a perceptive and readable guide to thinking about the flow of the course over the term.
- An excellent aid for preparing your syllabus is Grant Wiggins and Jay McTighe, *Understanding by Design* (Columbus, OH: Merrill Education/ASCD College Textbook Series, 2001).

Chapter 3

Meeting a Class for the First Time

The first class meeting, like any other situation in which you are meeting a group of strangers who will affect your well-being, is at the same time exciting and anxiety-producing for both students and teacher. Some teachers handle their anxiety by postponing it, simply handing out the syllabus and leaving. This does not convey the idea that class time is valuable, nor does it capitalize on the fact that first-day excitement can be constructive. Coldren and Hively (2009) have studied first impressions in class and found that projecting an authoritative presence works best. Fortunately, if you have prepared as suggested in the previous chapter, you're in good shape; the students will be pleased that the instructor seems to be well prepared, capable, and confident. Add that to focusing on their needs, and you convey that you are enthusiastic about the semester's work and ready to start.

To those ends, the following concrete suggestions are offered.

SETTING THE STAGE

One point to keep in mind on the first day, and throughout the term, is that yours is not the students' only class. They come to you from classes in chemistry, music, English, or physical education, or rushing from their dormitory beds or from parking lots. The first few minutes of a new class need to help this varied group shift their thoughts and feelings to you and your subject.

You can ease them into the course gradually, or you can grab their attention with something dramatically different, but in either case you need to think consciously about how you set the stage for learning. Even before the class period begins, you can communicate nonverbally with such actions as arranging the seats to fit the structure, posting an agenda, putting your name on the board or projecting it and the course identifier on the front screen, and chatting with early arrivals about what class they have come from or anything else that would indicate your interest in them.

BREAKING THE ICE

You will probably want to use the first period for getting acquainted and establishing goals. In large classes this involves finding some commonalities across the whole group. For example, because I teach a class taken by students from many different majors, I run through the most frequent ones and have folks identify themselves according to majors. This gives me and the students some idea of the composition of the class and gets students accustomed to participating. Then I try to explain how the course will help each group in its own area of study.

In a small class, you might ask all class members (including yourself) to introduce themselves, tell where they're from, mention their field of concentration, and answer any questions the group has. Sometimes I ask the students to tell one thing about themselves that isn't obvious from looking at them. We find out all kinds of skills and interests that are represented in the class. Or, you can ask each student to get acquainted with the persons sitting on each side and then go around the class with each student introducing the next, or each repeating the names of all those who have been introduced—a good device for developing rapport and for helping you learn the names, too.

Even if you remembered all of the students' names in the "Name Game," you may not recall them later; so it is helpful to supplement the memory in your head with an external memory device. I take a picture of each student or ask for a favorite picture. At the next class meeting I ask students to write their names, phone numbers, e-mail addresses, and other information on the photos for me. The "other information" might include previous experience relevant to the course, interests, distinctive characteristics that will help me remember them, possible major field, and so on. Some institutions now provide a photo roster of the class even before the semester starts, which means you can get started learning names before class begins! I've also found that name tents students put at the front of their desks for the first few weeks of the semester help me to call on students by their names instead of just saying, "Yes?" Eventually I can learn quite a few of the names just by that simple system.

ALLEVIATING ANXIETY

Most students are both curious and nervous about the course they're about to spend fifteen weeks of their life on. So it is important to alleviate some of that anxiety right away by explaining the course structure.

The Syllabus and Course Structure

These days, a lot of institutions require you to post your syllabus online before the class actually starts. Whether this is true of your university or not, bring paper copies to class. Or, you might bring a single page "highlights" outline, which then directs the students to the online syllabus for more detail. At this point in class you're just trying to let them know what to expect, so going over the entire syllabus is probably not worth it. Hit the key things like course goals and objectives, assignments and deadlines, daily class activities, and offer to answer any questions they have right then.

In discussing the class structure, you give the students some notion of the kind of person you are. The syllabus is a contract between you and your students. But a contract cannot be one-sided. Thus, it is important to give students time to read and discuss it. I usually tell the students that they can bring up any questions they have at the next class meeting, too, because I know it's hard to digest all that information in such a short time.

Testing, Grading, and Fairness

The students are, of course, interested in course requirements, but they are at least as much interested in what kind of person you are. One important issue is fairness.

Promoting the notion that you are objective or fair can best be handled in connection with marks and the assignment of grades (see the chapter "Assessing, Testing, and Evaluating"). A large part of the students' motivation in the classroom situation is (perhaps unfortunately) directed toward the grades they hope to earn for the course.

The very least that students can expect of you is that their marks will be determined on some impartial basis. Thus, it's important to give some time to discussing this section of your syllabus. Try to help the students understand how grading and assessment are tied to course goals.

The simplest way to show students that you are objective and fair is to let them know that you are willing to meet and advise them. Let them know they can tell you if they are likely to have special difficulties because of health or personal issues. Indicate your office hours and e-mail or other contact information. In addition, students appreciate it if you are willing (and have the time) to spend a few minutes in the classroom after each class, answering specific questions. Such queries most often concern questions of fact that can be answered briefly and would hardly warrant a trip to your office at a later time. If you teach an evening class, schedule some evening time to see students.

Strategies for Succeeding

One thing that really helps alleviate student anxieties about the class is realizing that you are as interested in their success as they are. Providing suggestions about how to learn your content, how to read the text materials, and even how to prepare for class (because your interpretation and theirs might be different) (Svinicki, 2008) can help the students feel like you are aware that they might be new to this content and need some extra help. Again, the information about how to get in touch with you or your assistants will be useful. You might also point out other help sites online or in the university where they can get some support, including other students in the class.

BUILDING COMMUNITY

Recent research on classroom climate has led us to a better understanding of what makes a class of students feel like a community. McKinney, Franluk, and Schweitzer (2006) have identified six qualities of a classroom that seem to be at the basis of feelings of community. They are connection, participation, safety, support, belonging, and empowerment. This is one of my own areas of research, so I can attest to its value in moving students toward wanting to learn and participate, not just get a good grade. Learning names and something about other students and the instructor goes a long way in creating these feelings in a class. Following are some ideas that have been discussed in the literature.

Reciprocal Interviewing (Case, et al., 2008; Foster and Herman, 2011)

This activity is usually combined with having the students fill out an information form and then "interviewing" the class by asking for a show of hands to see what the responses are to the various items. But it's the next step that is the reciprocal part; the students get to interview you. Have pairs or groups of three students sitting next to one another agree on one or two questions they'd like to ask you. Then ask a representative of each group to ask one of their questions. These might be about the syllabus or the course or about your own interests, serious or not so serious. You can reserve the right to postpone or not answer something. The intention is to show how you interact with a class and maybe have a life outside of class, too.

Question Posting

Question posting is a method of getting students involved and active that can be used in classes of all sizes. For this first class meeting you might say:

"What sorts of concerns or issues do you think we might deal with?"

"What are your expectations for this course?"

"What goals do you have for this course?"

"What have you heard about this course?"

You might ask students to write for a minute about their questions and then ask them what they have written. Your task then becomes that of recorder, listing responses on the board, overhead projector, or electronic smartboard. Lately, I've been projecting my computer in a word processing program to the front screen and just typing in what they suggest so everyone can see it. To make sure you understand, you may restate the response in your own words. If you feel that some response is ambiguous or too general, you might ask for an example, but you must be ready to accept all contributions, whether or not you feel they are important. It is crucial that the atmosphere be accepting and non-evaluative. Students should feel that you are genuinely interested in what they have to contribute.

By the end of the question posting the class normally has become better acquainted, has become used to active participation, has taken the first step toward attempting to understand rather than competing with one another, has reduced the attitude that everything must come from the teacher, has learned that the teacher can listen as well as talk (and is not going to reject ideas different from his or her own), and, I hope, has begun to feel some responsibility for answering its own questions rather than waiting for them to be answered by the instructor.

Prioritizing Class Goals

An interesting first-day activity is looking at the array of goals the instructor versus the students might have for the course. Ludy Benjamin (2005) suggests an interesting way to get students thinking about goals and their own responsibilities for them. He has created an inventory of about 17 different types of goals that one might have for a course. They include content and intellectual goals, as well as grades or personal growth goals. He has each student pick out his or her top three goals and then displays the results to the class as a whole. He normally does it the next class period, but with today's technology it's possible to do that instantly in class. Then he also talks about his top three and why he has them. They discuss where they are the same, where there is a lot of variability, and why that might be. He even offers to modify his own goals or add to them based on what the class has as a top priority. You'd probably want to create your own list, but look up his and you'll find yourself wondering about your own goals!

Assessing Prior Knowledge

The most important characteristic determining student learning is prior knowledge. Thus, you need to get some sense of the diversity of your class's background. You might simply ask questions such as, "How many have had more than *x* previous courses in this subject?" Or, you might give a short, noncredit test of relevant knowledge some time during the first few class sessions. Another strategy I've used is to list the main topics and then, using a scale of 1 to 5, I have the students indicate how familiar they are with each topic. For students who lack sufficient background, you might suggest materials for their own self-study. For those with very high scores, you might suggest supplementary materials that would be enriching and challenging.

QUESTIONS AND REACTIONS

Even in a large lecture it seems wise to interrupt these first descriptions of the course for student questions. Some of the questions will be designed as much to test you as to get information. Often the underlying questions are:

- Are you rigid?
- Will you really try to help students?
- Are you easily rattled?
- Are you a person as well as a teacher?
- Can you handle criticism?

Ask students to take two minutes at the end of class to write their reactions to the first day (anonymously). This accomplishes two things: (1) it indicates your interest in learning from them and starts building a learning climate in which they are responsible for thinking about their learning and influencing your teaching; and (2) it gives you feedback, often revealing doubts or questions students were afraid to verbalize orally.

WHAT ABOUT SUBJECT MATTER?

Many instructors dismiss class early on the first day. As the preceding sections indicate, I think the first day is important even though the students have had no prepared assignment. I like to give at least some time to subject matter. Typically, I give at least a brief overview of the course, indicate some of the questions we'll try to answer, and perhaps introduce a few key concepts. I like to give a couple of real-life examples that they're going to learn about during the semester so that they can see how the class relates to them.

But there is a limit to what you can do. The balance between content and other activities is one that different teachers will decide in different ways. My only admonition is to use the time. The first day is important, and by using it fully you communicate that you take class periods seriously. By the end of the class period, students should feel, "This is going to be an exciting course."

Supplementary Reading

- B. G. Davis, *Tools for Teaching*, 2nd ed. (San Francisco: Jossey-Bass, 1993), Chapter 3.
- Baron Perlman and Lee McCann, "The First Day of Class," *American Psychological Society Observer*, 2004, *17*(1), 13–14, 23–25.
- D. Duffy and J. Jones, *Teaching within the Rhythms of the Semester* (San Francisco: Jossey-Bass, 1995) has some good ideas about points throughout the semester and how to enliven the classes.

Part 2

Basic Skills for Facilitating Student Learning

Chapter 4

Reading as Active Learning

When I was an undergraduate psychology major, I had to take statistics, at which I was not very good. I blamed it on the topic because everyone knows that statistics is hard. It wasn't until I started teaching that I learned that a lot of my problems in statistics came from not knowing how to read the texts. As a math-phobic student, I glossed over the problem examples and read all the prose. It turns out that I had it backward. In courses like statistics and math, you should skip the prose and work the problems! Research today has demonstrated that working through the examples is one of the best strategies for this type of skill learning (Moreno, Reisslein, and Ozogul, 2009). If only someone had told me!

Along the same lines, most experts in learning through reading advise students to have goals for their reading. But when I ask my students to follow this advice, they have goals like "read and understand chapter 12." Pretty vague and pretty useless unless your goal is to just get through the reading. Unfortunately, that may be the goal that a lot of students actually have for their reading – read it start to finish, maybe highlight a few things, but mostly with the purpose of just gathering information, not really questioning what they read or integrating it into what they already know.

As teachers who believe in the value of learning from text, we are faced with two difficult issues. First, we want our students to learn the skills of reading like a professional in the field. Second, we want them to put those skills to use and actually read the text assignments we have so carefully selected. The purpose of this chapter is to help you teach students to be actively engaged in intentional reading and motivated to read what you assign.

TEXTBOOKS OR TEXTS?

For decades, the demise of the textbook has been eagerly predicted by advocates of each of the new panaceas for the problems of education. With electronic access becoming more and more available for a variety of materials, I think that we should stop thinking about the textbook as the only real book and start thinking about the "text" as any printed materials we want the students to access. Reading text will always be an important part of the teacher's compendium of tools, and the newer teaching methods and aids supplement rather than supplant reading. In fact, a substantial part of higher education is education in how to read—how to read poems, how to read social science, how to read legal briefs, how to read the literature of our culture and our professions. One of the best long-term outcomes of higher education could be the ability to read any kind of text for deep understanding.

RESEARCH ON LEARNING FROM READING

If you explore the literature on learning from reading, you'll find that there is a lot known about intentional reading, and also that there are some themes that run through it to describe what happens when good readers read. If I try to describe it as a psychologist, I would say that all the models have at their base "mindful learning" and "deep processing." These two ideas come from many sources, but the ones I like the best are Ellen Langer (1997) for mindful learning and Marton and Säljö (1976a) for deep processing.

Mindfulness refers to being aware and proactive in learning. Too many times we just read the words without thinking about why the author chose those words and where they fit with one another and with what we already know.

Let me illustrate mindfulness in a different context. Have you ever started driving home at the end of a tough day following the same route and suddenly find yourself in your driveway without any recollection of how you got there? Your driving was essentially "mindless" because it proceeded without your conscious attention. On the other hand, think about a time when you were in an unfamiliar environment, but you needed to get to a particular place using somewhat general directions. You would be consciously checking around to see where you were in relation to where you wanted to be, looking for landmarks, and using the big picture of what you know about the area to guide you. That would be "mindfulness." I think there's actually a third state in which the directions are *so* precise and complete, or you're using a GPS that tells you exactly where to go, that you never see much less remember anything else.

These three "states" may actually describe what happens to students when they read. In the first case, their automatic reading behavior kicks, in and they essentially read without being aware of what they are reading, blindly highlighting the first sentence of every paragraph. Suddenly they find themselves at the end of the chapter without much idea of what was in it. Skipping, for a minute, to the third state, if students are given extremely precise instructions (like very specific questions that have a right answer), they follow the instructions closely, answer the questions carefully, but miss the big picture. The middle state, "mindfulness," requires them to pay more attention to what they're reading because they have a general goal of understanding, with some directions that focus on the overall intent.

Deep processing could be said to result from such mindful behavior. Marton and Säljö (1976a) describe deep processing as going beneath surface features to see the underlying structure of an idea or a reading, one that makes clear how the idea fits with other ideas and what makes it unique. Keeping with our travel analogy, we learn the lay of the land as well as the landmarks and what they mean.

A Sample Reading Strategy Students Can Use

Most of the work on quality reading seems to reflect this notion of looking beneath the surface to construct a unique representation of the text that shows how its parts fit together and where they don't. In general, there are some fairly traditional models that have worked well over the years and can be tied to the modern theories of reading. I've picked just one to illustrate how we might teach our students to be more mindful and do deeper processing. The model reading process is the **SQ3R** (Robinson, 1961). You may have heard of it or even used it yourself. It's not perfect, but it follows the path that seems to be at the base of most reading strategies.

Survey The first S stands for Survey. Readers are encouraged to skim through the reading the first time to get a general impression of what the reading is about. They look at the title, the main headings, the figures and tables, not in depth yet, but just to construct a mental impression of the way the reading is going to lay out the content.

Question Then comes the Q, which of course stands for Questions. Jotting down what look like the main ideas and turning them into questions is the main task here. Preferably the questions are not restricted to "what" questions, which are more like definitions and rules. We should encourage the students to build in some "why," "how," and "when" questions because those are the questions that lead to deeper processing, especially the "why" questions. The questions then become the plan for intentional reading.

One idea that reading research advises for this phase is for the reader to create a visualization of the structure of the text. Examples of such visualizations would be a concept map, a flowchart, a decision tree, or even a metaphor. The visualization becomes the scaffold on which the reader builds an interpretation of the text by adding details, concepts, and insights. By representing the text in a different format, the reader may get a better map of the territory he's exploring (Caverly, Mandeville, and Nicholson, 1995; de Simone, 2007).

Sometimes as instructors we can provide the questions, especially for those new to the content. Study questions intended to guide the students' reading are often helpful, especially for novice or beginning learners. Marton and Säljö (1976b) found that questions designed to produce more thoughtful, integrative study were more effective than questions of fact. For example, in the assignment description, you might ask the students to compare the assertions of the author in one reading with those in another reading. How are they similar? How are they different?

Nevertheless, study questions do not automatically guarantee better learning. Marton and Säljö found that students sometimes tended to look only for answers to the questions while disregarding the other content of the chapter. Andre (1987) reviewed research on study questions and concluded that questions generally do aid learning and that higher-level questions, rather than low-level factual questions, increase the effectiveness of student processing of the reading. Similarly, Wilhite (1983) found that prequestions focusing on material at the top of the organizational structure (big ideas, for example) facilitated learning, especially for the less able students, who are less likely to think in those terms in general.

You need questions that get students to *think* about the material. One way to encourage thoughtful reading is to ask students to post their answer to a thought-provoking question on the class discussion board to share with peers. The posts then get discussed during class time, looking for common themes or points of agreement and disagreement.

Examples of Study Questions to Encourage Thought

Your assignment for Monday is to study the next chapter, "Memory." Here are some study questions:

1. How would you apply the idea of "depth of processing" to your learning from this chapter?
2. How does the limited capacity of working memory affect your learning in lecture classes?
3. How is the approach taken by researchers in memory like, and how is it different from, that taken by other researchers?

Another strategy that I have used involves having a set of questions that are asked about each reading or each theory. The repetition of the questions with different content helps students begin to have heuristics for reading, the way a professional reads. In my graduate class on instructional psychology, for example, we read sequentially about several different learning theories with a goal of being able to use them to design instruction. For every theory we ask the same four questions:

A Model for Learning about Learning Theory

How does this theory describe learning?

Given that description, what has to happen in order for learning to occur?

How should instruction be designed to make that happen?

When does this model of learning apply and not apply, based on learner or situational characteristics?

By the time we've looked at just three theories, this becomes the way they think when reading about learning theories.

Read, Recite, Review Getting back to the SQ3R model, the three Rs stand for Read, Recite, Review. Read is the actual process of reading the material. Recite is the part where the reader tries to answer the questions constructed at the beginning. And review is the self-monitoring step in which the reader compares his answers after reading to what was actually in the reading.

Examples of the recite phase might vary depending on the type of text. For example, echoing my own failures as a reader of statistics textbooks, there is strong evidence in the literature that when working with a problem-based text, a student should work out all the problems for him/herself, starting with the example problems that illustrate the author's point (Moreno, Reisslein, and Ozogul, 2009). These problems are models that the reader should be trying to understand. A corollary in a non-math based reading is to work out the author's argument for yourself. Why does the author makes the claims he or she makes? What kind of evidence is given? Do you agree or disagree with the conclusion?

There is ample evidence that students benefit from specific instruction in selecting main ideas, asking themselves questions, looking for organizational cues, and attempting to summarize or explain what they have read. Particularly in introductory classes, you will help learning if you make explicit reference to your goal in assigning a particular chapter and discuss ways in which students can best achieve that goal (McKeachie, Pintrich, and Lin, 1985; Weinstein and Mayer, 1986).

The above strategy is a general one that can be used for almost any kind of reading. It is also useful to show students how it might be modified to fit different types of texts. For example, Williams (2005) suggests what she calls the SQ6R, a modification of our model strategy expanded to fit the needs of reading the research literature. Her steps include: **S**urvey the reading first, write down some **Q**uestions that it seems to address, and then **R**ead, **R**eflect, **R**eview, **R**ehash, **R**ethink, and **R**e-evaluate. She has found that pointing out this strategy to her students opens their eyes about what it means to read carefully. For a fuller description of ways to help students become better learners, see the chapter "Teaching Students How to Become More Strategic and Self-Regulated Learners."

HOW DO YOU GET THE STUDENTS TO READ THE ASSIGNED READINGS IN THE FIRST PLACE?

The main reason students come to class unprepared is that they don't see what difference it makes. In many courses, reading assignments and lectures are independent parts of the course, sometimes overlapping, sometimes supplementary, but often not perceived as interdependent. Lei, Bartlett, Gorney, and Herschbach (2010) reviewed the literature on why students don't read assigned articles. They found that the students didn't have self-confidence in their ability to read articles, they weren't interested in the topic, or they didn't understand the importance of the readings for their learning. They also examined why more instructors didn't challenge the students to read at a higher level and found that instructor expectations and beliefs about student abilities was at the root of most of their reluctance. These authors, along with others, have made some suggestions with the caveat that each situation is different and there is no one right solution. Here are the most commonly suggested strategies.

Build Links to the Course as a Whole Frequently

Culver and Morse (2008) suggest that the first strategy for encouraging reading is frequent use of the phrase "As you read in your reading assignment for today…" or the question "What was your reaction to [the author of the reading]'s discussion of…?" They also suggest making the text material the basis for group work. The goal here is to help them understand how the readings related to the rest of the course.

Use the Readings in Class Exercises

A second strategy is to consistently use the readings as the basis of in-class activities. For example, have students write a one-minute paper at the beginning of occasional class periods on: "The most important idea (or two or three ideas) I got from the reading assignment for today." Alternatively, you can have students write a question—either something they would like explained or something that was stimulated by the reading. The class then revolves around what they've written.

One instructor (Roser, 2008) reports good results when she has her students participate in a jigsaw information-sharing activity. This method was developed by Elliot Aronson (1978) as a way to develop cooperation between ethnic groups. It has since been expanded for use in cooperative learning. In Roser's case, each student is assigned to two small groups: an expert group and a teaching group. Each expert group is assigned a different reading and works together to prepare a handout analyzing that reading and its main ideas for the rest of the class. These groups are then split into teaching groups, each teaching group having one representative from each of the expert groups. Each member of the teaching group then in turn uses the handout to explain their particular reading to the others. This technique has the students practicing critical reading (in the expert group) and summarization (in the teaching group), two key strategies in improving reading comprehension.

Build Reading Assessment into the Grading Structure

Probably the surest strategy is to announce that there will be a brief quiz of some kind on the assignment. A group of four faculty members at

Bucknell University decided to put this to the test by employing three different quizzing strategies in their courses (Carney, Fry, Gabriele, and Ballard, 2008). The three strategies represented different conditions, in terms of whether they were pop quizzes or non-random quizzes (announced or regularly scheduled), involved answering questions before coming to class or during class, and whether or not there was an element of chance involved with regard to which days, questions, or grading would be in effect. The most unusual version was called the Monte Carlo system, developed by Peter Fernald in 2004. Under this system the students had reading questions that represented different levels of Bloom's taxonomy that could be applied to any reading in the course. On the days when there were reading assignments, the instructor rolled some dice to determine whether or not there would be a quiz that day and which of the questions would be the quiz question (hence the name Monte Carlo quiz). The situation really increased students' preparation for every reading assignment, but also heightened anxiety. So our four curious faculty members modified that method in two ways. One way was to have a quiz whenever there was a reading (non-random timing) and allow the students to use their notes. The second way was to have the students write learning logs based on a set of questions while they were reading, which were turned in every time there was a reading due. This time the dice were used to determine if the answers were graded or not, and which of the questions was graded. While all three methods resulted in better preparation of the reading, the last one had the most positive reaction from the students.

Another strategy based on inclusion in the grading system is Team-Based Learning (Michaelsen, Sweet, and Parmelee, 2008), a method I use in my own class. On days when there is a reading assignment, we start class with each student taking a short quiz independently. Those are turned in and they take the quiz again but in their class groups (three students in a permanent group). Performance on the group quiz is added to the individual performance. Then we follow up by going through the items as an entire class, particularly those that students didn't do well on. Discussing why some answers are right and some are wrong has been a great way to spend class time because it goes more deeply into the reasoning behind answers.

The Bottom Line

As you might expect, it is giving credits to encourage reading that has the biggest impact on whether or not students read and to what depth. Students have busy lives and need to make strategic decisions about how they spend their time. Building the reading into the evaluation system makes the most direct connection from the readings to the grade; the associated benefits of better learning are more subtle outcomes that sometimes the students just don't see, but teachers do.

Supplementary Reading

- J. Hartley, "Studying for the Future," *Journal of Further and Higher Education*, 2002, *26*, 207–227. This article not only discussing reading, but changes in several other study skills that new forms of learning will require.
- F. Marton, D. Hounsell, and N. Entwistle (eds.), *The Experience of Learning* (Edinburgh: Scottish Academic Press, 1984). As an early proponent of deep processing, this book offers an argument for the kind of deep reading that we hope to encourage our students to do.
- C. Haas and L. Flower, "Rhetorical Reading Strategies and the Construction of Meaning," *College Composition and Communication*, 1988, *39*(2), 167–183. This really good discussion of the state of reading research informs the kind of higher level reading processes we'd like to see our students use. Reading is a lot more complex than we think, but if you really want to do some deep processing yourself, it's worth reading this paper.
- R. Fillipo and D. Caverly (eds.), *Handbook of College Reading and Study Strategy Research* (Mahwah NJ: Lawrence Erlbaum Publishers, 2000). This is a fascinating set of chapters covering not just reading, but test preparation, note-taking, and many more study skills that college students need.

Chapter 5

Facilitating Discussion

Active learning is the key word (or phrase) in contemporary higher education. Mayer (2008, p. 17) explains active learning as paying "attention to relevant information, organizing it into coherent mental representations, and integrating representations with other knowledge." The prototypic teaching method for fostering active learning has always been *discussion*:

> Leading a productive discussion, one that engages students and enhances their understanding, may be the most complex and challenging task in teaching. (Henning, 2005, p. 90)

Often teachers in large classes feel that they must lecture because they think discussion is impossible; but in reality, discussion techniques can be used in classes of all sizes. Generally, discussions in smaller classes *are* more effective, but perhaps they are needed *more* in large classes to avoid students going into passive learning mode. Chapter 18 will deal in more depth with how to integrate discussion into a large class setting, but as you read through this chapter, try to imagine how any interesting strategies you find could play out in a large class with a little tweaking.

Discussion techniques seem particularly appropriate when the instructor wants to do the following:

1. Help students learn to think in depth about the subject matter by giving them practice in thinking.

2. Help students learn to evaluate the logic of and evidence for their own and others' positions.

3. Give students opportunities to formulate applications of principles.

4. Develop motivation for further learning.

5. Help students articulate what they've learned.

6. Get prompt feedback on student understanding or misunderstanding.

7. Take advantage of the impact that social interaction has on learning and behavior.

Why should discussion be the method of choice for achieving such objectives? The first justification is a very simple extrapolation of the old adage, "Practice makes perfect." If instructors expect students to learn how to integrate, apply, and think, it seems reasonable that students should have an opportunity to practice these skills. To help students learn and think, both you and they need to find out what is in their heads. Discussion can help. A second justification is that recent research supports the assertion that having to explain your thinking is very effective in clarifying it and helping you learn from it (Fonseca and Chi, 2011).

TASKS IN TEACHING BY DISCUSSION

In teaching by discussion, the instructor is faced with several tasks:

1. Helping students prepare for discussion.

2. Getting and maintaining participation in the discussion

3. Facilitating the discussion in a way that progress is made.

4. Helping students learn and practice the process of civil discourse.

5. Listening to the students supportively to make the class a safe place to express ideas.

This chapter should help you make progress with each of these tasks.

HELPING STUDENTS PREPARE FOR DISCUSSION

As noted later in this chapter, it's hard to have a discussion if the students aren't prepared. But something to ask yourself very seriously is: What do you mean by prepared? If yours is a course that occurs very early in the students' sequence, they may have very little experience in discussing what they are learning, other than at a very low level that just confirms they read the material. Providing the students with higher cognitive level questions that ask for more than just details is one way of helping them use their preparation time wisely. The suggestions that were offered in the chapter on "Reading as Active Learning" for making their reading productive might be another good way to help them become better learners.

Other instructors have encouraged students to be prepared for class by beginning the class with a short quiz. Some instructors make them unannounced, but in my opinion, why not remove that anxiety and just make it a practice to start off the class with a student review of key points? This is the process in Team-Based Learning (Michaelsen, Sweet, and Parmelee, 2008). As I described in the chapter on "Reading as Active Learning," I use this process in my undergraduate class and the students really like it. At first each student takes the "readiness assessment" independently, and then again as part of a group. The combined points are part of their participation grade. In the group discussions a lot of confusion gets cleared up before the whole class discusses. That whole class discussion then can be devoted to the points that really need discussing.

Another example of something similar was described by McElwee (2009). He uses what he calls Participation Preparation Assignments that students work on before class. The PPAs are distributed at the end of the previous class and must be completed for the following class. The actual activities vary in format, from explaining a portion of the reading assignment in their own words to applying the reading content to a scenario appropriate to the topic. In the class period when these are due, the students spend some time working together in groups comparing their assignments and then presenting the result to the class as a whole. McElwee's students reported that they completed more of the readings because they knew what to do, which made them feel more prepared and more confident in their ability to participate.

There are also several examples of instructors who use participation in online discussions before class as a way of helping students prepare for the in-class discussion. For example, Lineweaver (2010) conducted a set of studies in which students were assigned different questions to be discussed online before the class on alternate class days. Students had to post their responses and respond to other students' posts before class. They received a small number of points for each completed discussion. She found that students reported reading the materials more closely and more regularly. I've used a similar procedure in my graduate classes with one addition. I make sure that I have read all the posts and brought them into the discussion in class so that students feel their work is valuable.

It's reasonable to assume that students want to do well in class discussions, and would do well if they only knew how to prepare. I think it is definitely worthwhile to get them started off knowing just that. As the semester progresses, they can use these strategies to get ready without prompting from the instructor.

CONDUCTING A DISCUSSION: GETTING STARTED

After a class has been meeting and discussing problems successfully, there is little problem in initiating discussion, for it will develop almost spontaneously from problems encountered in reading, from experiences, or from unresolved problems from the previous meeting. But during the first meetings of new groups, you need to create an expectation that something interesting and valuable will occur.

Starting Discussion with a Common Experience

One of the best ways of starting a discussion is to refer to a concrete, common experience through presentation of a demonstration, film, role play, short skit, or brief reading. It could be a common experience among all students, an issue on campus or in the media, or you can provide the experience. These days there is a wealth of material available on the web to spark a discussion. For example, the thought-provoking lectures presented at the TED (Technology, Entertainment, Design) website seem to be an endless array of short discussions of current issues from the annual conferences they sponsor (http://www.TED.com/talks). Teachers are encouraged to make use of this site to foster expanding understanding of current events. For example, in my own class, I showed a ten-minute lecture on neuroscience advances and whether mind control was possible. Following such a presentation it's easy to ask, "What are the implications of what you've just seen?"

Such an opening has a number of advantages. Because everyone in the group has seen it, everyone knows something about the topic under discussion. In addition, by focusing the discussion on the presentation, the instructor takes some of the pressure off of any anxious or threatened students who are afraid to reveal their own opinions or feelings.

Starting Discussion with a Controversy

A second technique of stimulating discussion is through disagreement. Experimental evidence indicates that a certain degree of surprise or uncertainty arouses curiosity, a basic motive for learning (Johnson and Johnson, 1995). Some teachers effectively play the role of devil's advocate; others are effective in pointing out differences in points of view. Some instructors invite the students to offer hypothetical contrary opinions or positions to be discussed.

I have some concerns about the devil's advocate role. I believe that it can be an effective device in getting students to think actively rather than accept passively the instructor's every sentence as "truth." Yet it has its risks, the most important of which is that it may create lack of trust in the instructor. Its success depends a good deal on the spirit with which it is played. Linc Fisch (2001) handles this problem by donning a T-shirt with "Devil's Advocate" on the front. My own compromise solution is to make it clear when I'm taking such a role by saying, "Suppose I take the position that ___" or "Let me play the role of devil's advocate for a bit."

In any case, the instructor should realize that disagreement is not a sign of failure, but may be used constructively. When rigid dogmatism interferes with constructive problem solving following a disagreement, the instructor may ask the disagreeing students to switch sides and argue the opposing point of view. Such a technique seems to be effective in developing awareness of the strengths of other positions. A good description of the "constructive controversy" strategy is found in an article by Johnson, Johnson, and Smith (2000) listed at the end of this chapter. They give not only the reasons behind using controversy but very practical suggestions about making sure students come away challenged to think differently.

Starting Discussion with Questions

The most common discussion opener is the question, and the most common error in questioning is not allowing students time enough to think. You should not expect an immediate response to every question. If your question is intended to stimulate thinking, give the students time to think. Five seconds of silence may seem an eternity, but a pause for five to thirty seconds will result in better discussion. In order to alleviate that awkward feeling in my own class, I actually endorse silence by saying, "I want you to think about the following question and no one can say anything for the next two minutes." In some cases you may plan for such a thoughtful silence by asking the students to write down one element that might help answer the question. Such a technique increases the chance that the shyer or slower students will participate, since they will know what they want to say when the discussion begins. In fact, you may even draw one in by saying, "You were writing vigorously, Ronnie. What's your suggestion?"

There are many different models for questions for both in-class and online discussions; several are described below.

Factual Questions There are times when it is appropriate to check student background knowledge with a series of brief factual questions, but more frequently you want to stimulate problem solving. You could start with a statement like, "Let's just make sure we all agree on some of the key definitions and facts before we start discussing," and then invite the students to suggest what the facts are. One common error in phrasing this type of questions is to ask in a way that conveys the message: "I know something you don't know, and you'll look stupid if you don't guess right." My former boss used to refer to these as "guess what's in my pocket" questions, guaranteed to annoy the students.

Application and Interpretation Questions Rather than dealing with factual questions, formulate discussions to get at relationships, applications, or analyses of facts and materials. Solomon, Rosenberg, and Bezdek (1964) found that teachers who used interpretation questions produced gains in student comprehension. A question of the type "How does the idea that ___ apply to ___?" is much more likely to stimulate discussion than the question "What is the definition of ___?" The secret is not to avoid questions or to lecture in statements, but rather to listen and to reflect on what is heard. Dillon (1982), a leading researcher on questioning, advises that once you have defined the issue for discussion, keep quiet unless you are perplexed or didn't hear a comment. Questions are tools for teaching, but as Dillon demonstrated, they sometimes interfere with, as well as facilitate, achievement of teaching goals. What happens depends on the question and its use.

Connective and Causal Effect Questions These questions involve attempts to link material or concepts that otherwise might not seem related. One might, for example, cut across disciplines to link literature, music, and historical events, or one might ask, "What are the possible causes of this phenomenon?"

Comparative Questions As the name suggests, comparative questions ask for comparisons between one theory and another, one author and another, one research study and another, and so on. Such questions help students determine important dimensions of comparison.

Evaluative Questions These ask not only for comparisons but for a judgment of the relative value of the points being compared; for example, "Which of two theories better accounts for the data? Which of two essays better contributes to an understanding of the issue?"

Critical Questions Asking critical questions is effective at getting the students to examine the validity of an author's arguments or discussion. Television, magazines, and other media provide opportunities for using critical or evaluative questioning. For example, "An eminent authority states thus and so. Under what conditions might that not be true?" Being so critical that students feel that their reading has been a waste of time is not helpful, but presenting an alternative argument or conclusion may start students analyzing their reading more carefully, and eventually you want students to become critical readers who themselves challenge assumptions and conclusions.

Starting Discussion with a Problem or Case

A discussion may arise from a case, or it may be a hypothetical problem. It may be a problem whose solution the instructor knows; it may be a problem that the instructor has not solved. In any case it should be a problem that is meaningful to the students, and for the sake of morale, it should be a problem they can make some progress on. And even if the teacher knows an answer or has a preferred solution, the students should have a chance to come up with new solutions. The teacher's job is not to sell students on a particular solution, but rather to listen and to teach them how to solve problems themselves. Don't be afraid to express your own curiosity, question, or "what if..." wonder about a topic. Ask the students what they think. It is better to be an open-minded, curious questioner than the fount of all knowledge.

Suppose you ask a question and no one answers, or the student simply says, "I don't know." Discouraging as this may be, it should not necessarily be the end of the interaction. Usually the student can respond if the question is rephrased. Perhaps you need to give an example of the problem first; or you need to suggest some alternative answer and ask the student what evidence might or might not support it; or you need to reformulate a prior question. More often than not, you can help the students discover that they are more competent than they thought by sticking with them as they struggle to answer.

One of the biggest problems in teaching by discussion is focus. Getting the discussion headed in the right direction and keeping it there requires that both students and the instructor be focused on the same questions. One of the better methods for producing focus is to use a problem or a case study as the main topic of discussion. The chapter

"Experiential Learning" discusses problem-based learning and the case method in more detail, but what follows here are some general ideas about working with problem-based discussions more efficiently.

Breaking a Problem into Sub-problems One of Norman Maier's (1952) important contributions to effective group problem solving, as well as to teaching, was to point out that groups are likely to be more effective if they tackle one aspect of a problem at a time rather than skipping from formulation of the problem, to solutions, to evidence, to "what-have-you," as different members of the group toss in their own ideas. In developmental discussion the group tackles one thing at a time.

One of the first tasks is likely to be a *clarification of the problem*. Often groups are ineffective because different participants have different ideas of what the problem is, and group members may feel frustrated at the end of the discussion because "the group never got to the real problem."

A second task is likely to be: *What do we know?* or *What data are relevant?*

A third task may be: *What are the characteristics of an acceptable solution?*—for example: What is needed?

A fourth step could be: *What are possible solutions?* and a fifth step may be to *evaluate these solutions* against the criteria for a solution determined in the previous step.

The developmental discussion technique can be used even in large groups, since there are a limited number of points to be made at each step regardless of the number of participants. Maier and Maier (1957) have shown that developmental discussion techniques improve the quality of decisions compared with freer, more nondirective discussion methods.

CONDUCTING THE DISCUSSION: MOVING THINGS ALONG

One of the important skills of discussion leaders is the ability to appraise the group's progress and to be aware of barriers or resistances that are blocking learning. This skill depends on attention to clues such as inattention, hostility, or diversionary questions.

Listening, Responding, and Modeling Discussion Behavior

There are some very good overviews of supportive teacher behaviors listed at the end of this chapter. Some are applicable to all discussion classes, such as Gray and Madson (2007) who provide ten ways to engage students in the class, such as maintaining eye contact (it puts subtle pressure on students to say something) and helping students take notes in discussion (which doesn't usually follow a linear path and therefore doesn't fit standard note-taking strategies). Henning (2005) offers ideas from discourse studies on how to move the conversation along, like follow a student's comment with your reactions, plus some additional related ideas that can be the basis for the next comment. A third instructor, Souha Ezzedeen (2008), focuses on strategies for dealing with controversial topics in the discussion, such as choosing reading materials that *don't* summarize all the arguments. Ezzedeen (and I) think that summaries might remove all the possible things a student might be able to offer as new ideas.

In general, however, all these instructors recommend one particular behavior pattern regardless of the content of the discussion, and that pattern involves actively listening to and acknowledging student comments and ideas. Not only does this pattern keep the discussion flowing because students believe their participation is welcome, but it also provides the model of civil discourse that we hope our students learn and take with them when they leave our classes. They also recommend that early in the semester, instructors draw the students into a discussion about the ground rules for appropriate behavior in the class, especially in discussions. It isn't that the students are unaware of appropriate behavior. Rather it is that by involving the students in the setting of behavior norms, the instructor gives them a stake in their adherence to the rules. In addition, if the students know that there are rules governing what will happen in the class even when things become tense, they will be more confident that things will remain manageable.

A new wrinkle in leading discussions comes along with the new students who have been labeled the "Millennials." Although much has been written about this generation of students born between 1980 and mid-2000, we still are learning about their thinking and ways of engaging in their education. In a recent study, Roehling and her colleagues (2010) interviewed multiple focus groups made up of students in this generational group to understand their views on class discussions and what would help them learn in those contexts. The study's results showed a remarkably perceptive analysis of discussion learning by the participants. They reported three reasons why they found discussions good experiences. First, this group of students values active learning. The students in this generation have grown up surrounded by fast-paced, interactive, and constantly changing media-based activities. To sit just listening is not their style. Discussion allows them to be active. The second quality of discussions that the students cited as positive was that discussion allowed them to develop a deeper understanding of what they were learning for themselves, not having to accept the authorities' versions of everything. Because they have been treated as special throughout their childhood, they have a strong sense of self and self-confidence. They believe that all perspectives should be honored in the discussion. This is also the third quality of discussion that they liked: everyone's input was valued and considered in drawing conclusions. They also depend on the instructor to create the situation in the classroom that allows these three qualities to be present in their discussions. In reality, the things that instructors would be advised to do to bring the Millennials into the discussion are just as applicable to many groups.

CONDUCTING THE DISCUSSION: COMMON PROBLEMS

Why Students Don't Participate

- Student habits of passivity
- Failure to see the value of discussion
- Fear of criticism or of looking stupid
- Push toward agreement or solution before alternative points of view have been considered
- Feeling that the task is to find the answer the instructor wants rather than to explore and evaluate possibilities

Students' Reluctance to Participate

A primary barrier to discussion is the students' feeling that they are not learning. Occasional summaries during the hour not only help students chart their progress but also help smooth out communication problems. A summary need not be a statement of conclusions. In many cases the most effective summary is a restatement of the problem in terms of the issues resolved and those remaining. Keeping a visible record on the board of ideas, questions, data, or points to explore help maintain focus and give a sense of progress. Asking students to summarize progress and what now needs to be done helps them develop as learners.

Another common barrier to good discussion is the instructor's tendency to tell students the answer before the students have developed an answer or meaning for themselves. Of course, teachers can sometimes save time by tying things together or stating a generalization that is emerging. But all too often they do this before the class is ready for it.

When you oppose a student's opinions, you should be careful not to overwhelm the student with the force of the criticism. Your objective is to start discussion, not smother it. Give students an opportunity to respond to criticisms, examining the point of view that was opposed. Above all, avoid personal criticism of students.

And perhaps the most common barrier is our own discomfort. During discussions we are not dispensing knowledge and not in control. It is all too easy to slip back into our old methods of teaching.

Involving Nonparticipants

In most classes some students talk too much, and others never volunteer a sentence. What can the teacher do?

Unfortunately, most students are used to being passive recipients in class. Some of your students may come from cultures whose norms discourage speaking in class, as discussed in the chapter on "Teaching Culturally Diverse Students." To help students become participants, I try to create an expectation of participation in the discussion. You can start to do this in the first meeting of the course by defining the functions of various aspects of the course and explaining why discussion is valuable. In addition to this initial structuring, however, you must continually work to increase the students' awareness of the values of participation. Participation is not an end in itself. For many purposes widespread participation may be vital; for others it may be detrimental. But you want to create a climate in which an important contribution is not lost because the person with the valuable idea did not feel free to express it.

What keeps a student from talking? There are a variety of reasons—boredom, lack of knowledge, general habits of passivity, cultural norms—but most compelling is a fear of being embarrassed. When students feel they are surrounded by strangers, when they do not know how critical these strangers may be, when they are afraid of the teacher's response, when they are not sure how sound their idea may be, when they are afraid of stammering or forgetting their point under the stress of speaking—the safest thing to do is keep quiet.

What can reduce this fear? Getting students acquainted with one another, and with you as the teacher, is one aid. Once students know that they are among friends, they can risk expressing themselves. If they know that at least one classmate supports an idea, the risk is reduced. For both of these reasons, the technique of subgrouping helps; for example, you can ask students to discuss a question in pairs or small groups before asking for general discussion.

Asking students to take a couple of minutes to write out their initial answers to a question can help. If a student has already written an answer, it's much easier to encourage them to speak, than if they are asked to answer a question immediately. Even the shy person will respond when asked, "What did you write?"

Rewarding infrequent contributors at least with a smile helps encourage participation even if the contribution has to be developed or corrected. Calling students by name seems to foster freer communication. Seating is important too. Rooms with seats in a circle help tremendously.

Getting to know the nonparticipant is also helpful. For example, I have found that it is helpful to ask students to write a brief life history indicating their interests and experiences relevant to the course. These self-summaries help me to gain a better knowledge of each student as an individual, to know what problems or illustrations will be of particular interest to a number of students, and to know on whom I can call for special information. One of the best ways of getting nonparticipants into the discussion is to ask them to contribute to a problem area in which they have special knowledge.

The technique of asking for a student's special knowledge deals directly with one of the major barriers to class discussion—fear of being wrong. No one likes to look foolish, especially in a situation where mistakes may be pounced upon by a teacher or other students. Students particularly avoid—or dread—questions that put them on the spot and only have one right answer, such as: "This is an example of what?" which is expecting the student to fill in the one correct word. There is an infinity of wrong answers, and obviously the teacher knows the one right answer; so why should the student risk making a mistake when the odds are so much against the student? And even if the answer is obvious, why look like a pawn of the teacher?

One way of putting the student in a more favorable position is to ask general questions that have no wrong answers. For example, you can ask, "How do you feel about this?" or "How does this look to you?" as a first step in analysis of a problem. Students' feelings or perceptions may not be the same as yours, but as reporters of their own feelings, they can't be challenged as being inaccurate. While such an approach by no means eliminates anxiety about participation (for an answer involves revealing oneself as a person), it will more often open up discussion that involves the student, than will questions of fact.

Another technique for reducing the risk of participation for students is to ask a question one class period before the discussion and ask students to write out answers involving an example from their own experience. Similarly, one can ask students to bring one question to class for discussion. This helps participation, helps students learn to formulate questions, and also provides feedback for you.

Finally, remember that out-of-class learning is often more important than that in class. E-mail, computer conferencing, and other interactive technologies can support active learning, discussion, and debate.

What about a Student Who Monopolizes?

If you have worked on nonparticipation effectively, the discussion "monopolizer" is less likely to be a problem, but there will still be classes in which one or two students talk so much that you and the other students become annoyed. As with nonparticipation, one solution is to raise the question of participation in discussion—"Would the class be more effective if participation were more evenly distributed?"

A second technique is to have one or more members of the class act as observers for one or more class periods, reporting back to the class their observations. Perhaps assigning the dominant member to the observer role would help sensitivity.

A third possibility is to audiotape a discussion, and after playing back a portion, ask the class to discuss what might be done to improve the discussion.

A fourth technique is to use buzz groups with one member chosen to be reporter.

Finally, a direct approach should not be ruled out. Talking to the student individually outside of class may be the simplest and most effective solution. This has been very successful for me as long as I am sensitive to that student's need for affirmation.

What If the Students Haven't Read the Material?

It's hard to have a discussion if students haven't studied the material to be discussed. What to do? Hopefully you've avoided this by following the advice at the beginning of this chapter. However, even the best laid plans....

One strategy is always to give students questions at the end of one class, asking them to get information on the questions before the next class. If they have the reading materials available in class either in hard copy or through the Internet, you could have them skim the material and formulate the questions that the material purports to answer. It would be a chance to have them practice the SQ3R strategies that we discussed in the chapter on "Reading as Active Learning." Using the jigsaw method also discussed in the chapter on "Reading as Active Learning," you could assign parts of the class to create the summary of parts of the reading and present the summaries to the class. You can ask students to evaluate the validity of different Internet sources providing relevant information to the topic at hand. You might even give different assignments to teams of students. The relative availability of in-class computers and network connections might allow you to set them a task of finding information on the web during the class that deal with the problem or topic of discussion.

If there are extenuating circumstances, you (or a student who is prepared) can summarize the needed points. Alternatively, you can give students a few minutes to scan the material before beginning the discussion. If used often, however, such strategies may discourage out-of-class preparation. It's better to deal with the behavior by having them do some of the work themselves in class, than having everything summarized for them.

If the problem persists, present it to the students. What do they suggest? One likely proposal is a short quiz at the beginning of class—which usually works. However, you'd like to have students motivated to study without the threat of a quiz. Usually the quiz can be phased out once students find that discussion really requires preparation and that the assignments are more interesting as they develop competence.

Handling Conflicts and Arguments

In any good discussion, conflicts will arise. If such conflicts are left ambiguous and uncertain, they, like repressed conflicts in the individual, may cause continuing trouble. You can focus these conflicts so that they may contribute to learning.

First, I hope you took the advice to set up ground rules for discussion before the class ever gets to this point. If things start getting heated, it's time to roll out those guidelines again and remind students of the principles of civil discourse. Then try to turn the discussion to one that is more productive by one of the following:

- Reference to the text or other authority may be one method of resolution, if the solution depends on certain facts.
- Using the conflict as the basis for a library assignment for the class or a delegated group is another solution.
- If there is an experimentally verified answer, this is a good opportunity to review the method by which the answer could be determined.
- If the question is one of values, your goal may be to help students become aware of the values involved.
- Sometimes students will dispute your statements or decisions. Such disagreements may often be resolved by a comparison of the evidence for both points of view, but since teachers are human, they are all too likely to become drawn into an argument in which they finally rest on their own authority. To give yourself time to think, as well as to indicate understanding and acceptance of the students' point, I suggest listing the objections on the board. (Incidentally, listing evidence or arguments is also a good technique when the conflict is between two members of the class.) Such listing tends to prevent repetition of the same arguments.
- In any case it should be clear that conflict may be an aid to learning, and the instructor need not frantically seek to smother it.
- If you're having problems with a particular student, check the chapter "Dealing with Student Problems and Problem Students."

The Two Column Method Another of Norman Maier's (1952) techniques, the two-column method, is a particularly effective use of the board in a situation in which there is a conflict or where a strong bias prevents full consideration of alternative points of view. Experimental studies (Gilovich, 1991) suggest that when people hear arguments against their point of view, they become involved in attempting to refute the arguments rather than listening and understanding. Disagreement thus often tends to push the debaters into opposite corners, in which every idea is right or wrong, good or bad, black or white. The truth is often more complex and not in either extreme.

The two-column method is designed to permit consideration of complications and alternatives. Before the issues are debated, all the arguments on each side are listed on the board or projected. The leader heads two columns "Favorable to A" and "Favorable to B" or "For" and "Against" and then asks for the facts or arguments that group members wish to present. The instructor's task is to understand and record in brief the arguments presented. If someone wishes to debate an argument presented for the other side, the instructor simply tries to reformulate the point so that it can be listed as a positive point in the debater's own column. But even though an argument is countered or protested it should not be erased, for the rules of the game are that the two columns are to include all ideas that members consider relevant. Evaluation can come later.

When the arguments have been exhausted, discussion can turn to the next step in problem solving. At this point the group can usually identify areas of agreement and disagreement, and in many cases it is already clear that the situation is neither black nor white. Now the issue becomes one of *relative* values rather than good versus bad. When discussion is directed toward agreements, some of the personal animosity is avoided, and some underlying feelings may be brought to light. The next stages of the discussion are thus more likely to be directed toward constructive problem solving.

Challenges and disagreements may be an indication of an alert, involved class. But the instructor should also be aware of the possibility that they may be symptoms of frustration arising because the students are uncertain of what the problem is or how to go about solving it.

CONDUCTING THE DISCUSSION: TEACHING STUDENTS TO LEARN THROUGH DISCUSSION

I have already implied that classes don't automatically carry on effective discussions. To a large extent students have to learn *how* to learn from discussions, just as they have to learn how to learn from reading. How can this occur?

First, they need to understand the importance of discussion for learning. Expressing one's own understanding or ideas, and getting reactions from other students and the teacher, makes a big difference in learning, retention, and use of knowledge.

What skills need to be learned? One skill is clarification of what the group is trying to do—becoming sensitive to confusion about what the group is working on and asking for clarification.

A second attribute is the students' development of a willingness to talk about their own ideas openly and to listen and respond to others' ideas. It is important for students to realize that it is easy to deceive themselves about their own insights or understandings and that verbalizing an idea is one way of getting checks on and extensions of it. Teachers can encourage development of listening skills by asking one group member to repeat or paraphrase what another said before responding to it, and repeatedly pointing out the purpose and values students gain from discussion.

A third skill is planning. Discussions are sometimes frustrating because they are only getting under way when the end of the class period comes. If this results in continuation of the discussion outside the class, so much the better, but often learning is facilitated if students learn to formulate the issues and determine what out-of-class study or follow-up is necessary before the group breaks up.

A fourth skill is building on others' ideas in such a way as to increase their motivation rather than make them feel punished or forgotten. Often students see discussion as a competitive situation in which they win by tearing down other students' ideas. As Haines and McKeachie (1967) have shown, cooperative discussion methods encourage more effective work and better morale than competitive methods.

A fifth attribute is skill in evaluation. If classes are to learn how to discuss issues effectively, they need to review periodically what aspects of their discussion are proving to be worthwhile and what barriers, gaps, or difficulties have arisen. Some classes reserve the last five minutes of the period for a review of the discussion's effectiveness.

A sixth attribute is sensitivity to feelings of other group members. Students need to become aware of the possibility that feelings of rejection, frustration, dependence, and so on may influence group members' participation in discussion. Sometimes it is more productive to recognize the underlying feeling than to focus on the content of an individual's statement. One way of helping students develop these skills is to use student-led discussions preceded by a training meeting with the student leader.

A more mundane skill is how to take notes in a discussion. I mentioned earlier that good discussions don't lend themselves to linear note taking, but many students don't know any other alternatives.

The two-column method described above is a good alternative strategy. Another is a concept map, showing how each point is connected to the overall discussion. The notes probably should mirror the purpose and flow of the discussion so there are myriad strategies. Just making the students aware that linear notes may not be their best bet would be a big help. But this next point is a more collaborative way of dealing with notes.

CONDUCTING THE DISCUSSION: MINUTES, SUMMARIES, AND DRAWING TO A CLOSE

One of the problems with discussion is students' feeling that they have learned less than they have in lectures where they have taken voluminous notes. One strategy that has worked for me is to assign one or two students to be the official minute takers for the class. This frees the other students up to be engaged in the discussion without worrying about getting the notes down. I think it is also useful to build in periodic progress checks so that students can see we're not going to go too far adrift before someone brings us back to the point. We can always decide to go ahead and continue our discussion, but I've found that by the time a progress check comes along, most students are ready to move on. At that time it might be beneficial to give the students a little self-reflection time to note some of their own thoughts or questions.

In order to convince the students that we've made progress, I like to go back to the beginning of the class period to see what goals we had and whether we've accomplished them. Then I like to summarize our progress or ask students to contribute to a summary. Better yet, use the last five to ten minutes for having the students summarize for themselves what they learned and give the group feedback. For example, ask students to write briefly a summary of the issues discussed, the pros and cons, and their conclusions. If the course schedule permits it, this is also a good time to make some action plans for what we'll all bring to the next class discussion.

STUDENT-LED DISCUSSIONS

In pioneering experiments in educational psychology and general psychology, Gruber and Weitman (1962) found that students taught in small, student-led discussion groups without a teacher not only did at least as well on a final examination as students who heard the teacher lecture, but also were superior in curiosity (as measured by question-asking behavior) and in interest in educational psychology. In a later study by Phillips and Powers (1979), the amount of student interaction was a function of the discussion leader. When students were leading the discussion, the amount of student participation was almost twice as great as when the discussion was led by the instructor. Phillips and Powers said that it was impossible to tell if this was because students as leaders facilitated discussion, or if the absence of an expert as discussion leader led to less inhibition of discussion, but it's an interesting question to ponder. Having a student as the discussion leader could easily change how the other students perceive their role in the class. In a more recent study, Casteel and Bridges (2007) found that students did indeed report being more comfortable disagreeing with others when it was students who were leading the discussion.

As it is probably the experience of disagreeing that causes the most self-reflection by a learner, and self-reflection causes better learning, feeling freer to disagree could lead to better learning from a discussion. This phenomenon has been described by Johnson and Johnson (1995) and referred to as "constructive controversy." After an extensive meta-analysis of the literature, Johnson and Johnson reported impressive effect sizes (the amount of difference made by an intervention) for studies that used formats that followed the creative controversy model. Johnson, Johnson, and Smith (2000) provided an excellent analysis of what is probably happening with that model, mentioned earlier. In this model of discussion, students are divided into groups of four and then each group is divided into pairs. One pair of the group researches the pro side of an issue and the other pair researches the con side. The pairs have to construct good arguments backed by literature and other forms of evidence. Once this has been done and each side has made its case and refuted the other, the pairs switch sides. They are required to come to some consensus on the best position with regard to the problem. Johnson and Johnson propose that such activity not only motivates students to dig deeply into the topic, but also causes them to experience the kind of conceptual conflict that research has shown leads to a re-examination of beliefs and attitudes. To learn more about this very interesting process, I recommend you read the Johnson, Johnson, and Smith (2000) article referenced in the Supplementary Reading list for this chapter.

ONLINE DISCUSSIONS

This is probably the most rapidly growing type of discussion in our arsenal today. As discussed in chapter 17, "Technology and Teaching," e-mail, list servers, computer conferences, and other online experiences extend the opportunities for discussion far beyond what is possible in the classroom. Online discussions also provide practice in writing. They can facilitate cooperative learning. The impersonality of e-mail may reduce the inhibitions of those who are shy in the classroom, but research suggests that it may also reduce inhibitions against rudeness. Thus, in initiating an online discussion, remind your students that respect for others and rational support for arguments are just as important online as in the classroom. For a really thorough discussion of this topic, I recommend going to chapter 17 or consulting some of the most recent work on the topic, which has been reviewed by one of the leaders in the field, Alfred Rovai. In a very thorough analysis, Rovai (2007) has recommended some key strategies. For example, he suggested providing rubrics for online discussion to help students understand the kind of thought you expect from them in the discussions. He has also emphasized the importance of creating a sense of community for students in courses that depend heavily on online discussion. He has been studying the issue of social presence in virtual classrooms, the idea that there is a real person behind the words on the screen. Although many of his recommendations apply to face-to-face discussions, it's good to remember that the ability to discuss serious issues online is a very different behavior than the social networking that many students are accustomed to, so we can't just assume that this level of thought will happen automatically.

IN CONCLUSION

Teaching by discussion differs from lecturing because you never know what is going to happen. At times this is anxiety-producing, at times frustrating, but more often it's exhilarating. It provides constant challenges and opportunities for both you and the students to learn. When you can listen for several minutes without intervening, you will have succeeded.

Supplementary Reading

- C. C. Bonwell and T. E. Sutherland, "The Active Learning Continuum: Choosing Activities to Engage Students in the Classroom," in T. E. Sutherland and C. C. Bonwell (eds.), "Using Active Learning in College Classes: A Range of Options for Faculty," *New Directions for Teaching and Learning*, no. 67, October 1996, 3–16.
- S. D. Brookfield and S. Preskill, *Discussion as a Way of Teaching: Tools and Techniques for Democratic Classrooms* (San Francisco: Jossey-Bass, 1999).

- J. T. Dillon, *Teaching and the Art of Questioning* (Bloomington, IN: Phi Delta Kappa Educational Foundation, 1983).
- S. Ezzedeen, "Facilitating Class Discussions around Current and Controversial Issues: Ten Recommendations for Teachers." *College Teaching, 56*(4), 2008, 230–236.
- T. Gray and L. Madson, "Ten Easy Ways to Engage Your Students." *College Teaching, 55*(2), 2007, 83–87.
- J. Henning, "Leading Discussions: Opening Up the Conversation." *College Teaching, 53*(3), 2005, 90–94.
- D. Johnson, R. Johnson, and K. Smith, "Constructive Controversy: The Educative Power of Intellectual Conflict," *Change Magazine*, January/February 2000, 28–37.
- P. Roehling, R. Vander Kooi, S. Dykema, B. Quisenberry, and C. Vandlen, "Engaging the Millennial Generation in Class Discussions," *College Teaching, 59*(1), 2010, 1–6.
- A. Rovai, "Facilitating Online Discussion Effectively" *Internet and Higher Education, 10,* 2007, p. 77–88.

Chapter 6

How to Make Lectures More Effective

The lecture is probably the oldest teaching method and still the method most widely used in universities throughout the world. Through the ages a great deal of practical wisdom about techniques of lecturing has accumulated. Effective lecturers combine the talents of scholar, writer, producer, comedian, entertainer, and teacher in ways that contribute to student learning. Nevertheless, it is also true that few college professors combine these talents in optimal ways and that even the best lecturers are not always in top form. Lectures have survived despite the invention of printing, television, and computers. Will they survive the web? Actually a lot of them have co-opted the web as their medium, bringing it into the classroom as the basis for an interactive, up-to-date lecture!

Is the lecture an effective method of teaching? If it is, under what conditions is it most effective? I will tackle these questions not only in light of research on the lecture as a teaching method, but also in terms of analyses of the cognitive processes used by students in lecture classes.

RESEARCH ON THE EFFECTIVENESS OF LECTURES

A large number of studies have compared the effectiveness of lectures with other teaching methods. The results almost invariably show that active learning methods are superior to straight lectures in student retention of information after the end of a course; in transfer of knowledge to new situations; in development of problem solving, thinking, or attitude change; and in motivation for further learning (Goldstein, 2007; McKeachie et al., 1990; Prince, 2004; Smith, et al., 2005; Yoder and Hochevar, 2005).

Similarly, text sources offer advantages over lecture. Students can read faster than lecturers can lecture, and they can go back when they don't understand, skip material that is irrelevant, and review immediately or later. Lectures go at the lecturer's pace, and students who fall behind are out of luck. But don't despair; lectures can still be useful.

WHAT ARE LECTURES GOOD FOR?

- Presenting up-to-date information (There is typically a gap between the latest scholarship and its appearance in a textbook.)
- Summarizing material scattered over a variety of sources
- Adapting material to the background and interests of a particular group of students at a particular time and place
- Helping students read more effectively by providing an orientation and conceptual framework
- Focusing on key concepts, principles, or ideas

Lectures also have motivational values apart from their cognitive content. By helping students become aware of a problem, of conflicting points of view, or of challenges to ideas they have previously taken for granted, the lecturer can stimulate interest in further learning in an area. Moreover, the lecturer's own attitudes and enthusiasm have an important effect on student motivation. Research on student ratings of teaching as well as on student learning indicates that the enthusiasm of the lecturer is an important factor in affecting student learning and motivation. You may feel that enthusiasm is not learnable. Clearly some people are more enthusiastic and expressive than others, but you can develop in this area just as in others. Try to put into each lecture something that you are really excited about. Notice how your voice and gestures show more energy and expressiveness. Now try carrying some of that intensity and animation over into other topics. Like other learned behaviors, this takes practice, but you can do it. Murray (1997) showed that enthusiastic teachers move around, make eye contact with students, and use more gestures and vocal variation, and that teachers could learn these behaviors. Both research and theory support the usefulness of enthusiastic behaviors in maintaining student attention.*

---

*Don't feel that you have to show high energy every minute. There will be times when calm, quiet, slow speech may be needed—times when you may need to wait and reflect before responding.

The lecturer also models ways of approaching problems, portraying a scholar in action in ways that are difficult for other media or methods of instruction to achieve. You can say, "Here is how I go about solving this kind of problem (analyzing this phenomenon, etc.). Now you try it." One of the advantages of live professors is the tendency of people to model themselves after other individuals whom they perceive as living, breathing human beings with characteristics that can be admired and emulated. So lectures can be effective—but sometimes more effective in stimulating our own learning and thinking than in stimulating that of the students!

PLANNING LECTURES

A typical lecture strives to present a systematic, concise summary of the knowledge to be covered in the day's assignment. Chang and associates (1983, p. 21) call this approach "conclusion oriented." While there are times when this is useful, more often your job is less knowledge dispensing, and more about teaching students how to learn and think. That kind of lecture involves analyzing materials, formulating problems, developing hypotheses, bringing evidence to bear, and criticizing and evaluating alternative solutions—revealing methods of learning and thinking and involving students in the process.

One of the implications of such an approach is that what is ideal early in a course is likely to be inappropriate later in the course. As noted earlier, the way students process verbal material depends on the structures that not only enable them to process bigger and bigger chunks of a subject matter but also give them tacit knowledge of the methods, procedures, and conventions used in the field and by you as a lecturer. Intentionally or not, you are teaching students how to become more skilled in learning from your lectures.

Because of this, you should go more slowly in the first weeks of a course, pause to allow students with poor backgrounds time to take notes, and give more everyday types of examples. Pausing to write a phrase or sketch a relationship on the chalkboard or projected image will not only give students a chance to catch up but also provide visual cues that can serve as points of reference later. Later in the term, students should be able to process bigger blocks of material more quickly because they have the necessary mental scaffold on which to hang new information.

Adapting to the differences in students' knowledge from the beginning to the later stages of a course is but one example of the principle that one key to good lecturing is an awareness of the audience, not only in lecturing but in preparing the lecture. In every class there is student diversity—not only in background knowledge but also in motivation, skills for learning, beliefs about what learning involves, and preferences for different ways of learning. Shulman (2002) described the skilled instructor's ability to balance all these things as "pedagogical content knowledge," the knowledge about how students actually learn the content and how to adapt teaching to support that learning.

PREPARING YOUR LECTURE NOTES

One of the security-inducing features of lectures is that you can prepare a lecture with some sense of control over the content and organization of the class period. In lectures, the instructor is usually in control, and this sense of controlled structure helps the anxious teacher avoid pure panic.

But no matter how thoroughly you have prepared the subject matter of the lecture, you must still face the problem of how to retrieve and deliver your insights during the class period. If you have plenty of time and are compulsive, you may be tempted to write out the lecture verbatim. Don't! Or, if you must (and writing it out may be useful in clarifying your thoughts), don't take a verbatim version into the classroom. Few lecturers can read a lecture so well that students stay awake and interested.

At the same time, few teachers can deliver a lecture with no cues at all. Hence, you will ordinarily lecture from notes of some type. Most lecturers use an outline or a sequence of cue words and phrases. Others use a series of questions to help them remember.

Day (1980) studied lecture notes used by professors at over 75 colleges and universities. She notes that extensive notes take the instructor out of eye contact with students so that students fall into a passive, nonquestioning role. Day suggests the use of graphic representations to increase teaching flexibility and spontaneity. Tree diagrams, computer flowcharts, or network models enable a teacher to have at hand a representation of the structure that permits one to answer questions without losing track of the relationship of the question to the lecture organization. Pictorial representations using arrows, faces, Venn diagrams, or drawings that symbolize important concepts may not only provide cues for the instructor but can also be placed on PowerPoint or the board to provide additional cues for students.

Projecting main points using presentation software is for many (myself included) a way of having notes without having notes. You *must*, however, resist the temptation to put everything up on the screen and read directly from it. That is absolutely the worst use of projected notes.

The use of such PowerPoint slides has gotten a lot of negative publicity mostly because of the lecturer's tendency to use them more as a crutch than an organizing system. Clark (2008) and Giers and Kreiner (2009) both did research on this point and found that the student complaints about such a lecture style were reduced when the lecturer build into the slide presentation variety of content (e.g., short videos, diagrams, pictures) and questions for the students to discuss.

Color coding your notes with procedural directions to yourself also helps. Because I try to get student involvement, I have a tendency to run overtime; I put time cues in the margin to remind myself to check. I also put in directions to myself, such as

- "Put on board." (usually a key concept or relationship)
- "Check student understanding. Ask for examples."
- "Ask students for a show of hands."
- "Put students in pairs to discuss this."

Allow time for questions from students, for new examples or ideas that come to mind during the lecture, and for your own misestimation of the time a topic will require. If perchance you finish early, let the students use the remaining time to write a summary. Finally, you can use your notes in a handout with a structure that students can use for filling in their own notes and asking questions. More on this later.

ORGANIZATION OF LECTURES

In thinking about lecture organization, most teachers think first about the structure of the subject matter, and then try to organize the content in some logical fashion, such as building from specifics to generalization or deriving specific implications from general principles. Too often we get so immersed in "covering" the subject that we forget to ask, "What do I really want students to remember from this lecture next week, next year?"

Some common organizing principles used by lecturers are cause to effect; time sequence (for example, stories); parallel organization, such as phenomenon to theory to evidence; problem to solution; pro versus con to resolution; familiar to unfamiliar; and concept to application. As I said earlier, stories not only interest students, they also aid memory. If you can make your story a mystery, you'll hold attention even better (see Green, 2004).

Leith (1977) has suggested that different subjects are basically different in the ways in which progress is made in the field. Some subjects are organized in a linear or hierarchical fashion in which one concept builds on a preceding one. The logical structure of one's subject should be one factor determining the lecture organization, but equally important is the cognitive structure in the students' minds. If we are to teach our students effectively, we need to bridge the gap between the structure in the subject matter and structures in the students' minds. As is indicated in all of the chapters in this book, you are not making impressions on a blank slate. Rather, our task in teaching is to help students reorganize existing cognitive structures or to add new dimensions or new features to existing structures. Thus, the organization of the lecture needs to take account of the student's existing knowledge and expectations as well as the structure of the subject matter. Analogies linking new ideas to similar ones that students already know can help. Remember that what you are trying to do is get an organization into your students' heads that will help them fit in relevant facts and form a base for further learning and thinking.

The Introduction

One suggestion for organization is that the *introduction* of the lecture should point to a gap in the student's existing cognitive structure or should challenge or raise a question about something in the student's existing method of organizing material in order to arouse curiosity (Berlyne, 1954a, 1954b). There is a good deal of research on the role of prequestions in directing attention to features of written texts. Prequestions in the introduction of a lecture may help students to discriminate between more and less important features of lectures. For example, before a lecture on cognitive changes in aging, I ask, "Do you get more or less intelligent as you get older?" and "What is a fair test of intelligence for older people?" Such questions may help create expectations that enable students to allocate their cognitive capacity more effectively. If students know what they are expected to learn from a lecture, they learn more of that material (sometimes at the expense of other material; Royer, 1977). In a recent study, Nevid and Mahon (2009) showed that putting these questions into a set of mastery quizzes before and after each lecture helped direct student attention to the key concepts and resulted in better unit-test performance at the end of the unit. Although there are other factors probably operating here, this is such a simple procedure, and students seem to like it. This is the basic model used in Team-Based Learning, which is discussed in the chapter on "Active Learning." I've been using it in my own classes and it has significantly increased student attention and interest in the rest of the class session. Students really want to know why their thinking was correct or incorrect!

Another approach is to begin with a demonstration, example, case, or application that captures attention. In many fields it is possible to begin some lectures with the presentation of a problem or case from a current newspaper or television show, then ask students how they would think about it in the light of this course, or alternatively illustrate in the lecture how experts in this field would think about it.

The Body of the Lecture

In organizing the *body* of the lecture, the most common error is probably that of trying to include too much. The enemy of learning is the teacher's need to cover the content at all costs. When I began lecturing, my mentor told me, "If you get across three or four points in a lecture so that students understand and remember them, you've done well." Lecturers very often overload the students' information processing capacity so that they become less able to understand the material than if fewer points had been presented. David Katz (1950), a pioneer Gestalt psychologist, called this phenomenon "mental dazzle." He suggested that, just as too much light causes our eyes to be dazzled so that we cannot see anything, too many new ideas can overload processing capacity so that we cannot understand anything.

As noted earlier, you can use the board, an overhead projector, or PowerPoint to give the students cues to the organization of the lecture. Progressively displaying points of an outline or key words is useful in three ways:

1. It gives a *visual* representation to supplement your oral presentation. Using a diagram or other graphic representation will help visualization.

2. Change helps retain (or regain) attention so everyone is on the same page at the same time.

3. It gives students a chance to catch up with what you have said (perchance to think!).

Using Examples Move from the concrete to the abstract. To link what is in your head with what is in the students' heads, you need to use examples that relate the subject to the students' experience and knowledge. I am not as effective a teacher today as I was decades ago because I do not know the students' culture and am thus limited in finding vivid examples of a concept in students' daily lives. Because no single example can represent a concept fully, you usually need to give more than one. Concept formation research suggests that examples differing from one another are likely to be most effective if you point out the essential features of the concept exemplified in each example. If you can find a cartoon or funny story that illustrates your point, humor helps maintain interest. But the danger is that students may remember the humor and not the concept, so repeat the concept. Harp and Maslich (2005) showed that "seductive details" are just as detrimental to learning from a lecture as they are from a text, so use them sparingly. And, most important, give students a chance to give examples.

Periodic Summaries within the Lecture From our knowledge of students' note-taking behavior, we know that students would be better able to learn from lectures if there were periodic summaries of preceding material. These give students a chance to catch up on material covered when they were not tuned in, and also give them a check on possible misperceptions based on inadequate or misleading expectations. Repeat main points once, twice, thrice, during the lecture. Such summaries can help make clear to students transitions from one theme to another, so that they are aided in organizing the material not only in their notes but in their minds. In fact, you might try thinking of your lecture as two or more mini-lectures separated by short periods for questions, discussion, or writing.

Checking Student Understanding Although it may seem irrational to cover material when students are not learning from it, you should not underestimate the compulsion you'll feel to get through your lecture notes. A remedy for this compulsion is to put reminders (to yourself) into the lecture notes to check the students' understanding—both by looking for nonverbal cues of bewilderment or of lack of attention, and by raising specific questions that will test the students' understanding.

Most lecturers recognize that they need to check student understanding periodically; so they ask, "Any questions?" and after three to five seconds without any response, they assume that everyone understands. Not so! If you really want to know, give students a minute to write down a question, then have them compare notes with students sitting near them before asking for questions. You'll get some.

However, the best way to check student understanding—as well as to maintain attention and support learning—is to incorporate activities into the lecture. The activities can be simple (e.g., have students summarize what was just said) or complex (e.g., use the personal response systems described below to get everyone in the class to respond to a content related question). Angelo and Cross's (1993) compilation of activities (called Classroom Assessment Techniques or CATs) can give you lots of ideas. Goldstein (2007) reports that students say they understand better when the instructor incorporates CATs. Gray and Madson (2007) have provided a very concise set of ways to involve students in large classes. There are more ideas discussed below.

The Conclusion In the *conclusion* of the lecture, you have the opportunity to make up for lapses in the body of the lecture. Encouraging students to formulate questions or asking questions yourself can facilitate understanding and memory. By making the oral headings of the lecture visible once again, by recapitulating major points, by proposing unanswered questions to be treated in the reading assignments or the future lectures, and by creating an anticipation of the future, the lecturer can help students learn. One good (and humbling) technique is to announce that you will ask a student to summarize the lecture at the end of the period. Another—less threatening—option is to have students spend three minutes writing a summary of main points, a technique sometimes called a "minute paper" (Wilson, 1986), and then asking one of them to read what they wrote. I also suggest collecting those minute papers as an ongoing assessment of what students are learning. Either method helps the process of elaboration, which is critical for memory. And, of course, as I mentioned earlier, a post-mastery quiz can serve to check students' understanding as well.

HOW CAN LECTURES BE IMPROVED?

The message of this chapter is that one way of improving lectures is to think about how students process lectures. What are students trying to do during a lecture?

As you observe student behavior during a lecture, the most impressive thing you might notice is the passive role students have in most classrooms. Some students are having difficulty in staying awake; others are attempting to pass the time as easily as possible by reading other materials, texting their friends, counting lecturer mannerisms, or simply doodling and listening in a relatively effortless manner. Most students are taking notes. Ideally, many students are attempting to construct knowledge by linking what the lecturer says with what they already know.

Attention

One of the factors determining students' success in information processing is their ability to pay attention to the lecture. Attention basically involves focusing one's cognitions on those things that are changing, novel, or motivating. Individuals have a limited capacity for attending to the varied features of their environment, despite claims of multitasking facility. The individual's total capacity for attention may vary with the degree of activation or motivation. At any one time, part of the capacity may be devoted to the task at hand (in this case listening to the lecturer), part may be involved in taking notes, and part may be left over to shift primary attention to distractions or daydreams when boredom occurs.

Wilson and Korn (2007) did a very good job of analyzing a lot of the research on the patterns of student attention during lectures in order to determine if students really did experience a waning of attention after about ten minutes. As is often the case with classroom-based research, the measures used to evaluate level of attention varied from the amount of notes taken to observational data on student behavior to retention of the material. And as is also often the case, they found that nothing was ever so simple as the definitive ten to fifteen minutes span of attention rule. They suggested that there are many individual variables of the student, the instructor, the content, and the environment that influence students' ability to maintain their focus. Wilson and Korn did suggest that you as an instructor would learn a lot from looking at what ends up in your students' notes, and that might be the best guide for estimating how well and how often your students are paying attention. If they're not getting down the main ideas, then you may begin to worry about how to help them pay attention at the right moments in the class.

What Can Be Done to Maintain Attention?

In determining how to allocate attention, students use various strategies. Any lecturer knows that one way of getting attention is to precede the statement by the phrase, "This will be on the test." In addition, students listen for particular words or phrases that indicate to them that something is worth noting and remembering. Statements that enumerate or list are likely to be on tests and thus are likely to be attended to.

Changes in the environment recruit attention. The ability of change to capture attention can work to the advantage of the lecturer. Variation in pitch, intensity, and pace of the lecture; visual cues such as gestures, facial expression, movement to the board; the use of demonstrations or audiovisual aids—all of these recruit and maintain attention to the lecture.

Auditory attention is directed to some extent by visual attention. Distracting movements in the classroom are thus likely to cause students to fail to recall what the lecturer has said. On the positive side, students' comprehension is greater when the students can see the speaker's face and lips (Campbell, 1999). Look at your audience; eye contact helps communication.

Motivation is important in holding student attention. Linking lectures to student interests, giving examples that are vivid and intriguing, and building suspense toward resolution of a conflict—these are all techniques of gaining and holding attention.

All of these devices will help, but the best device for maintaining attention is to break up the lecture rather than trying to hold attention for an hour or more. We've already looked at the value of active learning in keeping students engaged. If you spot signs of drowsiness or fidgeting, ask students to stand up and stretch. Bligh's research summary (2000) indicated that the gain in learning after such a break more than compensates for any learning that might have occurred in the time taken for the break.

A recent innovation that does wonders for student attention is the use of personal response systems, called "clickers," during the course of the period. These computer-input devices allow the instructor to interject activities throughout the class period and have the students respond by tapping keys on a small handheld device. These responses can then be projected in the aggregate for the entire class to see and captured to monitor individual student selections. The use of clickers is discussed in much greater detail in chapter 17 on the use of technology, but I mention it here because it is making a big difference in getting instructors to involve the students more actively during a lecture, and that is a wonderful way of maintaining attention. Recent research by Shaffer and Collura (2009) and Stowell and Nelson (2007) as well as the Mayer study mentioned below (2009) all come down on the side of clickers as supporting learning. Of course, you don't necessarily need to use technology for such opportunities for active responding; you can have students raise their hands to indicate their choice of answer to a question. This past semester I was using colored index cards, a low-tech version of clickers. They had some drawbacks, but for the most part, they had the same effect as the electronics. The technology has the advantage of allowing you to summarize and display the class's responses instantly, so they can inform what is happening in class immediately and retain the information for improvement purposes later. The recent study by Mayer and colleagues (2009) attempted to evaluate the educational value of using clicker-supported questioning during lectures in comparison to paper-based quizzes at the end of class and a control condition of no questions. They found that the class in which the clickers were used throughout the lecture had one-third of a grade higher than the other two conditions, which did not differ from one another. There are some methodological issues that might be a problem in interpreting the results of this study; but in general, the idea that clicker-based questioning in the course of the lecture resulted in better exam performance was supported. As it takes so little time to interject this type of questioning in class, it is certainly worth trying.

TEACHING STUDENTS HOW TO BE BETTER LISTENERS

We assume that listening is an innate skill, but you can train your students to be better listeners. For example, you might begin by asking students to write for one minute on "What do I hope to get out of this lecture?" or "What was the most important point in the reading assignment for the day?" Then explain how this strategy will help them to be more effective listeners in any lecture. Both of these strategies act as a "warm-up," focusing attention and activating relevant prior knowledge.

Another useful strategy is to ask students to listen to you (for five to fifteen minutes) without taking notes and then to write a summary. You might then ask them to compare their summaries with those of one or two classmates sitting near them.

A related strategy is to tell students that you will give them five minutes at the end of the lecture to summarize the main points of the lecture for someone sitting near them. At the end of the class period, ask them what effect this had on their listening to the lecture, and point out that they can use this approach to lectures even if they summarize them only in their own notes.

HOW DO STUDENTS PROCESS THE CONTENT OF A LECTURE?

Let's assume that students are allocating attention appropriately to the lecture. This alone, however, does not ensure that the content of the lecture will be understood, remembered, and applied appropriately. Even though students are trying to meet the demands of the situation, they may differ in the ways they go about processing the words that they have heard.

Marton and Säljö (1976a, 1976b) and other researchers at the University of Göteborg have described differences in the way students go about trying to learn educational materials. Some students process the material as little as possible, simply taking as many verbatim notes as they can. This would be described by Marton as a "surface approach." Other students try to see implications of what the lecturer is saying, relate what is currently being said to other information either in the lecture or in their own experience and reading, and try to understand what the author intended. They elaborate and translate the instructor's words into their own. They may question. This more thoughtful and active kind of listening is what Marton and Säljö refer to as "deep processing."

Experienced students can probably vary their strategies from surface to deep processing of concepts, depending on the demands of the situation. Generally, deep processing better enables students to remember and use knowledge for thinking and further learning. Pointing out relationships, asking rhetorical questions, or asking questions to be answered by class members are ways of encouraging deeper processing. You can also ask for examples of how students apply concepts to their own experiences, thus encouraging all students to realize that it is important to try to think about how concepts relate to oneself. Most of the active learning strategies we look at throughout this book are designed to foster deep processing.

SHOULD STUDENTS TAKE NOTES?

Note taking is one of the activities by which students attempt to stay attentive, but note taking is also an aid to memory. *Working memory*, or *short-term memory*, is a term used to describe the fact that one can hold only a given amount of material in mind at one time. When the lecturer presents a succession of new concepts, students' faces begin to show signs of anguish and frustration; some write furiously in their notebooks, while others stop writing in complete discouragement. Note taking thus depends on one's ability to maintain attention, understand what is being said, and hold it in working memory long enough to write it down. A study of students' lecture notes by Baker and Lombardi (1985) showed that "most students included in their notes less that 25% of the propositions judged worthy of inclusion and only 50% of the targeted main ideas" (p. 28). The students did, however, distinguish between main ideas and supporting details by recording more of the former and less of the latter in their notes. Finally, there was a relationship between the notes taken and their performance on test questions related to main ideas.

However, research does support two values of note taking. One is that the notes provide an external memory store that can be reviewed later; the other is that note taking involves elaboration and transformation of ideas, which aids memory (Babb and Ross, 2009; Hartley and Davies, 1978; Peper and Mayer, 1978). But note taking has costs as well as benefits. Individual student note-taking strategies differ. Some students take copious notes; others take none. We know that cognitive capacity is limited; that is, people can take in, understand, and store only so much information in any brief period of time. Information will be processed more effectively if the student is actively engaged in note taking—analyzing and processing the information rather than passively soaking it up—but taking notes requires capacity that may be needed for comprehension if material is difficult. Thus, encourage students to take *fewer* notes and to listen carefully when you are introducing new, difficult material. They can then fill in their notes after class.

Students' ability to process information depends on the degree to which the information can be integrated or "chunked." No one has great ability at handling large numbers of unrelated items in active memory. Thus, when students are in an area of new concepts or when the instructor is using language that is not entirely familiar to the students, students may be processing the lecture word by word or phrase by phrase and lose the sense of a sentence or of a paragraph before the end of the thought is reached. This means that lecturers need to be aware of instances in which new words or concepts are being introduced and to build in greater redundancy, as well as pauses during which students can catch up and get appropriate notes.

Snow and Peterson (1980) point out that brighter students benefit more from taking notes than less able students. For students with less background knowledge, note taking takes capacity needed for listening and comprehending, so they simply miss much of what is being said. This is not simply a matter of intelligence; rather, a student's ability to maintain materials in memory while taking notes and even to process and think about relationships between one idea and other ideas depends on the knowledge or cognitive structures the student has available for organizing and relating the material.

Hartley's research, as well as that of Annis (1981) and Kiewra (1989), suggests that a skeletal outline is helpful to students, but that with detailed notes students relax into passivity. It is better simply to provide an overall framework, which they can fill in by selecting important points and interpreting them in their own words. Because student capacity for information processing is limited, and because students stop and go over a confusing part of a lecture again, you need to build more redundancy into your lectures than into writing, and you need to build in pauses where students can catch up and think rather than simply struggle to keep up.

A question that I get asked a lot these days is whether the instructor should make lecture notes available beforehand to help students take better notes. Research on this will be ongoing forever because there are so many factors to consider in answering it. However, Babb and Ross (2009) conducted a well-designed study comparing attendance, participation, and exam performance of classes that received class notes either before or after the lecture. Contrary to popular beliefs among faculty, students who received the notes prior to the lecture actually attended class more regularly and participated more during class. The researchers speculated on why that might be the case. They suggested that having the notes alerted the students to things that would be discussed in class and allowed them to prepare more efficiently. However, there was no difference on the exam performance of the two conditions, which led the researchers to propose that there are many more variables that influence exam performance than the quality of the notes that students use to study, a reasonable conclusion. There were several more side conclusions of this research, but the main conclusion of these researchers was that giving notes before class is beneficial.

If I have to make a recommendation, based on all I know about learning, I would stick with giving outline notes prior to class and allowing students to fill in the details during class. That format seems to me to be most consistent with learning and motivation research.

IN CONCLUSION

What is the role of the lecturer in higher education? To communicate the teacher's enthusiasm about the subject.

The lecture is also sometimes an effective way of communicating information, particularly in classes where variations in student background, ability, or interest make feedback to the lecturer important. We have also shown that the organization and presentation of lectures may influence their effectiveness in achieving application of knowledge or in influencing attitudes. Active learning methods such as discussion, however, are likely to be more effective than lecturing in achieving higher-level cognitive and attitudinal objectives, and combinations of lecture and discussion may be optimal.

Becoming conscious of what is going on in the students' heads as we talk; being alert to feedback from students through their facial expressions, nonverbal behavior, and oral comments; and adjusting your strategies in reference to these cues—these will help you learn and help students to learn more effectively.

Supplementary Reading

- The most comprehensive book on lecturing is Donald Bligh's *What's the Use of Lectures?* (San Francisco: Jossey-Bass, 2000).
- A very practical guide for lecturers is George Brown's classic paperback, *Lecturing and Explaining* (London: Methuen, 1978).
- Barbara Davis's *Tools for Teaching*, 2nd ed. (San Francisco: Jossey-Bass, 2009), gives practical tips on preparing, delivering, and personalizing lecture classes.

Chapter 7

Assessing, Testing, and Evaluating: Grading Is Not the Most Important Function

When we think about evaluating learning, most of us think about examinations—multiple-choice tests, essay tests, oral examinations, perhaps performance tests. Currently there is much interest in other methods of assessment. In this chapter I begin with suggestions for conventional testing and then suggest other methods of assessing student learning.

Let me start with nine assertions:

1. What students learn depends as much on your tests and methods of assessment as on your teaching, maybe even more. What is measured is often what ends up being valued, so be sure your measures reflect what you want the students to learn.

2. Don't think of tests simply as a means for assigning grades. Tests should facilitate learning for you as well as for your students.

3. Use some nongraded tests and assessments that provide feedback to the students and you. The CATs (Classroom Assessment Techniques; Angelo and Cross, 1993) methods for gathering information about student learning can be a real boon to you and the students.

4. Check your assessment methods against your goals. Are you really assessing what you hoped to achieve: for example, higher-order thinking?

5. Some goals (values, motivation, attitudes, some skills) may not be measurable by conventional tests. Look for other evidence of their development.

6. Assessment is not synonymous with testing. You can assess students' learning with classroom and out-of-class activities, what the experts refer to as embedded assessment.

7. After the course is over, students will not be able to depend on you to assess the quality of their learning. If one of your goals is the development of lifelong learning skills, students need practice in self-assessment. Peckham and Sutherland (2000) showed that developing accurate student self-assessment requires training and practice. Peer assessment of one another's papers helps develop assessment skill and improves performance (Gibbs, 1999).

8. Don't rely on one or two tests to determine grades. Varied assessments will give you better evidence to determine an appropriate grade. This is what experts call *triangulation of data,* which means seeing it from multiple perspectives.

9. To summarize: Assessment is *not* simply an end-of-course exercise to determine student grades. Assessments can be learning experiences for students. Assessment throughout a course communicates your goals to students so that they can learn more effectively; it will identify misunderstandings that will help you teach better; it will help you pace the development of the course; and, yes, it will also help you do a better job of assigning grades.

PLANNING METHODS OF ASSESSMENT

The first step in assessment of learning is to list your goals and objectives for the course, as discussed on the chapter on course preparation. Once you have specified objectives, you can determine which kind of assessment is appropriate for each objective. Later in this chapter, you'll find ideas for assessing learning other than within class tests. Be open to trying something different if you're the person who gets to choose the assessment strategies. Also consider using some variety in assessing learning. Not every student can show understanding on high-stakes tests; some students might do better on written assignments or on projects or shorter assessments.

One way of maintaining a balance is to construct a grid, listing objectives along the side of the page and content areas along the top. If you then put a tally mark in the appropriate cells of the grid as you decide on assessment types you are going to use, you can monitor the degree to which your overall assessment plan adequately samples the objectives and content desired. Some objectives will be appropriate for in-class tests, some for out-of-class assignments, some for short periods of time, some for longer time periods. If you're having a hard time balancing content coverage in your assessment, this is one way to make sure you emphasize higher-level thinking along with basic information. The grid also helps you see gaps or overlaps so you can adjust the system as you create the syllabus or assignments. An example of this type of grid and how it was developed is found in chapter 2 of this book. Phyllis Blumberg's (2009) article on course alignment provides several good ways to chart not just course learning outcomes, but also recounts how the system was actually used in a physical therapy course.

Admittedly, it is more difficult to devise measures of complex, higher-level objectives. Yet the very effort to do so will, I believe, have an influence on student motivation and learning. Moreover, consideration of these objectives may help you break out of the conventional forms of testing. For example, in my classes in introductory psychology, the desired goals include developing greater curiosity about behavior, awareness of dimensions of behavior that might ordinarily be ignored, and increased ability to describe and analyze behavior objectively. To get at this I have sometimes used a video as a stimulus, and then had the students write in responses to questions that have to do with their reactions to the film; or I have asked students to leave the classroom for fifteen minutes and then return and report on some interesting behavior they observed. I have brought in scientific journals and asked students to find an article of interest and to write their reactions to it. I have asked for analyses of newspaper items to get at the degree to which students can read critically. These kinds of assessments embedded in the ongoing class activities are often not recognized as being "tests" and therefore do not fall prey to all the misconceptions and anxieties that students have about being tested. If you then have the students talk about what they have written, they often frame these assessments as learning activities rather than tests, which is a good way to think about them. Using materials with somewhat greater apparent relevance to course objectives than that of typical test items is more fun for the students taking the test—and more fun to grade.

Institutional Purposes for Your Course Assessments

As was mentioned in that earlier chapter on planning, most institutions are beginning to pay much closer attention to the learning outcomes of programs and courses to document the objectives of the institution as a whole. (See Figure 2 in the chapter on course preparation, for an example). Kinzie (2010) reviewed the results of a national survey on the assessment of learning outcomes. She reported that the concept of using assessments to satisfy accreditation requirements has taken hold and expanded as their value as a planning and evaluation tool became more evident. In her analysis, she says that involvement of faculty in incorporating assessment from their classes into the overall program and institutional process is critical. Being able to use information that faculty members have already collected as part of the class process, has been helpful in this regard. Kuh and Ewell (2010) caution that there is a lot of assessment going on, but the results are not being used as well as they should be. If the assessments are part of the teaching practice, they will more likely become the fulcrum for better learning as well as institutional improvement. A good source for advice on contributing to this kind of assessment is Palomba and Banta (1999), which is listed in the Supplementary Reading at the end of this chapter. Two examples of this practice are Blumberg (2009), at the institutional and individual course level, and Gerretson and Golson (2005), at the program level. If you can select assessment methods for your course that will also provide the kinds of data that are useful for program improvement, you'll be serving two important tasks of the university – student and organizational learning.

METHODS OF ASSESSING LEARNING

Tests: In and Out of Class

Because grades in many courses are determined to a great degree by test scores, tests are among the most familiar, but often most frustrating, aspects of the course to many students and arouse a great deal of overt and covert aggression. If teachers attempt to go beyond the usual practice of asking simply for memory of information from the textbook or lectures, they are immediately deluged with the complaint, "These are the most ambiguous tests I have ever taken!" This type of assessment is covered in chapter 8, "Testing: The Details," but just to put them in the context of assessment in general, I have included a few more general ideas here along with other assessment strategies.

Because some course examinations emphasize the recall of facts, many students demand *teaching* that emphasizes memorization of facts. One student wrote on a teacher evaluation, "The instructor is very interesting and worthwhile, but I have rated him low because he doesn't give us enough facts. The sort of job I get will depend on my grades, and I have little chance of beating other students out for an A unless I can get a couple of pages of notes each period."

Students may object at first to tests requiring them to think, but if you emphasize that the tests will measure their abilities to use their knowledge, you can greatly influence their goals in the course. This is indicated by another student comment: "More of the course should be like the tests. They make us apply what we've learned." Marton and Säljö (1976b) showed that questions demanding understanding rather than memory of detailed facts resulted in differing styles of studying for later tests and better retention. Foos and Fisher (1988) showed that tests requiring inferences enhanced learning more than those requiring memorized knowledge.

However, sometimes you just want to know if the students are getting the basics down before you move on to the bigger issues. For this level of assessment, in-class quizzes and tests are just the thing. There is a lot of interest in (and therefore research on) the kinds and frequency of quizzes that we should use (see Johnson and Kiviniemi, 2009, for online quizzes; Myers and Myers, 2007, for a comparison of shorter, more frequent exams; Padilla-Walker, 2006, for extra credit quizzes; and Roselli and Brophy, 2006, for anonymous quizzes). Summing it all up in a meta-analysis, Basol and Johanson (2009) conclude that frequent tests have a positive effect on student achievement, even though the actual frequency doesn't seem to matter as long as it's greater than two a semester. They don't have to be the major mid-semester type of marathon tests. The short pre- or post-lecture mastery quizzes and questions spread throughout a lecture can be both assessments and spurs to learning. Kuo and Simon (2009) came to a similar conclusion, although they reported that monthly tests paired with good feedback to students seemed to look like the best alternative.

In my own classes, students have commented that the quizzes make them read the textbook before we discuss something in class, which gives them a firmer foundation to understand the discussion. I have also noticed that my students rate practice exams as the thing that helps them prepare best for the real exams. So this next semester I'm going to call all the daily quizzes "exam practice" and see if this makes them more valuable in the students' eyes.

Performance Assessment (Authentic Assessment)

Over two decades ago, Alverno College in Milwaukee, Wisconsin, instituted a student-centered curriculum and performance assessment plan that has become a significant model for American colleges and universities. Faculty members construct learning situations in which they can observe student performance and judge the performance on the basis of specified criteria. The faculty has defined developmental levels in each of several abilities that students are expected to achieve. Since no one situation is sufficient for assessing a complex ability, the assessment plan stresses multiple modes of assessment related to real-life contexts. In addition, faculty actively train students in methods of self-assessment, an important outcome if students are to continue learning when there are no longer teachers around to evaluate their work (see Alverno College Faculty, 1994; Mentkowski and Loacker, 1985; Mentkowski et al., 2000).

Many other college teachers are using methods of evaluating learning that are more authentically related to later uses of learning than are conventional tests. For example, in chemistry, mathematics, and engineering courses instructors now use fewer standard abstract problems that can be solved by algorithms, and instead present more problems that describe situations in which more than one approach could be used and in which alternative solutions are possible. Such "authentic" assessments are particularly appropriate for service learning situations.

There is an interesting question about authentic assessment that was raised early on by Spence-Brown (2001). In analyzing the kinds of authentic assignments that foreign language instructors were adopting, she found that the key was how the students "framed" the assessment that affected its perceived authenticity. If they saw it as just another class assignment, their strategies for carrying it out were very different than if it was perceived as "real." The former perspective lowered the depth of processing and the motivation level of the students. I recommend that you do as much as possible to make the task a real task with real significance in order to avoid the class assignment mentality Spence-Brown found.

Simulations (on computers or role-played), hands-on field or laboratory exercises, research projects, and juried presentations (such as are used in music, art, and architecture) are also methods related more closely to later use of learning. Paper-and-pencil tasks used to evaluate these types of learning may require similarity judgments, sorting, or successive choices or predictions following sequential presentation of information about a case, scenario, or situation based on the real problems that a professional might face.

Graphic Representations of Concepts

An organized framework of concepts is important for further learning and thinking. Graphic representations of conceptual relationships may be useful both for teaching and for assessing learning. McKeachie's research group (Naveh-Benjamin, Lin, and McKeachie, 1989; Naveh-Benjamin et al., 1989; Naveh-Benjamin et al., 1986) developed two methods (the "ordered tree" and "fill-in-the-structure," or FITS) that they use to assess the development of conceptual relationships during college courses. In both of these methods the instructor chooses a number of concepts and arranges them in a hierarchical structure like that depicted in Figure 7.1 (which shows an example used in a Learning to Learn

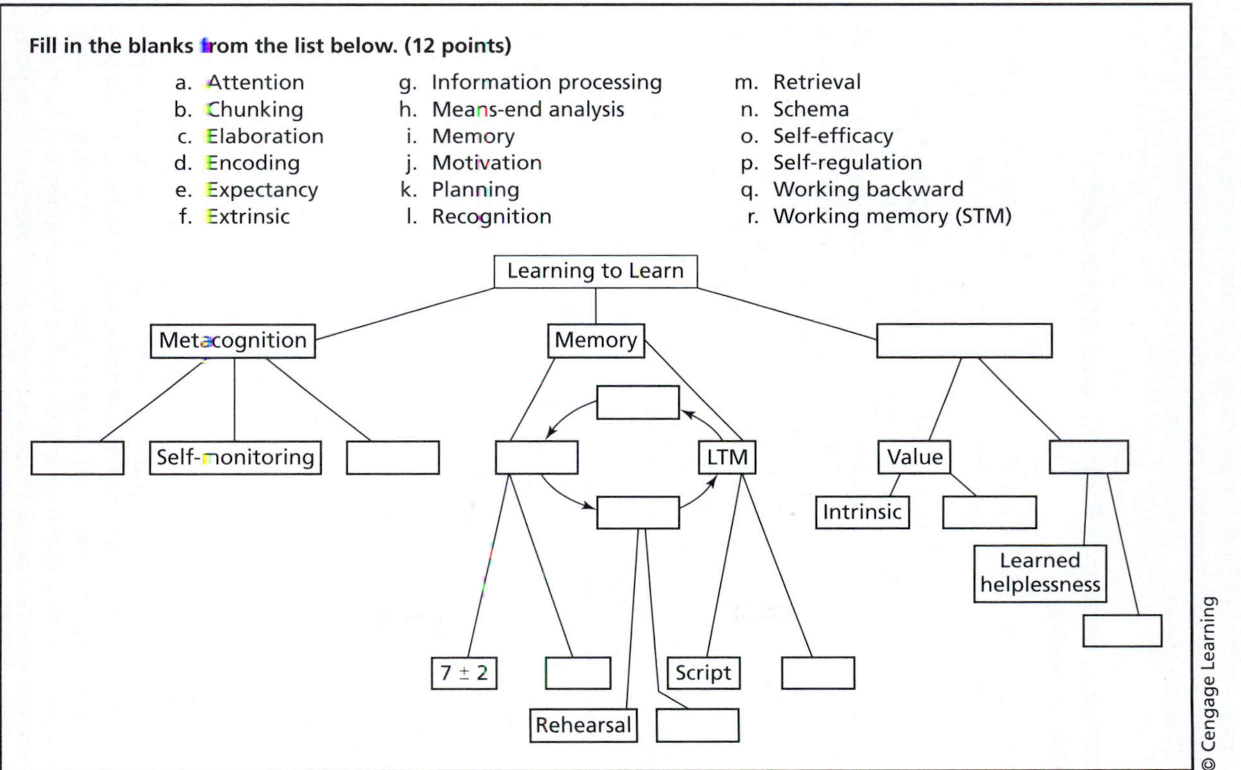

FIGURE 7.1 Learning to Learn Chart

course). For the FITS task the instructor gives the students a copy of the basic structure with some concepts missing. The students are then asked to fill in the blanks.

Journals, Research Papers, and Annotated Bibliographies

Journals, research papers, and reports come closer to the goals of authentic assessment than do most conventional tests. Journals are particularly useful in helping students develop critical reflection and self-awareness (Bolin, Khramtsova, and Saarnio, 2005; Connor-Greene, 2000; MacGregor, 1993; Rhoads and Howard, 1998). There has been some recent criticism of the claims made about student level of reflection prompted by journaling. Dyment and O'Connell (2010) summarized research on journal assignments and reported that the range of reflection shown was quite varied. They suggested that the quality of reflection can be improved by making expectations clearer, providing training for students, improving the relationship between the teacher and the students, and giving lots of practice with feedback. The chapter, "Using High-Stakes and Low-Stakes Writing to Enhance Learning," deals with such writing in detail. Annotated bibliographies can be a useful preparation for writing as well as a tool for assessment. Moreover, annotated bibliographies can be a resource for the whole class (Miller, 1998). Evaluating these products can be improved if you use the rubric method described in chapter 8 on testing details. A rubric is basically a carefully laid out analysis of the key characteristics of the assignment and how well the student met your expectations for each of them. Creating one prior to grading, and using it during grading, helps you maintain consistency in evaluating the papers and makes explaining the grades a lot easier later.

Portfolios

Traditionally used in art and architecture classes, portfolios are becoming popular in a variety of subjects and at all levels of education. Although there are many types of portfolios, they basically are used to highlight work that individual students have accomplished over a period of time. A portfolio might include early as well as later examples in order to demonstrate progress, or a portfolio may be simply a presentation of the student's best work or, better yet, the student's own descriptions of how the work helped his or her development. In mathematics or science a portfolio might consist of problems or lab reports representing various course topics written up to show the student's level of understanding. Portfolios in other courses might include entries from journals describing reactions to reading, classroom experiences, or learning occurring outside the classroom; papers; notes for presentations to the class; and other materials. A portfolio helps both the students and the instructor see how students have progressed. Students report increased self-awareness, and I frequently find evidence of learning (or the lack of it) that I otherwise would have missed.

Peer Assessment

Even if you use the best assessment and grading procedures, some students will be frustrated with their grades. You can prevent some aggression if you help students develop skills in self-assessment. As mentioned earlier, this takes practice, but a lot of instructors are beginning to incorporate peer assessment into their classes (Fleming, 2001; Fluckiger, 2010; Topping, 1998). In these instances, students learn about the criteria used for assessing their work, and they learn to apply those criteria to their work before they turn it in, a real benefit for the instructor. Some instructors have developed computer-based peer reviewing systems (called "calibrated peer review") that involve students grading other students' work online using a carefully refined rubric given by the instructor (Davies, 2000; Robinson, 2001).

On a more modest level, you can have your students evaluate one another's work in hard copy. After collecting tests or papers, redistribute them randomly with a rubric for evaluation. Encourage the students to write helpful comments as well as an evaluation. After students evaluate the papers they were given, ask them to exchange with a neighbor, evaluate the paper given to the neighbor, and then compare notes on their evaluations.

What you do next will probably depend on the size of your class. In a small class you can collect the papers and evaluations and review them before returning them to the evaluators and students evaluated. If the class is larger, ask the class as a whole to discuss the process, what problems they encountered, and what they learned.

Assessing Group Work

As teachers use more and more team projects and cooperative learning, one of the frequently asked questions is "How can I assess group work?" First let's be clear about what we're assessing. You might be assessing student learning in the form of papers or products produced by the group or by members of the group. Or you might be assessing the way in which students worked together in the group, focusing on group process and teamwork more than on content learning.

To measure how much content each student has learned, instructors sometimes ask group members to write individual reports. Students are told that purely descriptive parts, such as the research design, may be the same on all papers but that parts representing thinking are to represent the individual student's own thinking—although students are encouraged to read and discuss each other's papers before submitting them. You can also include an exam question relevant to the group projects on a unit test or final. Mostly, instructors ask each group to submit a single report, which the instructor evaluates.

To evaluate individual contributions to the group, I ask group members to simply describe the work contributed by other members without assessing its value. This allows them to be nonjudgmental, leaving the judgment calls up to me. Group members' descriptions of each member's contribution can be compared to get a more accurate picture of what each individual contributed. Other instructors have students distribute points according to the amount each student has contributed to the group's work. I find, however, that most students have difficulty offering any assessment other than reporting each person as doing an equal amount.

Some instructors develop group rating forms that list the key group contributions that each member is expected to make. Each group member evaluates the other members according to those criteria. I've found it very useful to include the students in the process of identifying those key contributions. At the beginning of a group-oriented project, I have a class discussion about what constitutes good group work. Once we all agree on the behaviors that fit that designation, I draw up a contract that all the students agree to. The peer assessment and my assessment of each student's work are then based on those criteria. Because they have contributed to defining the criteria, the students have a pretty clear idea about what is expected of them.

Embedded Assessment

Wilson and Sloane (2000) have provided a good description of the spirit behind embedded assessment. "By using the term *embedded* we mean that opportunities to assess student progress and performance are integrated into the instructional materials and are virtually indistinguishable from the everyday classroom activities" (p. 182). A great example of embedded assessments that has surfaced recently is the use of personal response systems in the classroom, as discussed in chapter 6 on lecturing and chapter 17, which focuses on technology. What sets embedded assessments apart from just plain classroom activities and makes them "assessment" is that the instructor can gather information about individual as well as class performance; this information can be used to diagnose student problems, provide feedback, and make adjustments, but also can be graded and figured into an overall grade. Another unique aspect of embedded assessment is that it can be repeated across the semester and give you an idea about student growth in understanding across time. Seeing that they are making progress serves as a good source of motivation for students, too.

You should think about what goes on in your class meetings and whether there are data that could be collected in the process of learning that would be useful. For example, in my class the students are constantly working on applying the ideas we are discussing to their future professional situations by responding to scenarios on an in-class activity sheet. The sheet forms the basis of our discussions and lets me and the students know if they are understanding the concepts. If the students were actually out in the field observing children's behavior, their field notes and write-ups could be used as assessments as well.

Classroom Assessment

The primary purpose of assessment is to provide feedback to students and the teacher so that learning can be facilitated. *Classroom assessment* is the term popularized by Pat Cross and Tom Angelo to describe a variety of nongraded methods of getting feedback on student learning. I described minute papers in the preceding chapter. Question posting (discussed in the chapter "Meeting a Class for the First Time") and the two-column method (in the "Facilitating Discussion" chapter) are ways of getting feedback as well as of facilitating student learning. Angelo and Cross (1993) describe a variety of classroom assessment techniques (CATs) discussed in the chapter on lecture that have been very popular. Regular use of such formative assessment may change the way students view what should happen in class. My own students consistently report how much they value these regular assessments.

IN CONCLUSION

1. Learning is more important than grading.
2. Tests and other assessments should be learning experiences as well as evaluation devices.
3. Providing feedback is more important than assigning a grade. You can use nongraded evaluation as well as evaluation for assigning grades.
4. Try to assess the attainment of all your objectives, even if some objectives (such as increased motivation for learning) are not appropriate criteria for grades.
5. Avoid evaluation devices that increase anxiety and competition.

Supplementary Reading

Paul Ramsden's chapter "Assessing for Understanding," in his book *Learning to Teach in Higher Education* (London: Routledge, 1992), presents a wise perspective on assessment and gives examples from chemistry, anatomy, materials technology, engineering, history of art, statistics, medicine, and physics.

Tom Angelo and Pat Cross's *Classroom Assessment Techniques* (1993) has become almost a bible for faculty interested in incorporating more ongoing assessment in their classes.

500 Tips on Assessment by Sally Brown, Phil Race, and Brenda Smith (London: Kogan Page, 1996) is a marvelous compendium of useful suggestions on all types of assessment, ranging from self-assessment through group assessment, multiple-choice tests, and assessment of performance, lab work, and dissertations.

Graham Gibbs discusses other methods of assessing learner-centered courses in his book *Assessing Student-Centered Courses* (Oxford: Oxford Centre for Staff Development, 1995). Chapters give case studies illustrating assessment of group work, projects, journals, skills, and portfolios.

Assessment Matters in Higher Education, edited by Sally Brown and Angela Glasner (Buckingham, UK, and Philadelphia: Society for Research into Higher Education and Open University, 1999), describes innovative approaches to assessment and current United Kingdom practices in a variety of disciplines. There is an entire section on peer assessment and self-assessment. (I suspect that the pun in the title was intentional.)

Assessment Essentials: *Planning, Implementing and Improving Assessment in Higher Education* by Catherine Palomba and Trudy Banta (San Francisco: Jossey-Bass, 1999) is a fine resource on all manner of assessment strategies and the rules that guide their use, particularly if your assessments are going to be folded into larger institutional evaluation issues.

Chapter 8

Testing: The Details

If your assessment plans call for the use of in-class testing (and they probably will), you can do a lot to make sure that the test you design serves the assessment purposes you had in mind. In this chapter, I'm going to get down to the nitty-gritty details of writing a test. Not all the details will fit every testing situation, but the planning and execution of most tests will follow this decision process.

WHEN TO TEST

Because tests are so important in making the goals of a course concrete and influencing student methods of learning, I give an ungraded quiz during the first week and a graded test after the third or fourth week of a fourteen-week semester. To reduce the stress I weight the early tests very little in determining the final grade. An early test gets students started—they don't delay their studying until the conventional midterm examination—and it will help you to identify problems early while they are still remediable. Thus, early tests should demand the style of learning you expect, and they need to be constructed carefully even though their purpose is more motivational and diagnostic than evaluative.

The amount and frequency of tests should depend on the background of your students and the nature of the content. In a first-year course in an area new to students, frequent short tests early in the term facilitate learning. Generally, however, I want to wean students from studying only for tests, so that they will become lifelong learners able to evaluate their own learning. This implies less frequent testing as learners become more experienced. It probably also implies questions requiring broader integration and more detailed analysis as learners advance.

CONSTRUCTING THE TEST

In planning your tests you may want to use a mix of different types of questions in order to balance measurements of the varied goals of education. The following sections describe the strengths and weaknesses of each type of question, as well as offer tips on constructing items.

Choosing the Type of Question

The instructor who is about to give an examination is in a conflict situation. The administration of an examination consists of two time-consuming procedures: (1) construction of the examination and (2) grading. Unfortunately, it appears to be generally true that the examinations that are easiest to construct are the most difficult to grade and vice versa.

Teachers often base their choice of question types solely on class size, using multiple-choice tests for large classes, short-answer questions for medium-sized classes, and essay questions for small classes. Class size is certainly an important factor, but your educational goals should take precedence. Higher level goals almost always will require the use of some essay questions, problems, or other items requiring analysis, integration, or application.

Problems In mathematics, science, and some other disciplines, a test typically consists of problems. The value of problems depends on the degree to which they elicit the sort of problem-solving skills that are your goals. Some problems are too trite and stereotypic to have much value as indicators of whether students understand the steps they are following. In other cases, the answer depends to such a large extent on tedious calculations that only a small sample of problems can be tested. In such cases you might provide calculations leading up to a certain point and ask students to complete the problem, or you might use a multiple-choice question about the proper procedure—for example, "Which of the following problems can be solved by procedure *x*?" Or you might have students set up the problem without actually calculating the final answer. Many instructors who have problem solving as their goal say that setting up the problem correctly is more than half the battle, yet students often jump right to a formulaic response. If the grade is based solely on problem setup, students will pay more attention to it. Many teachers use problems that may be solved in more than one way or that have more than one satisfactory answer. In this case, special emphasis in both teaching and grading should be on justifying the solution strategy rather than on the specific answer. This has the advantage of focusing students' attention on the process rather than on the product.

Short-Answer Items Here is an example of a short-answer item: "Give one example from your own experience of the concept of elaboration." In responding, a student might describe an experience of explaining a concept to another student or of thinking about the relationship of a fact to a general principle. Such a question is restricted enough that it is not often difficult to judge whether the expected answer is there. Furthermore, such questions can be presented in a format that allows only a small amount of space for the answer. The student tendency to employ the "shotgun" approach to the examination is thus inhibited.

Short-answer questions permit coverage of assigned materials without asking for petty details. Unfortunately, many short-answer questions only test recall of specific facts; however, they can do more. If you are trying to develop skill in analysis or diagnosis, for example, you may present case material or a description of an experiment and ask students what questions they would ask. You can then provide additional information that they can use in an analysis. Or a short-answer question can ask students to solve a problem or propose a hypothesis relevant to information learned earlier. An example is the following question from a course on the psychology of aging:

1. "Given the *differences* in ways in which men and women experience middle age, and the fact that depression rises as a psychiatric symptom in middle age, how might the *causes* of the depression differ for men and women at this time in life?"

Essay Items Although the short-answer examination is very useful in certain situations, I recommend that, if possible, you include at least one essay question on examinations in most college courses.

Experiments indicate that students study more efficiently for essay-type examinations than for objective tests (d'Ydewalle, Swerts, and de Corte, 1983; Monaco, 1977). Thus, in addition to the values of essay tests as evaluation devices, you should take into consideration their potential educational value as stimuli to students' reflection about conceptual relationships, possible applications, or aspects of thinking. One strategy is to pass out several questions the week before the test and tell students that these are the sorts of questions you will use—that, in fact, you may even use one of these very questions.

Where the tests can be returned with comments, essay examinations may give students practice in organized, creative thinking about a subject and an opportunity to check their thinking against the standards of someone with more experience and ability in the field. Johnson (1975) demonstrated that when marginal comments on earlier tests emphasized creativity, creativity on the final exam was improved.

In large classes where time is limited and in classes where the writing itself is not the point of the question, you can format the answer sheet to break a long, complex answer into its critical components, each of which has a space for an answer. For example, in my class the last problem on every exam is a case to which the students must apply whatever theory we have been studying. So at the top of the sheet, there is a short description of the scenario. Then there is a space headed: "In five sentences or fewer, describe your proposed solution to this scenario based on theory X." About two inches farther down the sheet there is another instruction: "In the spaces below connect the components of your solution to three aspects of theory X that are relevant and explain their relevance." That is followed by three spaces, each headed like this:

aspect one: (space)

connection to your solution and why: (space)

This considerably speeds up my grading time because rather than searching through a long essay organized (I hope) by the student, I can at a glance see if the student has provided a reasonable solution and tied it to the theory. I'm not "giving away the answer" because the prompts are fairly broad; I'm simply imposing a little organization on the answer to make my grading easier. And maybe students learn something about structuring an answer efficiently, too.

True-False Items Although true-false examinations are rather easy to make up, I don't advocate their use. Toppino and Brochin (1989) showed that after the test, students tend to remember the false items as being true—an outcome not conducive to achieving your objectives. If you do use true-false items, ask students to explain their answers. This will encourage reflection and help you understand why there were some common misunderstandings.

Multiple-Choice and Matching Items It is improbable that most teachers can adequately measure all their objectives with a test made up entirely of multiple-choice questions. Matching questions are similar to multiple-choice in that the student must discriminate between the correct answer and other choices. Nonetheless, for some purposes multiple-choice items are useful. They can measure both simple knowledge and precise discrimination. They can measure ability to apply concepts or principles; they can assess elements of problem solving. But they are not likely to assess organization of ideas, conceptual relationships, or many of the skills involved in higher-order thinking.

Good multiple-choice questions are difficult to construct. (The greater your experience in their construction, the more you realize how long it takes per item to construct a reasonably fair, accurate, and inclusive question.) Because of this difficulty, the construction of such items is probably not worthwhile unless they will be administered to several hundred students, either in a single year or in successive years. Some books that can help you write high-quality items, if you are so inclined, are referenced at the end of this chapter.

Even if you don't pretest the items on students, it is worthwhile to have someone take the test before it is in its final form. If you can persuade a skilled test taker who doesn't know the subject matter to take the test, you will probably be surprised at how many he or she gets right simply from cues that you provided in the questions.

How Many Questions Should You Use?

Obviously, the number of questions depends on the type and difficulty of each question. I prefer to give tests without a time limit, but the constraints of class scheduling usually require that you clear the classroom so that the next class can begin. Thus, you must plan the length of the exam so that the slowest students have time to finish before the end of the period. As a rule of thumb I allow about one minute per item for multiple-choice or fill-in-the-blank items, two minutes per short-answer question requiring more than a sentence answer, ten or fifteen minutes for a limited essay question, and a half-hour to an hour for a broader question requiring more than a page or two to answer. You can get a rough estimate of time requirements by simply timing how long it takes to actually read the items without answering them. That can serve as a minimum time requirement. If you ask someone else to take the test as suggested above, time that person, too.

Constructing Multiple-Choice Items

1. Teachers' manuals that accompany many textbooks contain multiple-choice items. You should not rely on a manual as the source of all your questions, because the manual probably will not contain many good questions and may cover only textbook material. You need to assess what students have learned in class as well as their understanding of what they have read.
2. A second source of multiple-choice items is the students themselves. They are not a particularly satisfactory source of test questions, because only about 10 percent of the items thus written will be usable. However, this technique is a useful pedagogical device because it gets the students to read their assignments more analytically. It also gives the instructor a good index of what the students are getting out of the various sections of their reading, and it gives you a chance to remind them of the goals of the course going beyond recall of details.
3. There are statistical methods for evaluating questions, but the best suggestions for improvement come from students themselves in their discussion of the test. It seems almost criminal to waste this experience with items; therefore I recommend a permanent file.
4. If you have a problem but no good distractor (incorrect alternative), give the item in short-answer or essay form and use the students' own responses for alternatives for a later use of the item in multiple-choice form.
5. Multiple-choice questions typically have four or five alternatives. Rather than wasting your and your students' time with extra alternatives that don't test a discrimination that is important, use only as many alternatives as make meaningful discriminations. Costin (1972) showed that three-choice items are about as effective as four-choice.
6. For measuring understanding, I like questions that require the student to predict the outcome of a situation, rather than questions that simply ask the student to label the phenomenon.
7. Multiple-choice items need not stand alone. You can use a sequence of related items to measure more complex thinking.
8. Grouping items under headings will improve student performance (Marcinkiewicz and Clariana, 1997).

TESTS FROM THE STUDENT PERSPECTIVE

It's not surprising that our students get so concerned about tests and other assessments. More is riding on their performance than just a grade in the class. All kinds of things depend on a student's grade point average, many of them with no apparent relationship to scholarly achievement. For example, in some areas, students with good grades get lower car insurance rates! Maybe the insurance companies figure that you must be home studying all the time to get such good grades, so you're not as likely to have an accident!

On a more serious note, no one is totally comfortable with being assessed, and, rightly or wrongly, students often equate grades with self-worth. We owe it to them to help them maximize their potential for good performance by dealing with some of the things that might get in the way.

REDUCING STUDENT FRUSTRATION AND AGGRESSION

Most beginning teachers find the aggression that students direct against them after a test very disturbing. It is likely to impair the instructor's rapport with the class and may actually be a block to learning. Thus, strategies for reducing the aggression seem to be worthwhile.

The most obvious solution to the problem is to reduce students' frustration when taking tests. You can do this by emphasizing the contribution the course can make to students' long-range goals. Explaining how and why you test as you do will also help. A nongraded practice test will provide guidance. Periodic assessments of learning (not necessarily graded) to help students assess their own progress and to help you identify problems, as well as frequent explanations of why and how you test and assess learning, should reduce students' anxiety and frustration about testing.

Yet no matter how much you emphasize long-range goals, the tests will in large measure determine what students do. Do you want them to memorize details? Then give the usual memory-of-details test. But if you want more, make your objectives clear, and make sure that your tests measure the attainment of those objectives. If you used the Bloom Taxonomy of Educational Objectives or Biggs's SOLO Taxonomy as suggested in the chapter "Countdown for Course Preparation," remind the students of these levels before each test.

Test instructions should indicate whether students are to guess, what the time limit is, and any other directions that define the nature of the expected responses. For the typical classroom examination, there is no point in a correction for guessing. Emphasizing in the multiple-choice test introduction that students should choose the *best* answer may help prevent lengthy discussion with students who dream up a remote instance in which the correct alternative might be wrong.

Research McKeachie did with his colleagues (1955) and research by Smith and Rockett (1958) demonstrated that on multiple-choice tests the instruction "Feel free to write comments," with blank space by each question for the comments, results in higher scores, especially for anxious students. A problem with this strategy is that students these days have been taught to make notes to themselves on the test, so you may find yourself reading a lot of stuff not really written to you. Here is one way to solve this problem and the problem of students who want to explain every item. Allow students to explain their choices for up to three questions. They star the question that they want to elaborate on; then on the last page of the test, called the "explanations page," they write their thoughts and indicate why they answered the way they did. Only read the explanations to questions that they have missed. This process greatly reduces their anxiety and saves you grading time. It also forces them to pick their battles; they can't simply write everything they know for every question in hopes that the correct answer is in there somewhere.

HELPING STUDENTS BECOME TEST-WISE

Particularly in the case of multiple-choice examinations, I have found that a good morale builder is spending fifteen minutes or so the day before the first test telling students how to take a test of this sort and familiarizing them with the format. Some of the points that I make in such a lecture follow in the sub-sections below.

Taking Multiple-Choice Tests

The student taking a multiple-choice examination is essentially in the same position as a poker player. The object is to get into a position where you are betting on a sure thing. If this is impossible, at least make your bet on the choice where the odds are in your favor. In poker, you are in the strongest position if you know exactly what your opponent has; in the examination situation, you are in the strongest position if you know the material. There is no substitute for study. Nevertheless, you are not likely to be absolutely certain of all the right answers, and when you are not, certain techniques may help.

What I recommend to the student is this. First go through the examination and answer all of the items you know. In addition to getting a certain amount of the examination done without spending a lot of time on single, difficult items, you probably will find that going through the complete test once in this way will suggest the answers to questions that might have been difficult had they been answered in numerical order. When you have gone through the test once in this fashion, go through it again and answer any questions whose answers are now obvious. Usually there will still be a few unanswered questions. It is in connection with these that certain tricks may be useful.

If the item is multiple-choice, don't simply guess at this stage of the game. See whether it is possible to eliminate some of the choices as incorrect. In a four-choice multiple-choice item, the probability of getting the answer right by pure guesswork is one in four; if you can eliminate two of the choices, your chances improve to 50 percent. So take advantage of the mathematics of the situation.

After completing the examination, go through the whole thing again to check your choices to make sure that you still regard them as correct and to make sure that you made no clerical errors when recording them. In this connection, it is worthwhile to point out to students the common misconception that when you change your answers, you usually change from right answers to wrong ones. Mueller and Wasser (1977) reviewed eighteen studies demonstrating that most students gain more than they lose on changed answers.

Taking Essay Tests

My instructions for essay exams are simpler.

1. Outline your answer before writing it. This provides a check against the common error of omitting one part of the answer.

2. If a question completely baffles you, start writing on the back of your paper, making note of anything you know that could possibly be relevant. This starts your memory functioning, and usually you'll soon find that you have some relevant ideas.

3. If you are still at a loss, admit it, write a *related* question that you can answer, and answer it. Most instructors will give you at least a few points more than if you wrote nothing.

4. Write as well as you can. Even if I intend not to grade on writing ability, my judgment is negatively influenced when I have to struggle to read poor handwriting or surmount poor grammar and sentence structure. Moreover, because I believe that every course is responsible for teaching writing, writing always enters into my grading.

Why Teach Test Taking?

Is it wise to give students these tips? The answer to this question depends on your purposes in giving an examination. If you want to test for "test-taking" ability, you will not want to give students such hints. At any rate, this orientation seems to have the effect of conveying to students the notion that you are not trying to "outsmart" them and are instead interested in helping them get as high a grade as their learning warrants.

Coping with Test Anxiety

Many students struggle with test anxiety because of the high-stakes testing they experienced in the past and the emphasis on grades they're experiencing now. A student may know the material but blank out during the test and be unable to show what he or she knows. If my students are having such problems, I can do several things to help:

1. I can lower the stakes of any given test. By having several assessments of learning, I can lower the overall importance of any one test and thereby lower students' anxiety about their performance on it.
2. I can offer "second chances" to students who experience difficulties while taking a test. This means allowing them after the test to earn back some of the points they missed. I describe this process later in this chapter. This is a good learning strategy, and more important for test-anxious students, it relieves some of the pressure and therefore some of the anxiety.
3. I already mentioned the strategy of allowing students to explain their answers more thoroughly on the test itself. This also removes some of the pressure that comes with uncertainty about a particular answer.
4. Prior to the test day I familiarize students with what the test will actually look like, the kinds of questions, any special procedures they'll need to follow, and how I'll grade the test. This removes a lot of the unknowns associated with the test, which are a big source of anxiety.
5. I offer ideas about studying and about getting physically ready for the test, relaxation strategies (taking deep breaths, putting down the pencil and flexing your fingers, and so on). Sometimes I even coach students to think about what they're saying to themselves that contributes to their anxiety—for example, saying, "I've *got* to get an A," instead of, "I'm going to do OK," is more likely to produce anxiety.

ADMINISTERING THE TEST

Handing out a test should be a simple matter. Usually it is, but in large classes, simple administrative matters can become disasters. It is hard to imagine how angry and upset students can become while waiting only ten minutes for the proctors to finish distributing the test forms. And if this doesn't move you, imagine your feelings when you find that you don't have enough tests for all of the students. (It has happened to me twice—deserving a place among my worst moments in teaching!)

How can you avoid such problems?

1. If you are having tests copied, ask for at least 10 percent extra—more if the test is administered in several rooms. (Some proctor always walks off with too many.) This gives you insurance against miscounting and against omitted or blank pages on some copies.

2. Unless there is some compelling reason to distribute the tests later, have your proctors pass out the tests as students come into the room. This protects students from mounting waves of panic while they wait for the tests to be distributed. Or prepare packets of tests for each row to speed up the distribution. The packets can be placed at the end of the row and passed along the row when the time for the test comes.

3. Minimize interruptions. Tell students before the exam that you will write announcements, instructions, or corrections on the board. Some exam periods are less a measure of achievement than a test of the students' ability to work despite the instructor's interruptions.

ALTERNATIVE TESTING MODELS GAINING FAVOR

Group or Team-Based Testing

Given the prevalence of group work in classes these days, some instructors have begun to administer group tests as well. Since the students have been encouraged and actually required to study and work in groups while learning, the logic is that asking them to perform in an individual situation on the test contradicts what they have learned about peer support. Although I may not agree with that logic, I do agree that taking a test in a group situation is a good learning experience for the same reasons that collaborative learning is a good teaching method: students learn a lot from one another and from having to explain their own answers.

The most common method for this strategy is to have the students initially take the test on their own. Then after turning their copy in, they get into a group (usually the one they've been working with all semester) and go through the test again to come up with a group response to the test. It is amazing how much energy there is during this activity! It has the advantage of giving the students immediate feedback on their test performance by comparing their responses to their group mates', and it also corrects any misconceptions right away—something that we can't do very easily in a regular test situation. Grades are a combination of individual test performance and group test performance.

There are many concerns about this strategy, most of them having to do with grading and with difficulties posed by room configurations. There is also the possibility of one student dominating the group's responses to the test. These are the same problems that arise whenever group work is suggested, and they must be at least acknowledged. Achacoso and Svinicki's (2005) descriptions of group testing by a couple of different instructors in different settings may inform your understanding of this trend.

Online Testing

Another new trend in testing is the use of testing online. In this model students take their tests on a computer, either their own or at a testing center. There are almost as many varieties of this strategy as there are instructors. Achacoso and Svinicki (2005) provide examples of different online testing strategies.

The advantage of online testing is that it can allow an instructor to give a customized test to each student through the miracles of technology and a large database of questions. Given what you know about computers, I'm sure you can imagine all the clever ways that the technology can modify, randomize, customize, and evaluate a student's test. For example, there is one format that calibrates the difficulty of each subsequent item based on whether the current item was answered correctly. This particular mode is being used with the large standardized placement tests, such as the GRE or LSAT. That's probably a little too fancy for a regular classroom test, but future developments in software may make it possible for individual instructors to design such systems just as we can now design online tutorials much more easily.

Another advantage of the online testing idea is that the instructor can include simulations that are interactive. Such questions would provide a much better test of student understanding than the static problems that can be included in paper-and-pencil tests.

The difficulty with such testing is maintaining testing integrity. Unless the test is administered under secure conditions—for example, in a computer lab or testing facility—the instructor may not be able to ensure that the person submitting the test is really the designated student or whether the student is making inappropriate use of support materials during the test. Many institutions are considering the feasibility of providing large computer-based testing centers, and it will be interesting to see whether such efforts are scalable to the kinds of large classes in which they might be the most useful.

WHAT TO DO ABOUT CHEATING

It may be hard for you to believe that your students would ever cheat—"Maybe other students cheat, but not mine!" Unfortunately, studies of cheating behavior over several decades invariably find that a majority of students report that they have cheated at some time (McCabe and Trevino, 1996). A recent Google search on "cheating in college" turned up over 157,000,000 pages! Most students would rather not cheat, but the pressures for good grades are so intense that many students feel that they, too, must cheat if they believe that other students are cheating. In my experience the most common excuse given by a student caught cheating is that other students were cheating and the teacher didn't seem to care, at least not enough to do anything to prevent or stop cheating. Many students thus feel less stress when an examination is well managed and well proctored.

Why Do Students Cheat?

The research on this question is alarmingly consistent. The most significant factor in a student's decision to cheat is peer influence (McCabe, Trevino, and Butterfield, 2001). McCabe and Trevino (1996) report that students don't believe they'll get caught because instructors are indifferent to their activities. Gerdeman (2000) reports students' belief that if they do get caught, they won't be punished severely even if the institution has policies for dealing with such misconduct. In today's high-stakes testing environment, where there is such a strong emphasis on grades, students believe there is a large reward for success at any cost (Whitley, 1998). Certainly they see on the news successful cheaters in the real world constantly getting away without severe penalties.

How Do Students Cheat?

1. Students pass information to a neighbor; for example, they may loan a neighbor an eraser with the answer on the eraser.
2. Students use notes written on clothing, skin, or small note cards.

3. Students store answers in calculators or recorders used during the exam.

4. Students peek at a knowledgeable neighbor's exam (sometimes seated in groups around the best student in the fraternity).

5. Students use tapping, hand code, cell phones, instant messaging, or other communication strategies.

6. Students accuse the teacher of losing an exam (that they never turned in).

7. Students pay someone else to take an exam or write a paper for them.

8. Students copy or paraphrase material for a paper without acknowledging the source.

Preventing Cheating

"OK, so we want to prevent cheating. What can we do?"

If it's true that cheating comes from some of the causes just mentioned, then there is a lot of proactive action that you can take to prevent it or discourage it from happening. Researchers are fairly consistent in many of their recommendations. Here are a few that I've gleaned from the now extensive literature on cheating in college (Gerdeman, 2000; McMurtry, 2001; Pulvers and Diekhoff, 1999; plus websites from teaching and learning sites at many of the major universities around the country such as the University of Illinois and the University of California at Santa Barbara). They're fairly consistent with my own practices.

An obvious first answer is to reduce the pressure. While you can't affect the general academic atmosphere that puts heavy emphasis on grades, you can influence the pressure in your own course, for example, by providing a number of opportunities for students to demonstrate achievement of course goals, rather than relying on a single examination. A second answer is to address the issue in your syllabus or have a discussion on the topic early in your course.

A third answer is to make reasonable demands and write a reasonable and interesting test. Some cheating is simply the result of frustration and desperation arising from assignments too long to be covered adequately or tests requiring memorization of trivial details. In some cases cheating is simply a way of getting back at an unreasonable, hostile teacher.

A fourth answer is to develop group norms supporting honesty. I frequently give my classes a chance to vote on whether or not we will conduct the tests on the honor system. I announce that we will not use the honor system unless the vote is unanimous, since it will not work unless everyone feels committed to it. If the vote is unanimous, I remind the students of it on the day of the exam and ask whether they still wish to have the test under the honor system. I haven't collected data on the success of this approach, but I've never had a complaint about it. Although only a minority of classes vote for the honor system, a discussion of academic dishonesty is itself useful in helping students recognize why cheating is bad. I've taken to having the students sign a pledge of academic integrity prior to each exam. I think it reminds them of my expectations and reinforces the impression that I care.

Fifth, if some students are not doing well in the course, talk to them and find out what has gone wrong and what they can do to improve. Try to reduce the stress that leads to cheating. If there are stresses originating beyond your course, suggest counseling.

What else can be done?

One principle is to preserve each student's sense that he or she is an individual with a personal relationship both with the instructor and with other students. Students are not as likely to cheat in situations in which they are known, as in situations in which they are anonymous members of a crowd. Thus, if a large course has regular meetings in small discussion or laboratory sections, there is likely to be less cheating if the test is administered in these groups than if the test is administered en masse. Moreover, if the test is given in their regular classroom, they may perform better because of the cues to their original learning (Metzger et al., 1979).

Even in small groups, cheating will occur if the instructor seems unconcerned. Graduate student teaching assistants often feel that any show of active proctoring will indicate that they do not trust the students. There is certainly a danger that the teacher will appear to be so poised to spring at a miscreant that the atmosphere becomes tense, but it is possible to convey a sense of alert helpfulness while strolling down the aisles or watching for questions.

The most common form of cheating is copying from another student's paper. To reduce this, ask to have a large enough exam room to enable students to sit in alternate seats. Write on the board before students arrive, "Take alternate seats." Some students fail to see the sign, so in large exams you not only need two proctors at each door passing out exams but at least one more to supervise seating.

In the event that you can't get rooms large enough to permit alternate seating, you probably should use two or more alternate forms of the test. Houston (1983) found that scrambling the order of items alone did not reduce cheating. Since I prefer to have items on a test follow the same order as the order in which the material has been discussed in the course, I scramble the order of answer choices. I typically write separate sets of essay questions for the two tests. It is difficult to make two tests equally difficult, so you probably will want to tabulate separate distributions of scores on each form of the test.

Whether you use one form or two, don't leave copies lying around your office or the typist's office. One of our students was nearly killed by a fall from a third-floor ledge outside the office where he hoped to steal the examination, and janitors have been bribed to turn over the contents of wastebaskets thought to contain discarded drafts of the test.

Handling Cheating

Despite preventive measures, almost every instructor must at some time or another face the problem of what to do about a student who is cheating. For example, as you are administering an examination you note that a student's eyes are on his neighbor's rather than on his own paper. Typically you do nothing at this time, for you don't want to embarrass an innocent student. But when the eyes again stray, you are faced with a decision about what to do.

Most colleges have rules about the procedures to be followed in case of cheating. Yet instructors are often reluctant to begin the procedure. The reasons for instructor reluctance vary. Sometimes it is simply uncertainty about whether or not cheating really occurred. Students' eyes do wander without cheating. Answers may be similar simply because two students have studied together. "If the student denies the charge, what evidence do I have to support my accusation?"

Again, unwillingness to invoke the regulations concerning cheating may be based on distrust of the justice of the eventual disposition of the case. Cheating is common in colleges; many teachers have been guilty themselves at some stage in their academic careers. Thus, most of us are understandably reluctant to subject the unfortunate one who gets caught to the drastic possible punishments that more skillful cheaters avoid. Such conflicts as these make the problem of handling a cheater one of the most disturbing of those a new teacher faces.

Unfortunately I've never been completely satisfied that I handle the problem adequately; so my "advice" should, like the rest of the advice in this book, be regarded simply as some ideas for your consideration rather than as dicta to be accepted verbatim. However, much of what I'm going to say is backed up by most writers in this field.

First, let me support the value of following your college's procedures. Find out what they are and what legal precedents may affect what you should do. Even though it may not have been long since you were taking examinations yourself, your role as a teacher requires that you represent established authority rather than the schoolyard code that rejects "tattlers." Moreover, your memories of student days may help you recall your own feelings when you saw someone cheating and the instructor took no action.

Further, student or faculty committees dealing with cheating are not as arbitrary and impersonal as you might expect. Typically, they attempt to get at the cause of the cheating and to help students solve their underlying problems. Being apprehended for cheating may, therefore, actually be of real long-term value to the students.

Finally, following college policies protects you in the rare case in which a student initiates legal action against you for an arbitrary punishment.

There still remain cases where the evidence is weak and you're not quite sure whether or not cheating actually occurred. Even here I advise against such individual action as reducing a grade. If you're wrong, the solution is unjust. If you're right, you've failed to give the student feedback that is likely to change his behavior. In such cases I advise talking to the student and calling the head of the committee handling cheating cases or the student's counselor. It's surprising to find how often your suspicions fit in with other evidence about the student's behavior. Even when they don't, advice from someone who has additional information about the student will frequently be helpful.

Finally, let's return to the case of the straying eyes. Here, you haven't time for a phone call to get advice; your decision has to be made now. Rather than arousing the whole class by snatching away the student's paper with a loud denunciation, simply ask the student unobtrusively to move to a seat where he'll be less crowded. If he says he's not crowded, simply whisper that you'd prefer that he move. He's not likely to refuse.

AFTER THE TEST

Grading Objective Tests

Of course the most wonderful thing about objective tests is they are easier to grade. Or are they? The important point to remember is to get the scoring key right! There's nothing more disconcerting to students than to find that the test was scored incorrectly. I strongly recommend that you check and double check the keys to be sure that the marks are correct. Then, before you give the tests back, it **really** pays to do a short analysis of overall student performance on each item. This is called an item analysis. It consists of figuring what percentage of the students missed each question, and how the performance of the top third of the class compares to the bottom third as measured by their overall score. You can short-circuit a lot of student complaints by identifying items that were troublesome and knowing why. For example, if an item is missed by more than half of the class, I always reread the item to see whether there was something unclear. Or if a large number of the students in the top group miss an item, I consider which answer they gave to see if for some reasons the question misled those who actually knew a lot, maybe too much. You still have time to make the necessary adjustments in the scoring to allow for poorly worded questions or a distractor that turns out to be correct after all. By making all these adjustments before you give the papers back, you avoid a lot of confusion about which items were right and which were wrong.

Once the students recognize that you are making a good-faith effort to identify or remediate poorly worded items, they are more likely to give you the benefit of the doubt. You also have the advantage of having at your fingertips solid data on each question so that if a student challenges a question after the test, you will know whether there is any merit to that challenge and you'll be able to respond immediately and authoritatively.

Grading Essay Questions

I recommend that you use some essay questions because of their powerful effect on the way students study, but there is a drawback. Instructors don't grade essay tests very reliably. One problem is that standards vary. First papers are graded differently than later papers. A paper graded immediately after several poor papers is graded differently than one graded after several good papers.

There are seven procedures you can initiate to improve your evaluation of essay examinations—but they entail work.

1. Establish a rubric or set of criteria—not just a list of facts to be included. Are you looking for integration, for analysis, for rational arguments for and against a conclusion? Be prepared to modify your criteria as you find student responses that you hadn't thought of. Learning to create a good grading rubric is worth the effort because it can help you write good questions, maintain reliable grading of answers, and, if shared with the students, help students understand how their answer was graded. Walvoord and Anderson (1998) have an excellent book on how to create rubrics based on "primary trait analysis."

Creating a good rubric through primary trait analysis involves laying out the key aspects (primary traits) of the response that figure into the grade. For example, on a given essay question, the analysis might list four main points that must be included in the answer, plus criteria for a clean argument and criteria for good writing itself. Then each "trait" is described along a scale of acceptability. Here is an example of a scale for the trait of "solid argumentation":

> Best answer (100 percent credit)—An answer at this level provides clear statements of the thesis or theses being asserted in a logical order that builds to the final conclusion. Each thesis is accompanied by sufficient reasonable

evidence to support it. Each thesis also considers and counters reasonable arguments against it. The theses stand together and are internally consistent with one another.

Acceptable answer (80 percent credit)—An answer at this level provides fewer theses but still provides reasonable and primary ones in light of the conclusion. There is evidence offered for each thesis, although possibly overlooking some minor supporting assertions. Several of the more obvious counterarguments are raised and refuted. The order is logical and builds to the conclusion. Transitions between theses are present but ordinary.

Unacceptable answer (no credit)—Any two or more of the following characteristics constitute an unacceptable answer. The answer contains many errors of assertion and omission. No evidence is given or the evidence given is incorrect or unrelated to the assertion. No attempt or a weak attempt is made to introduce and refute counterarguments. The order of presentation is not logical or convincing. The conclusion is not justified by the arguments.

Creating this type of rubric helps you clarify for yourself what you want in an answer. It also increases the reliability of grading across graders and across time within a single grader's work.

2. Read exams without knowledge of the name of the writer.

3. If you're unsure of what to expect, first read briefly through a random sample of answers. Then, having identified papers of differing levels of excellence, compare them to determine what the distinguishing features are. You will find some characteristics that were not in your original criteria. Now set up the criteria you will use, but don't be rigid. Give students credit when they come up with creative answers that don't fit the rubric.

4. Write specific comments on the papers. One of the problems in using essay exams and in assigning term papers is that students feel that the grading represents some mysterious, unfathomable bias. The more helpful comments you can write on the paper, the more students will learn.

I am finding that computer technology is a big help in my grading of papers (but not essay exams unless they're also done on the computer). I use the editing software available in common word processing programs to read and mark the papers that my students submit in electronic format. I can give a lot more feedback because I'm not limited by how much I can squeeze into the margins, and I can type a lot faster than I can write by hand. In addition, the students can probably read my typing better than my handwriting. (There is more about this in the chapter "How to Enhance Learning by Using High-Stakes and Low-Stakes Writing.")

5. Develop a code for common comments. For example, you might want to use a vertical line alongside paragraphs that are particularly good or "NFD" for "needs further development." Or you can identify the most

commonly occurring errors with numbers. When you grade, you can put the number next to the error on the paper and give students the numbered list of errors for reference. They may learn something from reading the whole list even if they didn't make any of those errors.

6. Don't simply give points for each concept or fact mentioned. Doing that just converts the essay into a recall test rather than a measure of higher-level goals of integration and evaluation. Developing rubrics like those described earlier can be helpful in increasing reliability of grading. However, don't use them mechanically. Your overall impression may be as valid.

7. If possible, do your grading in teams. My teaching assistants and I gather after administering a test. We bring in draft model answers for each question. We discuss what we expect as answers for each question. We then establish two- or three-person teams for each essay question. Each team picks eight to twelve test papers, which are circulated among the team members. Each team member notes privately his or her grade for the question. Team members then compare grades and discuss discrepancies until they reach consensus. A second group of tests is then graded in the same way, with grades compared and discrepancies discussed. This procedure continues until the team is confident that it has arrived at common criteria. From this point on, each member grades independently. When a team member is not sure how to grade a paper, it is passed to another team member for an opinion.

We stay with the grading until all the papers are done, but we make a party of it to alleviate fatigue and boredom. Funny answers are read aloud. Sandwiches are brought in from a delicatessen. Teams help other teams for a change of pace or to balance the workload.

If you don't have a team, try to develop your own strategies for maintaining motivation. If you begin to be bored, irritated, or tired, take a break. Or before beginning, pull out the answers of some of your most interesting students and read those when you begin to feel dispirited. Take notes to use in discussing the papers in class. Also take separate notes for yourself on what seem to be common problems that you need to correct in your teaching in the future.

Grading papers is still time consuming but does not become the sort of aversive task that makes for procrastination and long delays in providing feedback to students.

Helping Yourself Learn from the Test

Often we get so wrapped up in the pure mechanics of correcting and grading tests that we overlook the fact that measures of student performance not only can diagnose student weaknesses but also can reveal areas in which our teaching has failed to achieve its purposes. The item analysis process described earlier is especially helpful with this. Once you've achieved some ease with the grading process, look back at the papers to see what they reveal about problems in student understanding. There may be some things about which the entire class seems a bit shaky; in addition, there may be areas of difficulty experienced by certain subgroups of students—perhaps those with background knowledge or experience different from that of the rest of the class. In short, think about what *you* need to do as well as about what the *students* need to do.

Returning Test Papers

Remember that tests are important tools for learning and that discussion of a test can be a worthwhile use of class time. However, it's also a pretty emotional time for some of the students, and it might pay to delay the discussion until that emotion settles down. In fact, in my own class, I give students the opportunity to challenge the answer to a question in writing before the next class period. I've found that often once the student has had a chance to look over the items and tried to justify their incorrect answers, they realize what they did wrong much more readily than if I just tell them. Sometimes they are actually able to make a good case for their choice, in which case I'll give them credit for their answer. I don't think you should discuss every question in class, but when there are common errors, try to find out why the error occurred and suggest strategies for avoiding such problems in the future. Although you should avoid spending class time quibbling over some individual items, you should make known your willingness to discuss the test individually with students who have further questions.

Helping Students Learn from a Test

The most important function of testing is *not* to provide a basis for grading. Rather, tests are an important educational tool. They not only direct students' studying but also can provide important corrective feedback. The comments that you write on essay tests are far more important than the grade. Students do learn from their corrected papers (McCluskey, 1934). I recommend looking at the suggestions for giving feedback that are included in chapter 9 of this book. They apply equally to essays, papers, and objectively scorable tests like multiple-choice. If you have the time and the temperament, you can increase the probability that students will take that opportunity to learn if you give them a chance to redo an assignment based on your feedback, as described in the previous section.

Dealing with an Aggrieved Student

What about the student who comes to your office in great anger or with a desperate appeal for sympathy but no educationally valid reason for changing the test grade? First of all, listen. Engaging in a debate will simply prolong the unpleasantness.

Ask the student to think aloud about what he or she was thinking when answering the questions that he or she is unhappy about. Once you have heard the student out, if you have decided not to change the grade, try to convert the discussion from one of stonewall resistance to problem solving. Try to help the student find alternative modes of study that will produce better results: "What can we do to help you do better next time?" Encourage the student to shift from blaming you toward motivation to work more effectively. Ask the student to summarize what he or she plans to do before the next test. Although these suggestions may save the instructor some bitter moments, they cannot substitute for the time (and it takes lots) devoted to the construction of good tests.

What Do You Do about the Student Who Missed the Test?

In any large class some students are absent from the test. Their excuses range from very legitimate to very suspicious, but making that discrimination is not always easy.

Makeup tests can involve a good deal of extra work for the instructor. If you devise a new test, you may have trouble assigning a norm with which to grade the makeup comparable to grades on the original test. If you use the same test that the student missed, you cannot tell how much the student has learned about the test from students who took it at the scheduled time. One strategy is to simply average marks from the tests the student did take to determine the grade, counting the missed test neither for nor against the student.

Another strategy is to drop the lowest score or missed test out of all the tests a student takes. (This, of course, presumes you have enough exams during the semester that one can be dropped.) This also lowers test anxiety because the stakes on any one test are lower. Depending on how strongly you feel about final exams, you could allow students to use the final as the test they drop if they've taken all the other exams and are satisfied with their grade. You'd be surprised what an incentive that is for working diligently during the semester.

IN CONCLUSION

1. Consider using both graded and ungraded tests and moving from less frequent tests to more frequent, where each test can count less.

2. Select question types that target your educational goals.

3. Prepare your students to take the test.

4. Create a class atmosphere that values academic honesty and support and discourages cheating.

5. Develop grading strategies for essay questions so that you won't shy away from using them.

6. Be prepared to address students' complaints about test scores in a way that helps them learn.

7. Learn from the test yourself and show your students how to learn from it as well.

Supplementary Reading

Effective Grading: A Tool for Learning and Assessment by Barbara E. Walvoord and Virginia Johnson Anderson (San Francisco: Jossey-Bass, 1998) does a good job of describing how to create grading rubrics for all manner of written assessments.

Constructing Test Items: Multiple-Choice, Constructed-Response, Performance, and Other Formats, 2nd ed., by Steven J. Osterlind (Boston: Kluwer Academic Publishers, 1998) is a fairly complete discussion of the process of writing different types of test items. It may be a bit long on detail, but the guidelines for item construction are solid and fairly straightforward.

The following resources are drawn from the ERIC Digest series. This is a series of short summaries of research and best practices provided online for educators in a searchable database.

- www.ericfacility.net/databases/ERIC_Digests/index.
- Childs, R. (1989). *Constructing Classroom Achievement Tests*. ERIC Digest. ERIC Clearinghouse on Tests Measurement and Evaluation. ED315426.
- Grist, S., and others (1989). *Computerized Adaptive Tests*. ERIC Digest No. 107. ERIC Clearinghouse on Tests Measurement and Evaluation. ED315425.

- Kehoe, J. (1995). *Basic Item Analysis for Multiple-Choice Tests*. ERIC/AE Digest. ERIC Clearinghouse on Assessment and Evaluation. ED398237.
- Kehoe, J. (1995). *Writing Multiple Choice Test Items*. ERIC/AE Digest. ERIC Clearinghouse on Assessment and Evaluation. ED398236.

Readings about helping students:

- C. E. Weinstein and L. Hume, *Study Strategies for Lifelong Learning* (Washington: American Psychological Association, 1998). The American Psychological Association Division 15 has a whole series of publications on helping students improve their learning. Access them through the APA Publications site.
- D. Sadker and K. Zittleman, "Test Anxiety: Are Students Failing Tests—Or Are Tests Failing Students?" *Phi Delta Kappan*, 2004, *85*(10), 740.

The entire September 2004 issue of *Anxiety, Stress, and Coping* is devoted to test anxiety and research on it, including how to cope with it.
Readings about cheating:

- S. F. Davis, C. A. Grover, A. H. Becker, and L. N. McGregor, "Academic Dishonesty: Prevalence, Determinants, Techniques, and Punishments," *Teaching of Psychology*, 1992, *19*(1), 16–20.
- J. McBurney, "Cheating: Preventing and Dealing with Academic Dishonesty," *APS Observer*, January 1996, 32–35.

One might assume that it would be un-British to cheat. But Stephen Newstead, Arlyne Franklyn-Stokes, and Penny Armstrong found that British students are not much different from Americans in this respect. Their article "Individual Differences in Student Cheating," *Journal of Educational Psychology*, 1996, *88*, 229–241, is consistent with American data.

A particularly interesting set of recommendations comes from the website "On the Cutting Edge" of the National Association of Geoscience Teachers, which provides workshops for faculty in the geological sciences (serc.carleton.edu/NAGTWorkshops/index.html).

The Center for Academic Integrity at Duke University, Durham, North Carolina (www.academicintegrity.org/cai_research.asp), can provide a lot of information and sponsors workshops and research on academic integrity. They also have a searchable database of 700-plus articles on this topic.

Chapter 9

Good Designs for Written Feedback for Students

There is no such thing as good teaching without good feedback. The teacher, as knowledgeable expert, gives feedback to students with the intention of scaffolding their learning. By scaffolding, I mean supporting and helping students reach higher levels of learning and achievement but without doing the work for them. Students value the feedback comments that instructors write on their assignments, especially when these comments help explain gaps in understanding, are supportive in tone, and suggest ways of improving future work.

To get the best out of feedback comments, however, it is vital that students engage with them. No matter how much feedback the instructor delivers, students won't benefit unless they pay attention to it, process it, and ultimately act on it. Just as students don't learn to play basketball just by listening to the coach, so they cannot learn to produce a better essay or solve problems just by reading teacher feedback. Effective feedback is a partnership; it requires actions by the student as well as the teacher. Indeed, while the quality of teacher comments is important, engagement with and use of those comments by students is equally important.

In higher education, it is usual to think about the instructor as the initiator and provider of feedback. However, this is not the whole story.

This chapter was written by David Nicol, University of Strathclyde, Scotland.

Students frequently give each other feedback when tackling the same assignment (peer feedback). They also generate their own feedback while writing an essay or report; for example, they might consult a textbook to evaluate the accuracy of an argument or to identify gaps in a theoretical explanation. Significant learning benefits can be achieved when teachers harness peer feedback and build on these informal feedback processes (Nicol and Macfarlane-Dick, 2006).

It is also important that feedback is not too narrowly conceptualized as something that happens after the student has produced some work. Feedback is not always backward-looking and a consequence of action. It can also be forward-looking. In project supervision the instructor provides advice about what might be done next, while the work is in progress and not just at the end. Also, feedback does not occur in isolation; it is normally provided in relation to the assignment goals. When students understand and share these goals they are more receptive to the feedback they receive.

In the following sections I first provide a set of recommendations on how to improve the quality of teacher feedback comments. Then, consistent with a broader conception of the feedback process, I discuss ways of ensuring that these comments have maximum impact on learning. This involves creating structured opportunities for students to engage in feedback conversations with their teachers and with peers and to reflect on the meaning of feedback in relation to subject knowledge. In what follows, my assumption is that feedback is being generated in relation to a written assignment, for example, an essay or report, even though most of the discussion also applies to other feedback scenarios.

THE FORMULATION OF WRITTEN FEEDBACK COMMENTS

What are the features of good written teacher comments? The following is a set of recommendations for good practice. These are based on investigations of students' perceptions of what constitutes helpful feedback and on researchers' suggestions about how to translate these ideas into practice.

Understandable, Selective, and Specific

Overall, the research on feedback shows that students do value written comments on their work (e.g., Weaver, 2006). However, they also express concern when these comments are illegible, ambiguous (e.g., "poor effort, could do better"), too abstract (e.g., "lack of critical thinking"), too general or vague (e.g., "you've got the important stuff"), and too cryptic (e.g., "why?"). Sometimes this is a question of language, at other times of detail. Much feedback uses a disciplinary discourse that is difficult for students, especially beginning students, to decode. The teacher can remedy this by trying to write comments in plain language and by providing an explanation where disciplinary or technical terms are used. It is also important to provide enough detail so that students understand what the guidance means. This has led to the suggestion that comments should be formulated as small lessons, and that these should be limited to two or three well-developed points for extended written assignments (Lunsford, 1997). It can help students if teachers also point to examples in the submission where the feedback applies rather than provide comments with no referent. For instance, highlight a positive feature, explain its merit, and suggest that the student do more of that (e.g., a good example of logical transitions or of a disciplinary argument).

Research on Feedback Comments

Written feedback should be:

- **Understandable:** Expressed in a language that students will understand.
- **Selective:** Commenting on two or three things that the student can do something about.
- **Specific:** Pointing to examples in the student's submission where the feedback applies.
- **Timely:** Provided in time to inform the next piece of work.
- **Contextualized:** Framed with reference to the learning outcomes and/or assessment criteria.
- **Nonjudgmental:** Descriptive rather than evaluative, focused on learning goals not just performance goals.
- **Balanced:** Pointing out the positive as well as areas in need of improvement.
- **Forward-Looking:** Suggesting how students might improve subsequent assignments.
- **Transferable:** Focused on processes, skills, and self-regulatory abilities.

Timely

Numerous studies show that students receive feedback too late to be helpful, due to their receiving it after the next assignment. Students are also quite vocal about this problem. At one level, dealing with this issue is straightforward and might simply involve specifying turnaround times for grading and feedback on assignments; some institutions make a commitment to a three-week turnaround. However, the timeliness dimension is also related to opportunities to use feedback and the requirement that students get feedback when they experience difficulty rather than wait too long.

Multistage assignments can address some of these problems. If the assignment allows drafting with feedback provided on the draft, students are more likely to see the feedback as timely and make good use of it. Alternatively, teachers might provide feedback on aspects of the work in progress (e.g., essay plans, introductions, a sample of the argument and supporting evidence) with the task sequenced with each stage building to a more complex final assignment. Providing feedback on drafts need not necessarily increase teacher time; teachers can limit the feedback that they provide when they grade the completed assignment or students might give each other feedback at intermediate stages. A further concern is that on a graded assignment it is important that the student actually does the work and that the teacher does not rewrite the assignment as part of the feedback. This requires careful consideration of the kinds of feedback comments teachers provide.

Nonjudgmental and Balanced

Teachers need to consider the motivational as well as the cognitive aspects of feedback. Feedback comments can be discouraging, lead to defensiveness, or reduce confidence (e.g., "no, that's all wrong, you really have not understood the literature"). Kluger and DeNisi (1996) found that 30 percent of comments were of this type. Much motivational research has focused on whether feedback comments direct students' attention toward learning or performance goals, that is, toward the mindset that mistakes are part of learning and that effort can enhance achievement, or to the mindset that achievement depends on ability, which is more fixed (Dweck, 2006).

Research in this area also suggests that teachers should try to ensure that students perceive comments as descriptive rather than evaluative or authoritarian. One approach is for the teacher to reflect back to the students the effects of the writing, in other words, how the teacher has interpreted what is written (e.g., "here's what I see as your main point…"). This helps students see the difference between their intention and the effects that are produced. Some experts argue that faculty should start and end commenting on positive aspects of what the student has done, with a middle section focusing on those aspects in need of improvement. However, a word of caution is needed here; if the student perceives that praise is gratuitous or that it does not align with the grade awarded, then this can be confusing or have a negative effect on motivation.

Feedback could also emphasize learning goals by acknowledging the role that mistakes and effort play in learning and by avoiding normative comparisons with other students. Some teachers have addressed such issues by providing encouragement in their comments (e.g., "analyzing a case is complex and can be very demanding, but all students who put in the time and effort get there eventually"). This emphasizes success and lets students know that they have the capacity to succeed. Acknowledging the role that mistakes play in learning when giving feedback is another useful tactic (e.g., "this is a common misconception; when you identify the reason for this misconception you will have a good grasp of this topic").

Contextualized

Research suggests that feedback is more effective when it is related to the instructional context, that is, to the learning outcomes and the assessment criteria. Sadler (1989) defines feedback as information about the gap between what the student did (actual performance) and what was expected (the assignment outcomes), information that is intended to help the student close that gap. Hence, alignment of feedback to the instructional context is essential for learning. It also increases the likelihood that students will actually understand the feedback. Many teachers use feedback forms with assessment rubrics wherein feedback is written under or alongside the stated objectives or assessment criteria.

A related recommendation deriving from Sadler's definition is that students spend time at the beginning of an assignment actively unpacking what is required; for example, by translating criteria into their own words or by comparing samples of good and poor assignments submitted by classmates in earlier years so as to identify which is better and why. By enhancing their understanding of the requirements and criteria students are more likely to understand and use the feedback advice they receive. Glaser and Chi (1988) have also shown that the time experts spend constructing the initial representations of complex tasks partly accounts for their better performance when compared to novices.

Forward-Looking and Transferable

The most consistent request from students is that the feedback tells them about their strengths and weaknesses and specifically about what they need to do to make improvements in subsequent assignments. Knight (2006) calls the latter "feedforward" rather than feedback. Examples might include suggesting goals to focus on in future assignments or specific strategies that might apply. Some feedback sheets include an "action-point" box where the instructor can outline the specific actions that would lead to greatest improvement in the next assignment. Walker (2006) sees the focus as being on skills development rather than on specific content; developing the skills to solve problems or write essays in the discipline is more effective in the long run than solving a single problem or writing a specific essay. Another perspective is that comments should focus not on gaps in knowledge and understanding but on the students' representations of the knowledge in their discipline. Comments should help students find alternative ways of looking at the problem rather than simply highlight misunderstandings. The intention here is to promote new ways of thinking about concepts, their relationships, and their applications.

Hattie and Timperley (2007) identified four orientations to the provision of feedback comments; teachers could provide comments on the task, stating whether the assignment is correct or incorrect, or requires more input; they might be about the writing process (e.g., "this assignment could be better if you planned out the structure and sequence of arguments"); they might focus comments on the student's ability to self-regulate, for example, feedback on students' own assessments of their work would fall into this category (see below); or the comments might be personal (e.g., "that's a sophisticated response; well done"). Hattie and Timperley maintain that focusing comments on the process and on self-regulatory activities is most effective, if the goal is to help students transfer learning to new contexts.

I have discussed encouraging students to use feedback earlier in relation to multistage assignments. However, here is an additional example, based on a variation of a strategy used by a colleague. Students are required to write an essay, let's say on ethics. The instructor provides written feedback, usually a few paragraphs, on the subject content, the ideas, arguments, and evidence. Specifically, the feedback points to new ways of looking at the issues and refers briefly to other theorists. The students are then allowed to produce a second assignment in the same content area but using a different format (e.g., a report to the government on this ethics issue). Those who choose this option are told that to get a good grade on the second assignment they must go well beyond the ideas in the first assignment and demonstrate good use of the feedback. This is intended to encourage students to use the feedback, read more widely, and to interrelate and apply ideas from other sources in the report. Why is this design of interest? First, the students have a strong incentive to act on the feedback. Secondly, both the student and the teacher see the direct benefits of feedback in future action. Importantly, students do not repeat the same assignment, so they will not perceive this as duplication, nor will their teachers. This is a good example of the forward use of written comments.

FOSTERING FEEDBACK DIALOGUES

The advice on the formulation of comments above is a useful starting point in thinking about feedback. However, it does not really go far enough. Feedback is not a monologue. The meaning of feedback comments is not transmitted from the teacher to the student; rather, meaning comes into being through interaction and dialogue. So how might we enrich feedback and make it more meaningful to students?

First, teachers must, as far as possible, tailor their feedback comments to students' needs. Students differ in their understanding and in their reactions to feedback, so this is a challenge, especially with large classes. However, progress is possible by designing teacher-student interactions in ways that promote responsive and contingent feedback conversations. Second, teacher feedback must be supplemented by feedback from other sources. Students must be exposed to and interact with a greater variety of feedback responses. Multiple sources of feedback help students see their work from many perspectives, and this enhances understanding and capability. The most readily available source of supplementary feedback derives from peers enrolled in the same course.

Third, feedback must be geared to strengthening the students' ability to judge the quality of their own work. The long-term purpose of feedback is that students become independent of their teachers. Students already engage in inner dialogue and generate their own feedback when they produce an assignment. A systematic focus on strengthening these processes will not only make teacher and peer feedback more effective, but it will also help develop your students' ability to monitor and evaluate their own learning. Last, we must try to create the conditions that will motivate students actively to seek and use feedback. This, however, is more likely to happen if we strive to meet the other three conditions. The following sections develop these ideas and suggest strategies for implementation.

MAKING TEACHER FEEDBACK CONTINGENT ON LEARNERS' NEEDS

Wood, Wood, and Middleton (1978), in their work on contingent tutoring, demonstrated that there is no ideal level of feedback from a teacher. What is optimal is continual dynamic adjustment of the level of teacher input depending on the degree of learner understanding. More iteration is not necessarily better, neither is more specificity or detail; the point is to match the feedback to each student's needs. Unfortunately this can be difficult to achieve when student numbers are large.

One way of making teacher feedback more sensitive to individual needs is to have students express a preference for the kinds of feedback they would like when they hand in an assignment. Teachers, for instance, might ask students to request feedback, to attach questions with their submission identifying areas with which they would like help; while some might be about the writing process, others might concern concept understanding and use. The teacher would then focus the comments on these areas. Bloxham and Campbell (2008) tested this approach with first-year university students and found benefits, although they found that some students had difficulty formulating high-level conceptual questions. However, teachers can address this issue through better initial support for question formulation and/or by beginning with a collaborative essay task where groups of students work together to form questions. This procedure shifts the balance of responsibility for feedback toward the student. Requesting feedback based on their own concerns empowers students more than just receiving feedback based on the teacher's interpretation of weaknesses. However, this procedure need not stop teachers from using feedback to highlight additional issues not identified by students.

Elbow and Sorcinelli provide a structured version of the requested feedback approach (chapter 14 in this book); they ask students to write an informal cover letter to hand in with an essay, but they provide the framework using specific questions: What was your main point? What were your sub-points? Which parts of the submitted essay feel strong and weak? What questions do you have for me as reader? The cover letter ensures that the students' comments will form the beginning of a dialogue that is continued by the teacher through the feedback. They note that dialogue can extend further by having students respond to the teacher's feedback; for example, they might write a short note that tells what they heard in the comments and how they will use them. Importantly, when feedback comments are contingent on what the student does, it is more likely that they will actually meet the criteria for good commenting I discussed earlier, that is, be understandable, selective, specific, and even forward-looking.

Contingent dialogues could also start with teachers formulating their feedback as questions on students' work that are then followed through in face-to-face discussions, individually or in small group tutorials. A recent innovation is audio feedback. The teacher reads the student script and attaches audio files. Early reports suggest that students respond more positively to audio feedback, seeing it as closer to a dialogue. Teachers can produce reactions to the writing as they read, can ask questions, and suggest improvements. Variations in tone and the naturalness of the approach seem to give students more of a sense that teachers are interested in what students have written. Teachers or students could also build on the dialogues prompted through audio feedback in class. Early research shows, however, that it can take time for some teachers to get used to this feedback format.

SUPPLEMENTING TEACHER FEEDBACK WITH PEER FEEDBACK

It is natural to think about feedback as if only teachers are able to provide it. Yet, many learning benefits derive from peer feedback; it is not just about saving time (Boud, Cohen, and Sampson, 2001). It can be difficult for teachers to address all areas of weakness in students' work or to provide comments in an accessible language. Peers, however, who are tackling the same assignment, might be able to provide feedback in a student-centered discourse. Also, some students might actually be more receptive to teacher feedback if the comments they receive from peers agree with those from the teacher.

While consistency is important in marking and grading, this is less important in feedback. Indeed, there are significant benefits to be gained from variation. Having different readers respond to and comment on an assignment provides multiple perspectives, and this invokes multiple opportunities for scaffolding. Seeing examples of the work of others and commenting on them also helps students become more objective and critical about their own work. When students respond to others' work and receive comments on their own work, this enhances their understanding of what quality looks like, and how to produce it. They learn that quality does not come in a pre-defined form; rather, there is a spectrum of possibilities.

Collaborative Assignment Production

There are many ways of implementing peer dialogue in relation to written assignments. Informally, it can be provided during the execution of a task by getting students to work together collaboratively to produce an assignment. This is the approach that one teacher adopted in a first-year psychology course with an enrollment of 560 students. He required his students, in groups of six or seven, to collaborate and write six short essays online over two semesters (Nicol, 2009). All the group discussions and the final submission were recorded within WebCT (now Blackboard), the institution's learning-management system. Students remained in the same closed discussion group throughout the year with members of each group giving each other feedback while writing the essays and while negotiating about and agreeing upon the final submission.

The teacher provided online guidance that emphasized the value of peer feedback for learning and that instructed students in good practice in peer feedback. The teacher supplemented this with feedback through essay exemplars and with general feedback to the whole class through an open discussion forum. The exemplars were selected from the students' submissions and posted online after all groups had submitted their assignment. The students were encouraged to compare their submissions against the range of exemplars. This approach proved highly motivational and a majority of the students (64 percent) agreed that the peer dialogue increased their understanding of the topics studied. There was a significant improvement in essay performance in the final exams compared to previous years. One notable feature of this design was that the instructor organized rich and motivational feedback for 560 students without over-burdening himself with the provision of individual feedback to every student.

Peer Commenting on Assignments

A formal approach to peer feedback is to organize classroom sessions (or online opportunities) where students can critique each other's work. For example, students might write a short 500-word essay (e.g., 500 words) and bring three copies to a tutorial. The instructor distributes these across the tutorial group with the result that each student provides and receives three sets of peer feedback comments. Instructions might be to identify two weaknesses in the text and make recommendations for improvement or to identify whether the evidence sufficiently supports the argument. In some scenarios the instructor might provide the assessment criteria or rubric for the comments, whereas in others the students might derive the criteria during the act of assessing the work for peers. There are advantages in using both approaches.

Some students lack confidence in the ability or knowledge of peers. Hence they can show resistance to peer critiquing. This can be addressed through training and by linking peer to instructor feedback; for example, after peers have provided structured comments, the instructor could provide her own comments not on the assignment but on the comments provided by peers. Software has been developed to support peer commenting, which also makes it easy to implement this with large classes.

Learning through Peer Collaboration and Review

Although the findings from research suggest that students improve their writing in the disciplines through practice and feedback, most teachers are overwhelmed by the workload associated with providing this feedback. Hence a different approach is required. The approach I advocate here is that students learn writing through reviewing (see also chapter on writing). In collaborative authorship and in peer commenting, students analyze each other's writing, detect problems in understanding and in the writing process, and make suggestions for improvement. This is beneficial to all students but especially for those who might fail to detect their own misunderstandings or flaws in their writing, as well as for those who might overestimate their own understandings and capabilities. This approach can also give students more practice in writing without significantly increasing instructor workload.

Importantly, peer feedback builds on teacher feedback. It further optimizes the adaptation of comments to individual student needs, and it links comments directly to the production of a specific output. In effect, peer feedback helps ensure that comments meet the criteria presented earlier, that they are timely, forward-looking, and actionable. Finally, when students engage in peer-feedback activities, they are also put in the role of the assessor. This helps develop their ability to evaluate their own work.

ACTIVATING AND STRENGTHENING INNER FEEDBACK

When students engage in learning activities there is always a feedback dimension, even when there is no external source of feedback advice. For example, when writing an essay, students usually generate a great deal of inner dialogue and feedback during the act of production (e.g., "Have I expressed this clearly?" "What if I tried it this way?"). This inner dialogue leads to tracking maneuvers (re-workings of the text) that ensure a match between the student's goals and the finished essay. These inner or reflective dialogues are a natural consequence of engaging in any purposeful action.

Making these reflective dialogues more conscious and public offers many benefits. For instance, asking students to assess their own assignment either during its production or at the end before handing it in helps develop evaluative skills. These skills are important if students are to become less dependent on their teachers and more independent and autonomous. Also, if the products of these self-assessments are made public, teachers gain insight into how students think about their own work, which in turn enables them to better target their feedback.

It is also important to note that self-assessment is already embedded in students' use of teacher feedback (Black and Wiliam, 1998). When students receive teacher feedback, they must be able to use this information as a reference point to evaluate their own work; unless they do this, they will not be able to make subsequent improvements. However, through this evaluative process, students are in fact already engaging in acts of assessment not dissimilar to those carried out by their teachers when they produce feedback. So, as well as improving teacher feedback, it might be more productive in the long term to focus some of our effort on developing the student's own evaluative capabilities.

Harnessing Inner Feedback: More Frequent Tasks

To help students develop their self-assessment skills it is important to provide them with many opportunities to reflect on their work; this is relatively easy to do, for example, by replacing one large assignment at the end of a course with regular small assignments during the course. This gives students repeated occasions to benefit from feedback from their own evaluative activities; they will find out which concepts and ideas are difficult to express and where they have problems in writing. For some students this will be enough to trigger further study to clear up misunderstandings or even to seek out feedback from other students, which is also beneficial. And all this occurs without teacher feedback.

Support for the idea of regular and distributed assignments comes from the robust research finding about "time on task." This shows that the more time students spend studying in and out of class, the more they learn (Chickering and Gamson, 1987). This is not a consequence of practice alone; rather it is the result of the feedback students generate through that practice. The main drawback with numerous assignments is that teachers might feel they have to grade and provide feedback on them all. However, a small proportion of marks might be awarded for effort, for actually producing the assignment. And teacher feedback can be limited by using a simple rubric and/or by giving general feedback on a sample of these assignments to the whole class. Alternatively, peer feedback of the kind I described earlier might be appropriate.

Having Students Reflect on Teacher-Provided Comments

Students might also reflect on and evaluate the relevance of the comments that teachers provide. When a teacher provides comments, each student normally receives them in relation to their assignment. However, many students report that such comments do not meet their needs; for example, they might not address areas where they suspect they are weak. From the teachers' perspective, providing individual comments to students is a high workload activity that has low-benefit if the student does not find the comments helpful. The instructor could, however, multiply the benefits of comments if he collated all the comments for the same assignment and used them in new ways. A master list would suffice, although some software now enables comments to be stored in and accessed from a databank. For example, students might be asked to select from the collated list the comments that they consider most relevant to their assignment and to say how they might act on them. This would encourage inner reflection both on the comments and on their own work. Importantly, the students rather than the teacher would be the protagonist in identifying the relevance of comments. Engaging with the comments that other students receive for the same assignment alerts students to pitfalls they may not have noticed, puts individual feedback comments in a wider context, engages students actively, and helps them develop a better understanding of the assignment requirements.

Comments might be shared in many ways. The teacher might produce a printed summary ideally using an online environment, as this will give more flexibility for sharing. Importantly, this approach need not take more faculty time as the feedback comments produced in one year could be reused with new students in subsequent years, if the teacher set the same assignment. Taking this idea further, students could be encouraged to set up their own study groups where they meet and discuss their work and feedback comments. Some students are probably already doing this.

Strengthening Self-Assessment

It is also possible to structure assignments in ways that encourage formal self-assessments. Indeed, instructors can integrate such self-assessments into any course or assignment. Students might be required to make an evaluative judgment when they hand in an assignment (e.g., "What did you do well? Give examples," "Where do you think the assignment is weak?"). In a pharmacy course in my own university, an assignment cover sheet was developed for essay self-assessment. The students were required to rephrase the essay question in their own words, make a judgment about whether they had met some stated criteria, estimate the grade they expected, and provide a justification for this. Teachers then commented on these self-assessments. This approach not only encouraged students to stand back and evaluate their own essay but also provided the teacher with insights into how students' perceive and judge their own competence.

Self-assessment is even more powerful if the teacher asks students not only to judge their own work but also to formulate the criteria and standards that should apply. This often happens in later years in project classes, but it could be brought forward to earlier years. Students might, for example, be invited to generate the criteria by which to assess an unfamiliar assignment (e.g., a blog, a wiki) and then to carry out their own self-assessment of progress. The rationale is to move students away from dependence on the judgment of others to a greater reliance on their own judgment. This will better prepare students for professional practice and for future learning.

IN CONCLUSION

This chapter has provided many ideas and practical approaches to improving the power of written feedback. Some of these have been about the quality of the written feedback message, while many have been about improving students' interaction with and use of those messages. In this conclusion the essence of this advice is distilled into three overarching guidelines. Instructors should ensure that feedback:

1. *Is expressed in learner actions*. Make sure that feedback actually feeds forward into action rather than backwards. This is the most consistent recommendation from the research on written comments, both from the point of view of students and of faculty. Perhaps the ideal feedback scenario in higher education is project supervision, where the student has frequent meetings with the teacher to discuss and rework a developing assignment. If we could make large class feedback more like project supervision, feedback would have maximum impact.

2. *Is contingent on and responsive to student needs*. There is no right level of specificity or detail in feedback; it all depends on students' needs and your purpose in giving feedback. Contingency requires that students should have relevant and responsive feedback conversations not only with the teacher but equally with peers; this is necessary because the right level of specificity or detail cannot really be predicted in advance. It also means involving students actively in reflection on feedback and on their own work so that they are required to locate the contingency relationship, not just the teacher.

3. *Is perceived by students as nonjudgmental*. Feedback is about helping students succeed, not about exercising power over them. This means setting high expectations that challenge students while always assuring them that they have the capacity to succeed. Most of what has been suggested, if appropriately implemented, would lead to positive engagement with feedback; that is, reader-response commenting (Lunsford, 1997), contingent feedback, self-assessment, which gives students a sense of control over their learning, and peer feedback, which also fosters a sense of community.

The final word is about grading. Grading is often a concern given that many students focus more on their grades than on feedback comments. In this volume there is a chapter on grading (chapter 10) and on motivation (chapter 11). However, the essential advice here is to ensure that grading does not have a negative impact on feedback processes. Simple approaches might work, for example, asking students to respond to comments before giving the grade or asking them to come to class to discuss the feedback before distributing their grades. However, this all boils down to motivation; if the recommendations in this chapter are followed, then students will come to appreciate the value of feedback and how it helps them succeed in their learning.

Supplementary Reading

Nicol, D. J. and Macfarlane-Dick, D. 2006. Formative assessment and self-regulated learning: A model and seven principles of good feedback practice, *Studies in Higher Education*, 31(2), 199–218.

Nicol, D. (2009). Transforming assessment and feedback: Enhancing integration and empowerment in the first year, published by the Quality Assurance Agency for Higher Education, available at: http://www.enhancementthemes.ac.uk/documents/firstyear/First_Year_Transforming_Assess.pdf. Taking the perspective that the purpose of assessment and feedback is to help develop in students the ability to monitor, evaluate, and regulate their own learning, these two publications reinterpret and distill the research on feedback into a set of principles that can be used to guide practice. Seven principles of good feedback practice are suggested in Nicol and Macfarlane-Dick (2006), and numerous practical applications are suggested. These feedback principles provide another way of interpreting and implementing the ideas presented in this chapter. Nicol (2009) is a further development of the feedback principles but with a focus on first-year teaching. This publication includes a literature review, short definitions of each principle, a range of examples of their implementation, and strategic guidelines for senior managers. All this material and more can be found on the REAP (Re-engineering Assessment Practices) website (www.reap.ac.uk). REAP was a project funded by the Scottish government (£1m). Its goal was to show how technology might be used to enhance assessment and feedback practices in large enrolment classes.

Black, P. and Wiliam, D., Assessment and classroom learning, *Assessment in Education*, 1998, 5(1), 7–74. Paul Black and Dylan William provide the most comprehensive review of formative assessment and feedback available. They analyze the results of over 250 selected studies across all levels of education. This is the starting point for those with a passionate and deep interest in this topic.

Bryan, C. and Clegg, K., *Innovative Assessment in Higher Education* (London: Routledge, 2006). This book provides an up-to-date overview of thinking and research on formative assessment. It is grounded in the idea that assessment is *for* learning and that students should be active partners in assessment. The first part of the book provides frameworks for thinking about assessment and feedback while the second provides examples of innovative practice.

Grant Wiggins, *Educative Assessment* (1991). This is the best example of U.S. practice in this area. Although the book has a school perspective, its title "Educative Assessment" highlights the idea of assessment *for* learning rather than just assessment *of* learning. The focus is on designing assessments to inform and improve student performance.

Chapter 10

Assigning Grades: What Do They Mean?

Grading is almost always in the news. Grade inflation, grading leniency, contract grading, mastery grading—all of these stimulate heated discussion and cries of dismay. My own ideas about grading have become somewhat clearer as I have talked to my teaching assistants about grading policies. That may explain why I am not overly emotional about each of these issues.

First let's agree that grades are fundamentally a method of communication. The question then becomes, What does the professor intend to communicate to whom? When we put grading into this context, four things become apparent:

1. Evaluation is a great deal more than giving a grade. As we have seen in the preceding chapters, the major part of evaluation should be in the form of comments on papers, responses to student statements, conversations, and other means of helping students understand where they are and how to do better. A professor giving a course grade is communicating to several groups—individual students, professors teaching advanced courses, graduate or professional school admissions committees, prospective employers, and so on.

2. What professors communicate by a grade depends on the meaning of the grade to the person reading it—the effect that it has on that person.

3. Professors cannot change the meaning of grades unilaterally. The students' interpretations will be colored by their previous experiences with grades, and they are likely to be disturbed, or to feel that they are being misled, when a professor uses grades in new ways. This explains the strong emotional reaction to so-called grade inflation and to practices deviating from traditional meanings. Adams (2005) studied what students versus faculty think grades should be based on. He found that students believed that effort should have a bigger impact on final grades regardless of how much improvement they showed than faculty did. He also found a big difference in the number of hours the two groups felt constituted superior effort. I also believe the norms vary by discipline and across institutions. So an "A" isn't always an "A."

4. The meaning of As, Bs, and Cs has changed over the last fifty years. In the mid-1900s, C was the average grade. Today, B is more typical. This is not a problem as long as those who assign and interpret grades understand the current meaning. Whether they do is open to debate.

What are grades used for? I suggest that the person reading a grade typically wants information with respect to making a judgment about the student's *future* performance. Mastery systems of grading, pass-fail grading, and other alternative systems are resisted because they may not be efficient conveyors of information useful for predicting future performance.

DO GRADES PROVIDE INFORMATION USEFUL FOR DECISION MAKING?

One of the arguments against conventional grading is that grades do not provide useful information for the major purposes for which they are usually used. Teachers assume that grades have some informational and motivational value for students. Critics, however, argue that the threat of low grades is often a crutch used by poor teachers. Moreover, a heavy emphasis on grades is likely to reduce motivation for further learning and may even result in poorer achievement by the students who are most motivated by grades. In reality, those who achieve the most tend to have moderate grade motivation and high intrinsic motivation (Lin et al., 2003).

What about information for employers? Probably most human resources psychologists would agree that the best predictor of success on a job is successful performance on a similar job. For a young person entering the job market, the only previous employment has been in low-level part-time jobs. The employer's decision must then depend largely on other information, such as interviews, letters of recommendation, biographical data, family background, and test scores. Each source is only partially adequate. Insofar as the new job requires some expenditure for training, it seems likely that grades—representing the result of skills applied in study, learning, and problem solving—will add some useful albeit incomplete information. Grades might also be used by others as a surrogate measure of a strong work ethic, persistence, and flexibility in adapting to a wide range of situations. (I'm not saying that is an accurate interpretation of grades, however.)

Because grades are commonly used in combination with other variables, no one should expect grades always to correlate with success for the students who are selected. It is a simple mathematical truism that when we use several selection criteria—each of them having some validity—we should expect low positive, zero, or even negative correlations between any one selection variable and the ultimate criterion of performance. This outcome occurs because we balance criteria against one another. We select some people who are low in some important attributes because they have high grades, and we select others despite low grades because they are high in other important attributes. The common criticism that grades don't predict later performance is largely invalid because most of the studies cited were carried out in situations where grades and other predictors had already been used in selection.

CAN WE TRUST GRADES?

The information value of the grades we assign is heavily influenced by the methods used to evaluate learning. In chapter 7, "Assessing, Testing, and Evaluating," I described several ways of measuring student learning, from the typical in-class tests to out-of-class papers and authentic assessments. For grades to be truly useful, they need to be based on what the measurement field refers to as valid and reliable methods.

Validity of the Measurement

Assessments that are *valid* measure what they say they measure. For example, the best way to measure students' ability to structure a persuasive argument is to have students create their own unique argument on a topic and deliver it in either written or oral form. Answering multiple-choice questions about the parts of an argument isn't measuring the same thing. Even critiquing someone else's argument measures a different skill. When we grade argumentation skills with real argument-development activities, we have the most valid measurement and probably the best predictor of future argumentation success. The farther away from that situation we get, the less valid the measurement becomes.

One thing we should look for when determining the validity behind grades is what went into the grade calculation. Lots of instructors give or take away points for student actions that have little or nothing to do with measures of student learning. For example, they make deductions for late papers or failure to follow instructions. Although these are possibly valid surrogates for qualities such as personal responsibility, maturity, or professional behavior, they are not valid measures of what a student has learned. Including them in an assignment grade lowers the overall validity of that grade. I'd be tempted to have a totally separate grade category called something like "demonstrated responsibility" or "diligence" that would be used to measure things such as tardiness, late assignments, or inattention to class policies. These would be separate from the quality of the work itself yet still part of the overall evaluation of a student. I suspect that in many cases that type of measure would be as good a predictor of future success—perhaps even a better one.

Reliability of the Scores

Another important quality of an assessment is its reliability. An assessment that is *reliable* produces fairly consistent results either across time or across multiple graders. Multiple-choice tests, for example, are very reliable because no subjective judgment influences grading; the answer is either right or wrong. Essay tests and papers are less reliable unless you consistently use a rubric to grade them. If you have a reliable measure, everyone's grade indicates a very specific performance, and all individuals whose performance is the same get the same grade.

What does all this mean for you as the person giving the grades? It means that in order to communicate accurately with all the consumers of those grades, you need to be sure that the basis for your grading is both valid and reliable. If you can do that, then they can believe you when you provide them with evidence of student performance.

Of course, in reality, there are no grade police out there trying to make us all conform to the same exact standards. As a profession, we have to police ourselves. It's up to us to uphold our standards, not to keep grades from becoming inflated but rather to give honest grades that truly communicate what a student has achieved.

ASSIGNING GRADES: ON A "CURVE" OR AGAINST A STANDARD?

One of the persistent controversies in college teaching is whether to grade "on the curve" (norm-referenced grading) or against an absolute standard (criterion-referenced grading). These two positions are probably not as far apart as the argument would indicate. Even teachers who grade on the curve are influenced in setting their cutoff points between grades by their feelings about whether the class was a good or a poor one. Similarly, teachers who do not grade on the curve set their standards in line with what previous experience leads them to regard as reasonable accomplishment in the course. Personally, I believe that grading on the curve is educationally dysfunctional. If possible, your grades should, both in the students' eyes and in actuality, be more nearly based on absolute standards than on relative standing in a particular class.

The use of an absolute standard becomes easier if you formulated your major and minor objectives and tested their achievement. Travers (1950) proposed one set of absolute standards:

- A: All major and minor goals achieved.
- B: All major goals achieved; some minor ones not.
- C: All major goals achieved; many minor ones not.
- D: A few major goals achieved, but student is not prepared for advanced work.
- E or F: None of the major goals achieved.

Ideally, I should be able to list my goals for the course and at the end of the course assess each goal in such a way that I could use such a criterion-based system. In fact, however, my tests, papers, journals, research studies, and other elements of the assessment of learning are seldom pure measures of a single goal. For example, my tests assess knowledge and understanding of the major concepts and facts as well as ability to apply and think with these concepts. To separate each component would be almost impossible. Consequently, I assign points to each test, paper, and other assignment, and I give grades on the basis of the total percentage of points earned by the student over the term. This strategy at least avoids the detrimental effects of grading students' performances relative to one another and probably approximates the outcomes described by Travers.

There is a larger, more philosophical issue lurking behind the great norm-referenced versus criterion-referenced grading debate. The issue is the one we discussed earlier: What do grades mean? Is the purpose of the grade to identify the "best" students in a group (norm referencing), or is it to indicate what each student has achieved (criterion referencing)? Both are legitimate positions and can be and are argued for vociferously. There are no pat answers to the choice. For example, there are many times when we have to allocate limited resources or awards to only the best of a group. In those instances it makes sense to use intra-group comparisons. But what if everyone in the group does poorly or does really well? Do we pick "the best of a bad lot" or abandon good people who in another group would be the top performers? What if the skills needed for the next class or on the job are so critical that failure to achieve an absolute level of competence could have dire consequences? Should we pass only those who meet the standard? (Thinking of getting a shot from a nurse or doctor who was the top student in a class of klutzes, I'd much prefer that all medical personnel meet a set standard for shot giving, thank you!)

I don't have a pat answer for this dilemma. The choice rests on factors such as these:

1. How valid is the instrument on which the grade is based? How reliable is it? It may not be appropriate to use criterion referencing if the measures are not accurate or fair.

2. How select is the group being evaluated? If the group is very homogeneous, norm referencing is inappropriate because there's not really a distribution of skills across the group.

3. How critical is the content being evaluated? If it's critical, I favor criterion referencing every time.

4. Does future work depend on this content? If it does, then criterion referencing will at least be sure that everyone who passes has the prerequisites for that future work.

There are many more things to consider, but the important point is to consider them rather than choosing blindly.

REDUCING STUDENT ANXIETY ABOUT GRADES

Because to many students grades represent a fearsome, mysterious dragon, their anxiety can sometimes be reduced by encouraging the students to participate in planning the methods by which grades will be assigned. Students usually can recognize the instructor's need to conform to college policy in grade distribution, and the dragon seems less threatening if they have helped determine the system by which they are devoured (or rewarded).

Some instructors go so far as to let students determine their own grades or to have groups of students grade one another. I like the idea that students should develop the capacity for self-evaluation, but I recognize that many students resist this procedure, either through modesty or through fear that they will underrate themselves. If you use it, I suggest having a thorough discussion of the plan with students and an agreed-upon, well-defined set of criteria that all students should use.

Whether or not students participate, you need to be clear about your criteria. Examples of previously graded work may be helpful. Asking students to hand in their own estimates of their grades may help you to motivate them better and may also develop their abilities for self-evaluation.

In general, motivation is not helped simply by high grades; nor is it helped by tough standards. Students are most motivated when they feel that they can achieve success with a reasonable effort (Harter, 1978) and when they believe the grading is fair. In fact, Gordon and Fay (2010) have studied what influences students' opinions that grading has been fair. Amazingly they found that it was not clever strategies that we use to tweak the grades when they seem out of whack, for example, dropping the lowest grade or allowing students to redo an assignment to improve their grade. Instead Gordon and Fay found that it was the teaching strategies that we use to help the students do well in the first place (such as study guides, review sessions, practice tests, and so on) that were the best predictors of students' impressions of fairness. So if you want them to feel they've been treated fairly in the grading, you should put your emphasis on what happens before the test.

By keeping students informed during the course about where they stand, you help them control much of the anxiety they feel when the grading system is indefinite and unstructured. Sometimes it may seem easier to fight off grade-conscious students by being very indefinite about grades, but student morale is better when the students know the situation with which they must cope.

Whatever your grading strategy, if you are more generous in assigning grades to tests and papers than you are in the final distribution of grades, you are guaranteed visits from aggrieved students. One way in which you get yourself into this position is by providing opportunities for students to omit questions on an exam or to submit extra work for a higher grade. On the other hand, there is much to be said in favor of adopting procedures that take the sting out of the occasional failure by allowing a redo or throwing out the lowest grade. It will be a constant balancing act between measurement consistency and concern for student mental health. Any procedures you choose can have some educational justification, but you need to be able to convince administrators or colleagues that the pattern of grades you assign is appropriate for the achievement of your students.

WHAT ABOUT THE STUDENT WHO WANTS A GRADE CHANGED?

If you keep students informed about their grades on tests, papers, and other graded work during the term, you will avoid most complaints. But there still may be some. My basic strategy is the same as that used in returning tests or papers (see chapter 8): Listen first and then go over the criteria used. Try to understand the student's reasoning. This may be a learning experience for both of you.

In addition, of course, you may try to explain to the students the rationale of grades. Usually this doesn't seem to do much good. Both students and faculty sometimes confuse two possible criteria on which grades may be based. One is the relative amount of *progress* the student has made in achieving the goals of the course; the other is *achievement of the goals of the course* at the end of the term.

Progress, however, is relevant to prediction. A student who has made a great deal of progress despite a poor background may do as well in an advanced course or job as someone with somewhat better performance at the end of the course who made relatively little progress. My own solution is to assign grades primarily for achievement of course goals (total performance), but when a student's total points or overall performance is close to the boundary between grades, I assign the higher grade if there has been much progress.

No matter how you grade, some students will be unhappy. Be sympathetic, but beware! If you begin changing grades, the informal communication lines of the campus will soon spread the word. Be sure that you understand your institution's regulations with respect to grade changes. Check, too, on procedures that students may use to appeal capricious grading.

Don't finish reading this chapter with your own anxiety aroused by the dangers of grading. It is proper that good teachers should be humble, as they see how great is the power they have over the happiness of their students by printing a simple A, B, C, or D. Nevertheless, one of the real satisfactions of teaching is giving a good grade to an ordinarily average student who has come to life in your course.

GRADES VS. LEARNING: SOME RELATED RESEARCH

A lot has been written about goal orientation and its effects on learning. Carol Dweck (1986), among others, has discussed the finding that many learners seem to be pursuing goals that are focused on *appearing* competent rather than on actually learning anything. This is the phenomenon of goal orientation. Some students are pursuing mastery goals (they really want to learn and are what we might call non-grade-conscious); others are working primarily for a grade (called in this literature "performance oriented"). You will find a more complete explanation of this theory in chapter 11 on motivation, but here is how the theory is relevant to grades.

Although originally these orientations were thought to be related to some personality traits, more recent literature relates these orientations to the conditions of learning, to what rewards and punishments are in place for success. The researchers even assert that a single person can have both types of goals in the same situation but for different aspects of the task. All of us have had students whose only interest seemed to be in their grades. The research on this topic has shown that these students are usually very literal-minded, not willing to try anything new, and likely to stick to the familiar so they know they can succeed. And yet they are motivated, just not in the way we would like. Sometimes you run across a student who wants to learn no matter what it takes. The research literature shows that students like this are willing to risk mistakes, to interpret failures as something to learn from rather than avoid or hide. Obviously we'd all like to have the latter students rather than the former. The great thing is that we can influence which type of goals students will work toward in our classes: learning or grades. Ames (1992) and Maehr and Midgley (1991), all researchers in the area of motivation, have given some very good guidelines about how to turn students into learning-oriented learners. Their recommendations* include the following:

1. Focus on meaningful activities that students can see are related to their own future. This helps them focus on becoming skillful rather than on simply earning a grade.

2. Make the learning interesting through the use of variety and novelty. The goal is to distract the students from focusing on grades by making the learning worthwhile in and of itself.

3. Make the learning challenging but doable. Challenge is a big source of motivation for students, but only if there is hope of success.

4. Give learners some choice in what they are going to do. When you are able to choose, you are more likely to work toward something in which you have a vested interest.

5. Focus on individual improvement rather than on comparisons with others. This is probably the most important but most difficult thing to control. Students have a long history of comparing themselves to others with their grades.

6. Make evaluation private rather than public. This actually supports item 5. Private evaluations make it harder for students to focus on how they compare to others.

7. Recognize effort and progress. Try to get students' minds off getting the right answer as the only goal.

---

*These recommendations are adapted from a set created by Pintrich and Schunk (2002, pp. 238–239), who combined the findings of all these researchers into a coherent set.

8. Help students see mistakes as opportunities for learning. This is best done through the way you react when a student makes a mistake. Do you criticize, or do you try to help students work through their thought processes? These two behaviors result in very different reactions by students.

9. Encourage collaborative learning. Students who are working together toward a common goal are less likely to be comparing themselves to others.

The research on student goal orientation indicates that if you can structure your class along these lines, students will be more comfortable in putting grades aside and focusing on learning because they can trust you to help them accomplish as much as they can. Perhaps that will help take the sting out of grades and as a result decrease their importance overall.

IN CONCLUSION

1. Grades are not just a communication between teacher and student; they are a decision-making tool for future professors, employers, admissions committees, and others.

2. Useful assessments are both valid and reliable.

3. Involving students in the planning of assessment methods can reduce grade anxiety.

4. Grading on the curve can have detrimental effects. Tread carefully.

5. Try to focus students on learning rather than on grades.

Supplementary Reading

What grades mean to faculty, parents, personnel directors, and students is described in O. Milton, H. R. Pollio, and J. Eison, *Making Sense of College Grades* (San Francisco: Jossey-Bass, 1986).

A fine vignette about the problem of assigning grades is Linc Fisch's "Students on the Line," in *The Chalk Dust Collection: Thoughts and Reflections on Teaching in Colleges and Universities* (Stillwater, OK: New Forums Press, 1996), pp. 132–134.

Barbara Davis describes a number of systems for determining grades and gives sensible advice in her chapter "Grading Practices," in *Tools for Teaching*, 2nd ed. (San Francisco: Jossey-Bass, 2008).

Another good resource is B. E. Walvoord and V. J. Anderson, *Effective Grading: A Tool for Learning and Assessment* (San Francisco: Jossey-Bass, 1998).

Read more about goal orientation and its relationship to grading practices in D. H. Schunk, P. R. Pintrich, and J. Meece's *Motivation in Education: Theory, Research and Applications*, 3rd ed. (Upper Saddle River, NJ: Merrill/Prentice Hall, 2008).

With the change in instructional methods comes the need for a change in grading practices. Rebecca S. Anderson and Bruce W. Speck's "Changing the Way We Grade Student Performance: Classroom Assessment and the New Learning Paradigm," *New Directions for Teaching and Learning*, no. 74, July 1998, gives some good suggestions about new ways to grade student work.

Grading Students by Lawrence H. Cross (ERIC Digest, 10/1995). The ERIC Digests were very good summaries of research and practice provided by the ERIC Clearinghouses on different issues. The service has been discontinued, but some of the materials are still available. A site that provides access to the material is www.ericdigests.org.

Part 3

Understanding Students

Chapter 11

Motivation in the College Classroom

Few topics concern teachers at all levels as much as the motivation of students. We worry over the students who appear disengaged, who attend sporadically, or whose laptop use in class seems more directed toward social networking than note taking, and we may disparage those who appear to care only about grades. We delight in the students who share our passion for the subject matter, who are eager to ask intelligent questions, who view grades as informational feedback, and who not only prepare for class but seek us out to learn more. We marvel when we compare notes with a colleague and learn that these contrasting motivational profiles sometimes describe the same student—but in different courses, suggesting that motivation is something other than an abiding characteristic of an individual.

We all want students who are motivated to learn. These are the students who choose to attend class regularly, participate constructively, persist when learning is difficult, make the effort to prepare for class and to study effectively, who solicit help when they need it, and who translate all this into academic success. Knowing more about how students are motivated, and what you can do to structure a class that positively affects student motivation, can make a significant difference in student engagement and learning. A classroom of motivated learners affects *our* motivation

This chapter was written by Barbara Hofer of Middlebury College.

as well and can make teaching a more satisfying experience for the instructor. Particularly in an era where we are competing for student attention among so many technological and communication devices, knowing more about classroom motivation is increasingly relevant.

MOTIVATIONAL THEORIES: AN OVERVIEW

Researchers typically consider three indices of motivation: choice, effort, and persistence; achievement is an outcome of these variables. Accordingly, students who are motivated to learn choose tasks that enhance their learning, work hard at those tasks, and persist in the face of difficulty in order to attain their goals. So it should be no surprise that motivation is important to consider if we want to enhance student learning. Why students vary in their motivation is a compelling question, and several theoretical frameworks help provide answers.

Some students may be driven by a high *need for achievement* (McClelland et al., 1953). Need for achievement may be characterized as an individual trait or disposition, and it is likely to be the outcome of early environments in which parents set high standards and valued achievement. In general, students differ from one another in the degree to which achievement for its own sake is meaningful to them, but this difference explains only one aspect of motivation, which is considered to be contextual and malleable, and a function of classroom instruction, tasks, and activities (Maehr and Zusho, 2009) as well as interest. A particular student may exhibit a striving for achievement on the soccer field but not in your class, or perhaps appears more motivated to achieve in some parts of your course than in others; and we have all known students who did not appear motivated at the start of a course but became deeply engaged. Most importantly, classroom environment and instructional practices can foster certain types of motivation over others, as can the overall climate of an educational institution.

Autonomy and Self-Determination

Many psychologists posit that human beings have a fundamental need for autonomy and self-determination (Deci and Ryan, 2000). In general, individuals want to be in charge of their own behavior, and they value a sense of control over their environment. We can enhance students' sense of control by offering meaningful opportunities for choice and by supporting their autonomy, which in turn enhances motivation. Quite often these opportunities for choice can be relatively simple things such as a choice of paper topics, test questions, due dates, or reading assignments, yet they go a long way toward acknowledging a student perspective. For example, I typically list on my syllabus three due dates for papers and tell students that they can choose which of these dates work best for them. The actual assignments are similar at each of these points, but draw on material from that section of the course, and I list four or five topics from which students can choose. Too much choice, however, is not helpful, as Barry Schwartz (2004) has shown in *The Paradox of Choice*. Thus students typically don't benefit as much from highly open-ended assignments such as being allowed to "write about anything" they choose. Providing some parameters and guidance, and some choice within that framework, seems most effective (and simplifies your assessment).

Intrinsic and Extrinsic Motivation

Most educational researchers acknowledge that what matters is not only whether a student is motivated but also what type of motivation the student has. Instructors at the college level often complain of student preoccupation with grades, typified by the perpetual classroom question "Will that be on the test?" *Extrinsically* motivated students are likely to engage in the course for reasons of external rewards, such as grades, recognition, or the approval of others (notably instructors and parents). Individuals who are *intrinsically* motivated engage in an activity for the value of the activity itself, rather than for an external reward. These students learn for the pleasure of learning and have a sense of self-determination about their educational path. Intrinsic motivation has been shown to foster conceptual understanding, creativity, involvement, and a preference for challenge. Research on college-student learning indicates that students with an intrinsic orientation are more likely to use cognitive strategies such as elaboration and organization, resulting in deeper processing of the material (Pintrich and Garcia, 1991).

Although the image of a classroom of intrinsically motivated learners might sound ideal, students are also driven by the desire for grades, approval, praise, and other rewards, and understandably so. Intrinsic motivation and extrinsic motivation exist not on a single continuum but on two separate ones, and students may often have multiple goals for the same course. A student enrolled in a required course, for example, may be deeply interested in the material and may also see it as a step in her professional development; she may desire to earn an A so that she will be likely to gain admission to graduate or professional school. Even students who initially appear only extrinsically motivated to take a course, perhaps viewing it merely as a requirement toward graduation, can become more intrinsically motivated if the instructor arouses their curiosity, provides appropriate levels of challenge, and offers them choices that enhance their control (Lepper and Hodell, 1989). Faculty members are also excellent models for intrinsic motivation, and talking about your own enthusiasm and passion for the field can be contagious. Motivation that begins as extrinsic can become internalized over time and we can help students come to an appreciation of learning that is not so driven by external rewards and approval.

Although studies have indicated that external rewards may diminish intrinsic motivation by undermining self-determination (Ryan and Deci, 2000), recent research seems to support the judicious use of external rewards as a complement to other motivational approaches. Extrinsic rewards may be particularly useful when intrinsic motivation is lacking—and it is reasonable to assume that students are not always going to be intrinsically motivated to learn everything they are expected to learn during the college years. Students may also find extrinsic rewards to be productive during the early stages of learning a new subject before they feel they can begin to master it and when the necessary nature of the tasks (such as memorizing vocabulary in a foreign language or learning a large number of terms in the sciences) may not be intrinsically interesting. There is also evidence from a study of intrinsic motivation in college undergraduates that the pursuit of grades may not be all bad (Covington, 1999), in that the attainment of grade goals can foster an increase in interest, at least among those whose goals are not driven by the desire to avoid failure.

Extrinsic rewards are most beneficial when they *contain informative feedback* and enable students to focus on improvement. Thus grades alone are less helpful than grades accompanied by narrative feedback that addresses specific directions for change. It is also possible to defer awarding grades and provide comments for improvement only. In the required Research Methods course that I teach, I give feedback—but no grades—on the first draft of research proposals, conveying how students might improve their work in the next version. With no grade to focus on, they seem to attend more deeply to the comments. Helping students separate feedback and grades, as well as providing opportunities for revisions, can help them tune more to improvement.

Taking the time to provide students with constructive feedback on papers as well as using class time when returning tests as an opportunity for further teaching can facilitate student engagement and motivation. Students appreciate knowing that their learning matters to you, and that you can help guide them toward success. I typically do a frequency count of missed items on a test, for example, and I use a few minutes of class to review any questions that more than a few students missed so that I can address misunderstandings. If more than half of the class misses an item, I don't count it and try to determine if it was simply a poorly written question or if I need to spend more time re-teaching the material.

Expectancy-Value Theory

Students typically direct their behavior toward activities that they value and in which they have some expectancy of success (Wigfield and Eccles, 2000). From this social cognitive perspective, motivation is viewed as the outcome of multiplying these two forces; if either one is absent, the resulting product is zero. Instructors can benefit by knowing that they need to foster both. Students need to feel that there is a reasonable possibility of success and that the work is of value. Thus even students who believe they can do well in an introductory course might not continue with the subject if they do not see that learning the material is worthwhile; likewise, even those who entered with professional ambitions dependent on the course may not persist in the field if they think that they cannot expect success. You may assume that students know the value of your field or of your particular course, but often this is not the case, and it may be worth the time to explain the relevance of what you are teaching. Fostering expectancy for success is equally important. Students benefit when instructors have high expectations for success and also provide the conditions for achieving it. Informative feedback is also critical here, as is availability in office hours or providing access to tutors, whether graduate student assistants or undergraduate peers.

Mastery and Performance Goals

Motivated behavior is directed toward goals, and goals related to learning tend to reflect two broad types of purposes: mastery goals and performance goals (Ames, 1992). Students who adopt *mastery goals* are those whose primary desire is to understand and master the material, with the goal of developing competence. By contrast, students with *performance goals* are more likely to focus on their achievement relative to the performance of others, directed more toward the demonstration of competence rather than its development. The classrooms we create may implicitly foster either type of goals (Meece, Anderman, and Anderman, 2006), depending on grading practices, classroom climate, and other such factors. Researchers have increasingly demonstrated the relevance of this model to higher education Zusho, A., Karabenick, S., Sims, B.C., and Rhee, C.K. (2007), and faculty members can be particularly influential in affecting productive motivational beliefs.

In a class that is focused on mastery, instructors generally use criterion-referenced grading rather than normative (grading on a curve), foster a supportive climate where students can take intellectual risks, and provide opportunities for students to demonstrate improvement. A mastery orientation may be visible in classroom discussions when students ask genuine questions to which they do not already know the answers, driven by a desire to better understand the material, rather than to impress their peers and the instructor. Mistakes are viewed as an opportunity for learning, rather than as a measure of worth, subject to the judgment of others.

In a class that is focused on performance, instructors often use normative grading practices, which imply that only a specified percentage of students are likely to succeed no matter how hard the entire class works, and provide no opportunities for revising and improving written work. Student questions may be formulated to present the inquirer in the best light and to gain recognition and reward. In contrast to students with mastery goals, students who are ego-involved with their performance may compare grades with one another and take academic shortcuts, such as avoiding more effort than is necessary to acquire the desired grade or engaging in academic dishonesty (Jordan, 2001).

Overall, mastery goals lead to more adaptive outcomes, for such students are likely to focus on learning, use effective cognitive strategies, and experience less performance-impeding anxiety (Pintrich, 2003). Students in highly competitive college classrooms, however—which are performance oriented by design—may find it adaptive to pursue a performance orientation (Harackiewicz, Barron, and Elliott, 1998). Faculty members thus may have considerable power in shaping goal approaches within their classrooms. Fostering a particular goal orientation begins with course design and syllabus construction, when we make choices about evaluation and grading practices and how we plan to communicate them to students. Take time the first day of class to explain your grading practices and, if you are using a criterion-referenced grading system, to make it clear that students are not competing with one another for grades. This also makes it evident that it is advantageous to form study groups and support one another's learning. Students in required courses that are essential for their progression toward professional goals (medical school, business school, etc.) can benefit from an environment that teaches them that their success does not come at the expense of others.

Goal orientation is also reflected in an array of teaching practices. Mastery orientation thrives in a classroom climate of warmth and acceptance where instructors support and value intellectual risk-taking and avoid comparisons among students. Research indicates that student perceptions of classroom goal structures matter. For example, college students who view their instructors as promoting a mastery orientation, and whose instructors appear caring and supportive of questioning, show higher academic achievement in those courses. These perceptions of mastery goals have been linked to positive outcomes in a range of studies, including a preference for challenging tasks, enjoyment of learning, help-seeking, and adaptive learning strategies (Maehr and Zusho, 2009).

When professors foster a performance orientation by stressing competition and acknowledging only high-achieving students, students are less likely to exhibit such outcomes.

Social Motivation and Other Goals

Students are obviously motivated by more than academic achievement, and the focus on mastery and performance may overlook other goals students have (Zusho and Clayton, 2011). For example, they also have social goals that are operative in the classroom: they want to be socially responsible and to form social relationships with peers (Patrick, Hicks, and Ryan, 1997; Wentzel and Wigfield, 1998). Culture also shapes goals, and social goals may be particularly relevant to students from more collectivist cultures, where relational and group-oriented goals are common, rather than the individualistic ones suggested by the mastery and performance research (King and Watkins, 2011). (See chapter 12 for more information on teaching culturally diverse students.)

Although most studies of the relation between social goals and academic motivation and achievement have been conducted with younger adolescents, certainly no college instructor would doubt that social goals are operative in the college classroom. Enabling students to make new acquaintances in your classroom in conjunction with meeting academic goals may enhance student motivation to attend class and to participate in academic work. For example, a brief moment to discuss a question with a partner works well from a cognitive perspective because it fosters elaboration and retention and provides opportunities for clarification, but it also gives students an opportunity to get to know one another. Helping students form study groups prior to exams fosters preparation and also addresses social needs. Group projects, as long as they are well structured and include individual accountability, can also be ways for students to meet new people and make friends with common interests.

Social goals are not met solely in the classroom, nor are many of the other goals students might have. Given the various demands on their time, it may be no surprise that in spite of the best efforts of instructors, students are often weighing the benefits of how deeply to invest in a course or assignment. What may appear to instructors as an aversion to work or a disappointing level of effort, may be the result of a pragmatic decision on the part of students, as they balance an array of demands. Helping them learn how to be strategic in their choices in a way that does not hinder their academic work can be especially effective (e.g., when to read deeply and when to skim). Again, allowing choices of due dates in the syllabus also helps, as it offers students more control about the timing of tasks and helps alleviate some of the pressure they may feel.

Attribution Theory

When individuals need to seek an explanation for unexpected outcomes, they make attributions about the probable causes, and these attributions have motivational consequences (Weiner, 2001). In the academic sphere, this often arises when students fail to perform well on a test or get a grade that differs from what they had expected. Typical attributions are effort ("I didn't study hard enough"), ability ("I'm just not good at this subject"), or luck ("The test emphasized the material I actually studied!"). Attributions can be categorized along three dimensions: locus, stability, and responsibility, which refer respectively to whether the cause is internal or external, stable or unstable, and whether the cause is controllable or not. Students who explain their disappointments with internal, controllable attributions ("I know I didn't prepare adequately for the test") are likely to do better next time, because they believe they can affect the outcome. Students who attribute failure to stable, uncontrollable causes ("I will never understand statistics") are less likely to be motivated for improvement and understandably pessimistic about future outcomes.

Instructors can assist students in making adaptive attributions, particularly by helping them attribute failure to effort rather than ability, as well as by communicating their own positive attributions about students' capabilities to learn. When meeting with students to confer about low performance or an unexpected poor grade, you can help them reframe their thinking about the cause of their difficulties and help them gain a sense of control over future outcomes by helping them think diagnostically and rationally. Ask them to describe how they studied (or went about writing the paper), review the types of questions they missed or the most significant flaws in a paper, and help them know how to prepare or write more effectively in the future. In addition, referring students to a study skills center on your campus in order to improve their learning strategies can communicate that the problem is remediable and that they can take charge in addressing it. Overall, helping students endorse controllable attributions as explanations for failures can lead to increased performance, as attribution retraining with first-year students shows (Perry et al., 2010).

The Motivational Power of Beliefs about Intelligence

Fostering students' beliefs about the power of effort and hard work also reinforces the notion that intelligence is incremental and can be developed, a powerful motivational belief, according to Carol Dweck, author of *Mindset* (2006). Students with this "growth mindset" are likely to take on challenging work, learn from mistakes, and approach new learning with enthusiasm, as these are opportunities for improvement. By contrast, individuals who believe in an entity view of intelligence, or what she calls a fixed mindset, are dedicated to preserving their own and others' impressions of their ability. Such students fear that having to work hard for accomplishment simply displays a lack of ability and talent, so even if they do exert effort they may try to hide it. Those with a growth mindset are more likely to appreciate how they have developed in the process of applying themselves well.

Dweck's research, supported by a large number of experimental studies, shows that the feedback of teachers (and parents and coaches and employers) has dramatic effects on how students perceive their own intelligence and what mindset they adopt. A student who does well on a paper and is told, "You're really very smart at this," will do what it takes to protect that image, perhaps not speaking in class unless they are confident of the answer, choosing less demanding assignments, and avoiding novel tasks. A student who is told, "You did well at this and must have worked hard to reach such a level of understanding," is likely to feel acknowledged for the effort and want to continue to seek challenges.

PUTTING MOTIVATION THEORY INTO PRACTICE

These principles can be used in many ways to structure classes that foster student motivation to learn. Here are a few suggestions:

1. When planning assignments, consider issues of choice and control. If you would like students to write two papers during the term, provide assignments during three time periods and let them choose which two to complete. This enables students to take charge of planning their work in the context of requirements from other courses and allows them to select issues of greatest interest. (This also has the advantage of spreading out the grading that you will need to do, an added bonus.) Similarly, provide a choice of topics for each assignment and consider a range of options that engage interest. Foster initiative by allowing students to propose alternative topics that meet the intent of the assignment.

2. Project your own motivation—for the subject matter and for the students. Take opportunities to describe your own intrinsic motivation for both research and teaching and your mastery orientation to learning. Too much of the literature on faculty "rewards" has focused on the extrinsic reinforcement for teaching, neglecting our own intrinsic motivation for academic work (as well as the intrinsic satisfaction of teaching). You are a powerful role model for your students as they develop their own passion

and motivation for learning as well as for their future professions. Get to know your students as individuals with lives beyond your classroom.

3. Foster students' intrinsic motivation to attend class by being well prepared, making lectures and discussions interesting, varying the instructional format, inducing cognitive dissonance and stimulating thought, and adding interactive elements where appropriate. Students are more motivated to come to class when the learning experience clearly exceeds what can be copied from another's notes. Engagement is more than being present, of course; they are also less likely to be texting under the desk or viewing Facebook rather than taking notes if the material is presented in an engaging way and supplements the reading they can do outside of class.

4. Make the value of your courses explicit, and take time to help students understand why what they are learning matters. Teach with a sense of purpose.

5. Promote adaptive attributions, helping students value the application of effort and learning strategies, and communicate your belief in their capability. Avoid praising students for ability or talent.

6. Foster mastery by encouraging students to revise their writing. Although it might not be reasonable for you to read drafts of every paper, you might do this for the first written assignment and then create peer review groups for additional papers. Or you can vary this process by responding to outlines for one paper and then reading drafts of opening paragraphs for the second. You can further foster mastery by uncoupling feedback and grading, so that early drafts receive written comments but no grades.

7. Adopt a criterion-referenced approach to grading rather than a normative one. Outline course requirements so that the point value for each assignment is clear from the beginning, and students know what they need to do to succeed—and know that they can succeed without worrying about their standing relative to others in the course. This fosters a sense of control, creates a cooperative rather than a competitive climate, and appeals to both intrinsically and extrinsically motivated students.

8. Test frequently enough that students become accustomed to the format and have opportunities to learn from their mistakes; at the very least, consider a similar format for the midterm and final. Allow students to justify and elaborate on their multiple-choice answers (which enhances control), and give partial or full credit for acceptable and reasonable justifications of alternative answers. Provide choices of essay questions to answer (e.g., "Answer five of the following six questions"). Consider providing one of the essay questions in advance, particularly one that might require more thoughtfulness and preparation.

9. When grading tests, consider dropping questions missed by a large number of students—and then re-teach the material when you return the tests. This sense of shared responsibility for the learning process heightens student awareness that you are committed more to their mastery of the material than to penalizing them for what they do not yet know (or for exam questions that might have been confusing).

10. Provide feedback that is constructive, noncontrolling (e.g., avoid words like "should" and "must"), and informative, thus enhancing student desire to improve and to continue to learn. View problems as something that can be addressed, not as evidence of an individual's worth.

If you are at a large university and involved in supervising teaching assistants, you can also make the motivational implications of your instructional decisions explicit to them. I am indebted to Paul Pintrich, Bill McKeachie, and Scott Paris, who were extraordinary role models in their design of graduate seminars that fostered student motivation, but who also provided me with opportunities as a teaching assistant to understand the motivational structure of their undergraduate courses, which I have enjoyed putting into practice in my own teaching.

Supplementary Reading

Although some of the following works are directed more toward the motivational issues of K–12 schooling, the theories and many of the suggestions are useful to those who are interested in the issue of motivation in the college classroom.

- J. Brophy, *Motivating Students to Learn* (Mahwah, NJ: Erlbaum, 2010). Writing for teachers, Brophy distills the motivation research into key principles that guide suggested classroom strategies.
- C. Dweck, *Mindset, The New Psychology of Success* (New York: Ballantine, 2007). This book makes the research on beliefs about intelligence highly accessible to a wide audience and gives examples for teaching, coaching, and parenting.
- D. H. Schunk, P. R. Pintrich, and J. Meece, *Motivation in Education: Theory, Research, and Applications*, 3rd ed. (Upper Saddle River, NJ: Merrill/Prentice Hall, 2007). This primer for instructors on a wide variety of motivational theories and their application surveys the research thoroughly and addresses how it can best be used.
- M. D. Svinicki, *Learning and Motivation in the Postsecondary Classroom* (San Francisco: Jossey Bass, 2004). The only motivation book focused on college and university teaching, this book addresses both motivation and learning theories, with clear examples for implementation.

Chapter 12

Teaching Culturally Diverse Students

Responding to the individual student may be the most important way to improve your instruction. Appreciating the unique needs and characteristics of your students sets an educational environment that will better enhance learning by each student.

Many dedicated teachers seek feedback in the classroom either by observing students' reactions or by directly soliciting comments: "How am I doing?" "Am I being clear?" "Is this too basic—do you want me to speed up?" For the most part, such feedback will enable you to accurately gauge the pace of student progress as well as the effectiveness of your approach to teaching. However, with a culturally diverse class, some basic differences in the students' and the teacher's backgrounds may cause feedback communications to fail. This chapter suggests some common cultural characteristics of some students coming from culturally diverse heritages. It highlights some illustrations of how a faculty person of a white, European American background—which I will refer to here as a "Western" background—may stumble in working with a student from a different cultural background.

Cultural advice can provide useful general guidelines, but those guidelines are not necessarily appropriate for all ethnic students. Keep

---

This chapter was written by Richard Suinn of Colorado State University.

in mind that just as "All Asians are not alike," all students within any ethnic group are not going to be alike—for two reasons. First, there are different nationalities and cultures even within an ethnic category. Among Asians, for instance, are over 60 different cultural groups, among them Chinese, Japanese, Hmong, Korean, Vietnamese, and others (Kim, Wong, and Maffini, 2010; Tewari and Alvarez, 2009; Vea, 2008). Second, within each subgroup there may be individual differences. Varying levels of acculturation, or being raised in a nontraditional ethnic family, might invalidate the cultural premises in this chapter (Suinn, 2010). For instance, to apply these suggestions to a highly acculturated, westernized ethnic student would be equivalent to employing a stereotype (Stuart, 2004).

Having offered this caution, I would like to offer some insights from a nonwhite cultural perspective. At a minimum, I hope that instructors will gain a perspective that avoids the deficit model, the view that inadequate performance from an ethnic person automatically means the student is academically deficient, unmotivated, uninterested, or poorly prepared. Instead I will highlight new ways of understanding the communications of culturally diverse students, and I will suggest ways in which your own behavior can be adapted to enhance the students' learning environment.

CULTURE AND COMMUNICATION

Nonverbal Communication

Eye Contact You are giving a complicated lecture. One student in the audience looks at you and nods and smiles occasionally. Another student never looks at you. Instead, he continually looks down. He is not even taking notes. Which of these students is interested in the lecture? Which is listening attentively? Which is daydreaming?

The bread and butter of teaching is the act of communication as a two-way interactional process. You as the instructor usually communicate verbally. Students also communicate, not only when you ask them a question, but also nonverbally when they are listening. Nonverbal cues provide important feedback that influences your further communication (Gifford, 2011; Manusov and Patterson, 2006).

What we observe, we interpret. And our interpretations influence our actions. Our meaning comes from our culture as Westerners. But to be culturally sensitive teachers, we must keep in mind that behaviors from different cultures have different meanings. The interpretation from a Western perspective of a student not making eye contact is that the student is inattentive, distracted, uninterested, or daydreaming. What is the consequence in your behavior? You might spend more lecture time going over the same point to arouse interest, or even talk louder (maybe the student will hear you the second time!). You might glare at the student or call him in for a conference. You might even dismiss this student as a lost cause.

Are you aware that for some ethnic groups, such as Asian Americans, African Americans, and Native Americans, looking away may be indicative of careful attention rather than inattention (Baruth and Manning, 1991; Dovidio, Hebl, Richeson, and Shelton, 2006; Garwick and Auger, 2000; Gudykunst, 2004)? It is estimated that white Americans make eye contact 80 percent of the time when listening and look away 50 percent of the time when speaking, and that African Americans make more eye contact when speaking and less when listening (Sue and Sue, 2007). In addition, among Asian cultures, staring at a person of higher status is considered rude (Sue and Sue, 2007); and mutual gaze among Mexican American parents and youngsters is also uncommon (Schofield et al., 2008). So eye contact or the lack thereof is not an automatic sign of attentiveness or inattention.

Nonparticipation In the middle of your lecture, you want to know not only if the students are listening, but whether they are also understanding and grasping the topic. So you ask, "Have I been clear? Anyone have any questions ... any questions at all?" And what happens is ... nothing. No one offers a question. No one even raises a hand.

From a Western perspective, because no one speaks up, and no hands are raised, or you might even see a smile, you might be congratulating yourself: "All right! My presentation is clear. I must be a great communicator!" Consequently, you rapidly complete your discussion and move speedily on to the next topic. But silence among ethnic minorities can have various meanings (Matsumoto, 2006; Schrader-Kniffki, 2007). Are you aware that in some cultures it is very important to show great respect for elders or for persons with wisdom greater than one's own, and it may be considered disrespectful and insulting to raise a question (Calzada, 2010; Nagata, Cheng, and Tsai-Chae, 2010)? Doing so may imply that the elder (or instructor) is at fault for being unclear. Thus an ethnic student who fails to understand a teacher might blame himself or herself for being poorly prepared. For a Westerner, receiving a smile would generally signify that the student understands what is being said, yet in some cultures the smile is actually a polite way of hiding confusion (Matsumoto, 2006).

Questioning the speaker can also imply that the student is challenging the teacher. And such a challenge may be a taboo either because a challenge shows arrogance or because it disrupts harmony. Native

Americans and Asian Americans value nonconfrontational interpersonal styles as a way to protect harmony in the interpersonal system. It would be unseemly to act otherwise (Apfelthaler et al., 2007; Dixon and Portman, 2010; Swinomish Tribal Mental Health Project, 1991).

Other culturally based reasons for nonparticipation include the following:

- ***A Culturally Ingrained Value of Humility*** Some cultures value modesty, not standing out in a crowd (Stickney, 2010). A Japanese saying observes that "The nail that sticks out is hammered down." Another saying proclaims that Westerners place a premium "not only on knowing but on saying what you know," while the Asian "values knowledge but discourages verbalizing knowledge" (Nishida, 1996). Such a background might lead to what I call the "spotlight" effect. Like a deer that freezes in the glare of headlights, the ethnic student may freeze when the teacher focuses attention by directing a question to that student. Standing up and providing the correct answer conflicts with the humble image of remaining unobtrusive. It also reduces any impression of competition against classmates or showing off.
- ***A History of Distrusting the Motives or Intentions of Others*** Students coming from experiences of racism, of being put down, and of experiencing the deficit model may feel especially vulnerable (Bowser, Young, and Jones, 1993; Trimble, 2010; Vontress and Epp, 1997). Out of caution, an African American student might be reluctant to volunteer or might be close-mouthed when asked a question. "Am I being picked on to make me look dumb in front of the class?" a student might wonder. "Are you setting me up so you can criticize my answer and show how much better a white student can talk?"

What You Can Do A better understanding of the actual meaning of student behaviors will put you in a better position to respond to nonverbal feedback. Your first step is to avoid the false assumption that lack of eye contact and nonparticipation mean lack of attention, disinterest, or boredom. Also avoid the false assumption that a lack of questions means that your presentation has been well understood. Consider the possible cultural meanings of nonverbal behaviors and silence in communications. Once you have rapport and trust with students, gather them informally and solicit their input. Be open about how you are puzzled about the nonverbal signals you think you're receiving.

Finding out what is going on will require gaining verbal participation from students at some point, if the nonverbal cues are not reliable indicators. This leads us to the topic of cultural aspects of oral communication.

Verbal Communication

Reluctant Speech You stop your lecture to obtain feedback. You directly ask a student to tell you whether your lecture has been clear; or you ask whether the student has any questions; or you even ask the student to explain in his or her own words what you covered. The student gets up slowly, looks sheepish, shifts from foot to foot, keeps her head down as though she is carrying the weight of the world, and quietly offers a very brief reply ... that leaves you wanting more. You are still in the dark about how much the student has understood your presentation.

If you were not feeling so sympathetic toward the tongue-tied student, you might feel mystified about what's going on and speculate that she is being evasive and uncooperative. But as you saw in the earlier examples, there are possible cultural explanations for the student's reluctance to verbalize much. Perhaps the student is being careful to remain respectful by not challenging or insulting the higher-status expert—you, the teacher (McGregor, 2006). Or perhaps the student feels the need to get away from the focus of the spotlight as quickly as possible through a brief answer. Or perhaps underlying distrust about your intentions prompts her cautiousness.

What You Can Do How might an instructor overcome an ethnic student's reluctance to respond more extensively even to a direct prompt? There are various strategies an instructor could try, yet still be sensitive to various cultural concerns.

Concern about Insulting the Teacher How you word your prompt can make a difference. "Is my explanation clear?" is a very difficult question for a respectful student. Instead restructure the situation so that the student's reply is collaborative rather than critical. For example, "By the way, you know I've covered this topic with so many classes that sometimes I forget how familiar this topic is to me, and I leave out some important details, so you can help me … ."

Concern Related to a Collectivist vs. Individualistic Orientation Many cultures emphasize that outcomes are best achieved as a group and for the benefit of the group. In a Western society like the United States, individual effort, performance, and reward are more the norm. Hence a Western student is likely to be quicker to speak up or to volunteer an answer. To encourage participation of a student who is more used to a collectivist orientation, assign them to work as a group. A technique called "Think-Pair-Share" assigns students to a group, then gives the group time to consider their answer, then has one member orally present the consensus response (Hoover, Klingner, Baca, and Patton, 2008). This approach has the advantage of de-emphasizing attention and focus on one individual. As a consensus answer, it also bypasses the issue of how to maintain humility.

Concern about Being in the Spotlight Despite many years of experience as a lecturer and classroom teacher, at times I feel this discomfort, such as when I'm taking part in a discussion with a group of people I've just met. It is a feeling of embarrassment, of suddenly being aware that everyone is quiet, that all eyes and ears are focused not on the discussion leader but on me! All of my cultural sensitivities become stirred: avoid standing out, do not embarrass yourself, be modest and defer to others to take the lead, you can be seen but certainly not heard, avoid arrogance.

One solution to discomfort from being in the spotlight is to shorten the exposure. Turn the spotlight off or away. Let the students know that you are going to ask a question, but you want them to limit themselves to a brief reply because you want to quickly move to other students' replies to obtain a group viewpoint. Or indicate that you want to hear the student's first thought as 'brainstorming' to limit the concern about the answer being evaluated as correct or incorrect. The prime characteristic of brainstorming is that it is to stir ideas without evaluation. This strategy shines the spotlight on any individual for only a brief moment. Further, it enables a gradual exposure while the student becomes more and more comfortable participating. You might also add that students need not stand up when called on. Addressing your question to other students first can give the reluctant student time to be ready.

Concerns Related to Trust It takes time to build distrust and to establish trust. Individuals with difficult life experiences sometimes learn to be very observant and to attribute meaning to the tone associated with statements, to the implied meaning of terms, to the signals of posture, or to other nonverbal behaviors. Often these serve as guides for survival, particularly in an unfamiliar environment. So how a teacher words a question, what tone or posture accompanies the query, and what an instructor says after the student replies—all offer information influencing trust/mistrust.

When you ask a student to answer, could it seem as though you are issuing a challenge, or is it clear that you honestly want to know what the student has to say—no strings attached? To improve trust, carefully consider the wording of your questions, perhaps taking a bit more time to explain why you are asking ("So I know how to think up more examples that help make sense out of this messy topic"). Avoid abruptness not only in wording a question but in your comments following a response. Consider what you say after the student replies. Is your follow-up comment supportive, or is it a correction that implies that the student was wrong or that you didn't like the reply? A little bit of encouragement and a positive attitude will go a long way to building bridges. Remember too, that your nonverbal behavior will be immediately considered the real message to a student used to reading the environment. Such a student often believes that "what is said is not always what is meant" (Brown and Kysilka, 2002).

Concern Relating to Lack of Verbal Fluency Writing assignments before or as a follow-up to a classroom session can help especially those for whom English is not their first or preferred language. Pre-assigned written tasks before a class can aid a student in organizing personal thoughts to then be orally presented. Having students summarize what they took out of classroom discussion is not only effective active learning, but can provide you with feedback on the clarity of the discussion. To those with access to specialized equipment, a different form of feedback from students to instructors involves technology. Lectures are recorded, then reviewed by students after class. By using electronic clickers, students establish a signal when a topic is unclear. These are summed so that faculty can readily calculate which topic needs more explanation. Only one's imagination will limit how today's instant messaging devices can be creatively used for such feedback.

Circularity vs. Linearity At your initial class meeting you decide to establish rapport by asking for a simple personal opinion: "Did you enjoy your vacation?"

You receive a fairly extensive response: "Well, like, you know, spent first day at home. ... My brother is getting another job soon. Some of us watched *Star Wars* on TV. ... Got back yesterday ... back with my roommate ... was an interesting visit."

This roundabout, rambling reply might feel confusing rather than informative. The generic "an interesting visit" conveys everything and nothing. But this response might represent an ethnic "circular" style of oral communication rather than a more "linear" Western one (Gudykunst, 2004; Park and Kim, 2008). Western thought and language tend to proceed in a linear fashion. You ask a question; you expect a direct answer. "What did you have for breakfast?" "Bacon and eggs." "Where and when shall we have lunch?" "There's an excellent menu today in the student center. Let's meet there at 11:30." "How was the movie?" "Excellent! I liked the part about ... " A linear reply to the question "Did you enjoy your vacation?" would ultimately communicate a yes or a no. Many details might be offered, but the basic question to be answered is "Did you or didn't you?"

A teacher with a Western background who hears a student's roundabout reply may think, "The student is being evasive and is avoiding my straightforward question. Is there a reason? Maybe I'm not trusted, or maybe the student had a bad experience during vacation and doesn't want to talk about it. Maybe the student did something that was shameful, maybe even criminal ... This student rebuffs my overtures to be sociable. He is rejecting my attempts to reach out. Maybe the student just has low social skills." The teacher may be unaware of a number of cultural issues giving rise to circular communication (Gudykunst, Ting-Toomey, and Nishida, 1996; Park and Kim, 2008; Ting-Toomey and Chung, 2005):

- The student's reply may reflect a cultural tradition deriving from a preliterate period in which knowledge was passed on orally, storytelling was the medium for education, and lengthy tales or proverbs were used to convey information. Gay (2010) refers to this style as "topic-chaining" or "topic-associative" discourse. The student begins in an indirect fashion well suited for imbedding a moral, a message, or the main answer. In this student's culture, grasping the overall context of the "story" is more important than the meaning to be found in specific words, and general conversation may precede any serious interaction. Such seemingly superficial chatting or small talk develops a comfort level and establishes rapport (Gay, 2010; Ruiz and Padilla, 1977).
- A circular response might be another way of maintaining a respectful attitude toward the teacher-authority-expert. Carefully phrased replies avoid the impression that a student is so presumptuous as to offer advice, instruct the instructor, or even tell the teacher something the teacher does not know. Occasionally, the student's first reply simply conveys respect, and pending the teacher's acknowledgement, the student can then feel free to proceed with his/her answer. So answers might be cached in a two-phase bundle.
- A level of defensiveness may prompt the circular reply, as it keeps the student from being personally evaluated. Circularity may enable the student to avoid committing to a firm statement or being pinned down, but not because the student has anything to hide. Instead it is simply a way of keeping distance, especially if the question is perceived as personal. Instead of using a "I ask ... you answer" approach, designing your interaction more like a conversation between two people on a common topic might prove productive.

What You Can Do Here again you can take the initiative in setting the stage for improved responsiveness from the student. Keep in mind that some of the behaviors of a culturally diverse student come from a long tradition or repeated socialization. His or her way of behaving is thus neither conscious nor intentional but rather habitual or even traditional. Thus, it may require a dedicated teacher to get the best from the student.

Patience, of course, is essential. Control your own need for a quick, precise, linear response. Permit the serpentine narrative to unwind at its own speed. Listen carefully for the overtones and the hidden theme. Wait for the student's follow-up comments as the 'story' unfolds. As you summarize or paraphrase the essence of what is said, this will provide the encouragement for the student to elaborate.

Beware of phrasing questions that can put the student on the spot. Develop your own version of nonlinearity (Block, 1981; Sanchez and Atkinson, 1983). Instead of "Tell me how you would solve this problem?" consider asking "What might be at least one approach to dealing with this problem?" or "Suppose someone you know is facing this problem, how do you think that person would start attacking it?" or "What have you seen others do?"

MOTIVATION AND STRESS

"Why don't these students perform like they should?" "They just don't respond to encouragement like other students. Obviously, they don't care!" "I can't seem to get through to them. I know they can do better—after all, they made it this far." "I even tried sharing what has personally motivated my actions."

Such concerns about inadequate student performance might be explained by two contributing cultural factors: differences in motivation across cultures and cultural stressors. Increasing a student's performance toward his or her potential might be enhanced through culturally appropriate incentives or through reduction of interference from certain stressors.

Cultural Differences in Motivation

There is a fundamental difference between Western and certain ethnic motivational orientations. The former emphasizes an individualistic orientation, the latter a collectivistic orientation.

Westerners tend to be spurred by goals such as individuation, independence, self-development, self-reliance—"being the best you can be," experiencing the satisfaction of personal achievement. Other cultures tend toward collectivism, perhaps tracing back to the era of tribes but now focused on the family unit. Within ethnic cultures goals are group goals, achievement honors the family, and personal failure is agonizing because it reflects negatively on the family (Calzada, 2010; Dixon and Portman, 2010; Lee, 2008). Thus, appeals based on individual recognition and accomplishment might fail to motivate an ethnic student, but putting the focus on family values might be more successful.

"Family" Defined For various ethnic cultures, family means more than the nuclear family or even blood relatives (Dolbin-MacNab, 2009). For some Hispanics, there are terms for a type of family member, *compadrazo* or *compadre/commadre,* referring to godparents who function as family (Arredondo, 1991; Ruiz, 1995). For African Americans, family roles may be assumed not only by grandparents but even by individuals outside the household, ranging from neighbors to ministers (McAdoo, 1999).

Collectivism and Family Goals Calling upon family ties can be an effective approach to use with a student who requires motivational inspiration (Ojeda, Navarro, and Morales, 2011). One underachieving Hispanic undergraduate improved his study habits when faced with the question, "If you drop out, what do you think your younger brother will do with his life?" This was a more telling argument than the entreaty, "You are throwing away your life unless you shape up!"—an individualistic appeal.

With family support, an ethnic student achieves great strength and feels a powerful desire to work toward goals (Lee, Donjan, and Brown, 2010; McGregor, 2006; Walker and MacPhee, 2011). Once when discussing weekend plans, I tentatively asked a Latina graduate student if her new boyfriend's visit might distract her from attending to her assignments for the week. Her immediate and no-nonsense reply was "No way! My parents and I agreed: I have only one reason for being here ... my studies come first. Dropping out is not an option. My boyfriend understands that!" She has since earned her doctorate, married her boyfriend, and is employed in a university position.

Family-based values can also influence what defines success (Sage, 1991). For some older-generation parents, success by their adult offspring might be finding a secure job with a steady income. Thus, the value of an education is measured in those terms.

For a Native American, the collectivistic orientation may involve tribal members, who not only influence values but also offer support. Solving problems "the Indian Way" refers to seeking the wisdom of tribal members, often by returning to the reservation (Attneave, 1982; Gone, 2008; P. Thurman, personal communication, 2004).

The sharing of one's own personal motivations can be impactful, as the prior chapter suggests. However, this is partly a function of whether this strategy is a fit for the student. Would an ethnic student agree that your characteristics are a model to be adopted if you are not of the same ethnic heritage or upbringing? Having a role model with which the student can identify can be quite productive. Invited speakers or appropriate readings can be a way to offer such models.

Cultural Stressors

Keep in mind that underachievement might be caused by impaired performance due to the stressors that the culturally diverse student faces (Cervantes and Cordova, 2011). There are several possible unique stressor conditions: the imposter syndrome, the first-generation condition, and acculturation anxiety.

The Imposter Syndrome This is the stress caused by self-doubt as the ethnic student is aware of his or her minority status. Surrounded by majority white students who are from different sociocultural backgrounds and whose English may seem more fluent or without accent, culturally diverse students cannot help but feel different. In fact, they are at least outwardly different in physical appearance.

The imposter syndrome raises questions such as "Do I really belong?" and "Perhaps it is a mistake for me to be here" (Cokley, McClain, Enciso, Jones, and Martinez, 2010; Gould, 2008). Despite all facts to the contrary, it is often difficult to avoid such a feeling. During my own career, I was successful in being elected to several important committees and boards of the American Psychological Association. Though basically confident about my abilities, I still felt discomfort at my first meeting—the vague, gnawing sense that everyone else was familiar with one another and I was the only outsider. I finally ended my unease by reminding myself that the election procedure meant that three new people were always reporting in, so there had to be two others who were in the same situation as I. Further, instead of acting as though I didn't belong, I immediately introduced myself to the others and took my place at the table as they did.

On occasion the imposter issue is worsened by accusations from others. I recall a disgruntled, unsuccessful white applicant claiming that an ethnic student took "his" place only because of affirmative action. I also remember the experience of an African American who tested at the gifted level on standardized tests normed on white children, entered a school for the gifted, and continuously confronted other students' beliefs that she couldn't possibly have qualified on her own merits.

The First-Generation Condition "First-generation students" are the first in their families to attend school at a level higher than the level their parents attained, such as being the first admitted to college. As such, they sometimes experience stress caused by lack of familiarity with the new environment—that is, university life (Pike and Kuh, 2005). Entering college may be like entering a foreign country as the student faces decisions about what courses to take, misses home and family, struggles to engage with a world consisting mainly of the white majority, and tries to make sense of unfamiliar customs (Latus, 2007). The student's normal familial support system might be unable to help. Because no family members ever experienced the demands of that level of schooling, they might not understand the new pressures and strains the student is experiencing and may be unable to offer even sympathy (Aguayo, Herman, Ojeda, and Flores, 2011; Gardner and Holley, 2011).

For students from an ethnic minority cultural environment, certain concepts or procedures may be difficult to grasp. Here are some that are associated with college enrollment:

- Being on time. Some Native Americans believe that taking the time to do things well is more important than doing things quickly but poorly. Thus, the requirement to complete an assignment "on time" might initially seem to be a troublesome demand because the student is inclined to focus more on doing a complete, high-quality job (Sutton and Broken Nose, 1996; Verbos, Kennedy, and Gladstone, 2011).
- Having grades based on class participation. The requirement to speak out in class can come into conflict with the issues I cited earlier regarding reluctance to participate. These include not standing out, being humble, avoiding competition, cautiousness, etc.
- Being graded on the curve. For ethnic groups that value cooperation and collectivism (working for the common good), the idea behind being graded on a curve may be hard to comprehend, because it involves an individual competing against everyone else for an individual goal. The criterion-referenced approach cited in the prior chapter is one solution.
- Seeking help from strangers. Well-meaning friends might warn an ethnic student, "You're going to be at a disadvantage. Remember, no one there will want to help you succeed. So you must be tough, be prepared to deal with things yourself" (Thompson, Bazile, and Akbar, 2004). Under these conditions, especially if the student feels any shyness with strangers for other reasons, it takes a strong student to ask for help from a teacher, to locate a tutor, or to identify a mentor. Yet a caring mentor is often a major factor in academic success.

Acculturation Anxiety I remember a Native American student whose tribal elders were hesitant about her leaving the reservation. There was fear that she would find life more attractive elsewhere, and that her core identity would be diminished through acculturation into the mainstream society.

Each of the four American ethnic minority groups has a term for group members who lose their ethnic identity through exposure to the Western culture. These are persons who have exchanged their cultural roots for an identification with the white culture. They are variously called "apples" (red on the outside, white on the inside), "bananas" (yellow on the outside, white on the inside), "coconuts" (brown on the outside, white on the inside), or "Oreos" (black on the outside, white on the inside) (LaFromboise, Coleman, and Gerton, 1998; Lone-Knapp, 2000; Maruyama, 1982; Tatum, 1993). What does this imply? It represents another source of stress for the ethnic person, who now is not only coping with academic tasks and possibly adapting to a new environment, but also facing the risk of denigration from his or her own cultural group.

Educational experiences often aim at enhancing personal growth and development of new knowledge, conducting inquiry, and opening new vistas into the world at large. As personal knowledge and skill levels expand, so does the sense of self. One's identity may be solidified, expanded, or even dramatically challenged. If changes in identity were without social consequences, the transformation would be easy. However, for an ethnic student with strong traditional ties, serious discomfort can be an outcome instead (Cano and Castilo, 2010; Smith and Silva, 2011). "Am I selling out … betraying my own group?" "What am I? I am neither fish nor fowl now! And is the person I've become better or worse that what I was before?" "Am I now such a hybrid that I am an outcast from both the majority and the minority cultures?" It is easy to imagine how such a significant conflict can disrupt attention to academic studies and even raise thoughts of dropping out.

A teacher can enhance an ethnic student's learning and performance in a number of ways. The most important first step is to continue to be aware that low achievement may be due not to low ability but to motivational issues or interference from stressors. If motivation or stress is involved, then the following approaches might be useful.

Increasing Motivation

What You Can Do Remember that individualistic goals may not be as meaningful as collectivistic goals. Working on tasks alone might not prove as motivating as working in a group setting. For the student who values cooperative engagement instead of individual achievement, a group task is more satisfying. As cited earlier, for the student who is reluctant to be personally visible, sharing a task is a good way to overcome this reticence.

In some instances, a first generation student has yet to broaden career perspective to other than concrete vocations. In covering topics, a valuable principle to remember is to continuously create examples of the day-by-day relevance of a topic being discussed. This might be how the topic, information, or skill will help the community, be the foundation for broader employment opportunities, or be an illustration of something within the student's life experience. Whenever possible, connecting the task or topic to the student's cultural experiences can increase interest and motivation and understanding. For most white students, undergraduate studies may be seen as laying the foundation for future graduate or professional education. The ethnic student might not respond to goals other than immediate ones. Hence it becomes crucial for teachers to link tasks to perceivable outcomes. Ambiguous motives lack the power of concrete goals.

In discussing goal setting with an ethnic student, it is always valuable to understand the family background. Find out how he or she came to be in school to begin with, and gain a sense of the familial values and expectations. Identify the strength of these familial ties, and determine if there are special family or community members whose opinions carry more weight (Freyberg and Markus, 2007). Try to differentiate between personal goals and familial goals, and be prepared to deal with conflicts between familial goals and expectations and newly developing personal desires—the student whose family expects to have "my son, the doctor" or "my daughter, the lawyer" while the student is now dreaming about being a philosophy major.

Consider inviting significant family or community persons to work with the underachieving student. This could even include problem solving.

James, an African American student, lived at home while entering his freshman year of college. As the eldest child, and now the first to attend college, James was looked up to by his family and friends. Six siblings of all ages also lived in the apartment, and the environment was lovingly described as "organized chaos." A grandmother also shared a room and helped in daily cleaning, cooking, and babysitting the younger children while James's mother worked. Although James had been able to keep up with high school work, he soon discovered that in college the extra reading assignments and pressure from deadlines added new demands. Because the college campus was two hours away by public transportation, studying at home after school was the only option. However, the lack of privacy, the constant flow of activity, and the noise level were problems.

A teacher thinking along majority-culture lines would inquire about a move to a dormitory, which would provide quiet hours, have student tutors, enable being integrated into "college life," and promote individuation. However, that solution would overlook certain cultural values, beyond the issue of expenses. James would be forced to leave his major support system, his responsibility as the "man in the family," and a cultural environment that is an integral part of his current psychological development. His presence in the community and church is an inspiration to the neighborhood, a role that embarrasses him, but that he recognizes as coming with the turf.

As a culturally sensitive alternative, one of James's professors, who saw the need for James to have study time, paid a visit to James's home for a conference with the entire family present. It quickly became apparent that everyone understood the problem and wanted James to be successful in his schooling. The family discussed options such as studying at a neighbor's place, but this would have been an imposition on others so it was temporarily tabled. Eventually, one solution was suggested by the grandmother. In a firm voice, she declared that henceforth all children would participate in a nightly "Help James Time." One room would be vacated and would be "James's college room" for two hours. During this period, James's grandmother, with the help of James's next eldest sibling, would arrange for each of the children activities such as story time, TV time, and outside play-time to ensure quiet. The children would rotate through the activities. A chart was posted on which James would note his study progress after each evening's session. As James completed assignments and received grades, he would share these with the family before the next "Help James Time." With this solution, James and his family eventually were able to celebrate his bachelor's degree.

Dealing with Stressors

What You Can Do Understanding the source of a student's stress may assist you in offering appropriate help. Familiarize yourself with reports that offer ethnic students' personal views of the academic environment (Garcia-Sheets, 2008; Maton et al., 2011). The imposter syndrome may have its roots in a history of racism, or it may be an issue of simply entering a new and unfamiliar setting, including new social/interpersonal settings. A mentor who believes in the student, who knows how to teach the student to use his or her strengths, and who recognizes the value of taking one step at a time can be a major positive influence.

The specter of presumption of special privilege through affirmative action may contribute to the imposter syndrome. There is no one action that would erase such feelings. However, the following argument might be valuable: If detractors interpret affirmative action as special privilege, it is equally important for them to recognize that "white privilege" also exists but goes unexamined. Because of white privilege a white person in the majority community never needs to be aware of how she or he is viewed by others when entering a store, restaurant, or class, or when boarding a bus, waving down a taxi, or standing up to express an opinion (Sue, 2006; Todd and Abrams, 2011). Being accepted as belonging, never standing out, never worrying about below-the-surface evaluations, and not having your comfort level displaced in interactions are privileges. An ethnic person is continuously faced with looking different or sounding different and is unable to alter those facts. This person will adapt, of course, but will never fully acquire white privilege.

It is entirely legitimate for schools, businesses, and industries to set criteria for selection of personnel based on goals. Athletes are recruited; merit scholars are enticed into undergraduate programs; students with special life experiences, those who show evidence of high motivation and excellent work habits, or even those representing geographic diversity are offered admission to limited graduate programs. These represent opportunities, not guarantees of eventual success. To those of your students who might be vulnerable to the imposter syndrome I would quickly point out, "The door has been opened for you to enter. Whether you deserve to remain will be up to you to prove."

The first-generation condition is not unique to ethnic students, although a history of poverty, poorer educational preparation, or recent immigration might lead to more ethnic students being the first generation in college. Because these students lack information about the school environment that is likely to be a key factor in their success, any steps your school can take to increase their familiarity will help.

One useful solution is precollege visitation days, at which incoming students and their families can become familiar with the campus and procedures. Putting together a survival guide for culturally diverse students or distributing a section from an existing guidebook might provide an excellent resource (the American Psychological Association has one for graduate students; see American Psychological Association, 2010). Informative roundtable discussions sponsored by ethnic student services offices can be important, as well as a way of matching upper-division ethnic student mentors with new students.

Many students experience homesickness when they leave their homes to attend school elsewhere. The homesickness compounds the difficulty of sudden geographic displacement, separation from a support system of family and friends, being confronted with the unfamiliar college culture, and the stress of the immediate need to adapt to numerous new challenges.

Most students manage their initial homesickness, develop a new sense of freedom and self-confidence, and become comfortable with their new identities. As I mentioned previously, the ethnic student may also adapt quickly and discover the new "self" that emerges, but may also be confronted with the identity conflict this brings. For some white students, brief visits home or even phone calls to family serve as a connection that smoothes the transition. Similarly, for a culturally diverse student, making this connection can provide a refreshing energy to move forward. For some Native Americans, a powerful spiritual renewal comes from even a brief return to the reservation or tribal environment.

TAILORING YOUR TEACHING METHODS

In addition to being sensitive to cultural differences among students, you can make your classroom more welcoming and effective for ethnic minority students by your choice of teaching approaches.

Offer Multiple Ways for Students to Learn

Try this exercise: Close your eyes. Using your imagination, develop a clear image in your mind of a very large plane flying over you. It's very close as it passes over you. Now stop and describe this airplane to a friend in as much detail as you can. How did the airplane appear in your imagination? As you described it, what details were salient? Visual ("The plane had a long body with windows")? Auditory ("It roared past me")? Tactile ("I felt the wind rush by")? Have some friends repeat this exercise, and compare the results. Notice the individual differences in the way a person experiences the world around him or her.

Likewise, different students—both majority and minority—may have different preferences in the way they like to learn (DeVries, Golon, Castellano, 2011; Roig, 2008). Some students prefer to learn through listening to or reading a description of an idea. Others prefer to see the idea in graphic form. Some prefer a step by step breakdown of an idea, while others like to see the "big picture" before getting the details. Research in this area continues, although this is a very difficult construct to measure accurately even though it seems so close to our own experiences.

It is impossible to find a teaching method that fits everyone's preferences since every class is made up of a mix of individual preferences. However, offering multiple ways for students to learn allows them to choose what works best for them and gives them some control over their situation as well. Even if you can't give each person his or her own choice, you can vary the way you present the material using two or three different methods. That also helps students learn how to learn from different teaching styles.

Be Concrete

Being concrete is another generic principle of teaching, but there are different ways of achieving this. You can use a demonstration/exercise, use metaphors, or use examples from students' personal life experiences. Understanding the cultural experiences of an ethnic student can help bring academic material to life in concrete ways. It is also useful to discuss the practical applications of classroom topics to satisfy the pragmatic interests of ethnic students (Reyes, Scribner, and Scribner, 1999).

Enhance Performance Measurement

Earlier, I described some differences between Western and ethnic groups' concepts of time. Native Americans, we saw, value doing a task well rather than doing it quickly. Therefore, timed tests might be a poor indicator of their actual knowledge. Also the commonly used timed multiple-choice examinations rely extensively on memory skills. Useful alternatives would be take-home examinations that can measure analytic skills, creativity, and comprehension without the side issue of time.

One interesting approach is testing based on the triarchic theory of intelligence, which postulates three elements: analytic, creative, and practical. Sternberg (2003; Sternberg and Grigorenko, 2008) found that measures of analytic/creative/practical knowledge predict college grade point averages more accurately than the traditional SAT verbal/math test scores, and that students taught with attention to these educational priorities perform better on traditional course examinations (Bray and Kehle, 2011; Sternberg and Kaufman, 2011).

Choose Appropriate Nonverbal Behaviors

Just as the way a student speaks, listens, and stands creates an impression on you, the impact you have on your students results not only from your explicit verbal communications, but also from certain nonverbal behaviors:

- *Conversational pauses.* Typically, a Westerner pauses one second before continuing to speak; therefore, any longer pause signals that the speaker has finished. Native Americans pause a bit longer, four to five seconds, before completing a sentence or thought (Baruth and Manning, 1991). Failing to understand the meaning of this longer pause, a Westerner may begin to talk, thereby interrupting the conversation and communicating rudeness, disinterest or disrespect, or a dominating attitude.
- *Personal space.* Different cultural groups interact normally at different distances (Matsumoto, 2006). The space each group prefers is known as personal space. If one person steps into another's personal space, this is experienced as an intrusion. Similarly, if too much distance is maintained during an interaction, this may be interpreted as aloofness (Harrigan, 2005). African Americans and Hispanics tend to stand closer to someone they are conversing with than do white Americans, and Asians tend to prefer greater distances (Jensen, 1985; Mindess, 1999). An understanding of personal-space norms is important for maintaining good interpersonal communications.

For some cultures, touching is not acceptable. Hence, a teacher reaching to offer support or encouragement, and just lightly touching a student can have the opposite effect.

An interesting teaching exercise will point out the rigid but unconscious American rules about space. Read the following questions about elevator behaviors and see if you are aware of these rules:

1. What are the rules for standing in the elevator? Where do people stand when there are only two or three people (strangers to one another)? What happens when a fourth person enters the elevator?

2. How would you feel if there were two people on the elevator and a third stranger entered and stood right next to you?

3. What happens when the elevator becomes more crowded and there are four or more people?

4. How close will people stand? What are you allowed to "touch"?

5. What do people look at in a crowded elevator?

6. When is it permissible to talk to the other people?

Compare your answers against the rules in the Appendix, which are rules typically followed in the United States.

Be Accessible

Cultures can be viewed as either horizontal or vertical in their interpersonal structure. A vertical, hierarchical culture establishes high- to low-status roles associated with titles of address (Feldman and Rosenthal, 1990; Gudykunst, 2004; Lee, 1999). The structure of Western cultures tends to be horizontal—everyone is on the same level. A student raised in a vertical culture may prefer to address you by your title and may be puzzled by your insistence on a more familiar mode of address (Dever and Karabenick, 2011; Yamauchi and Tharp, 1995). For students from a horizontal culture, the invitation to "Just call me Bill" or the remark "I'm Janet" confirms the desired message of equality. You can use a title to allow ethnic minority students to be comfortable, while still conveying by other actions your openness and accessibility.

A research study found that the dropout rate among Hispanic high school students was nearly three times higher than that of white students and two times higher than that of African American students (Fry, 2003). A study of factors associated with persistence in school identified teachers as the second most influential factor for Hispanics (Fuentes, Kiyana, and Rosario, 2003). Most interesting is how these teachers were described. They were seen as encouraging their students to succeed, having high expectations, and believing that their students could meet these expectations. Rather than being viewed as aloof or regimented, the teachers were described as "playful." In essence, they were seen as approachable, interested in their students, and inclined to find potential rather than deficits in the young people they teach.

It is important for you to take the initiative to be accessible and to convey genuine interest and to be welcoming in words and in behaviors (Suinn, 2007). A simple greeting helps, in the classroom, in the hallways, and outside of school.

- Take time to chat. At first you may need to take the lead, avoiding the spotlight effect.
- Have consistent office hours, but encourage drop-in visits.
- Be encouraging and positive, supportive and solution oriented, and by all means listen.
- Work on problems and engage in positive reappraisal: "Persistence will work." "A step at a time is progress." "You can make it."
- Help students identify their strengths, find ways to cope and succeed, and leverage those strengths.

IN CONCLUSION

Pay attention to your students in order to learn about them and truly understand them. Be a caring person, a welcoming person, an interested person. Identify and build on strengths, and encourage them!

Take heed from a set of studies showing how context alone can enhance or interfere with student achievement. One group of African American students took a test under the belief that their intellectual abilities were being measured, while another received no such pressure. The first group underperformed in comparison to whites in the first condition, which made salient the stereotype that ethnics are deficient. However this discrepancy did not occur in the second condition (Steele and Aronson, 1995). A follow-up study eventually named "When white men can't do math" faced white students with taking tests for which Asians were "known to excel over white students." Again those white students exposed to the stereotype which suggested whites to be deficient, actually performed poorly, thereby confirming the stereotype (Aronson, Lustina, Good, Keogh, Steele, and Brown, 1999).

The moral: as a teacher, the support, confidence, and assurance you convey to your students can not only help reduce consequences of discrimination among your students, but can help them reach their highest potential (Fischer and Massey, 2007)!

Suggested Readings

Davis, B. Diversity and complexity in the classroom: Considerations of race, ethnicity, and gender. http://teaching.berkeley.edu/bgd/diversity.html

This chapter is retrievable from the referenced website and comes from the book *Tools for Teaching* by Barbara Gross Davis. The chapter directly addresses strategies for classroom teachers of culturally diverse students.

Farmer, V. and Shepherd-Wynn, E. (eds.), *Teaching Culturally Diverse College Students in a Pluralistic Society.* (Lima, Ohio: Wyndham Hall Press, 2002). This is a well-organized set of readings by college faculty experienced with culturally diverse students.

Mushi, S. (2001) Teaching and Learning Strategies That Promote Access, Equity, and Excellence in University Education. http://www.eric.ed.gov/PDFS/ED449760.pdf. This is actually a report of surveys and interviews of seventeen groups of undergraduate and graduate students over seven years from the United States, Canada, and Tanzania. Through quotes, the report provides rich insights into how ethnic students perceive the university environment, how they see themselves as university students, and concrete teaching strategies which they feel enhances their ability to learn. The author also provides detailed suggestions for the classroom instructor based upon these results.

Gudykunst, W. and Kim, Y. Communicating with Strangers, 4th edition. (New York: McGraw-Hill, 2002). This is a comprehensive, well-written coverage of principles needed to understand cultural communication patterns. It provides essential background and advice for interpreting interpersonal messages and for communicating effectively with persons across and within cultures.

Manusov, V., and Patterson, M. L. (eds.) *The Sage Handbook of Nonverbal Communication.* (Thousand Oaks, CA: Sage Publications, 2006).

This handbook is a scholarly overview on the many ways in which nonverbal communication is present and an influence in everyday interactions. Concise chapters touch on nonverbal behavior as reflection of gender, age, culture, or personality.

Sue, D., and Sue, D. *Counseling the Culturally Diverse: Theory and Practice,* 5th edition. (New York: Wiley, 2008).

Although written for psychotherapists, this book provides comprehensive discussion of cultural characteristics on African Americans, Asian Americans, Native Americans, and Hispanic Americans including their histories, family characteristics, and value systems. Valuable details also cover gender, the elderly, persons with disabilities, immigrants, Arab Americans, and Jewish Americans. "Case incidents" activities enable readers to learn useful insights about working with these diverse populations.

APPENDIX

According to Judie Haynes, the following are the typical behaviors governing personal space in elevators by Americans:*

1. If there are only two or three people on an elevator, each person usually leans against the walls. If a fourth person boards the elevator, the four corners are normally occupied.

2. Being in a crowded elevator would be a breach of our personal "space." We would feel very uncomfortable and move or get off the elevator at the next stop.

3. When more than four people are on an elevator, the occupants begin to follow a complex set of rules for behavior. Everyone turns to face the door. Hands, purses, and briefcases hang down in front of the body. People usually scrunch up, rounding their shoulders, so that they take up as little space as possible.

4. People don't touch each other in any way unless the elevator becomes very crowded, and then they only touch at the shoulders or upper arms. If you see an overcrowded elevator, you will probably choose to wait for the next one.

5. Everyone usually looks at the floor indicator located above the door.

6. It is unusual for people (who are strangers) to speak to each other in an elevator unless they are sharing some kind of similar experience (such as a conference). People who do know each other will usually speak softly. When a group of people enter the elevator and do not follow these rules, other occupants usually feel very uncomfortable.

---

*See the full article, "Proxemics and U.S. Culture" at: www.everythingesl.net/inservices/proxemics_elevator.php

Chapter 13

Different Students, Different Challenges

There isn't a teacher in the world who hasn't had to deal with challenges that arise from the fact that students are unique individuals, sometimes very different from us as you read in the chapter on cultural differences. Somehow it is reassuring to know that you are not alone in having this problem and that the problem is probably not due solely to your own inadequacy as a teacher. This chapter discusses some common challenges that teachers at all levels face, and it suggests some strategies to try. I organized the chapter into three categories of challenges, ranging from those directly related to the academic side of teaching, to those stemming from the fact that we are working with humans engaged in the process of growing and maturing.

First, a word of general advice: It is human nature to perceive the challenge as the other person's fault; but before focusing on changing the student's behavior, take a few moments to look at what you are doing that might be related to that behavior. Interpersonal clashes involve at least two people.

INTELLECTUAL / ACADEMIC CHALLENGES

The challenges examined in this section arise from things that affect how people learn and what happens when they have difficulties doing it.

Argumentative Students

There are many reasons why one or more students might be inclined to be argumentative and always challenging what is said in class. The most desirable reason might be that they are interested in the topic and have a lot of prior experience or knowledge to contribute, even if that prior knowledge is actually wrong. Or they might be challenging you because there is genuine disagreement about a particular topic and they're flexing their academic mental muscles against someone (you) who is very knowledgeable in the area. You usually can tell the difference between these students and those who convey, both verbally and nonverbally, hostility toward you and the whole enterprise. Sometimes the attitude is not so much hostility as a challenge to your (or any) authority.

Faced with the first of these two alternatives, you should be pleased! Consider this a "teachable moment." By disagreeing or always adding their two cents, these students are giving you an opportunity to accomplish two very important teaching tasks. The first is to delve more deeply into the logic behind the facts and principles that sometimes pass for content in students' minds. Rather than blindly accepting everything you say, students should try to reconcile new information with their preconceptions. They should be asking for greater depth, more examples, more explanation. These challenging students are out in the forefront of that student push. The second teaching task that these students are allowing you to do is to model what it means to be a critical thinker in the face of challenges to your ideas. In what passes for political dissent these days, students seldom have the opportunity to see two individuals actually discuss their disagreements rather than talk past one another about a controversial point. When students challenge you, you can demonstrate scholarly debate, including careful listening, thoughtful reflection, respectful disagreement, and reasonable compromise where appropriate.

Later in this chapter, in the section on emotional problems, I'll discuss what to do with students who really are hostile or angry about everything.

Students Who Are at Different Stages of Cognitive Development

You just gave a superb lecture comparing two competing theories. A student comes up after class and says, "That was a great lecture, but which theory is right?"

All too many students feel that the teacher's task is to tell them the facts and larger truths and the student's task is to listen to the truth, learn it, and be able to give it back on exams. This conception seemed to William Perry of Harvard University to be particularly common among first-year students.

As you read in the chapter on motivation, individual differences in student responses to teaching may be conceptualized in terms of stages of cognitive development, from dualists (there is a right answer) to multiplicists (all opinions are equal) to relativists (right is situated in the conditions of the moment). Students in the final stage of commitment are ready to commit to values, beliefs, and goals, and to make decisions and act on their values, despite their lack of complete certainty. Sixteen years after Perry's article was published, Barbara Hofer (1997), the author of the chapter 11 on motivation, found that dualists were rare at the University of Michigan, where she conducted her research. Rather, college students were more likely to believe that multiple perspectives are equally valid. Students like those studied by Hofer might be the very students who challenge everything that you or any other authority says. How should you respond to the challenge?

Researchers like Perry and Hofer would agree that teachers need to help students understand how knowledge is arrived at in their own disciplines, what counts as evidence, and how to read critically and evaluate knowledge claims. For development in such epistemological beliefs, students need to debate and discuss issues in which competing ideas are challenged and defended; they need to write journals and papers that are responded to by the teacher or by peers. Baxter-Magolda, King, and Drobney, writing about the challenges facing first-year students (2010), found that engaging in deep analysis and exploring perspectives different from their own were some of the developmental tasks these students needed to engage in the most to make the leap from a reliance of external authority to a belief in their own ability to think critically.

Recently there has been a lot of talk about generational differences in students, particularly in what is called the "Millennial Generation" (Howe and Strauss, 2000). These are students born between 1982 and 2002, as opposed to Boomers (like myself) and the "Greatest Generation," those who lived during World War II. It has been proposed that individuals of different generations are formed by critical events that occurred within their formative years. For the "greatest" it was WWII; for Boomers, it was Vietnam; for Generation X it was the rise of technology; for the Millennials it was 9/11. Those events are proposed as affecting how we think, what we value, how we see our place in the world, our response to authority, and many other crucial aspects of life and living. The Millennials are said to be hard-working, socialized to expect and attain success, active in service and interested in social problems, and team oriented with high confidence in their own futures. They have also been characterized less positively as self-centered, protected, "special" in a bad way, over-reliant on technology, and having a short attention span (Elam, Stratton, and Gibson, 2007).

Several authors, especially those interested in information technology and business, have written about the kind of training that might be most attuned to their needs (Holman, 2011; Werth and Werth, 2011). Of these articles, the one I like the best is by Maureen Wilson (2004) about "Teaching, Learning and Millennials." I like it because she tries to tie the characteristics of the Millennials to the recommendations made by Chickering and Gamson (1987) called the "Seven Principles of Good Practice in Undergraduate Education." You'll notice that this article, which has had a huge impact on undergraduate teaching ever since it was published, actually came out only five years after the first of the Millennials were born. It's not that Chickering and Gamson were psychic about what those students would need. Instead they were writing about what *all* students need and the Millennials are no exception. They recommend things like student/faculty contact, high expectations, collaborative learning, diverse ways of knowing, and so on. As you might guess by now, I'm not a big believer in the specialness of each generation, and I'm not alone. Eric Hoover (2007, 2009) has written several pieces for the *Chronicle of Higher Education* tracking the quality of the research that is used to back up this generational segmentation of the population. As is the case with most attempts to categorize people into a small number of types, the differences between groups are often smaller than the differences within groups. Mano Singham (2009) also writing for the *Chronicle*, suggests that these kinds of characterization and stereotyping, and higher education needs to move beyond them, no matter how seductive they seem. So for now, I think it's safe to say that good teaching for any age has many of the same qualities, especially those listed by Chickering and Gamson, whose principles are based on learning and motivation research.

Most important of all, all students need good models of how to think about the quandaries that are a constant in higher-level thinking and learning. As I said in the previous section, they need to see how you deal with contradictions and inconsistencies, how you solve problems when you don't have enough information, how you cope with the frustration of never being sure of the "right" answer.

Students Who Are Underprepared for the Course or Struggling

One of the most influential differences among students is their prior knowledge and experience with the content of a course. Sometimes students come into our classes without the appropriate background. Perhaps they didn't have the right prerequisites, or they didn't apply themselves diligently in their previous courses. It really doesn't do you or them any good to rail against their previous efforts or castigate them for imagined or real previous failures. That was then; this is now. What are you going to do with them now?

If the gaps in students' backgrounds can be remedied by pointing students toward supplemental or remedial resources, that's a good first step. It puts the students back in charge of their own learning, which is a good source of motivation, especially for those who are behind through no fault of their own. These days a lot of remediation can be made available electronically. Resources available on the Internet might be helpful for basic skill development, such as math skills or writing skills. Alternatively, you can prepare tutorials on the most commonly occurring deficits that you've seen in students in prior semesters. Your department may even want to create a common website that helps students with key skills needed in all courses in the discipline or that provides definitions, examples, and activities to practice the basics of the discipline. You also can put materials or alternative textbooks on reserve in the library or online for those students who may not have had the appropriate content in prerequisite courses. Include sample questions or old exams to help them decide whether they understand well enough to go on.

Another type of help that has had a lot of success with underprepared students is the use of Supplemental Instruction (Martin and Hurley, 2005). This strategy integrates instruction in learning strategies into the substance of the course. Although the original format for Supplemental Instruction involved trained peers who conducted extra study sessions for those interested in learning how to learn, Drake (2011) had better success when it was the course instructor who conducted those special sessions. Regardless of the format, building suggestions for how to learn the content into the course itself is a simple and yet powerful strategy for helping these students. (See the chapter on learning strategies for ideas about what to include in this training.)

You know the value of working with someone else when you're having problems. So, if you can, encourage students to form study groups to work together throughout the semester, not just when there's a test coming. The hardest part of this for students is finding a time to get together. A colleague of mine who teaches a mega-course (500 students) set up an electronic matchmaker that allows students to indicate when they're free to study and where they'd like to get together. Such a system helps struggling students find others who are not struggling and are willing to help them as a way of earning extra credit (all instructor certified, of course). Another way of providing help is to set up a class discussion board where students can post questions and get responses from other students or from the instructor. If enough students ask the same question, you might create a FAQs page with the best solution to the problem and make it available to everyone, including future classes.

Some students are having trouble that requires additional help. I give quizzes and tests early in the term to help students identify and diagnose their difficulties. I invite those who do not do as well as they hoped to come in to see me. Sometimes students who are underprepared have trouble recognizing when they don't understand, however. Zabrucky and Bays (2011) help their students develop the metacognitive skill called "calibration of comprehension" by a simple check. They have the students predict how well they think they will do on a test or assignment before they begin it. Then they compare that prediction with what they actually did. Combining these two understanding estimates with a discussion of what the students did to study and what helped them the most helps build the students' ability to monitor their own achievement, an important skill for self-regulation of learning. Providing students with scaffolding for such skills, for example, checklists, rubrics, and helpful e-mails has also been shown to help students learn self-regulation (Fleming, 2001).

Sometimes I refer students to other resources on campus, such as a student learning support center. I keep learning-center handouts in my office to provide to students who might need a nudge. If they see how helpful such folks can be, they might be more inclined to go and see them. I check with students later to see whether they tried any of my suggestions, and I watch later performance to see if further help is needed.

CLASS MANAGEMENT CHALLENGES

Sometimes the problems we have with students are really issues of policy or rule keeping. It's amazing how much effort some students will put into trying to get around the rules. The best way to save yourself time and effort in this area is to have fair policies that you state clearly in a readily available source (such as the syllabus or the class website) and that you enforce consistently (but not inflexibly). Let's consider some specifics.

Attention Seekers and Students Who Dominate Discussions

In *The College Classroom*, Dick Mann (1970) and his graduate students describe eight clusters of students, one of which is "attention seekers." Attention seekers talk whether or not they have anything to say; they joke, show off, compliment the teacher or other students—they continually try to be noticed (Mann et al., 1970). I've talked a bit about these students in the chapter on discussion.

At the beginning of the term, when I am trying to get discussions started, I am grateful for the attention seekers. They help keep the discussion going. But as the class develops, both the other students and I tend to be disturbed by the students who talk too much and interfere with other students' chances to talk. What do I do then?

Usually I start by suggesting that I want to get everyone's ideas—that each student has a unique perspective and that it is important that we bring as many perspectives and ideas as possible to bear on the subject under discussion. If hands are raised to participate, I call first on those who haven't talked recently.

If all else fails, I ask an attention seeker to see me outside class, and I mention that I'm concerned about the class discussions, and that although I appreciate the student's involvement, it would be helpful if he or she would hold back some of his or her comments until everyone else has been heard. Sometimes I phrase it like this: "The other students are starting to depend on you to do all the work, so let's make them speak up more." Put this way, the comment makes the two of us accomplices in furthering the education of the rest of the class!

Some dominant students are knowledgeable, fluent, and eager to contribute relevant information, contribute real insights, and solve problems. We prize such students; yet we must recognize the potential danger that other students will withdraw, feeling no need to participate because the dominant student is so brilliant or articulate that their own ideas and questions will seem weak and inadequate. Here, subgrouping may help, with the stipulation that each student must present his or her question, idea, or reaction to the task of the group before beginning a general discussion.

In his newsletter *The University Teacher*, Harry Stanton (1992), consultant on higher education at the University of Tasmania, suggests that each student be given three matches or markers at the beginning of a class. Each time students speak, they must put down one of their markers, and when their markers are gone, their contributions are over for the day. Perhaps subgroups could pool their markers or one group could borrow or bargain for an extra marker for a really good idea that needs to be presented.

Inattentive Students

Periodically, I have a class in which two or three students in the back of the room carry on their own conversations. This is annoying not only to me but to students sitting near them. What to do?

First consider whether the problem is with the material rather than with the students. Is the lecture material too difficult? Too easy? Does the topic of discussion arouse anxiety? If the answer to these questions is "no" and the behavior persists despite changes in topic or level of difficulty, what next?

My first attempt is typically to break the class into buzz groups assigned to work on some problem or to come up with a hypothesis, and to move around the room to see how the groups are progressing, making sure that I get to the group including the disruptive students to see that they are working on the group task. Usually this works, and sometimes this gets the students re-engaged in the class for the rest of the class period.

But suppose that in the next class period the same problem recurs. This time I might have the class write minute papers and call on one of the inattentive students to report what he or she has written, or alternatively I might call on someone seated near the inattentive group, centering activity toward that part of the classroom.

Another possibility is to announce that, because research evidence indicates that students who sit in front get better grades (you can explain why seeing an instructor's face and mouth improves attention and understanding), you have a policy of rotating seats periodically and next week you will expect those sitting in the back row to move to the front row and all other students to move back one row.

If all else fails, I might have a general class feedback discussion on what factors facilitated, and what factors might have interfered, with learning in the class thus far in the term. Alternatively, I might ask one or more of the students to see me outside of class to ask them about their feelings about the class and to express my concern about not being able to teach in a way that captures their attention.

Students Who Come to Class Unprepared

There are often good reasons why students come to class unprepared, but some students are chronically unprepared for no apparent reason. What can we do? Here, I'll elaborate on the suggestions made in the chapters "Facilitating Discussion" and "How to Make Lectures More Effective."

In my introductory course I try to communicate from the beginning that I expect students to read the assignments before class. I announce that on the second day of class I will give a brief quiz based on the first lecture or discussion and the assignment for the second day of class. I give the quiz and then ask students to correct their own papers, indicating that this quiz had two purposes: to start the habit of reading the assignment before class, and to give them an idea of whether or not they were getting the main points of the assignment. I give a second quiz a week later and a longer one three weeks later. By this point I hope that my students have established a routine for keeping up with their assignments.

Such a procedure assumes that students know what is expected of them. One of the most common causes of underpreparation is that students don't really know what is expected. Often instructors say something like "You might want to look at the next chapter of the book before the next class," or they state that the next lecture will be on topic X but don't indicate that this is also the topic of the next reading. Giving students some questions to think about as they study the next assignment can help, as will announcement of an activity in the next class that depends on the assignment. One of the advantages of a well-written syllabus is that it communicates your expectations. You also need to communicate expectations by frequent use of phrases such as "As your assignment for today demonstrated" or questions such as "What does X (the textbook author) say about...?" or "What evidence from the assigned readings would support (or not support) your position?" I wrote a piece for the National Teaching Learning Forum entitled "The Scout's Motto: Be Prepared" (Svinicki, 2008) to offer a range of suggestions about this very problem. It really helped me to clarify for myself what I meant by being prepared for my class and sharing that with the students. You might find that even the definition of "read" varies from student to student and class to class.

Students Who Are Uncivil

It's a sad thing to think that the behavior of some college students is being characterized as uncivil. You would hope that they would know how to behave in public, but if you ask any professor, and even some of the students, you'll hear of students being disruptive in class, coming in late, doing other classwork while the instructor is trying to talk, and speaking rudely to the instructor and other students. The list goes on. This has become enough of a problem that people have done research on it. In much of the research, the questions are about how faculty versus students see incivility in their classes. Two pairs of researchers who have done a lot in this area are Bjorklund and Rehling (2010) and Braxton and Bayer (2004).

In the case of Bjorklund and Rehling's work the focus was on student behavior and the extent to which students and faculty agreed on what constituted incivility. Giving each group a list of behaviors that might be considered inappropriate, such as "continuing to talk after being asked to stop," "coming to class under the influence of alcohol or drugs," or "sleeping", the researchers calculated the average score of a scale indicating degree of incivility. These were then ranked from highest to lowest level. The general results indicated that faculty and students regarded the same behavior as uncivil, but the difference was in how disruptive they felt the behaviors to be. Faculty rated the behaviors as more uncivil than students rated them. At the same time, students reported the behaviors to be more frequent than faculty felt they were. Both faculty and students rated "continuing to talk after being asked to stop" as the most uncivil behavior of the list they rated.

The difference in the Braxton and Bayer (2004) work was that it included faculty incivility as one of the behaviors being measured. Of the six behavior categories that were evaluated, inattentive planning (not being ready; not taking student needs into account, etc.) was the one behavior pattern that had the highest incidence reported having been experienced by students. However, even that was reported as seen "sometimes" by only 19 percent of the students responding. When the same behavior categories were evaluated by faculty, "inadequate planning" was joined by "inadequate course design," "inadequate communication," and "inadequate syllabus," but still at a very low level of occurrence.

On the student side of incivilities Braxton and Bayer developed two broad categories, "disrespectful disruptions," which included such things as repeatedly interrupting others during the class session and regularly leaving class before the class has been excused, and "insolent inattention," which included such things as coming to class intoxicated and sleeping during class. The second of these was more commonly seen as uncivil by the students than the first.

In both of these sets of studies, the authors suggest that institutions create statements of normative behavior that is acceptable and unacceptable in their classrooms. The broad support of such rules of conduct would help to back up faculty and student efforts to raise the level of civility in each classroom and other sort of activity sponsored by the institution. Barring such general statements, you might enlist your class in creating local norms that they believe will make the classroom more conducive to learning.

EMOTIONAL CHALLENGES

Now we come to the type of problems that are the most difficult for every teacher to face: those that involve emotional issues rather than the cold academic or managerial issues I've been describing up to this point.

Angry Students

Earlier I described students who are argumentative in challenging ideas. Some students, however, are actually angry at you or your authority and express their anger verbally or nonverbally in or out of class. What should you do with them?

Probably the most common strategy is to try to ignore them. This strategy often succeeds in avoiding a public confrontation and disruption of the class. But it may not result in better motivation and learning for the student, and sometimes it's hard to keep from reacting hostilely in return. Hostility would be a mistake because it doesn't provide a good model of how to deal with emotional situations, either for that student or for the rest of the class.

I try to forestall situations like this by becoming better acquainted with the student. If I have had students turn in minute papers or journals, I read the angry student's writings especially carefully to try to understand what the problem is. I may ask the student to come in to see me and discuss the paper. During this meeting I ask how the student feels about the course, what things he enjoys, what topics might be interesting to him. (I use the masculine pronoun deliberately because these students are most likely to be males, although I have also encountered hostile female students.) Sometimes you will feel in such a conversation that you have to drag each word from the student, yet the student will accept your invitation to come in for another discussion. Sometimes you may need to invite a small group of students to meet with you (including the hostile student) in order to make the situation less threatening for the hostile student who hides fear with aggressiveness. Whatever your strategy, it seems to me important to let the student know that you recognize him as an individual, that you are committed to his learning, and that you are willing to listen and respond as constructively as possible.

What about overt hostility—the student who attacks your point of view during a lecture or class discussion, or the student who feels that your poor teaching or unfair grading caused his or her poor performance on a test? First of all, *listen* carefully and respectfully. Remember that nothing is more frustrating than to be interrupted before your argument or complaint has been heard. Next, acknowledge that there is a possibility that the student may be right, or at least that there is some logic or evidence on his or her side. Recognize the student's feelings. Then you have at least three alternatives:

1. State your position as calmly and rationally as you can, recognizing that not everyone will agree. If the issue is one of substance, ask the class what evidence might be obtained to resolve or clarify the issue. Don't rely on your own authority or power to put the student down or to make it a win-lose situation. If the issue is one of judgment about grading, explain why you asked the question, what sort of thinking you were hoping to assess, and how students who did well went about answering the question. Acknowledge that your judgment may not be perfect, but point out that you have the responsibility to make the best judgment you can, and you have done so.

2. Present the issue to the class: "How do the rest of you feel about this?" This tactic has the obvious danger that either you or the aggressor may find no support and feel alienated from the class, but more often than not it will bring the issues and arguments for both sides into the open and be a useful experience in thinking for everyone. This might be a place to use the two-column method described in the chapter "Facilitating Discussion," listing on the board, without comments, the arguments on both sides.

3. Admit that you may have been wrong, and say that you will take time to reconsider and report back at the next class session. If the student really does have a good point, this will gain you respect and a reputation for fairness. If the student's argument was groundless, you may gain the reputation of being easy to influence and have an increasing crowd of students asking for changes in their grades.

What about the student who comes into your office all charged up to attack your grading of what was clearly a "very good exam paper"? Again, the first step is to listen. Get the student to state his or her rationale. As suggested in the chapter "Assessing, Testing, and Evaluating," you may gain some time to think if you previously announced that students who have questions or complaints about grading of their tests should bring to your office a written explanation of their point of view and the rationale for their request for a higher grade.

But, once again, don't be so defensive about your grading that you fail to make an adjustment if the student has a valid point. I have on rare occasions offered to ask another faculty member to read the paper or examination to get an independent judgment.

If you don't feel that the student has a valid point and your explanation is not convincing, you may simply have to say that, although the student may be right, you have to assign the grades in terms of what seem to you the appropriate criteria. If you have been clear about the rubric you use in grading, both before giving the assignment or test and when you returned the papers, grievances should be rare.

Discouraged, Ready-to-Give-Up Students

Often after the first few weeks you will spot some students who seem depressed and discouraged. Sometimes they come to class late or miss class; often their papers are constricted and lack any sense of enthusiasm or creativity. In my introductory classes, some students begin with great enthusiasm and energy and a few weeks later seem to have lost their energy. Interestingly, we spot the same phenomenon in our pro-seminar for beginning PhD students. In both cases the transition to a new level of education brings demands greater than those students have experienced in the past. Often their familiar supports from family and friends are no longer available; they begin to doubt their own ability to achieve their goals.

There is a magic elixir for this problem that research has demonstrated to be surprisingly effective. This is to bring in students from the previous year who can describe their experiences of frustration and self-doubt during their first year and report that they surmounted them and survived. The theory explaining why this works basically states that the task is to convince the discouraged students that their problems need not be attributed to a lack of ability that cannot be changed but rather is a temporary problem. By developing more effective strategies, investing more effort, or simply becoming less worried, students are likely to achieve better results (Van Overwalle, Segebarth, and Goldchstein, 1989; Wilson and Linville, 1982).

Students with Emotional Reactions to Sensitive Topics

In almost every discipline there are some topics that will arouse strong feelings in some of your students. In a psychology class the sensitive topic might be "group differences in intelligence"; in biology it might be "evolution" or "animal experimentation"; in sociology it might be "the role of birth control and abortion in population policy." Often we are hesitant to open such topics up to discussion. But if the topic is relevant and important, it is probably wise to acknowledge the sensitivity of the topic, admit that it may be hard for some members of the class to feel free to contribute their ideas, and explain why the topic is relevant to the goals of the course. Comparing alternative approaches, perhaps using the two-column method described in the chapter "Facilitating Discussion," may help students see the complexity of the issue.

When you are conducting the discussion of a sensitive topic, it is important to stress that each student should listen to other students with respect and try to understand their positions. You might ask a student to put in his or her own words what other students have said. If feelings are running high, you might cool things off by asking students to write for a couple of minutes on one thing they have learned or one point that needs to be considered. Having students write a short essay advocating a position opposed to their own is an effective way to open their minds.

Be sure to allocate enough time for adequate discussion. Students may be reluctant to participate until they feel that it is safe to speak honestly. Such fear of rejection also suggests that you schedule controversial topics late enough in the term to ensure that students have developed trust in you and in their classmates.

Dealing with Psychological Problems

There seems to be a lot of agreement in the literature that the frequency and length of psychological problems in today's students are increasing and causing a crisis in university counseling centers (Erdur-Baker, Aberson, Barrow, and Draper, 2006). Many things are contributing to this trend, but it is becoming more likely that at some point you will suspect that a student needs psychological counseling. Some of the signs are belligerence, moodiness, excessive worry, suspiciousness, helplessness, emotional outbursts, or depression. Sometimes you will spot symptoms of drug or alcohol abuse. How do you get the student to the help needed?

The first step may be to get the student to talk to you. Usually you can do so by asking the student to come in, perhaps to discuss a paper or test. Typically the student is aware that things aren't going well, and you can simply ask, "How are things going?" or "What do you think is the reason for your problems?" Listen rather than intervening. After listening and expressing concern, you might then say, "What do you think you can do?" One alternative, probably the best, is to seek professional help. (Take the time to find out what is available on campus before you need it.) If the student agrees that professional assistance might be a good idea, I've found that it helps to pick up the phone and say, "I'll call to see when they can see you." In fact, most counseling agencies will at least carry out an initial interview with any student who walks in. But the sense of commitment involved when a faculty member has called seems to make students more likely to follow through than if they simply agree that they'll go in. Even if the student does not immediately get professional help, your concern and support will be helpful, and awareness of the availability of professional help may be valuable later.

Potential Suicides

The increasing concern with suicide risk among college students prompts a few words on the early recognition of the kinds of depressed states that accompany such risks. If you were to notice a sudden falling off of a particular student's faithfulness in attending class, you might want to inquire further, especially if you noted signs of neglect of personal grooming and hygiene, lethargy, and any marked weight changes, or a facial expression that is atypically gloomy or distressed. Your interest in the student should include concern with any other changes he or she has been experiencing, including major separations or losses and mood states. You should listen for talk of death or references to suicide or to getting one's personal and legal affairs in order.

Your major concern should not be to reach an accurate assessment of suicide risk. In fact, it is definitely not within your purview to become the student's counselor; that would be inappropriate, even unethical. But you are one of those in a position to recognize a change in the student. A student manifesting any of these characteristics is surely troubled and should be urged to seek whatever professional counseling is available. A good source for advice on college student mental health is the National Academic Advising Association. Their website has materials for you to consult, overviews of common problems faced by college students, and bibliographies dealing with various issues. Getting the student to a source of help should be your primary objective. On one occasion, I walked with a student to the clinic to be sure that he got there. On a couple of occasions when a student seemed unlikely to seek help, I asked the university health service to call the student in. Sometimes the idea that someone really cares is enough to get the student through the down times.

IN CONCLUSION

1. Don't duck controversy. Use it as an opportunity to model good problem-solving skills and critical thinking.

2. *Listen*, and get students to listen to one another.

3. Keep your cool. You don't have to respond immediately.

4. Paraphrase, question, and summarize, but delay suggesting alternatives until you are confident that you understand.

5. Talk to colleagues. Ask what they would do.

6. Remember that your problem students are human beings who have problems and need your sympathy and help.

Supplementary Reading

An excellent review of the attributional retraining research dealing with motivation of discouraged students is R. P. Perry, F. J. Hechter, V. H. Menec, and L. Weinberg, *A Review of Attributional Motivation and Performance in College Students from an Attributional Retraining Perspective,* Occasional Papers in Higher Education, Centre for Higher Education Research and Development, University of Manitoba, Winnipeg, Manitoba, Canada R3T 2N2.

Two interesting compilations of research and thinking on problems in classrooms are Steven M. Richardson's "Promoting Civility: A Teaching Challenge," no. 77, March 1999, and John Braxton and Alan Bayer's

"Faculty and Student Classroom Improprieties: Creating a Civil Environment on Campus," no. 100, 2005, in the *New Directions for Teaching and Learning* series.

In A. W. Chickering, *The New American College* (San Francisco: Jossey-Bass, 1988), the chapter by Jane Shipton and Elizabeth Steltenpohl provides a useful perspective on the broad issues faced by academic advisors. The typical schedule of fifteen minutes per advisee is clearly insufficient for planning an academic program in relation to lifelong goals.

In *Tools for Teaching* (San Francisco: Jossey-Bass, 2009), Barbara Davis offers good practical advice in chapter 44, "Holding Office Hours," and chapter 45, "Academic Advising and Monitoring Undergraduates."

Also see Alice G. Reinarz and Eric R. White (eds.), "Teaching Through Academic Advising: A Faculty Perspective," *New Directions for Teaching and Learning*, no. 62, 1995.

Chapter 7, "One-on-One Interactions with Students," in Anne Curzan and Lisa Damour's book *First Day to Final Grade* (Ann Arbor: University of Michigan Press, 2000), provides good advice on counseling students who have a variety of problems.

A helpful source is Mary Deane Sorcinelli's chapter "Dealing with Troublesome Behaviors in the Classroom," in K. W. Prichard and R. M. Sawyer (eds.), *Handbook of College Teaching: Theory and Applications* (Westport, CT: Greenwood, 1994).

Barbara Hofer and Paul Pintrich review the various theories about epistemological beliefs and learning in "The Development of Epistemological Theories: Beliefs About Knowledge and Knowing and Their Relation to Learning," *Review of Educational Research*, 1997, *67*, 88–140.

One particularly relevant reading is R. Harper and M. Peterson, "Mental Health Issues and College Students," *NACADA Clearinghouse of Academic Advising Resources*, 2005. Retrieved May 27, 2009 from www.nacada.ksu.edu/Clearinghouse/AdvisingIssues/Mental-Health.htm. This article particularly targets what advisors can do to recognize and help troubled students.

For advice on college student mental health the National Academic Advising Association's website is: www.nacada.ksu.edu/Clearinghouse/Advisingissues/Mental-Health.htm.

Part 4

Adding to Your Repertoire of Skills and Strategies for Facilitating Active Learning

Chapter 14

Active Learning: Group-Based Learning*

THE VALUE OF ACTIVE LEARNING ITSELF

Before we start talking about how to get students active in their learning by using groups, I thought it might be worthwhile to talk about *why* to get them actively learning in the first place. Throughout this book I've tried to include ideas from the research literature on learning, and if there is one thing that the literature agrees on universally, it is the value of involving the learner in the active processing of incoming information. There is a big difference between hearing and learning. In fact, there's a difference between simply listening and listening mindfully. Despite the fact that some instructors believe that telling is teaching, a learner really hasn't stored new information in long term memory until he or she does something with that information. It might be that the learner makes a connection between what he's hearing and what he already knows. Or it might be that she creates an example or image to represent the new

*I use the term *group learning* to include "collaborative" and "cooperative" learning. Some authors distinguish collaborative from cooperative learning, but both involve peer learning in which there is interdependence of students working toward a common goal. Similarities in and differences between collaborative and cooperative learning are discussed in Cooper, Robinson, and Ball (2003).

information and its structure. Whatever the processing act is, even if it's taking lecture notes that are summaries of what's said instead of verbatim, the learner makes that information unique to his or her understanding. So some form of active learning is necessary.

Another value of active learning is that it helps eliminate the "illusion of understanding." This is that wonderful experience we've all had, of listening to an expert describe a process and thinking we understand it only to find out that we can't replicate it when we try to do it ourselves. You've heard your students say, "I understood it when you talked about it in class, but when I tried to do the homework, I couldn't!" That's an instance of this phenomenon. We feel like we understand something just because we've seen it or heard it or read it before. It takes the attempt to apply the information to prove to us that we don't understand it yet. Active learning during class breaks that cycle, rather than waiting until the exam to show the students that they didn't really understand.

Finally, active learning opens up the opportunity for motivation. Doing something is generally more motivating and interesting than just taking notes. And when we do something and get it right, that's a real motivator! The inclusion of questions, nongraded quizzes, and opportunities to apply ideas can all be done very quickly and without the need for the instructor to grade or even review each student's work. A perfect example of active learning that is becoming more popular is the use of personal response systems (clickers) in lecture classes. (See chapter 17 on technology for a more detailed description of this equipment.) This technology allows the instructor to periodically ask everyone in the class to answer a question by clicking their answer choice; the results are then immediately displayed to the class and used as feedback. If you've ever used one of these systems or seen someone else use it, you know how interested the students are to see if they got the right answer and what a great teaching moment it is when they didn't.

Although the feedback system just described is great for active learning, not all active learning requires feedback from the instructor. Sometimes it's enough to just get the students to stop and write briefly about what they are thinking at that moment. Writing is an excellent opportunity for individual active learning. (See chapter 16 for more ideas on writing as learning.) I've already referred to the "minute paper" strategy of having the students spend five minutes at the end of class writing a summary of their current understanding of the topic for the day. Usually they hand these in for the instructor to read, but the writing doesn't have to be graded. It can just be read and digested to form the basis of a further conversation between the instructor and the class.

THE VALUE OF ACTIVE LEARNING IN GROUPS

The bottleneck in educational efficiency is that learning to think requires thinking and communicating one's thinking through talking, writing, or doing, so that others can react to it. Unfortunately, a professor can read only one paper at a time, can listen to only one student's comments at a time, and can respond with only one voice.

The problem is not one of communicating knowledge from professors to students more efficiently. Printed materials have done this very well for years, and for most educational purposes are still superior to any of the modern alternatives. The problem is rather one of interaction between the learner and teacher. Fortunately, interactions that facilitate learning need not be limited to those with teachers. Often, those with peers are more productive.

WHY DOES PEER LEARNING WORK?

The best answer to the question "What is the most effective method of teaching?" is that it depends on the goal, the student, the content, and the teacher. The next best answer may be "students teaching other students." There is a wealth of evidence that peer learning and teaching is extremely effective for a wide range of goals, content, and students of different levels and personalities (Johnson et al., 1981). Moreover, skill in working cooperatively is essential for most vocations. Miller and Groccia (1997) found that cooperative learning produced positive results in ability to work with others as well as better cognitive outcomes. Marbach-Ad and Sokolove (2000) found that cooperative learning in biology courses resulted in higher-level student questioning.

A very thoughtful review of the processes underlying group learning was written by Angela O'Donnell (2006). She describes the social/motivational as well as the cognitive basis for the advantages of group learning. For example, motivationally, peer learning has the advantages of interaction with a peer—an opportunity for mutual support and stimulation. One piece of evidence for the motivational value of peer learning (Schomberg, 1986) is that it reduces absenteeism. Knowing that your teammates are depending on you increases the likelihood of your doing your work. Cognitively it provides an opportunity for elaboration—putting material into one's own words—as well as a chance to begin using the language of the discipline. It communicates that the locus of learning is in the students' heads. An effective partner can act as a model of useful strategies as well as a teacher.

Several of the effective peer learning techniques involve alternating between listening and summarizing or explaining. Structures of peer learning (such as the learning cell, described in detail later in the chapter) that reduce the chance that one participant is simply a passive recipient seem likely to be better for both motivation and learning.

The task of the successful student in peer learning is to question, explain, express opinions, admit confusion, and reveal misconceptions; but at the same time the student must listen to peers, respond to their questions, question their opinions, and share information or concepts that will clear up their confusion. Accomplishing these tasks requires interpersonal as well as cognitive skills—being able to give feedback in nonthreatening, supportive ways, maintaining a focus on group goals, developing orderly task-oriented procedures, and developing and sustaining mutual tasks. It is little wonder that peer learning sometimes fails; the wonder is that it so frequently works. And it does.

Students are more likely to talk in small groups than in large ones; students who are confused are more likely to ask other students questions about their difficulties or failure to understand than to reveal these problems with a faculty member present. Students who are not confused must actively organize and reorganize their own learning in order to explain it. Thus, both the confused and the unconfused benefit.

GROUP LEARNING: VARIATIONS ON THE THEME

Peer Tutoring

"Pay to be a tutor, not to be tutored" is the message from studies of peer tutoring. For example, Annis (1983) compared learning of students who read a passage and were taught by a peer and students who read the passage and taught it to another student.

The results demonstrated that teaching resulted in better learning than being taught. A similar study by Bargh and Schul (1980) also found positive results, with the largest part of the gain in retention being attributable to deeper studying of material when preparing to teach. These results fit well with contemporary theories of learning and memory. Preparing to teach and teaching involve active thought about the material, analysis and selection of main ideas, and processing the concepts into one's own thoughts and words. However, this does not mean that those being tutored fail to learn. Peer tutoring also helps those being tutored (Cohen, Kulik, and Kulik, 1982; Lidren, Meier, and Brigham, 1991). Hartman (1990) provides useful suggestions for training tutors. Peer tutoring need not be one on one. Group tutoring is also effective.

The Learning Pair: From Learning Cells to Think-Pair-Share

We don't often think of pairs of students as constituting a "group," but as an easy way to start using more active learning, they are simple to implement and don't take much time. One of the best-developed systems for helping pairs of students learn more effectively is the "learning cell" developed by Marcel Goldschmid of the Swiss Federal Institute of Technology in Lausanne (Goldschmid, 1971). The learning cell, or student dyad, refers to a cooperative form of learning in pairs, in which students alternate asking and answering questions on commonly read materials.

1. To prepare for the learning cell, students read an assignment and write questions dealing with the major points raised in the reading or other related materials.

2. At the beginning of each class meeting, students are randomly assigned to pairs, and one partner, A, begins by asking the first question.

3. After having answered and perhaps having been corrected or given additional information, the second student, B, puts a question to A, and so on.

4. During this time, the instructor goes from dyad to dyad, giving feedback and asking and answering questions.*

A variation of this procedure has each student read (or prepare) different materials. In this case, A "teaches" B the essentials of his or her readings; then asks B prepared questions, whereupon they switch roles. Research by Goldschmid and his colleagues demonstrated that the learning cell is effective in a variety of disciplines (Goldschmid, 1975; Goldschmid and Shore, 1974). Training students to generate thought-provoking questions enhances learning (King, 1990; Pressley et al., 1992).

The simplest form of pair work is called the "Think-Pair-Share" strategy. The actual origins of this strategy are hard to pin down, but it has been listed by virtually every author who writes about group learning in the classroom. The basic idea is to ask the class a question and have each person "think" about it for a little bit. The class forms "pairs," and each pair member "shares" with one another what they thought about; then that gets shared with the class as a whole. To recapture student attention and stimulate deeper processing, I often ask students to think about a problem for a minute, write for a minute, and then share

*Students can also use the learning-cell technique outside of class. My students use it in preparing for tests. A similarly structured method is "Ask to Think—Tell Why" (King, 1997).

their thoughts with a neighbor. Students then feel freer to participate in a general discussion of the problem. Pairing can also be effectively used for interviews, discussion of an issue or questions, analyzing a case or problem, summarizing a lecture or assigned reading, or even just checking if they understood what the instructor just said!

Another type of pair sharing is the use of creative controversies (Johnson and Johnson, 1995), which I discussed in chapter 5 as a technique for discussion. In this format each student of the pair is given one side of an argument to research and develop. Then the pair compares their arguments and tries to come up with a compromise that will satisfy both sides.

Team Learning: Syndicate and Jigsaw

The term *syndicate* has a faintly evil connotation in the United States, but in Great Britain and other countries, *syndicate* is used to describe a team-based system of learning that has proved to be effective. In syndicate-based peer learning, the class is divided into teams (or syndicates) of four to eight students. Each syndicate is given assignments (perhaps three or four questions). References are suggested, and members of the syndicate may divide the readings. The findings are then discussed by the various syndicates as they meet in small groups during the regular class period. The syndicate may then make a written or oral report to the class as a whole.

I have found that I get more interesting reports when I remind students that they have probably sometimes been bored by student reports. Hence, they need to plan not only the content of the report but also how to make it interesting. I'm impressed by student creativity; my students have developed graphic and audio aids, skits, class participation, and other devices for motivating their classmates.

The *jigsaw* method, first developed by Elliot Aronson, begins like the syndicate by dividing a class into groups that are given assignments. Members of each group report back to their group, which agrees on what and how to present to the rest of the class. However, instead of a presentation to the entire class, each member of the group meets with one member from each of the other groups, forming a new task group. In this new task group each student is responsible for teaching the students from the other groups what his group has learned. Because every student is thus in a group in which every group is represented, all students have the opportunity to learn the essence of all the assignments.

Students often form groups to study difficult material together or to prepare for an exam. Yan and Kember (2004) interviewed students from a variety of disciplines and found that some groups collaborated to minimize the work for the individual group members. Others, however, collaborated to gain a better understanding of an issue or concept.

Online Groups: Synchronous and Asynchronous

The advent of technology has made it possible to have students work together even when they can't get together in the same place at the same time. Many of the same strategies that I have described for in-class group work could be replicated online, but in general the online group work tends to be asynchronous, meaning that it doesn't have to happen at the same time. (This use of technology to support student-to-student and student-to-instructor learning is discussed much more completely in chapter 17 on teaching with technology.) Uses include discussion boards, e-mail, wikis, and probably many more by the time this book is published. It's hard to keep up with the changes in technology. The technology actually allows me to bypass the common complaint that students have about group work that is supposed to happen outside of class. Because class-management software allows me to form group spaces that are unique to each group in my class, it's easy for them to "meet" whenever they can or to share their ideas at the time and place most convenient for them. In addition, for some students, especially international students whose English may not be as good as their peers, this asynchronous group work allows them the time they need in order to interpret what their peers are saying and to craft a response and edit it before making it public.

A particularly interesting use of synchronous online groups came in very handy this past year when I had two deaf students in my class. Because small group work is so important in my classes, I set up chat rooms for any group that one of these students was in. All the students in that group would log in to the chat and everyone was able to make their contributions without having to go through an interpreter. It was very satisfying for me and for *all* my students, and resulted in a much greater inclusion of the deaf students in the class conversation.

A colleague of mine uses synchronous chatting in her class in order to get a permanent record of the discussion for later analysis by her and the students. This characteristic of online groups highlights an interesting phenomenon in the literature. Because technology allows researchers to capture a permanent record of the discussions they are studying, there is a huge literature building up around computer-mediated communication, and we know more about it than most other teaching methods. A review of the literature by Romiszowski and Mason (2004) provides all kinds of perspectives on how to use online discussions. As for my colleague, she uses it because she is interested in studying how students come to understand ideas. Her students use it to review the discussions and write papers drawing on what was said. On a more mundane level, it does give her a permanent record of who participated and what the quality of their contribution was.

Team-Based Learning

This type of group learning is a very well-developed and structured strategy for getting students to learn from one another rather than exclusively from the instructor. It was developed by Larry Michaelsen in large management classes at the University of Oklahoma in the late 1970s, and has since spread far and wide. There are two valuable references about this technique listed in the supplementary readings section of this chapter, but here's a brief overview. Students are formed into groups of seven to nine students who work together through the entire semester. Before coming to class the students read the text assigned for the day. Upon arrival at class, each student independently answers a "readiness" quiz about the reading and turns it in. Then the group gets together and retakes the quiz as a group. The discussion runs hot and heavy when students disagree about the correct answer, and therein lies one of its strengths: You have to be able to convince the others that you are right, which means you'd better be sure of your answer so you don't lead the group astray. Being able to articulate your reasoning is an extremely valuable learning method and it is the core of this method. Eventually each student's grade for that quiz is a combination of his or her own performance and the performance of the group.

Learning Communities

There is currently a big movement in postsecondary education to use all of these advantages of group learning in what are called "learning communities." Gabelnick and colleagues (1990) reported on the growth of learning communities in higher education early in their development. There are several ways to think about learning communities, but the one most relevant for our purposes is the "classroom community." The idea behind such a system is to harness all the benefits of group learning in the context of a class. Students and instructor would work together to achieve learning goals rather than the instructor assigning a task and the students carrying it out. The class makes group decisions about how to proceed and supports one another in the process. Each student would feel like a member of that community, learning from and helping others learn from the class. A critical component of this whole process is the active learning that takes place within the class. Classroom communities provide a safe place for the tough business of learning new things.

ISSUES IN DESIGNING GROUP WORK

Here are some tips that may be helpful in initiating a variety of types of cooperative learning methods:

1. You should be the one to form the groups rather than letting students form their own. You are more likely to create diverse groups and less likely to have friends (especially couples) in a group (which can lead to some difficult group dynamics). I find that my students actually prefer to be in a group that is not the same as their social group. And they are more likely to stay on task. I suggest forming groups that are based on characteristics and skills that students bring to the group. For example, in one of my graduate classes, I have students coming from a range of fields and the goal of the class is to understand how the theories apply across fields. So in that class, I try to create groups that have one representative of each of the fields present in the class. When they work on a theory, each person is representing his or her field to the representatives of the other fields. However, in an undergraduate class made up of future teachers who are going to be teaching at a wide range of grade levels, and the goal is to be able to apply the theories to designing instruction for your future students, I form the groups by grade levels: all the pre-K teachers in one group, all the first grade teachers in another, and so on. That way they will get the maximum benefit out of working on the applications. There might be some similar groupings in your class. Some instructors form groups on the basis of personality inventories. I don't recommend this for a lot of reasons, but mostly because most instructors are not trained in the use of such inventories and put too much faith in their validity and reliability. Better to ask your students straight out how they like to work in a group and put students with similar preferences together.

2. Once the groups are formed, have students discuss what contributes to effective group functioning. (See the box on group behavior for ideas to raise with the class.) Explain why working together is important and valuable even for students who don't like to work in groups. When they come to an agreement on what good group behavior is, have them sign a contract that they will abide by those rules or suffer the consequences of being booted out of their group. If that happens, they either have to find another group that will accept them or do the work

themselves. Some instructors adopt the philosophy that students have to learn to work with others they don't get along with and refuse to rearrange the groups. That might be a good idea, but the instructor should also probably facilitate a discussion about how the group can get back on track. One strategy that seems to be fairly successful if groups are going to work together for the entire semester is to have a mid-semester feedback survey that provides each group member an assessment of what he or she contributes to the group and what changes the other group members might suggest. I have a colleague who has an elaborate online system that allows this to happen anonymously and privately and it seems to work fairly well at bringing errant members into line.

3. Make sure students know what their task is; for example, if it involves out-of-class work, give teams a few minutes before the end of the class period to make plans. At this time they should also report to you what they plan to do and when and where they will meet.

4. For in-class group work, move around and listen in to be sure students are not lost and confused. Use this time to get and keep them on the right track, but don't let them suck you into doing their thinking for them.

5. The trickiest part of group work is grading it. Johnson and Johnson, the most widely published proponents of collaborative learning, recommend that you have both individual measures of accountability for learning and productivity as well as group measures. Each student's grade then is a combination of the two. I have found it helpful to ask the group members to describe in writing what each of their peers has contributed to the group across the life of the project. I do this in lieu of having them actually assign a grade. I then use those descriptions to look for strengths and weaknesses and consensus about each student's contributions.

Suggestions for Students: How to Be an Effective Group

1. **Be sure everyone contributes to discussion and to tasks.**
2. Don't jump to conclusions too quickly. Be sure that minority ideas are considered.
3. Don't assume consensus because no one has opposed an idea or offered an alternative. Check agreement with each group member verbally, not just by a vote.
4. Set goals—immediate, intermediate, and long term—but don't be afraid to change them as you progress.

(*continued*)

(continued)

5. Allocate tasks to be done. Be sure that each person knows what he or she is to do and what the deadline is. Check this before adjourning.
6. Be sure there is agreement on the time and place of the next meeting and on what you hope to accomplish.
7. Before ending a meeting, evaluate your group process. What might you try to do differently next time?

IN CONCLUSION

1. Students often learn more from interacting with other students than from listening to us. One of the best methods of gaining clearer, long-lasting understanding is explaining the topic to someone else.

2. This does not mean that we can be eliminated or have time to loaf. More of our time will be spent in helping students work together effectively, less time in preparing lectures.

3. Cooperative peer learning is one of our most valuable tools for effective teaching.

Supplementary Reading

One of the preeminent scholars of cooperative learning in higher education is Jim Cooper, who in 1991 initiated the newsletter *Cooperative Learning and College Teaching*, an excellent source of ideas for different ways of using cooperative learning. You can subscribe by writing:

Network for Cooperative Learning in Higher Education

Dr. James L. Cooper

HFA-B-316

CSU Dominguez Hills

1000 E. Victoria St.

Carson, CA 90747

Small Group Instruction in Higher Education, edited by J. L. Cooper, P. Robinson, and D. Ball (Stillwater, OK: New Forums Press, 2003) is a fine resource.

Another good resource is Philip Abrami's book *Classroom Connections: Understanding and Using Cooperative Learning* (Toronto: Harcourt Brace, 1995).

Two comprehensive books on cooperative learning are D. W. Johnson, R. T. Johnson, and K. A. Smith, *Active Learning: Cooperation in the College Classroom* (Edina, MN: Interactive Book Co., 1991), and B. Millis and P. Cottell, *Cooperative Learning for Higher Education Faculty* (Phoenix: ACE & Oryx Press, 1998).

Cooperative learning does not imply absence of controversy. D. W. Johnson, R. T. Johnson, and K. A. Smith describe the use and value of controversy in their book *Academic Controversy: Enriching College Instruction Through Intellectual Conflict* (Washington, DC: ASHE/ERIC, 1997).

Team-based learning can be explored further in L. K. Michaelsen, A. B. Knight, and L. D. Fink, *Team-Based Learning: A Transformative Use of Small Groups* (Westport, CT: Praeger, 2002) and in L.K. Michaelsen, M. Sweet, and D. X. Parmalee, *Team-Based Learning: Small Group Learning's Next Big Step, New Directions for Teaching and Learning Series*, no. 116 (San Francisco: Wiley Periodicals, 2008) online.

For online group work, the review by Romiszowski and Mason, "Computer-Mediated Communication" in D. Jonassen (ed.) *Handbook of Research on Educational Communications and Technology* (Mahwah, NJ: Lawrence Erlbaum, 2004) can answer a lot of questions with conclusions based on the research literature (although it does get kind of technical at times).

Experiential Learning: Case-Based, Problem-Based, and Reality-Based

Chapter 15

THE ARGUMENT FOR EXPERIENTIAL LEARNING

One of the biggest criticisms of education in general is that things that are learned in school are never used in real life. And even if they could be used in real life, students don't seem to be able to transfer what they learned from school to use in the real world. Sometimes blame is placed on schools for being too far removed from the needs of everyday experience. Sometimes blame is placed on the students for not being able to generalize what they've learned, as if it were a deficit in their character, intellect, or motivation. It may be a little bit of both. But psychologists have begun to describe this phenomenon of transfer failure as "situated learning" (Lave and Wegner, 1991). This isn't an easy thing to describe, but in essence it means that knowing something is closely tied into a context, and when we learn, we learn not only the facts and skills but that context. When we try to remove the knowledge or skill from its context, we no longer have the same situation and therefore we no longer have the same response. (This is somewhat similar to what we all do when we try to remember where we put our car keys. We try to think back to the last time we remember using them, and low and behold, that triggers our memory of where we were and where they probably still are. We are taking advantage of the fact that our memories are tied to a specific place and time.) The failure of transfer can then be ascribed to the lack of the situation cues that were part of the original learning. The learned skill is "situated" in the original learning context and can't be separated from it easily, if at all. Think of it this way. Have you ever bought a new computer that used software slightly different from your old computer and found that all the skills you had learned within that old software environment were now not only useless, but sometimes interfered with using the new computer? Your computer skills were "situated" in the environment of the old computer. It then takes a lot of mindful effort to figure out which skills transfer and which don't. If your new computer was identical to your old computer, you'd transfer immediately. The greater the differences between the old computer and the new, the harder it is to use the new computer. That's sort of the point of experiential learning. If you want students to be able to transfer what they learn to the real world, it helps if the learning takes place under conditions that approximate that real world.

The second part of the argument for experiential learning is that the learning in the real-world environment should reflect the real skills and activities that the students will need to use someday. The more the students are involved in real problem solving, the greater the probability that they'll be able to use what they learn after they graduate.

The final argument for experiential learning is not as obvious until you really think about it. Learning from a real environment is difficult work and requires a lot of mental effort. To be able to transfer what is learned, it helps to be "mindful" about what is learned. That means that the learners' attention should be brought to the fact that they *are* learning, and it's important to reinforce what it is they are learning, so they're not just going through the motions. Therefore, a key part of experiential learning is reflecting on the experience.

THE ESSENCE OF EXPERIENTIAL LEARNING

In light of the above discussion, the following components are incorporated into almost all experiential learning methods:

1. The learning uses real-world situations, problems, equipment, or actions to the extent possible.

2. The situations involve complex, ill-defined problems that don't have a simple answer and may even have more than one possible answer.

3. The situations involve the learners in solving a problem that reflects the kinds of problems they would encounter in the real world using the real tools of the discipline.

4. The instructor is a resource, but not the leader of the problem-solving task.

5. When the learners have come to a solution, they spend an equal amount of time reflecting on how they reached their solution and getting feedback about the quality of their proposed solution.

For example, if I were teaching a psychology class about early childhood development and wanted the students to understand the kinds of learning activities that are appropriate at different ages, I might assign them to design a playground for a real daycare center that would fit the needs of all the students and teachers at that center. It's a real problem situation (using what they know about development to select appropriate playground equipment) that is ill-structured (there is no one right design) and involves a set of skills that they might be called upon to use some day. (I teach mostly teachers, by the way.) Teams of students would be assigned to study the center and create a proposal for the playground development based on what they learned about the children there and what they learned about children in general in the class. They'd be given a budget within which to work, and the real-world children and teachers' likes and dislikes to consider. I'd have each group present its proposal to the center director and staff for selection of the top two designs. We might even go so far as to bring the designs to the attention of the center's governing board and ask for the top playground design to be implemented. Once the designs have been judged, the class would spend time individually, as well as in a group, reflecting on the outcome of their design choices. What did they learn? What did they omit? How effective was their process? And most important of all, what did they learn about children's needs as a result of doing this project?

Of course, not all experiential learning can be this elaborate, so a whole range of levels of complexity can be substituted for the full blown situation I just described. The following alternatives have all been used in real classes in one form or another for many years, but they all boil down to asking students to come up with solutions to real-world problems and to learn something in the process.

TYPES OF EXPERIENTIAL LEARNING REPRESENTING LEVELS OF REALITY

The Case Method

The case method has been widely used in business and law courses for many years and is now being used in a variety of disciplines. Generally, case method discussions produce good student involvement. Case methods are intended to develop student ability to solve problems using knowledge, concepts, and skills relevant to a course. Cases provide contextualized learning, as contrasted with learning disassociated from meaningful contexts.

Cases are often paper descriptions of actual problem situations in the field in which the case is being used; sometimes they are syntheses constructed to represent a particular principle or type of problem. For example, in medicine, a case may describe a patient and the patient's symptoms; in psychology, a case might describe a group facing a decision; in biology, a case might describe an environmental problem. So while cases are not done in the actual environment in question, they represent the best possible portrayal of that environment that can be made without actually being there. Whatever the case, it typically involves the possibility of several alternative approaches or actions and some evaluation of values and costs of different solutions to the problem posed. Usually cases require that the students not only apply course content but also consult other resources.

Finding the Right Cases You can write your own cases, but you may be able to find cases already written that are appropriate for your purposes and are motivating for your students. For example, Silverman and colleagues (1994) have published cases for teacher education. Other cases can be found on the Internet.

Typically, the case method involves a series of cases, but in some case method courses the cases are not well chosen to represent properly sequenced levels of difficulty. Often, in order to make cases realistic, so many details are included that beginning students lose the principles or points the case was intended to demonstrate. Teachers attempting to help students learn complex discriminations and principles in problem solving need to choose initial cases in which the differences are clear and extreme before moving to more subtle, complex cases. Typically, one of the goals of the case method is to teach students to select important factors from a tangle of less important ones, which may nevertheless form a context to be considered. One does not learn such skills by being in perpetual confusion, but rather by success in solving more and more difficult problems.

The major problem in teaching by cases involves going from the students' fascination with the particular case to the general principle or conceptual structure. In choosing a case to discuss, the teacher needs to think, "What is this case a case *of*?"

Tips for Teaching with Cases Usually, cases are presented in writing, but you can use a video, or you can role-play a problem situation. (Role-playing is like a drama in which each participant is assigned a character to portray, but no lines are learned. The individuals portraying specific roles improvise their responses in a situation—a situation that presents a problem or conflict.)

Whatever method you use to present the problem, you should allow class time for students to ask questions about the process they are to use and to clarify the nature of the problem presented.

You should clarify ways of going about the case study, such as:

1. What is the problem?

2. Develop hypotheses about what causes the problem.

3. What evidence can be gathered to support or discount any of the hypotheses?

4. What conclusions can be drawn? What recommendations? Make it clear that there is no one right answer.

Very likely you will want to form teams (as described in the preceding chapter on active learning) and take time during class for the teams to agree on when to meet and to determine what they will do before their meeting. Some problems may involve work extending over several meetings in class and out of class.

When the teams report, your role is primarily to facilitate discussion—by listening, questioning, clarifying, challenging, encouraging analysis and problem solving, and testing the validity of generalizations. You may want to use a chalkboard, overhead visuals, or a computer to keep a running summary of points established, additional information needed, and possible ethical or value considerations. Don't forget to include the evidence supporting alternative approaches.

If the case is one that actually occurred, students will want to find out what actually was done and how it worked out. You can have a productive discussion about how the actual process, variables considered, or strategies used differed from those in the class. Sometimes you might bring in someone working in the field so that the students can see how an expert analyzes the case, and also ask questions about what really happens in practice.

Problem-Based Learning

Problem-based learning is (along with active learning, group-based learning, and technology) one of the most important developments in contemporary higher education. The ideas embodied in problem-based learning have a long history, ranging back at least to the use of cases in Harvard Medical School in the 19th century and extending through John Dewey's philosophy, Jerome Bruner's discovery learning, and the development of simulations in the 1960s. The current surge of interest stems from McMaster University, where in 1969 the medical school replaced the traditional lectures in first-year basic science courses with courses that started with problems presented by patients' cases. A chemical engineering professor at McMaster, Don Peters, developed a problem-based approach for his courses; and another engineering professor, Charles Wales of West Virginia University, had a little earlier developed a problem-based method called "guided design." In a few years, courses and curricula in various disciplines in universities all over the world were using similar problem-based methods. The biggest difference between problem-based learning and case-based learning is in the presentation. In most instances, case-based learning situations provide the learners with all the details of the case, sometimes even the outcome, at the very start, and the students are more involved in critiquing what was actually done and suggesting alternatives. In most problem-based situations, the students are given just the "nugget" of the situation, the problem, and some introductory material and have to figure out how they'll solve the problem rather than critiquing how someone else did it.

Problem-based education is based on the assumptions that human beings evolved as individuals who are motivated to solve problems, and that problem solvers will seek and learn whatever knowledge is needed for successful problem solving. Even in cultures where students do not expect to participate actively in classes, problem-based learning (PBL) can be successfully implemented; Marjorie McKinnon (1999) describes the introduction of problem-based learning at the University of Hong Kong in her article "PBL in Hong Kong." If a realistic, relevant problem is presented before study, students will identify needed information and be motivated to learn it. However, as in introducing any other method, you need to explain to students your purposes.

The steps involved in one recommended form of PBL, called "guided design," described in the box "Steps in Problem-Based Learning," are representative of those likely to be involved in many variations of problem-based learning. Note the emphasis on assessment of constraints, costs, benefits, and evaluation of the final solution. Helping students develop skills of self-assessment is an important goal of education.

Problem-based learning does not mean that you can sit back and relax once you have presented the problem. You have to check on each group's progress regularly. If you have set a time when groups must report, you may have to help a group clear up a misconception or get out of a blind alley. It's frustrating to start a problem and not have a chance to finish.

In the McMaster model of problem-based learning, students meet in small groups with a tutor who acts as a facilitator. Although the facilitator is typically a faculty member, teaching assistants or peers can also be successful if trained. Typically, after the students have presented their recommendations, classroom discussion summarizes the learning that has occurred and integrates it with students' prior skills and knowledge.

Steps in Problem-Based Learning (Guided Design)

1. State the problem and establish a goal that will be pursued in resolving it.
2. Gather information relevant to defining the problem and understanding the elements associated with it.
3. Generate possible solutions.
4. List possible constraints on what can be accomplished as well as factors that may facilitate getting a solution accepted.
5. Choose an initial or possible solution using criteria that an acceptable solution must meet. The criteria can include tangible and monetary costs and benefits, the likely acceptance of the solution by others, and discipline or other standard criteria normally applied to such problems.
6. Analyze the important factors that must be considered in the development of a detailed solution. What has to be done, who does it, when it should happen, and where the solution would be used are possible factors to explore.
7. Create a detailed solution.
8. Evaluate the final solution against the relevant criteria used earlier, to ensure that it meets at least those requirements and others that now appear to be necessary.
9. Recommend a course of action and, if appropriate, suggest ways to monitor and evaluate the solution when it is adopted.

Source: Wales, C. E. and Nardi, A. (1982, November). *Teaching decision making with guided design* (Idea paper no. 9). Kansas State University, Center for Faculty Evaluation and Development.

Games, Simulations, and Role-Playing

An educational game involves students in some sort of competition or achievement in relationship to a goal; it is a game that both teaches and is fun. Many games are simulations; for example, they attempt to model some real-life problem situation. Thus, there are business games, international relations games, and many others. Whatever the topic, the planner of the game needs to specify the teaching objectives to be served by the game, and then plan the game to highlight features that contribute to those objectives.

Early educational games often involved large-scale simulations in which participants played the roles of individuals or groups in some interpersonal, political, or social situation. Now many more simulations are available on computers. Research and laboratory simulations are available for courses in the sciences, and interactive social simulations can be used to teach foreign languages and the behavioral sciences. Computer simulations are often more effective in teaching research methods than are traditional "wet labs." Simulated worlds, such as "Second Life," have reached levels of sophistication that had not been possible before. While this level of simulation seems very desirable, it's also fairly complex and requires skills that most instructors don't have. However, progress is being made on software that could allow even novices to design simulated environments for problem-based learning.

As with other teaching methods, the effectiveness of simulations depends to some extent on the degree of instructional support or structure. Research on traditional as well as nontraditional teaching has shown that students with low prior knowledge tend to benefit from a higher degree of structure than students with greater knowledge or intelligence (Cronbach and Snow, 1977). Veenstra and Elshout's research (1995) on computer simulations in heat theory, electricity, and statistics found even more complex relationships. The degree of structure made little difference for high-intelligence students; more structure enhanced learning for students with low intelligence and low meta-cognitive strategies (poor analysis, planning, evaluation, and work methods).

The chief advantage of games and simulations is that students are active participants rather than passive observers. Students must make decisions, solve problems, and react to the results of their decisions. Lepper and Malone (1985) have studied the motivational elements in computer games. They found that key features are challenge, self-competence, curiosity, personal control, and fantasy.

There are now a number of well-designed games that have been used in enough situations to have the kinks worked out. Some use computers to implement the complex interaction of various decisions. One classic example is SIMSOC (Gamson, 1966), a sociology game in which students are citizens of a society in which they have economic and social roles; for example, some are members of political parties, and some have police powers. Games like this are useful in getting students to consider varied points of view relevant to the issues addressed in the game. Like the case method, an educational game may be either too simple or complex to achieve the kind of generalization of concepts or principles that the teacher desires. The biggest barrier to the use of games is logistic. Often it is hard to find a game that fits the time and facilities limitations of typical classes. Devising one's own game can be fun but also time consuming. Nonetheless, games are potentially useful tools for effective teaching.

Field Experience

All the previously mentioned instructional strategies involve some degree of artificiality because they don't take place in the real world. To get the full benefit of experiential learning, you would want the students to experience that world firsthand. In most cases this is done in some kind of field experience, such as research studies or internships. However, those experiences are often reserved for more advanced students and have as their goal an academic outcome primarily. The idea of experiential learning has been manifested in the various forms of "service learning," an instructional situation in which students take the skills they are learning and put them to use in real service projects in real community projects (Canada and Speck, 2001; Eyler, Giles, and Astin, 1999). The key to distinguishing service learning from community service is the emphasis on the learning component (Furco, 1996). The activity has learning goals as well as service goals, and the interests of the learners and the community are equally represented.

IN CONCLUSION

Whether one uses cases, PBL, games, simulations, or service learning, experiential learning is a valuable part of one's armamentarium of teaching strategies. In fact, even if you don't use experiential learning in its traditional forms, the general principle that students like to solve problems that offer a challenge but are still solvable is important. And motivation isn't the only reason to use problems. If students are to learn how to think more effectively, they need to practice thinking. Moreover, cognitive theory provides good support for the idea that knowledge learned and used in a realistic, problem-solving context is more likely to be remembered and used appropriately when needed later.

Supplementary Reading

Guided design is fully described in C. E. Wales and R. A. Stager, *Guided Design* (Morgantown: West Virginia University, 1977).

Kenneth France has a nice article on using PBL in service learning: "Problem-Based Service Learning: Rewards and Challenges with Undergraduates," in Catherine Wahlburg and Sandra Chadwick-Blossey (eds.), *To Improve the Academy*, 2004, 22, 239–250.

Donald Woods has published three useful books on problem-based learning: *Problem-Based Learning: How to Gain the Most from PBL* (written for students), *Helping Your Students Gain the Most from PBL* (written for teachers), and *Resources to Gain the Most from PBL*. All three are published by Donald R. Woods, Department of Chemical Engineering, McMaster University, Hamilton, ON L85 4LT, Canada.

For comprehensive help in using PBL, see Dave S. Knowlton and David C. Sharp (eds.), "Problem-Based Learning in the Information Age," *New Directions for Teaching and Learning*, no. 95, September 2003. Also see Maggi Savin-Baden, *Facilitating Problem-Based Learning* (Maidenhead, UK: Open University Press, 2003).

The Harvard Law and Business Schools were pioneers in using the case method. The following reference provides a good description of the methods they developed: C. R. Christensen and A. J. Hansen, *Teaching and the Case Method* (Boston: Harvard Business School, 1987).

A sophisticated description of the use of the case method in medical education as well as two experiments on activating and restructuring prior knowledge in case discussions may be found in H. G. Schmidt, *Activatie van Voorkennis, Intrinsieke Motivatie en de Verwerking van Tekst* (Apeldoorn, The Netherlands: Van Walraven bv, 1982). (Don't worry. Despite the Dutch title, the text is in English.)

The use of active learning in geography is described in M. Healy and J. Roberts (eds.), *Engaging Students in Active Learning: Case Studies in Geography* (Chettenham, UK: University of Worcestershire, 2003).

Linc Fisch's article "Triggering Discussions on Ethics and Values: Cases and Innovative Case Variations," *Innovative Higher Education*, 1997, 22, 117–134, has a lot of practical tips.

Hank Schmidt and Joseph Moust describe four types of problems used in PBL—explanation problems, fact-finding problems, strategy problems, and moral dilemma problems—in "Towards a Taxonomy of Problems Used in Problem-Based Learning Curricula," *Journal of Excellence in College Teaching*, 2000, *11*(2), 57–72.

Information about the implementation of service learning is offered in Mark Canada and Bruce Speck, *Developing and Implementing Service Learning Programs*. New Directions for Higher Education, no. 114 (San Francisco: Jossey-Bass Publishers, 2001).

To read about experiential learning in general, a good resource is Jennifer Moon's book, *A Handbook of Reflective and Experiential Learning: Theory and Practice* (New York: RoutledgeFalmer, 2004).

Chapter 16

Using High-Stakes and Low-Stakes Writing to Enhance Learning

A LITTLE THEORY: HIGH STAKES AND LOW STAKES

Because writing is usually learned in school (where it is nearly always graded or evaluated), and because writing tends to be used for more serious occasions than speaking ("Are you prepared to put that in writing?"), most people see writing as a high-stakes activity. But it isn't *inherently* high-stakes. Indeed, writing is better than speaking for *low-stakes* language use—for exploring and experimenting—because writing can easily be kept private or revised before being shared. Of course we need high-stakes writing assignments in our college courses, but high-stakes writing will go better and lead to more learning if we also exploit the resources of low-stakes writing.

High-Stakes Assignments

If we ask students to articulate in clear writing what they are studying, we help ensure that they learn it. Without these carefully written essays and essay exams, we can't give trustworthy final course grades—grades that reflect whether students actually learned and understood. For if students take only short-answer tests or machine-graded exams, they may *appear* to have learned what we are teaching, but they don't really understand. Besides, writing is a central skill for higher education, and students won't improve their writing skills if they write only for English or writing teachers.

This chapter was written by Peter Elbow and Mary Deane Sorcinelli of University of Massachusetts Amherst.

Low-Stakes Writing

The goal here is to increase how much students think about, understand, and learn what we teach. Low-stakes writing is usually informal and tends to be ungraded or graded informally. You could describe the goal this way: We can throw away low-stakes writing itself, yet keep the neural changes it produced—the new insights and understandings.

LOW-STAKES WRITING

Kinds

The most obvious approach is to ask for comfortable, casual, exploratory writing about a question or topic, and urge students not to struggle too much to get the thoughts exactly right or the writing good. Make it clear that the writing is for exploring and processing course material—and will not be graded. Low-stakes writing also increases fluency and confidence in writing and helps with creativity and risk-taking. These benefits are maximized if you sometimes ask for low-stakes writing in the mode of *freewriting*—asking students to write without stopping, putting down whatever comes to mind even if it doesn't make sense.

Occasions

In Class Many teachers ask for five or ten minutes of low-stakes writing at the start of class—to help students recall the homework reading or explore their thoughts about the day's topic. Or in the middle of class, to ponder a question—especially if discussion goes dead. Or at the end of class, to summarize and reflect. Students will have more to say in discussion, and be less afraid to speak up, if you start with a few minutes of freewriting. (For more on freewriting, see Elbow (1994).)

Out of Class Many teachers ask students to keep a journal of informal reflections on readings and classes. The goal is to get students to process what they study and connect it with their experiences, thoughts, and feelings. Because students sometimes experience journal writing as an artificial exercise and resist it as useless "busywork" (especially if no one else reads it), many teachers ask instead for weekly *letters* that students write to a classmate or friend, in which they reflect on the course material (Sorcinelli and Elbow, 1997). Many teachers now ask students to post letters or journal entries on a class website—or simply have students send entries to a group e-mail address.

Benefits of Low-Stakes Writing

Some faculty members are nervous about inviting students to write loosely and informally, but there are many benefits:

- Low-stakes writing helps students involve themselves in the ideas or subject matter of a course. More students focus their minds on the course material during low-stakes writing than during a lecture or discussion.
- Low-stakes writing helps students find their own language for the issues of the course; they stumble into analogies and metaphors for academic concepts. Theorists like to say that learning a discipline means learning its "discourse," but students don't really know a field unless they can write and talk about the concepts in their *own* language. Parroting textbook language can mask a lack of understanding.
- Frequent low-stakes writing improves high-stakes writing. Students will be warmed up and fluent before they write something we must respond to. When they turn in an impenetrable high-stakes essay (and who hasn't tangled up prose through extensive revising?), we don't have to panic. We can just say, "Come on. You can revise this more into the clear, lively voice I've already seen in your low-stakes writing."
- Low-stakes writing helps us understand how student minds work: how they understand the course material, feel about it, and react to our teaching.
- There's a special application of low-stakes writing to math and science courses—and to problem-solving in general: Ask students to write the story of the paths their minds followed as they tried to solve a problem. These paths are idiosyncratic, and it's instructive to have students share these meta-cognitive stories.
- Regular low-stakes assignments can easily help students keep up with assigned reading, so they contribute more and get more from discussions and lectures. Quizzes can do this job, but they invite an adversarial climate and don't bring the other benefits described here—including pleasure.
- And don't forget: Low-stakes writing takes little of our time and expertise. We can require it but not grade it. We can read it but not comment on it. In many cases, we don't even need to read it. Yet we can get students to read each other's informal pieces—and (if we want) discuss them.

Handling Low-Stakes Writing

Plenty of students still aren't used to low-stakes writing—or don't expect it in a "hard-nosed disciplinary course." They assume that all writing must be read and graded by the teacher. So it's important to explain to them why you require it but don't grade it. You can point out that much writing in the world gets no response at all. Or you can say, "This *is* graded. You get 100 if you do it; 0 if you don't."

Most teachers set up a combination of audience relationships for low-stakes writing: some is private and some is shared; some of the shared writing goes to the teacher and some only to fellow students. Sometimes students are invited to *discuss* the thinking they've heard in one another's low-stakes writing—but not give feedback on the writing's quality. If you have time to give a nongraded response to some low-stakes writing, that can be useful, but most of us need to save most of our responding time for high-stakes writing (but see the section later in the chapter on "middle-stakes writing").

Some teachers read journals; others treat them as private and just check that students have written. Some teachers ask students to trade journals weekly with a peer—perhaps for a response, perhaps not. Letters are natural for sharing, and lots of learning comes from this sharing.

When we start a new class with students who don't trust us and might resist writing anything we don't see, we often collect the low-stakes writing for a few sessions. We stress that we won't grade it or comment on it—just check quickly to make sure they explored the topic. They learn that nongraded or even private writing isn't busywork but, in fact, leads to new insights and better enjoyment of writing.

Many students have never had the experience of writing with their *full attention* on their thoughts. Their writing has always been for a teacher and a grade, and therefore much of their attention has leaked away in worries about mistakes in language, spelling, or wording. After a few sessions, we can stop collecting and let these pieces be entirely private—or just for sharing with classmates.

When students do low-stakes writing in class, it's important that the *teacher* writes too. This helps students see it as a process that professionals and academics use to develop their thinking.

Some teachers fear that low-stakes writing will promote carelessness. This is a problem only if teachers fail to emphasize the sharp distinction between low-stakes and high-stakes writing—and don't insist on high standards for the latter.

HIGH-STAKES WRITING

We cannot give fair course grades unless we get a valid sense of how much students have learned and understood. For this, we need high-stakes writing. The stakes are high because the writing bears directly on the course grade. Most readers of this book are not trained as teachers of writing and understandably feel some apprehension about high-stakes writing—especially about devising topics, writing comments, and grading. The stakes are high for teachers as well as students.

If your campus has a writing center, it can help with high-stakes writing. Tutors there can help students at *all stages* of the writing process: understanding the assignment; brainstorming; and giving feedback on drafts. A writing center isn't a "copyediting service," but tutors can *help* students learn to copyedit better.

Topics and Assignments

When devising assignments, try to choose topics that will lead to writing that interests the writer—and the reader. Try to avoid assignments that ask for regurgitation of material from textbooks or lectures.

It's often assumed that students should learn to write in the academic forms used by professionals in the field. In a graduate course, this makes sense; perhaps also for majors. But most students in undergraduate courses will never have to write like professional physicists, sociologists, or literary critics (for example). Perhaps you feel nevertheless that they should have *experience* with those forms and genres. You get to decide. But we question the value of requiring academic genres and styles for non-majors.

Our goal, instead, is what is sometimes called "essayist literacy": the ability to organize an essay around a main point, to support that point with clear reasoning, and to illustrate it with apt examples. In truth, an academic genre with all the rituals of academic style can sometimes *get in the way of* clear exposition and argument. We think students learn more from explaining course concepts or making an argument to readers *outside the field*.

Most of us are best acquainted with two essay genres: arguing a position and analyzing complex data or a text. But other genres can be very useful to assign—especially because some students fall into stale, formulaic writing when they write in genres they are tired of. Alternative genres include: papers written as a dialogue between two figures you are studying—or other interested parties; personal papers that start from a disagreement that came up in class discussion and analyze the issue or take a side; papers that describe an event or person or era from inside the mind of a participant or bystander. (Students sometimes understand better how an enzyme or molecule functions if they explain what it does "in its own voice," as though it were talking.) Collaborative papers can lead to pooling of knowledge. Letters to the editor constitute a *short* high-stakes assignment that still takes careful thought; papers in the form of a collage are much easier to write but still ask for good thinking and writing (see Elbow 2000a, 2000b).

Criteria for Evaluation

"What are you actually looking for in this paper?" This can be an annoying question from students, but it's a valid one and deserves an answer—ideally on the handout stating the assignment. (Teachers often regret it when they don't put assignments on a handout.) We cannot fairly comment or grade if we're not conscious of the criteria that underlie our judgments. How much will we care about factors like correct understanding of concepts, application of concepts to new instances, creative original insights, organization, good examples, clarity of sentences and good word choice, spelling, and grammar? Certain assignments will suggest other criteria (documentation, correct format for lab reports, voice). There are no right answers—professionals differ in their priorities—but it's not fair to keep your priorities hidden.

Multiple Papers and Multiple Drafts

There are two powerful ways to improve student writing and student learning: multiple papers and multiple drafts.

We suggest assigning several short papers rather than one long term paper ("terminal" paper!). Students often delay writing term papers, they tend to pad them, and they seldom learn from our comments because the course is over before they pick their papers up (*if* they pick them up). Short papers are quicker to read, and we can give shorter responses.

It is enormously useful to require students to write drafts of high-stakes papers, get feedback, and revise. But does this require you to spend twice as long responding? No. Our time is limited, so we need to think strategically: How can we use our scarce response time to do the most good? (Consider the guiding principle for our better-paid medical colleagues: "Do no harm.") If we devote the most time to feedback on a *draft*, we have a better chance of getting students to improve their writing *and* their understanding of concepts. By responding to drafts, we coach improvement. If we respond only to final drafts (autopsy-like), students have a hard time using our feedback to improve future papers (especially if there are no other papers in the course—or if the next paper is quite different). But if we spend the bulk of our limited time commenting on a draft, we need to *save* time on final versions: We can do this by reading through them once and grading them with a rubric. Here's a simple generic example:

	Weak	OK	Strong
Content, thinking, mastery of ideas	☐	☐	☐
Organization, structure, guidance for readers	☐	☐	☐
Language: sentences, wording, voice	☐	☐	☐
Mechanics (spelling, etc.) and correct citations	☐	☐	☐
Overall	☐	☐	☐

With a rubric of this sort, teachers who have many students can limit themselves to reading each paper once and merely checking the boxes. Using multiple criteria provides feedback about strengths and weaknesses—feedback notably lacking in conventional, one-dimensional grades. Because each criterion has only three levels, you don't have to stop and "compute a grade" each time. You need only read the paper and hold each criterion briefly in mind to see whether the paper seems *notably strong* or *notably weak* in that dimension. If neither, the verdict is "OK." (See the discussion later in the chapter on three-level grades and twelve-level final course grades.)

Criteria can be chosen to fit different genres, your priorities, or a writing skill you want to emphasize (e.g., research, considering both sides of an issue, revising, audience awareness). It helps to state your criteria in plain, everyday language. (See the chapter "Assessing, Testing, and Evaluating" for more on rubrics.)

One of the most useful criteria to set for final drafts is *substantive revising*. When we ask students to revise, they often settle for small corrections in wording, spelling, and grammar. When we ask for revising, we can usefully startle students by saying, "Don't worry about spelling and grammar at this stage: Your job now is to make substantive revisions to create the very best essay you can." (And surface features often improve from work on substance.) Many students need help understanding the difference between revising and correcting. Revising is *substantive*: improve the ideas, reasoning, and organization of a paper and clarify badly tangled sentences. Correcting is a *surface* matter: Fix mistakes in spelling and grammar and make small improvements in wording. There's no point in sentence-level editing till the substance has reached its final form. If your teaching conditions permit it, you can help students by separating revising and surface editing: Set one due date for the revision and a slightly later date for the final version. (Just hold on to the revision and wait for the final version to give your response.)

Worst-Case Scenario

Teachers with large classes or heavy teaching loads (and no training in the teaching of writing) will feel, understandably, that they have no time for the "luxury" of multiple papers and multiple drafts. The situation is not so hopeless, however, if we look closely at some undeniable facts: When we assign writing and get students to write, we can trust that we are helping them learn more and probably write better; but when we comment on their writing and grade it, we can't be so confident that it helps them. Research reveals some disturbing findings. Comments by faculty members are often unclear. After all, we write comments in great quantity, working slowly down through thick stacks of papers. It is often late at night, and we're usually in a hurry and perhaps even discouraged or grumpy. Almost inevitably, we write quickly and fail to read over and revise what we've written.

Even when our comments are clear, they are not always trustworthy. When we write that a certain reason is weak or that a particular section should be moved, respected colleagues might well disagree. Grades on papers are notoriously unreliable (as students sometimes prove by turning in the same paper to different teachers). It's not surprising that many bright students are cynical about teacher response. And even when we manage to write comments that are clear, valid, and helpful, students often misunderstand them because they read through a distorting lens of discouragement, resistance, cynicism, or downright denial. And many students don't even read the comments we labored over, looking only at "what matters," namely the grade. So even though teachers may have very little time per student, strategic *assigning* of writing yields the biggest payoff from their scarce time. They can increase learning even more by assigning *two* or more shorter papers and save responding time by using a rubric instead of writing comments. Remember that rubrics give feedback about strengths and weaknesses in the writing, whereas conventional grades give nothing but a number on a "yea/boo" meter.

If your teaching situation is particularly dire, you can tell students openly that you don't have time to give them feedback on their drafts but that you will help them use a more productive writing process and end up with a better paper. Set a due date for a required *draft* of each high-stakes paper—perhaps one week before the final version is due. Collect the drafts and subtract points severely for drafts not turned in, but just glance at each one to see that it seems to be a draft on the chosen topic. Then, a week later, collect final versions and respond with the rubric. This doesn't *force* them to revise, but most students will think of ideas for a better paper during the week after they turn in their drafts. Even more students will revise if you devote some class time for students to read their drafts aloud to each other in pairs or trios. (See below for more about sharing or peer feedback.)

Responding to High-Stakes Papers

Response as Dialogue Commenting is easier and more productive if we ask students to write a brief, informal *cover letter* to hand in with the draft or final version. It should answer questions like:

> What was your main point and what were your major subpoints? How did the writing go? Which parts feel strong and weak to you? Most important of all: What questions do you have for me as reader? And when it's a revision: What changes did you make—and why?

With this cover letter, our comment isn't the *start* of a conversation about the writing, but the *continuation* of a conversation begun by the student. Cover letters help us decide what to address with our comment. Often we can agree with much of what the student has said—and sometimes even be more positive about the essay than the student was. (Students write better cover letters if, on the first couple of due dates, we take ten minutes to write cover letters in class and hear a couple of examples—so we can make suggestions.)

On a couple of occasions when we *return* papers to students, we can continue the dialogue by giving students five minutes to write a short note telling what they heard us saying in our comment and how they are reacting to it. These short notes tell us when our comments are unclear or when students misinterpret us.

Read the Whole Piece *Before* Making Any Comments Students seldom benefit from criticism of more than two or three problems. And we can't decide *which* problems to highlight until we read the whole paper. When we write marginal comments while reading, we get into trouble: wasting time on something that turns out to be minor; making a brief comment that the student misunderstands; saying something that's actually wrong (such as, "you don't understand X," although later on it's clear that the student does understand X); or getting caught up in a spasm of unhelpful irritation. If we settle for making straight and wavy pencil lines during our first reading (for passages that are notably strong or weak), these will serve as reminders after we have read it all and are trying to decide what few issues to address. Even when we want to give "movies of the mind"—that is, to tell the story of our reactions as we were reading—we can usually do this more clearly and helpfully by waiting until we've read the whole piece.

Write Comments on a Separate Sheet Rather Than in the Margins This helps us comment *as readers* about what works and what doesn't and how the writing affects us—rather than falling into the trap of trying to be *editors who fix the text*. Sometimes, of course, we write something brief in the margin ("I'm lost here" or "Shrewd insight"), but most of us save time by writing comments on a computer—which means using a separate sheet.

Use Everyday Language Comments about the writing are usually more effective when we use everyday language instead of technical grammar terms. How much better to say, "I'm having trouble understanding who did what" than to say, "Too many passive verbs."

About Criticizing and Encouraging There's an essential learning principle that is too often neglected: It's easier to learn if teachers say, "Do more of this," than if they say, "Do something you've never done." Thus students can improve more in a weak area (say revising) if we look for a useful revision (even a small one) and tell them to do more of it. For example:

> Your paper has big problems with organization. I often got lost. But I've indicated several paragraphs that hang together just fine; and also several paragraphs that are linked well with good transitions. Give us more of that! You've shown you can do it.

Another useful kind of response is often overlooked because it seems too simple: *Describe the paper* as you see it. For example, "Here's what I see as your main point: … . Here's what I see as your subsidiary points: … . Here's what I see as your structure: … ." This helps students learn to *see* their writing from the outside (a difficult skill), and it tells them what got through and what didn't.

MIDDLE-STAKES ASSIGNMENTS: THINK PIECES

Consider using assignments that are not essays and don't have to be organized around a single point, but are not mere freewriting. Ask for short exploratory pieces that think through a topic. The task in a think piece is to *work at thinking—and also* clean things up a bit so it isn't unpleasant to read. We can describe them as thoughtful letters to an interested friend. A good think piece, like a good letter, might pursue one line of thinking, then discover a problem, and finish by rethinking the matter and taking a different tack.

If your teaching load permits, consider requiring a think piece every week or two (say one to three pages). You can respond to each one with just a check, check-plus, or check-minus—with or without a few words from you (not about the writing but about the ideas). No think piece would be due on weeks when a high-stakes draft or revision is due. Think pieces can also function as exploratory drafts for high-stakes essays.

Think pieces help students get more out of readings, class discussions, and lectures. Topics can be completely open (e.g., "Write about something that interests you in this week's reading"). Or topics can focus on a slippery concept, or ask students to practice particular intellectual tasks. Examples: "Compare these two concepts from the reading." "Use X concept from the reading or lecture to describe and analyze something you have encountered in your life." "Write a true or fictional story that uses the technique of flashback or unreliable narrator." "Write about this historical event from inside the head of one of the participants." Students can take intellectual and rhetorical chances because they know their grade will be fine if they throw themselves into the task and the result doesn't really work. Learning is vastly enhanced if you take a few minutes on due dates for students to read think pieces aloud in pairs or in small groups.

PEER RESPONSE

Most readers of this essay won't be teaching a writing course, so our advice is to emphasize peer *sharing* more than peer response. By reading drafts and final versions aloud to classmates, students experience how each sentence fits in the mouth and sounds in the ear, and they can usually tell which sentences work and which ones don't. And not just sentences: Reading an essay aloud gives students an almost visceral feel for the organization and train of thinking—and when that train goes off the rails. Best of all, sharing—reading aloud—takes very little class time. Sharing isn't just about writing: When three students hear one another's drafts (and lots of low-stakes writing too), they are hearing different understandings of the *course content*.

Teachers and students who haven't used sharing in this way will be surprised at its power—not just to help with writing and learning course material but also to build community. Nevertheless, students may need encouragement and cajoling to make them read slowly and loudly enough that peers will understand. And both reader and writer can feel awkward about the silence of no response at the end of a reading. There's a simple ritual that deals with this problem: Listeners simply say "thank you," then move to the next reader.

The sharing of writing can be a good occasion for discussing the content ("I don't see it the way you do. In my view... "). And if you want to ask for a *bit* of peer feedback, here are two simple quick forms of response: (1) *pointing:* "Here are passages and ideas that seem strong or interesting"; (2) *say back* or *summarizing*: "Here's what I hear as your main point; and you also seem to be saying.... " (For those who want to make a bigger commitment to peer response, see Elbow and Belanoff (2003).)

ABOUT CORRECTNESS: SPELLING AND GRAMMAR

We can't teach grammar and spelling in a college course. But that doesn't mean we can't demand it. (We often demand logic and math skills). The main thing students need to learn about correct spelling and grammar is schizophrenic: Correctness is *not* important for rough exploratory writing, but it's *crucial* for final drafts.

For high-stakes essays, it makes sense to require not only clear, well-organized writing but also good copyediting. Here is a useful formulation: "Your final drafts must be virtually free of mistakes." Many students can't manage this without the help of friends, so it's not realistic to demand that they reach this standard entirely on their own. But we can demand that they learn to get whatever help they need for good copyediting. *This* is the skill and the habit they need when they write on most other occasions they'll encounter. (Most of *us* ask for help in copyediting our own writing, and we get professional help when we publish.)

It doesn't make sense to penalize students for surface mistakes on in-class writing since they have no time to revise and no access to help. For exploratory think pieces written out of class, we can require what's appropriate for an informal letter to the teacher: Clean it up enough so it's not annoying or hard to read because of mistakes or messiness, but don't struggle to catch all mistakes.

This approach to correctness takes most of the worry out of dealing with writing from ESL students. It asks the same of them as of native speakers: "Learn to get whatever help you need to correct virtually all mistakes in grammar and spelling." But *don't* require ESL students to get rid of all unidiomatic language and "foreign" phrasing. To make this demand could pressure them to find someone to completely rewrite their papers. And we can tolerate more mistakes from ESL students on low-stakes or think pieces.

TECHNOLOGY AND WRITING

Technology gives writers an incredible array of tools. Some enthusiasts for technology have argued that students write better papers using computers—but the evidence comes up short (see Moran, 2003). Tools don't, in themselves, improve writing. What they give us are potentialities—with upsides and downsides. See chapter 17 in this book for an extended treatment of technology and teaching in general; here are a few matters that bear on writing.

The Process of Writing

Since the onset of computers, e-mail, text messaging, blogging, and social media, students have become less afraid of the blank page—less hesitant to put their thoughts and feelings into writing at a moment's notice. It used to seem like a big deal to sit down to write something—physically and psychologically. Before e-mail, most writing by young people was done for teachers in school, where judgmental feedback was almost inevitable. But now most students write much more out of school than in. Writers no longer feel that written words are "set in black and white." Words are just pixels on a screen—easily changed.

Students have always been able to talk to friends and classmates about their topic, but now they can explore it through writing in the form of e-mail, threaded discussion, and chat. For many students, the stumbling block in writing papers was once the transition from talking to writing, but now many students have already passed that stumbling block before they "really start." Moreover, technology has led a huge proportion of students to become fast, comfortable typists; this used to be rare.

Nevertheless, these tools don't always produce good writing. The newfound comfort with writing can tempt students to use casual prose that's not carefully thought through for their *final* drafts, not just for their exploratory writing. Also, we forget how messy papers used to be when they were typed or handwritten; now they are pristine. But lovely surface appearance can tempt students into thinking that papers are more "done" than they are. And they can be tempted to think that spell checking removes all misspellings.

Revising

Revising used to mean retyping or rewriting everything; computers have removed the drudgery. Students can easily navigate all their notes and passages and various drafts—and notes from others. It's a cinch to cut and paste. Deleting turns out to be the hard part. Computer-written papers may not be better, but they are on average longer. One of the big problems is the temptation to do all revising on screen, where it's hard to see the structure and movement of thought: we see only the trees and not the forest.

The Dialogic, Collaborative Dimension of Writing

It's now much easier for students to share their drafts and get responses online—from peers and also from teachers. Collaborative writing is now far less awkward and complicated: Drafts and responses can shoot back and forth between co-authors—and more than one person can have access to the same paper. Students' frequent use of sites like Facebook has tended also to make them less nervous about audience in general—about letting strangers see their words and respond, even when those readers might wildly disagree.

The Teacher's Role with Technology

Even the simplest technology can enhance teaching. You and your students can use basic word-processing features like "comment" and "track changes" when responding to or revising drafts. And students can easily trade those drafts or send them to you by e-mail. You can also set up a web-based discussion page, letting students post and receive messages. Start where you feel comfortable and add technologies where they make sense for your teaching goals.

Most campuses now support web-based course management software such as Blackboard/Moodle. These let teachers post syllabi, assignments, and readings and host various kinds of class discussion—threaded, blogs, journals, and chat. You can ask students to comment, perhaps once or twice weekly, about the reading, lectures, or discussion. These sites are ideal for posting low- and middle-stakes assignments. Fellow students can easily read the posted writing and respond in real time or at any time; discussion can continue outside class. All this tends to improve both learning and writing.

It's common for teachers to ask students to submit their high-stakes papers digitally. Especially with course websites, teachers can organize submissions by topic, set deadlines, and comment or grade directly while reading responses. The danger is that some teachers get sucked into commenting as though they are editors—pointing out all weaknesses and even fixing errors. We must learn the old skill of writing comments from a more global perspective so we can focus on just a couple of weaknesses that are most fruitful to work on and on the strengths that need to be generalized.

Remember, too, that sometimes you may want to turn the computers off. Class discussion is often more focused and fruitful when it's face to face. There can be tactile pleasure in handwriting in a notebook or journal—even with devil-may-care cursive. Teachers can promote "old school" social networking by having students read their writing to each other, face-to-face. Technology is a powerful tool, but only when it helps you become a better teacher and your students become better writers.

ABOUT GRADING

A whole chapter in this book is devoted to grading. (See "Assigning Grades: What Do They Mean.") We'll make a few points that bear on writing. It's particularly hard to give a fair grade to a piece of writing because a conventional grade like B-minus represents with just *one dimension* the quality of a *multidimensional* performance. (A spelling test, in contrast, asks for a fairly one-dimensional performance.) Also, teachers disagree about which dimensions should count most (e.g., accuracy of course content, validity of thinking, originality, structure, sentence/word clarity, mechanics).

Grading rubrics mitigate this problem by spelling out individual judgments for individual dimensions. Rubrics don't get rid of grading's inherent subjectivity (How *bad* is "weak content"? How *good* is "strong clarity"?), but they reduce it. For final course grades, most of us must settle for a one-dimensional grade, but we can still use a rubric to communicate the grade's meaning to students. Here our criteria can encompass many dimensions, and we can communicate whether we count things such as effort, improvement, or attendance.

Our sample rubric (earlier in this chapter) shows only three levels of quality (weak, OK, strong). This may seem crude; people hunger for fine distinctions. But the more levels of quality we use, the more work we give ourselves, the more chances we have to be wrong (that is, to differ from how other respected readers would judge), and the more chances we have to make students disagree with us and resist our teaching. Of course, most of us have to give a course grade with something like twelve levels of quality (counting pluses and minuses). But there are simple ways to add or average four or five crude three-level grades to yield a twelve-level final grade.

Portfolios

If we base grades on a portfolio (using either a rubric or a single grade), we draw on a more trustworthy picture of the student's ability or learning (thus enhancing "validity"). And portfolios have other advantages. The grade seems fairer because students can choose a *selection* of their best writing and aren't so penalized for having started out the semester unskilled. Most of all, portfolios enhance student learning because they support retrospective meta-thinking; the final piece in a portfolio is typically a reflective analysis in which the student looks back at everything included and says what he or she has learned. For the sake of this reflection, it's helpful for students to include some low-stakes writing and at least one example of an "instructive failure."

Contract Grading

The chapter "Assigning Grades: What Do They Mean" discusses contracts, but we want to mention a little-known hybrid contract that can be very productive in certain courses. Students get a list of *all* course activities that the teacher thinks are important sources of learning, and students are guaranteed a course grade of B if they simply *perform* them all with good faith or decent effort. Typically, this list involves things like attendance, meeting deadlines, genuinely revising drafts, giving feedback to other students, copyediting, and any other activities that are important for learning—such as labs or special projects. The teacher gives normal feedback on these activities when appropriate—even criticism of what's wrong or doesn't work—but for the grade of B, these judgments of quality are irrelevant. This system gives students a large safety net, yet it tends to get more of them to do more work. And it reduces the degree of student resistance to grading. For grades higher than B, however, criticism and judgments of quality come into play.

PREVENTING—AND HANDLING—PLAGIARISM

We can't catch all plagiarism—and if we try, we'll turn ourselves into suspicious cops. It's hard to track down the sources in Internet cheating. But many schools and teachers use Internet tools such as google.com or turnitin.com to *detect* plagiarism. The issue of plagiarism gets more complicated as more students from other countries and cultures enter our classrooms with different understandings about intellectual ownership and using sources and references. Thus it's far easier to *prevent* plagiarism than to handle it after the fact. See "What to Do About Cheating" in chapter 8 for a fuller treatment of cheating. Here we treat plagiarism in writing.

Despite our best efforts, plagiarism happens. But when we get work that looks plagiarized, we must withhold judgment in the absence of trustworthy evidence. In particular, it's no fair saying, "This work is better than you can do." Most students are capable of work that's astonishingly better than what they often turn in.

Some teachers who suspect plagiarism meet the student right away and present their account of the situation. They may bring samples of the student's earlier writing. If the student cited sources, they ask that he or she bring the source materials. If the student pleads guilty, they may conclude, nevertheless, that the plagiarism was not intentional. Such cases can be resolved informally—for example, by allowing the student to rewrite the assignment rather than lowering the grade for the assignment or course.

But many campuses, understandably, have academic dishonesty policies that forbid imposing any penalty without reporting the case to an official committee and allowing the student to appeal. This may seem bureaucratic, but there are two good justifications. Many students have been falsely accused and penalized with no chance for appeal; and more than a few students have been found working out informal arrangements with teachers over and over again—convincing each teacher that they are naïve and have never plagiarized before. Learn the procedures at your institution.

Ways to Prevent Plagiarism

- Clarify in your syllabus what constitutes plagiarism. Tell students what documentation is required for essays, including for Internet sources. Tell students what collaboration is acceptable and unacceptable.
- Encourage students to meet or e-mail you if they are in doubt about citations. Try to persuade them that admitting they don't know something is better than making a mistake that could constitute plagiarism.
- Ask students to check their syllabi to see if there are weeks in which they have too many writing assignments due at once. Allow students to hand in an assignment early to balance their workload, or negotiate a deadline delay.
- Collect lots of low-stakes writing so students know that you know their style and voice.

(*continued*)

(continued)

- On high-stakes essays, where students might be more tempted to cheat, assign specific, idiosyncratic topics so they can't lift things from books, the Internet, or other courses. Examples: "Apply this theory to that set of data"; "Describe your reactions to X and then go on to ..."; "Give a sympathetic summary and then a critical summary of what X writes on page 134, and then write an essay of your own reflections about it"; "Write a short story that explains and illustrates the principles we've studied this week."
- Require drafts and revisions and cover letters that explain the revisions. Require students to hand in all previous versions and notes with every final draft.
- Write fresh topics each year so students aren't tempted to recycle papers from previous years.
- In large courses with different section leaders, have each leader create different assignments for think pieces and essays, so students aren't tempted to copy work between sections. Circulate copies of new (and old) topics to all instructors.
- Students are less tempted to plagiarize from the Internet if you project that you know what's out there. One of our colleagues deters problems with this note in his syllabus: "Last year, we suspended paper writing in favor of hour tests while we studied Internet plagiarism and how to detect it. Now we're ready."

IN CONCLUSION

Teachers can enhance student learning if they use a combination of high-stakes and low-stakes writing. High-stakes writing tests whether students have learned what we are teaching. If we base grades on nothing but short-answer exams, we don't get a trustworthy picture of whether students genuinely understand course concepts and how to apply them.

Low-stakes writing—without pressure for quality or correctness—helps students in many ways. They can explore and figure out new ideas; connect personally with those ideas, using their own language; become more active learners; and become fluent and comfortable in writing before they produce the high-stakes essays that determine their course grade. And low-stakes writing takes little teacher time or skill. Students learn and improve more if they are assigned two or three essays, not just one, and if they have to turn in a draft of each essay for feedback before revising it.

Teachers can handle the increased demands implied by the previous suggestion by (a) keeping essays short; (b) giving their main response time to drafts, when their responses can actually help students improve; and (c) spending less time responding to final drafts by using a multi-criterion rubric and just checking boxes—rather than writing comments. The multiple criteria make the final grade more valid and reliable.

It's easier to *prevent* plagiarism than to catch and prosecute it. Methods for preventing plagiarism include making essay assignments particular and idiosyncratic so that students cannot find anything written by someone else that fits the assignment; insisting on drafts of essays and then revision on the basis of feedback to those drafts (along with a note about how they revised); and seeing lots of students' low-stakes, informal, in-class writing so we know their writing voice and they know we know it.

Supplementary Reading

- P. Elbow and P. Belanoff, *Sharing and Responding* (New York: McGraw-Hill, 2003). A short pamphlet that explains eleven kinds of response to a text (with illustrative examples)—many of them descriptive rather than judgmental. It's written to help students with peer feedback, but it helps teachers give more kinds of responses to student writing.
- Susan H. McLeod, "Responding to Plagiarism: The Role of the WPA," *WPA: Writing Program Administration*, 1992, *15*(3), 7–16. A short and particularly thoughtful and practical exploration of methods for responding to plagiarism.
- Moran, Charles, "What We Have Hoped For," *Computers and Composition*, 2003, *20*(4), 343–358. A shrewd exploration of research on writing with computers. Moran shows the limitations of some inflated claims.
- M. D. Sorcinelli and P. Elbow (eds.), *Writing to Learn: Strategies for Assigning and Responding to Writing Across the Disciplines. New Directions in Teaching and Learning*, no. 69, February 1997. A collection of essays by faculty in various fields giving practical suggestions about assigning and responding to writing in different disciplines.
- Stephen Tchudi (ed.), *Alternatives to Grading Student Writing* (Urbana: NCTE, 1997). A collection of essays that offers innovative options and suggests ways to introduce alternative methods to students.

Chapter 17

Technology and Teaching

As network computing and tools for learning, teaching, and administration gain more power and accessibility, integrating technology into the educational process is becoming a major thrust for most colleges and universities. Some instructors are embracing technology whole-heartedly, while others feel skeptical or left behind. Based on our work with instructors, we believe that the essential questions of technology integration are threefold: (1) How will technology enhance teaching and learning? (2) What considerations go into teaching with technology? (3) What is the impact of technology on teaching and learning? In this chapter, we will address each of these issues.

HOW WILL TECHNOLOGY ENHANCE TEACHING AND LEARNING?

When instructors ground their choice of technology in individual course goals, personal teaching philosophy, and disciplinary values, technology tools are capable of enhancing teaching and learning. Instructional technology can serve a number of very useful functions in college and university classrooms, including the following:

This chapter was written by Erping Zhu and Matthew Kaplan, University of Michigan.

Providing new opportunities for engaging students and creating an optimal learning environment that would otherwise be impossible or very difficult. Course or learning management systems allow you to post reading/study questions, guides, notes, and other resources that might be prohibitively time consuming or costly to create and share, especially for larger classes. The assessment tool in a learning management system enables an instructor to create and administer quizzes and exams with immediate feedback to students in large courses. The inherent flexibility, openness, and ubiquity of the web and web-based applications have made them useful tools for creating learning activities that foster critical thinking, problem solving, written communication, and collaboration, core skills of a liberal education (e.g., see Uchida, Cetron, and McKenzie, 1996). For example, in class blogs and wikis, students can pose questions, share and exchange ideas, work collaboratively on assignments, and reflect on their own learning process to create a better understanding of course content. Thanks to web conferencing programs, lectures are no longer restricted to classrooms, since students can easily attend live lectures on their laptops. As a result, students and faculty in online, distance, or hybrid learning courses can work together from multiple geographical locations in real time in ways that are simply impossible without technology. Instructors can use technology tools to make their classrooms more student-centered, incorporating active and collaborative learning strategies (Felder, 2003). For example, an instructor in a philosophy course can set up a class discussion forum and ask students to work in small groups to generate questions for quizzes with answers. Each group would then post the questions to a class discussion forum where peers could discuss and defend their answers. In the process, students deepen their understanding of the important points of each lecture with the instructor guiding the learning process.

Addressing specific learning goals more effectively. For example, in learning to illustrate, create sculptures, and design structures, students need to be able to read and think visually, spatially, and critically. To help students acquire these skills, instructors teaching art and design can post examples in a variety of media, including video clips, images, and text, enabling students to reflect on the work of others or post their own work for feedback and critique from colleagues. By using e-mail lists, chats, blogs, or other communication tools, instructors in any discipline can extend discussions beyond the classroom, so that students are engaged in comparing and contrasting opinions, in critical analysis of readings, and other course materials, and there is a written record of the conversation that they can return to and review. Similarly, by integrating games, simulations, and virtual worlds into teaching, you can help students practice and reach a level of accuracy and facility before engaging in real-world lab tests or activities.

Taking advantage of the rich information now available online. From searchable databases, government documents, and reports to technical information and primary sources, a wealth of information is now at students' fingertips. Instructors can take advantage of these resources to incorporate real-world applications into their courses, a strategy that promotes learning and long-term retention (Halpern and Hakel, 2003). For example, access to the online resource Papyri offers students rare opportunities to study ancient texts written in Greek and Latin (http://www.lib.umich.edu/pap/). Data and mapping "mashup" technology opens possibilities for deep understandings of events in specific contexts and geographical locations. Instructors can use such tools to involve students in research, requiring them to manipulate archival data and think critically about patterns and relationships (The EDUCAUSE Learning Initiative, 2006).

Preparing students to succeed in the 21st century. While many students now come to higher education having used technology, joined various online social networks, and interacted with peers who may not live in the same neighborhood, city, state, or even country, they may not have developed skills to collaborate effectively with people from different backgrounds and cultures. Students may also have extensive experience in surfing the web and searching multiple databases, yet be unable to navigate and sift through excess information efficiently or critically evaluate the information they find. Student learning in the digital age occurs in a variety of ways, through completion of courses, personal networks, and communities of practice. Students will need to learn continuously and be able to organize information and use technology to enhance, extend, and even amplify personal capacities (Siemens, 2004; Wheeler, 2010). Such skills are taking on increasing significance in the workplace and beyond, and students will benefit from exposure to a variety of technologies and thoughtful consideration of sources of information and their validity. For example, instructors can ask students to discuss issues of etiquette and privacy in the digital world, or examine the connection between sources of information and issues of copyright when consuming and producing information and data for the Internet.

There is, of course, no guarantee that instructional technology will accomplish these ends effectively. Just as with any tool, technology can be used poorly or inappropriately. Successful incorporation of technology tools will depend upon the extent to which they are connected to course goals, combined with effective pedagogies, and designed to improve student learning, rather than being used for their own sake.

TEACHING WITH TECHNOLOGY

The phrase "teaching with technology" may conjure up a variety of different images depending on our own experiences as instructors, students, or even conference attendees. For some it might mean using PowerPoint or student classroom response systems in lectures; others may think of podcasting lectures; and still others may think of specific disciplinary applications, such as designing web-based interactive learning modules and simulations to teach skills and concepts. While it is natural to think of the tool itself as a starting point, the use of instructional technology is more likely to be effective and appropriate (i.e., facilitate student learning and increase your own productivity) if it is integrated into a careful planning process that takes into account the various factors involved in teaching and learning.

From a systems approach, teaching with technology involves four major components: the students, the instructor, course content, and technology tools (see Figure 17.1). We need to attend to each component in order to make technology integration as successful as possible. **Content** can be examined in terms of learning outcomes and the discipline being

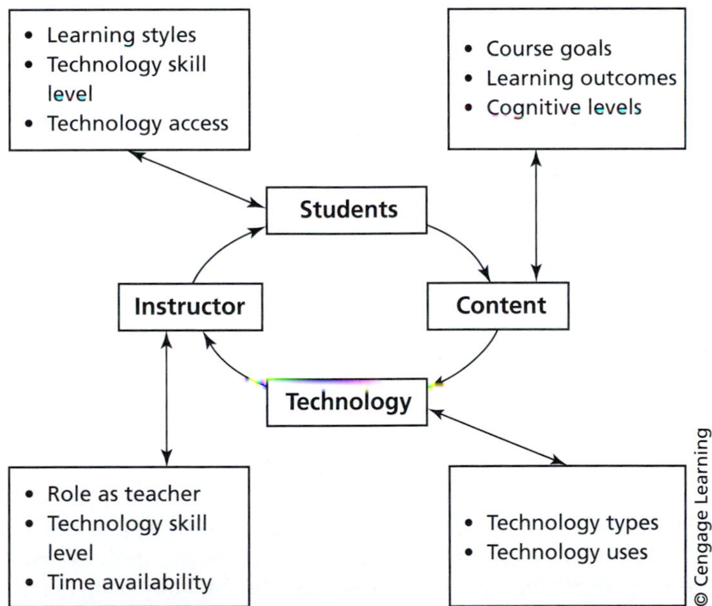

FIGURE 17.1 Teaching with Technology

taught and how technology may promote specific types of learning. As **instructors**, we can think of our own experience with technology, the amount of time we have for planning and teaching, and our view of our role in the teaching and learning process. We also need to think carefully about our **students**, their exposure and access to technology as well as their preferred learning styles and expectations. Finally, we analyze the **technology** itself according to its functions and relevance to our teaching. This approach to teaching and learning with technology assumes that the four component parts are interrelated and that effective changes in one part will require reconsideration of the other three as well.

Content

In order to use technology effectively in teaching, we must examine our course goals as we do when we plan a new course. What do you expect students to learn from the course? What skills and knowledge do you want them to acquire by the end of the term? What teaching strategies (lecture, discussion, group work, case studies, etc.) will best help students achieve these goals? (See the chapter "Countdown for Course Preparation.") Once you have answers to these questions, you can choose the appropriate technologies and design learning activities to help students reach the learning goals, and even employ technology to assess student learning.

To help make the connection between goals and technology tools, we can turn to the taxonomy of educational objectives developed by Benjamin Bloom (1956) and revised by Anderson and Krathwohl (2001). Objectives at the lower levels of the taxonomy involve acquisition of factual knowledge or development of basic comprehension. Higher-level learning involves skills such as analysis, evaluation, and creation. Figure 17.2 briefly illustrates the basis for selecting technology in accordance with this taxonomy of objectives.

For example, if you want students to record and remember materials effectively, you could use software programs such as Microsoft PowerPoint to ensure clear, readable outlines and post them online so that students have easy access for review and correction of their own notes. However, if you also wish to promote critical thinking through active learning during lectures, software programs alone may not be the best choice. Presentation software can lead to a teacher-centered mode of instruction in which students are relatively passive spectators (Creed, 1997). To avoid placing students in a passive learning mode, you will need to incorporate activities that engage students in performing tasks, actively thinking, and reflecting on their own actions. In this case, you

Level of Thinking

Use of Technology

Understanding	Applying	Analyzing	Evaluating	Creating
Presentation & Distribution	**Drill, Practice, & Integration**	**Communication & Interaction**	**Review & Comment**	**Creation & Manipulation**
■ Taking notes on slides ■ Watching recorded lectures ■ Accessing readings electronically	■ Using clickers for well-defined problems ■ Completing online grammar exercises ■ Completing and submitting problem sets online	■ Editing and providing feedback to peers online ■ Participating in a threaded discussion ■ Posting responses to course readings in an online journal	■ Commenting on each other's work ■ Examining existing hypothesis and testing new ones ■ Reviewing Wikipedia entries	■ Creating course-related websites ■ Creating and posting podcasts on a course topic ■ Writing Wikipedia entries
Receiving	Responding	Exchanging	Critiquing	Constructing

Nature of Student Engagement

FIGURE 17.2 Technology and Learning Objectives

can supplement PowerPoint slides with the use of a classroom response system ("clickers") to involve students actively in the lecture and reinforce their understanding. You could also extend the discussion of difficult concepts or problems beyond the class in an online space such as a discussion board or a blog space.

The discipline you teach, as well as the goals you set for student learning, will affect your decisions about which technologies are most appropriate for a given course. In some disciplines, technology is a standard part of professional work in the field, and planning for technology integration needs to take these realities into account.

The Instructor

Once you have a clear view of the course goals and learning objectives and how technology can support students' achievement of the goals, you will need to ask some questions about your own skills and confidence: (1) How skilled and experienced are you in using technology? (2) How much time do you have for course planning and selecting teaching strategies suited to your choices of technology? (3) What is your role as an instructor?

If you have little or no experience using technology, it might make sense to start slowly with tools that are established and easy to use so that you build your confidence and support your students' learning. You can learn from colleagues in your department or attend a technology workshop to get started with software programs commonly used at your institution.

The time you have available for course planning and skill development should also influence the extent to which you undertake the integration of technology into your courses (see Table 17.1). The more complex and unfamiliar a particular tool is, the more time you will need to dedicate to course planning, development of materials and learning activities, and your own skill development. Time for starting up and managing such activities throughout a term may be greater than you expect or wish to spend on teaching. You need to be aware of this and be ready for such a time commitment when you make the decision to integrate technology into your courses. Failing to do so could negatively impact your teaching and student learning.

As part of your course planning it is also important to consider the most appropriate teaching strategies for using specific technology tools. Many campuses now have teaching centers and offices of instructional technology staffed by consultants who can work with you and help you explore teaching strategies best suited to selected technology tools. In addition, you may solicit ideas and feedback from graduate and undergraduate students who have experience with technology and who usually know what tools helped or didn't help them learn.

Easy *(Commonly available and easy-to-learn tools)*	**Moderate** *(More complex learning curve)*	**Complex** *(Specialized software and special training may be necessary)*
Examples: ■ E-mail, listserv ■ Text-based presentation software ■ *Course Management Systems* ■ Chat, blog, and bulletin board ■ Classroom response system (e.g., clickers)	*Examples:* ■ Multimedia presentation ■ Audio or video clips ■ Websites ■ Web-conferencing ■ Podcast ■ Wiki ■ Social networks ■ Collaboration tools	*Examples:* ■ Complex animation ■ Simulation/game ■ Interactive database ■ Virtual world or learning environment

TABLE 17.1 Common Technology Tools and Their Uses

You also need to understand students' expectations of technology use in class and set clear expectations of what you will or will not do with technology, and the reasons for your decisions. Students' expectations in this area may vary widely. It is important for you to find out their expectations and think carefully about the technology you may or may not use in your teaching. If you collect information from students on the first day of class, you may want to ask them about their expectations and backgrounds with respect to technology.

Technology can support student learning, but it can also become a distraction (Lloyd, Dean, and Cooper, 2007). Research indicates that multitasking (e.g., surfing the web, texting, or using social networks during lecture) has a negative impact on learning (Clapp, Rubens, Sabharwal, and Gazzaley, 2011; Ellis, Daniels, and Jauregui, 2010; Hembrooke and Gay, 2003). You may want to establish ground rules in your class to ensure students get most out of their technology tools, rather than being distracted by them. Having such policies on your syllabus, for example, can help avoid misunderstandings by making your expectations clear from the outset. The following examples can be adapted for your own teaching context:

> Do not use laptops for entertainment during class and do not display any material on the laptop which may be distracting or offensive to your fellow students. (Northern Michigan University, 2010)

> Laptops may be used only for legitimate classroom purposes, such as taking notes, downloading class information from TWEN, or working on an in-class exercise. E-mail, instant messaging, surfing the Internet, reading the news, or playing games are not considered legitimate classroom purposes; such inappropriate laptop use is distracting to those seated around you and is unprofessional. (Mazzie, 2008)

When you notice students using laptops in lectures only to check Facebook pages or browse websites that are unrelated to lectures, you can ask them to close the laptop until it is needed for a specific activity. You can also designate a specific laptop-free location for students who do use computers in class and do not wish to be distracted by others who do.

One final issue we need to consider in this category is how the instructor views his or her role in the teaching process and how technology integration can support or conflict with that view. If you see your main role in teaching as that of an expert, an authority in a given field whose main task in teaching is to convey information, you may find it disconcerting to discover that the incorporation of technology can situate you as a guide or facilitator. Moreover, in some cases you may discover that your students know more about—and are more comfortable with—technology than you are. It is best to think carefully about your own view of teaching and learning, how your use of technology might challenge your teaching philosophy and change the dynamics in your class, and whether you are willing to make that shift.

Students

As you adopt technology tools into your courses, you will need to consider students' previous experience with technology, their expectations and access to technology, and the variety of learning styles they bring to your course.

Many instructors report that student comfort and experience with technology seems to increase each year. Data from national studies confirm that overall, Americans are gaining greater access to technology. In 2007, about 75 percent of U.S. households were connected to the Internet, and broadband connections have increased in the Internet generation. Access to computers in the public schools had already increased greatly to 99 percent by fall 2002 (Kleiner and Lewis, http://nces.ed.gov/surveys/frss/publications/2004011/2.asp#one). The generation that grew up with the personal computer is now on campus, and relies on the Internet in every dimension of college life. For this generation, computer technology has become as much a part of the learning environment as the overhead projector and blackboard were for the previous generation.

Despite these encouraging statistics, there are still segments of the population that may be far less familiar with technology. While the digital divide has narrowed over the past several years as Internet connectivity and home ownership of computers have increased, there are still disparities in groups of people who have Internet and broadband access and the use of specific technologies. For example, recent reports indicate that households earning higher incomes ($75,000+) use the Internet at much greater rates than lower income households, have higher levels of computer ownership, and are much more likely to use the Internet multiple times each day for a variety of tasks (Jansen, 2010). Similarly, individuals living with disabilities use the Internet at much lower rates than those who do not report disabilities (Fox, 2011).

Thus, it is important not to assume that all students have had the same exposure and access to the technology you plan to use in class. Instead, you can conduct a brief survey at the beginning of the semester to find out where your students stand. Even students who come from households where technology was present might not have spent much time with it and might not be familiar with the applications you expect them to use. For example, a large number of students on college campuses know how to use iTunes and have MP3 players or iPods, but they may not necessarily know how to create a podcast. When you ask students to do a podcast project, a brief orientation to the technology, as well as some tasks that would allow them to learn the technology, will help all students succeed in completing the project and accomplishing course-specific goals. It is also important for you to tell them about the resources available and where they can go for help with technology questions. Finally, you can seek out the office on your campus that supports students with disabilities to learn more about services they offer so that you can be proactive (in your syllabus and in introducing the technology) about discussing accommodations for disabled students. (For more information on differences among students, see chapter 12, "Teaching Culturally Diverse Students.")

Beyond addressing differences among students, you will need to consider how technology alters the roles students need to take on in your classes. When you use technology in teaching, students may be required to assume new responsibilities, such as monitoring their own learning goals, setting priorities, and controlling the pace of learning. Some students may not be ready or willing to take on these responsibilities. They may even be resentful of new expectations and challenges because they are used to learning in a passive and responsive way, rather than being active and taking the initiative. If you adopt a more student-centered approach, some students might see it as an abdication of responsibility, rather than a positive development. As you move toward greater student involvement and autonomy, you will need to explain your rationale for doing so and build in enough structure so that students do not feel lost. The following suggestions should help.

- Be clear about your expectations for using technology for any projects and assignments and tell students how these activities will benefit their learning.
- Build in multiple milestones for independent or group projects so that you can check student progress.
- Provide opportunities for feedback about the class so that you can make minor adjustments when problems arise.
- Discuss options for support should students encounter difficulties.

Technology Tools

Now that we have carefully considered the context of teaching and learning, we can turn to an examination of the technology itself. One of the challenges we all confront is the need to understand the possible uses and functions of an ever-expanding array of technologies. You need to consider which applications are appropriate for your students, disciplinary learning, course content, and teaching style. Not all tools are the same. Some are better at promoting learning in specific content areas while others are useful for a wide range of disciplines. Some technology tools are built for specific instructional goals, while others are more generally applicable.

In order to explore appropriate uses of technology, we can categorize various technology tools into groups according to function. For example, a large group of tools can be used to help students communicate and interact with each other or with the instructor. Software programs such as PowerPoint, Keynote, and Prezi assist users in organizing and displaying information in text and/or graphic format. Course or learning management systems make it easy for instructors to distribute course materials to students, give quizzes, and even manage students' grades. And instructors can take advantage of a variety of discipline-specific technology tools and programs such as MetLab (numerical computing environment and programming language) and Finale (music composing and notation software). Our discussion will focus on general technology tools rather than tools that are designed for specific content and learning needs. Below we divide the general technology tools in four major groups: (1) communication, (2) presentation, (3) information searching and resource management, and (4) course or learning management systems.

Types	Examples	Instructional Uses
■ Bi-directional	E-mail, text message, audience response and polling system, Internet Relay Chat (IRC), bulletin board, listserv	Distributing/delivering information, providing instant feedback
■ Multi-directional	Audio/video conference, web conference, blog, wiki	Interacting with others, and collaborating on tasks

TABLE 17.2 Communication Technology: Type, Example, and Instructional Use

Communication technology can facilitate exchanges between the instructor and students or among students themselves, both within the classroom and beyond it. (See Table 17.2.) These tools fall into two main categories: those that allow for communication between the instructor and a single student or a group of students, either in class or online, and others that enable a more multivocal conversation among students and the instructor, usually via the web.

Bi-directional instructor-student(s) communication via electronic mail or Short Message Service (SMS or "texting") is probably most familiar to instructors. E-mail in particular can be used for a variety of tasks, from communicating with individual students about logistics (e.g., office-hour appointments), handling questions, or submitting student work. E-mail and listservs can also be used to communicate with the whole class or subsets of students for announcements, clarifications, etc. The downside of e-mail is its ubiquity, which causes some students to have unrealistic expectations for rapid responses from instructors, and others to abandon it in favor of texting or social networking sites such as Facebook or MySpace as their primary means of keeping in touch. Table 17.3 provides some tips for using e-mail effectively in teaching.

Instructors can also take advantage of technology to communicate with students in class by using student response systems (commonly called "clickers"). These polling devices enable a large number of students to send their individual responses to an instructor's computer. The instructor is then quickly able to assess students' prior knowledge of a subject or check their understanding of new concepts during lecture. Clickers have been shown to be particularly effective when used to gauge students' conceptual understanding and when combined with strategies for active learning, such as peer instruction (Mazur, 1997; Smith et al., 2009). Clickers seem to be less effective when used strictly for classroom management. In surveys at the University of Michigan,

- Set up rules for class e-mail, for example:
  - Establish conventions for subject lines and subheadings (e.g., ECON 101 – Assignment and ECON 101 – Requesting for Appointment).
  - Clarify wait time for the instructor's response (e.g., a student who sends an e-mail at 3 a.m. can't expect an immediate response from the instructor).
  - Ask students to use consistent attachment formats (e.g., saving documents in MS Word or Text format)
- Don't assume that your students will keep all the messages you send; keep a copy of important correspondence.

TABLE 17.3 Tips for Using E-mail

students responded negatively to clickers when the instructor used them primarily to check students' lecture attendance (Zhu, 2007). See Table 17.4 for tips on using clickers effectively. The book *Teaching with Classroom Response Systems* provides additional ideas for creating active learning environments with clickers (Bruff, 2009).

While clickers require specialized devices both for students to transmit answers and instructors to receive them, services provided by "Poll Everywhere" (http://www.polleverywhere.com/) now make it possible for students to use their cell phones to respond to instructor questions. Researchers and instructors are now experimenting with a variety of ways to use personal communication technology like cell phones as tools for interactive teaching and learning and for bringing student culture into the classroom (Kolb, 2008).

In addition, students and instructors sometimes use texting via cell phone or Twitter to communicate, learn, and even improve social presence in online courses. Although texting may be a very convenient tool for sending students updates, distributing resources and reminders, and for scheduling appointments, its use as an interactive device within lectures is relatively new and the implications for teaching and impact on student learning, especially reading and writing, are unclear.

Backchannel communication is another method to engage students, especially in large lecture class. Backchannel communication, with conversations taking place in the background of a class lecture, allows students to contribute to the class by offering suggestions for discussion topics, asking questions, helping each other, and sharing resources. Instructors and students can use a variety of technology tools to communicate in the background. For example, some professors at the University of Michigan use the chat function in LectureTools to encourage students to comment on lecture slides or ask questions. Professors or

- Establish clear goals for using clickers in class and explain those goals to students.
- Clearly articulate your expectations of students and also establish rules and student responsibilities (e.g., it is the students' responsibility to bring clickers to lecture every time).
- Develop a pool of thoughtful and effective clicker questions for each lecture. Questions that ask for conceptual thinking in technical courses or critical thinking in any class are particularly effective.
- Use clickers in conjunction with teaching strategies such as "Peer Instruction" or "Think-Pair-Share" to improve students' conceptual understanding of the content, as well as their critical thinking, problem-solving, and decision-making skills.
- When using clickers for the first time, consider the first couple of class sessions experimental so that both faculty and students will have a chance to practice. It is not a good idea to give students tests using clickers on the first day of class.
- Be sure not to allocate too many points to a single test that is given to students during lecture using clicker technology, since it may create anxiety and also increase the temptation to cheat.
- If clicker technology is used to track attendance, be sure to use the system for other purposes as well, such as assessing student understanding, generating ideas for class discussion, or engaging students in thinking critically about course content.
- When using clickers in a lecture class, be sure to use them regularly and consistently.
- When using clickers to diagnose students' understanding, be sure to comment on or explain students' responses, give students another question on the same topic if needed, or adjust lecture pace and sequence if necessary to clarify confusion or misconceptions.

TABLE 17.4 Tips for Using Clickers

teaching assistants monitor the backchannel communication and discuss students' questions either during the lecture or in the follow-up discussion sections. Such approaches can help students overcome the intimidation of raising their hands in large classes and ensure broader participation from students. Other institutions have created systems for students to communicate in the background of a lecture. For example, students use tools like Hotseat at Purdue University (http://www.itap.purdue.edu/studio/hotseat/) and Live Question Tool at Harvard University to comment on the lecture and ask questions. These tools allow them to comment on one another's posts and "vote up" their peers' comments or questions, so that the instructor or teaching assistants can easily identify the pressing issues and address them immediately.

In addition to these course-specific applications, some instructors now use backchannels that are public, such as Twitter, allowing those outside the class to participate in and contribute to the discussion. Guest speakers and experts or alumni can easily help answer questions and provide guidance to students' projects that are created with real world-problems.

Multi-directional communication tools via threaded electronic discussions[1], blogs, and wikis, allow students to share information, discuss issues, and collaborate on learning tasks. Asynchronous online discussion tools make it possible for students to start a discussion before class and continue it after class ends (Table 17.5). For example, a musicology professor at the University of Michigan asks students to listen to musical excerpts and discuss their reactions with each other in a "threaded" discussion in the course management system. He can then start the face-to-face discussion with topics that interested or perplexed the students. "The online discussion quickly became a core component of the course and its organization. The threaded discussion complemented the classroom experience, encouraging a richer, more open, more respectful and thoughtful dialogue" (Clague, 2004). These tools also allow students to reach experts beyond campus walls and collaborate on learning tasks with peers in other countries.

Blogs have become another popular tool for sharing information, comments, and media-based resources. They are sometimes used in ways similar to a discussion space, where students can discuss and comment on questions, share insights and information about course materials, projects, or relevant events on campus. Students can also post pictures, video clips, and any digital media to blogs in ways that are not possible with a threaded discussion. The Educated Nation is one such a blog space (http://www.educatednation.com/). Blogs also have the potential to encourage students to write and to engage them in sharing and commenting on one another's writings.

Like blogs, wikis are a great tool for collaborative learning, including group projects, writing, editing, and presentations (Table 17.6). The best-known is Wikipedia, an online, free encyclopedia that anyone can edit. While skepticism about the quality of entries on Wikipedia abound (along with consternation about student willingness to start and end their research with this particular source), some instructors are actually using this site for creative assignments. For example, an instructor at the University of Michigan organized student groups to evaluate chemistry

---

[1] A threaded discussion is an online dialogue or conversation in which the original message and all of its replies are linked together. The "thread" is analogous to a conversational thread. One online forum or conference usually contains many threads covering different subjects.

Preparation

- Define clear goals and objectives for the online discussion.
- Design a clear organizing structure for the online discussion.
- Create an outline of different types of discussion activities.
- Make the online discussion an integral part of the course. (Do not separate what is happening in the conference from what is happening in the face-to-face class meetings.)
- Establish a clear starting and ending time for each discussion topic.
- Provide detailed instructions for students, including student roles and responsibilities.
- Establish rules for appropriate and inappropriate behaviors before starting a discussion.
- Assign points or grade percentage to students' participation in the discussion.
- Establish clear expectations and standards for assessing students' performance in the online discussion.
- Direct students to technology training classes, online tutorials, and any other assistance when necessary.

Facilitation

- Create a comfortable atmosphere for the online discussion, for example:
  - Be an active participant.
  - Bring your own experiences to the discussion.
  - Use personal anecdotes when appropriate.
  - Do not dominate a discussion or let a few students dominate it.
  - Challenge students without silencing them.
- Ask questions at different levels (e.g., knowledge, comprehension, application, analysis, synthesis, and evaluation).
- Paraphrase a message if it is not clear.
- Encourage active student participation.
- Energize the online discussion if needed (e.g., using role plays, simulations, and pros and cons).
- Bring closure to an online discussion (e.g., summarizing learning points).

TABLE 17.5 Tips for Using Asynchronous Online Discussion

- Set clear goals and objectives for class blogs and wikis (e.g., gather, apply, and synthesize new ideas).
- Connect the blogs or wikis to other learning activities in the course.
- Establish clear expectations and specific standards for assessing students' learning.
- Clearly define your and students' roles and responsibilities for the class blogs or wikis.
- Collectively create ground rules for behavior for the class blogs and wikis.
- Direct students to technology training, online tutorials, and any other assistance if necessary.

TABLE 17.6 Tips for Using Blogs and Wikis

entries in Wikipedia. They would then select chemistry topics to research and update (or create) for a general audience. Similarly, instructors at Louisiana State University and James Madison University ask students to evaluate selected articles in Wikipedia and then learn to improve the entries (Rae, 2011).

Many instructors are finding that wikis are a useful teaching tool because they enable collaboration and public knowledge creation. One instructor at the University of Michigan engaged students in co-creating an online textbook in a wiki. Other instructors create wikis as resources for coordinating teaching in large classes. The wiki provides a large number of teaching assistants (TAs) with access to resources such as lesson plans for weekly discussions, instructions for interactive activities, and responses to frequently asked questions. In addition, there is a space where TAs can share questions and concerns that have arisen in their own sections or comment on the effectiveness of particular activities and readings.

Wikis can even serve as a very flexible course management environment. A professor at University of Michigan taught an entire business information technology course using a wiki to house all elements of the course: syllabus, assignments, lecture slides, class notes, project presentations, blogs, feedback comments, and other class interactions. This wiki-based course changed the dynamics of the classroom, with the professor and students teaching and learning from each other throughout the semester. The class time was devoted to project-based work and interaction, rather than the delivery of information, which was moved to the wiki in the form of notes, lecture videos, etc. For example, one student was responsible for posting notes after each class, and others could correct and add to them. In the process, students were able to take control of their own learning as they gathered, analyzed, and evaluated information. They then wrote up and published their findings on the Internet, with the professor providing guidance throughout the process. Wikis have enormous potential to engage students in learning and creating knowledge both inside and outside of the classroom.

Communication tools are essential for distance and online students to attend "lectures," meet the instructor and other students in class, interact with the instructors and peers, perform learning tasks, and form online learning communities that connect learners at diverse locations. Students can hold group meetings, discuss course assignments and projects, or provide feedback on one another's work using asynchronous tools (such as threaded discussions, blogs, and wikis) or synchronous tools (such as chat). Communication technology tools allow instructors to easily deliver lectures, facilitate discussions, and offer office hours to on-campus students who are confined to the dorms because of a flu outbreak or other pandemic, or are away from the campus for one or two classes. For example, a professor at the University of Michigan broadcasts live lectures to students and enables those who are studying abroad or on an internship in the spring term to join the class and participate in live discussions.

Table 17.7 outlines the various types of presentation and organization technology and how they can be used.

Presentation technology allows instructors to organize and display information in text, graphic, animation, or multimedia formats. It is easy to prepare lecture notes/outlines in text and graphic format with software programs such as Microsoft Word or Microsoft PowerPoint. As they develop fluency with these tools, instructors should be careful not to overload students with slides in lectures, which can quickly

■ Text ■ Text/Graphic ■ Text/Graphic/ Sound/ Animation	Presentation software (e.g., PowerPoint and Keynote) Webpage editor Animation and video software (e.g., Flash and iMovie) Lecture capture tools	Organizing, presenting information Creating learning modules

TABLE 17.7 Organization and Presentation Technology: Types, Examples, and Instructional Uses

overwhelm students' note-taking capacities and attention spans. While instructors hold differing opinions on whether to make slides available in advance of lectures, research on note taking suggests that students learn more when they have skeletal outlines to structure their notes (DeZure, Kaplan, and Deerman, 2001).

It is important to keep in mind that PowerPoint's linear structure and bullet outlines may dilute thought, narrative, and data (Tufte, 2003) and may not facilitate brainstorming and foster creative thinking. You need to be aware of possible pitfalls of a presentation tool that encourages a linear path. If your goal is to explore relations among concepts or ideas, you may want to choose tools like Prezi or Cmap that enable you to map out concepts easily and move them around depending on paths you choose to explore. See Table 17.8 for additional tips on using presentation tools.

- Plan interactive activities to use with presentation.
- Use fonts 24 points or larger for the text.
- Ensure that your slides are legible (e.g., watch your color choices for type and background).
- Avoid USING ALL CAPS. The normal use of upper- and lowercase characters is easier to read.
- Use italics or color rather than underlining to emphasize a point. Underlining makes some characters difficult to read.
- Limit the information to essentials (e.g., generally no more than six words per line and six lines per slide).
- Clip art and graphics should enhance and complement the text, but not overwhelm the viewer (e.g., no more than two graphics per slide).
- Be consistent with effects, transitions, and animation.
- Use the slide as a guide for presentation.
- Face the audience when presenting.
- Distribute a copy of the slides to students ahead of time if possible.
- Keep the room lights on and avoid showing slides in a dark room for more than fifteen minutes.
- Avoid putting students in a passive mode of receiving information by combining the slide presentation with chalkboard/whiteboard use or other learning activities.
- Have a backup plan in case of a power outage or equipment failure.

TABLE 17.8 Tips for Organizing and Presenting Content

The learning curve for making a PowerPoint presentation with graphics and images is not steep, and the time you need to learn the skills should be manageable. However, integrating digital media into your presentations or telling a story digitally may require specific skills, especially if you need to convert the media format or learn a new software program. On most campuses, instructional technology labs or centers help faculty with various media conversion projects such as digitizing film clips and creating multimedia presentations.

Instructors may be able to find useful video clips from Internet websites such as YouTube (http://www.youtube.com). Like a picture, a video may be useful and effective for illustrating abstract concepts or points, and hierarchical relationships, as well as for motivating students, sustaining their interest, or starting class discussions (see Table 17.9). A psychology professor at the University of Michigan uses video clips in two ways: In large lecture courses, he shows short, humorous clips (not necessarily on topic) embedded in PowerPoint to break up the lecture and help students "reset" their attention span; in small seminars, he uses iMovie to create videos of patients with disorders covered in the class.

Assigning students to create their own videos can engage them in deeper learning of course content. A number of studies have shown that presenting novel and difficult concepts to learners in both auditory and visual symbolic modes results in more learning than information presented exclusively in either mode (Halpern and Hakel, 2003; Mayer, 1997; Mousavi, Low, and Sweller, 1995).

Video is also very useful as a means of archiving course lectures, demonstrations, and so on. Lecture capture technology has simplified the process of recording and posting lectures for either traditional or online courses. Many institutions have installed automated lecture capture systems in large lecture halls that allow instructor to simply press a button to start and stop recording a lecture. The recordings will

- Have a clear goal for using a video clip or clips. Ask yourself why you are using the clip and what you want students to learn from it.
- Provide proper context for your clip(s) (e.g., explain that a clip comes from a sequence or part of a story or conversation).
- View the entire clip before showing it in class and develop activities to accompany the video.
- Limit the length of video clips. No matter how interesting they may be or how motivated students are, video clips longer than ten minutes may fail to hold students' attention.

TABLE 17.9 Tips for Using Video Clips in Presentation

be available for students a few minutes after a lecture. Programs such as Camtasia and iShowU also allow faculty to record and synchronize their lectures with a slide show or other multimedia presentation. Students can then watch the full lecture as often as they need, with time to review segments that were unclear. The ease of use of lecture capture and its potential to make course materials accessible to wider audiences have drawn the attention of many instructors and students on college campuses across the country. Institutions including Duke University (http://itunes.duke.edu/); Stanford University (http://itunes.stanford.edu/); University of California, Berkeley; (http://itunes.berkeley.edu/); University of Michigan (http:// itunes.umich.edu); and University of Wisconsin-Madison (http://www.uwebi.org/news/uw-online-learning.pdf), are experimenting with providing lecture podcasts as supplementary learning material to students, including those who registered for distance-learning courses. Students can have access to lecture archives for reviewing material, revisiting demonstrations of difficult concepts, or seeing talks given by guest lecturers.

Recording and posting lectures in advance opens the possibility of freeing up in-class time for practical, hands-on work (problem sets, discussions, and team work). A number of faculty members at the University of Michigan are already capturing lectures and creating podcasts and/or screencasts as additional learning resources for on-campus students.[2] For example, CRLT offers a short-course on college teaching for postdoctoral scholars. The course meets weekly for three-hour sessions. Participants complete readings and watch podcasts in advance of each session so that we can devote class time to discussion and active learning.

Although lecture capture offers many potential benefits (Coghlan et al., 2007), it also presents a set of challenges for instructors, including mastery of the technology (for students as well as instructors), recording and replay quality, intellectual property issues, and possible passivity of learning when viewing long lectures and using them to substitute face-to-face classroom experience. See Table 17.10 for suggestions about how to get the most from this technology tool.

Information searching and resource management technology helps users find and manage the wealth of information available on the Internet. College instructors across the curriculum identify the skills associated with searching for, managing, and evaluating information on the Internet as important student learning objectives and survival skills for the 21st century. However, navigating the web of information to find

---

[2] Examples of U-M faculty using lecture-capture technology are available at http://www.crlt.umich.edu.

- Before you start, make sure of the following:
  - You have clear goals for podcasting lectures and the time to prepare them consistently throughout the entire semester.
  - Your students are receptive to and prepared for lecture podcasts. Don't assume that all students have the same level of access to or comfort with using podcasts.
  - You know the copyright policies regarding podcasts (e.g., copyright clearance of materials and release forms from students if their questions and answers will be recorded).
  - You have adequate and continuing technology support and podcast hosting if you don't teach in a room with automated lecture capture system/service.
- Once you decide to podcast, make time to experiment with recording quality. Choose a reasonable podcast quality since poor sound quality may not encourage students to use the recorded lectures.
- Make podcasts available as soon as possible after a lecture, since most students download podcasts within a few days, as well as right before an exam.
- Devote additional classroom time for interactive discussion, demonstrations, or active learning activities if podcasts can replace lectures.
- Podcasts should not replace more traditional methods of providing supplemental material to students, such as putting materials in the course management system, before you know for sure that all your students have access to devices to download and play back podcasts.
- Make reference to podcasts during lectures or when responding to students' questions, if appropriate, so that students will be more likely to take advantage of the available resource.
- Make accessing and using podcasts easy and fast by providing detailed instructions for downloading, and ensure that the file format is compatible with common media-playing devices (e.g., MP3 players, iPods, and computers).
- Provide students with a clear explanation of instructional goals and technical requirements if podcasts are used for student projects or assignments.
- Be aware of any potential implications of your lecture podcasts for other courses in a program or in the curriculum.

TABLE 17.10 Tips for Using Lecture Capture

resources that support learning and teaching can be quite challenging for both instructors and students. For example, students' self-reports from a survey of University of Michigan undergraduates (2010) showed that 62 percent had trouble narrowing their research topics, and 72 percent reported having trouble defining their topics.

Types	Examples	Instructional Uses
■ Information searching and managing	The Internet, electronic databases Procite, EndNotes, Refworks Excel, and other data management tools	Searching, manipulating, analyzing information/data Evaluating and researching

TABLE 17.11 Information Search and Research Management Technology: Type, Example, and Instructional Use

You can start helping students develop information search skills by embedding in a course small assignments that teach students to use a variety of information tools to search a variety of sources and formats. (See Table 17.11 for examples.) The assignment's goals could include teaching students how to focus on a topic, select search terms and appropriate data sources (e.g., Google and fee-based databases), improve search results by constructing search strategies, and evaluate search results. An undergraduate research course at the University of Michigan, for example, addresses the students' needs in this area, teaching them skills and ability to conduct research from defining a topic and locating proper supporting sources, to evaluating the sources.

In addition, many university and college libraries also provide resources to help students develop their research skills. For example, the undergraduate library at the University of Michigan provides "DIY Toolkit: Modules for Teaching Research Concepts" (http://www.lib.umich.edu/shapiro-undergraduate-library/diy-toolkit-modules-teaching-research-concepts), and the University of California at Berkeley has useful information on Internet search engines and Website evaluation (http://www.lib.berkeley.edu/TeachingLib/Guides/Internet/Evaluate.html).

When asking students to use the Internet for writing projects, the instructor should teach students good practices for evaluating and using online resources and for recognizing and avoiding plagiarism. The instructor should also encourage students to use media in their projects when appropriate, as digital storytelling is a powerful way to engage students in classroom (Robin, 2011). Resources for instructors and students on academic integrity, copyright issues, and creative commons licenses (http://creativecommons.org/) can easily be found on the Internet or at institutions' websites. For example, the University of Michigan has a website with extensive resources on academic integrity (http://www.lib.umich.edu/acadintegrity/). Penn State University's information technology services gather useful resources on plagiarism (http://tlt.its.psu.edu/

Types	Examples	Instructional Uses
■ Open source ■ Proprietary	Sakai CLE (collaborative learning environment), Moodle, CTools[3] Blackboard, Angel Learning, eCollege	Providing a space/ environment for students to engage in a wide range of learning tasks

TABLE 17.12 Course Management Systems: Types, Examples and Instructional Uses

copyright-plagiarism) including examples of acceptable and unacceptable paraphrases. The creative commons website at http://creativecommons.org/ explains how to attribute others' work properly and how to create a license for your own digital work. The Educational Uses of Digital Storytelling website (http://digitalstorytelling.coe.uh.edu/) provides cases to explain how to handle copyrighted materials in a presentation.

Course management systems were created over a decade ago. Some systems are built on an open source architecture, allowing each institution to customize the system. Others started with proprietary technology but may have opened part of the system for customize later on. They all provide a virtual course space for distributing resources, communicating with students, giving quizzes and tests, and managing students' grades without requiring high-level programming or web-design skills. Tools for collaboration and reflection, such as wikis, blogs, eportfolios, and streaming media (e.g., podcasts), are common in the current generation of course management systems. They have evolved to include features of learning management that allow instructors to track data concerning students' use of instructional materials or other site features. Such information can help instructors determine which website usage patterns and behaviors correlate with student success in a course or series of courses, information they can share with students to help them navigate the course more effectively. (See Table 17.12.)

Even course management systems that contain only administrative features have the potential to guide instructors through a course-planning process anchored in effective pedagogy and adapted to diverse student needs. As instructors use course management systems to store and distribute information and engage students in online discussion, small changes in teaching may later become the impetus for more ambitious changes. For example, a language instructor at the University of Michigan started using a course management system to post a syllabus

[3] CTools is an advanced web-based environment that combines course management features with project and research collaboration features.

- Identify the features of a course management system you will use and decide how you will use them.
- Start with a few features if you are a novice user of the course management system.
- Provide specific instructions to students if you use online discussion or other interactive features.
- Set clear deadlines and enforce them if you use assignments, quizzing, and testing features.
- Be aware of student privacy and ethical issues when you use learning analytics generated by a course or learning management system.
- Allocate appropriate time for preparation if you decide to create online learning modules.
- Prepare students for the use of advanced features in a course management system and arrange student training if necessary.

TABLE 17.13 Tips for Using Course Management Systems

and make class announcements, but subsequently learned how to use online reference tools, as well as peer writing, critiquing, and online editing. It is comparatively easy to use a course management system to post a syllabus, lecture notes, assignments, and resources, but more complex features may require training (see Table 17.13).

Course management systems are particularly useful for distance learning. They provide "one-stop shopping" for the various tasks and resources that could otherwise become difficult to juggle without the face-to-face interaction with instructor and peers. Some learning management systems capture information and data about online students' behaviors, such as social presence in the online space, cognitive ability in completing the assigned work, and usage patterns in the learning environment, enabling the instructor to provide timely guidance to students who may have difficulties in the course.

Instructors can also create their own websites for teaching, taking advantage of tools such as reflective blogs and collaborative wikis to engage students in creative thinking, involve them in the development of content, or expose them to new ways of teaching and learning. For example, the Valley of the Shadow project (http://valley.vcdh.virginia. edu), which appeared on the web in the early 1990s, introduced a new way of learning and studying history. The technology skills required to start a simple course website are similar to those needed to create a multimedia presentation. Many wiki and blog tools like WordPress provide online templates ready for you to add content. Current HTML editors like Dreamweaver are also straightforward and easy to learn. If you wish to

- Allow plenty of lead time for planning the course and designing course webpages.
- Be sure that the course webpages are functional and contents are accessible to students with disabilities.
- If you have interactive activities on the course website, be sure that security and privacy issues are discussed and well understood by students.
- Have a back-up plan for lectures (e.g., also save critical information or images locally).
- Be well prepared for lecture when using your own course website, for example:
  - Verify links, especially the external links.
  - Check the room lighting to see if it is suitable for both viewing the projected screen and taking notes.
  - Check the set up (e.g., browser and software for audio/video and animation).
  - Arrange for technical support staff to be in your classroom at the start of class to help with the setup if necessary.
  - Always know whom to call for help if technical problems occur.
- Emphasize the need for filtering, interpreting, and evaluating information found on the Web when encouraging students to use online resources.
- Remind students that only a small fraction of the whole archive of knowledge is available on the web.

TABLE 17.14 Tips for Creating Course Websites

publish your pages on your institution's server, you will need to find out how to access designated spaces on the web server of your department or institution (see Table 17.14).

You can also build website creation into student projects. Creating their own websites and making their work available to a larger audience may motivate students to learn and raise their expectations about the quality of their work and the time they are willing to invest in a class. At the same time, such projects present challenges for both students and instructors. While students may be new to using this kind of medium for class projects, the instructor also might not have much experience designing or assessing this type of project (see Table 17.15).

For example, in "Zoom," a course in "Big History" at the University of Michigan, the professor guided students to see history through the perspectives of other disciplines, such as astronomy, geology, biology, and anthropology. Students worked in groups to create a set of wiki pages describing their discipline and examining how different disciplines relate to one another. Students collaborated across

- Work with students to define specific goals for webpages or other technology projects.
- Work with students to set up guidelines for student projects.
- Discuss expectations and standards for assessing student projects.
- Make student webpages or other technology projects an integral part of student learning experiences in the course.
- Encourage students to share and review one another's projects.
- Set periodic check-in points for a semester-long technology project.
- Arrange technology training for students if necessary.

TABLE 17.15 Tips for Assigning Student Technology Project

groups in order to create linkages, both literal hyperlinks and intellectual connections, among wiki pages and disciplines. The students found that the experience enhanced their intellectual and technical skills, and they were excited about creating work for a "real" audience. One student noted, "Asking us to create a knowledge base that's not only part of our grade but potentially viewed by hundreds of people encouraged us to research both the subject we were teaching and the audience we were catering to" (Northrop, 2011)[4].

TEACHING ONLINE OR AT A DISTANCE

Teaching at a distance may include all the technology tools listed above. In addition, distance learning courses can be delivered via videoconference systems (one- or two-way audio and video) as well as web-conferencing programs (such as Adobe Connect and Elluminate). Effective teaching strategies and good teaching practices work in all instructional situations. Instructors, whether teaching on campus, online or at a distance, will face similar challenges and issues. However, instructors teaching online or at a distance may encounter several additional challenges due to the lack of in-person contact with students, heavy reliance on technology for delivering instruction, and differences in student population. For example, online and distance teaching may require special attention to course planning, facilitation, and assessment of student learning.

---

[4] http://www.umich.edu/%7Eece/about.html#comments; this site contains useful directions for setting up a similar project.

A good start for an online or distance learning course is to develop a thoughtful plan that includes not only course goals and learning objectives, but also methods of teaching and assessing student learning outcomes. The following is a list of areas you may want to consider when planning an online or distance learning course. (See also chapter 2, "Countdown for Course Preparation.")

- Course design
  - Clearly defined course goals and measurable learning objectives
  - Meaningful activities (assignments) that help students reach learning objectives
  - Student and instructor responsibilities in learning and teaching
  - Level of student participation and involvement in the teaching/learning process
- Delivery of instruction
  - Methods of teaching that match well with course goals (e.g., case studies and pre-recorded or interactive lectures via web-conferencing program)
  - Technology tools that support teaching and learning activities (e.g., course management systems, blogs, wikis, threaded discussion forums, and synchronous chat rooms)
- Communication and interaction
  - Effective means of communication and interaction between instructor and students and among students themselves
  - Frequent feedback from and to students on teaching and learning
  - Supportive learning community for students to share and exchange (avoid leaving students in isolation)
- Assessment of student learning
  - Clear expectations and standards for assessment (aligned with learning objectives)
  - Variety of assessment methods that address different learning styles
  - Flexible assessment methods, but rigorous standards

Ideally, the online teaching/learning environment will provide ample opportunities not only for the dissemination of information, but also for the interaction that is so important for helping students to develop higher level thinking skills (e.g., through discussion, reflection, collaborative learning, interactive real-world case studies, etc.). Incorporating such strategies may challenge some teaching practices that you may have been using for years. This learning and teaching environment may also prompt you to take on a new role, that of a guide or facilitator, monitoring and supporting students and leading them through the process of information gathering, evaluation, and knowledge construction (Berge, 2000).

In addition, while a medium to high level of technological competency in using online tools (such as discussion forum, blogs, wikis, and tools for online grading and progress tracking) is optional for face-to-face teaching, it is now required for teaching online and at a distance. Thus, learning adequate skills and tactics for communicating with students, interacting with them, giving feedback, and responding to their needs are now essential for teaching effectively online or at a distance.

Some institutions offer faculty development programs for online or distance instructors, especially for those teaching this way for the first time. Those training programs often include principles for course design, effective practices and strategies for online teaching, facilitation, communication, and proper assessment methods. It is useful to participate in all or part of such programs to gain a deeper understanding of exactly what online teaching entails. Most higher education institutions also offer workshops and seminars on using course or learning management tools and other software programs for administering and facilitating online communication and discussion for either face-to-face or online and distance teaching. Research indicates that some part of faculty online or distance teaching training be conducted online (Ko and Rossen, 2001) in order to give faculty the experience of being online learners.

While preparing yourself for distance teaching (e.g., learning about technology tools and developing online communication and facilitation skills), it is important to think about your students and what activities you may create to enable them to study and learn effectively online or at a distance. Student backgrounds and preparation are always important factors in planning for teaching online or at a distance, as they are when you plan to integrate technology into teaching on campus.

HANDLING THE TECHNOLOGY BOOM

Finally, we need to mention Web 2.0 technology, especially social networking sites such as Facebook and cloud-based collaboration tools such Google Apps. These tools have already made their way into on-campus, online, and distance teaching and learning in higher education. The whole suite of Web 2.0 technology, and even newer and emerging technology tools that may appear tomorrow, may confuse us and leave us wondering about what to use or integrate into teaching. One of the effective ways to deal with this challenge is to apply the basic principle of integrating technology into teaching and learning we introduced at the start of this chapter. Technology decisions are essentially teaching and learning decisions. Therefore, when contemplating use of a new tool, you certainly need to understand the technology and its potential implications for teaching and learning; however, you also need to think carefully about your course goals and learning objectives, as well as the abilities and backgrounds of your students and how the technology will enhance your course and your students' learning. Finally, while you remain an expert in a field, a guide and a mentor to your students, technology tools and the new teaching and learning environment may change how and when you perform your role as an expert, mentor, and guide. You want to be able and ready to adjust yourself to teaching in this new and technology enabled environment.

WHAT IS THE IMPACT OF TECHNOLOGY ON TEACHING AND LEARNING?

According to a 2008 report, leaders in both higher education and business agree that technology has and will continue to have a significant impact on college teaching (The Economist Intelligence Unit, 2008). That trend has only accelerated in the past few years as technologies have proliferated and students have become ever more proficient in using them. Given the ubiquity of technology and the accelerating pace of change, it is important for faculty and institutions to have reliable data about the impact of technology. Data concerning how technologies can best support specific learning goals can inform institutional decisions about how best to invest resources. In addition, systematic research studies of teaching and learning with technology can help faculty avoid potential pitfalls in integrating technology into teaching. Areas for scholarship of teaching with technology could vary from examining students' learning outcomes and describing their strategies for engaging with technology, to investigating how technology affects pedagogies, strategies, and effectiveness of instructors. Some examples of faculty pursuing these types of questions can be found on the website for the Visible Knowledge Project (http://crossroads.georgetown.edu/vkp/), which focuses in part on applying methods from the scholarship of teaching and learning to technology. The website contains short descriptions of individual faculty projects that focus on a specific technology and its impact on student learning and attitudes. For example, faculty members are "examining under what classroom conditions one is more likely to create intellectual communities that mirror and cultivate disciplinary thinking" (Elmendorf and Ottenhoff, 2009).

Similar examples of faculty investigating student learning and the impact of technology can be found at the University of Michigan. One engineering professor is studying the impact of posting recordings of lectures along with homework and quiz solutions, on student learning, studying, and problem solving. A large-scale study focused on examining the use of a student response system (Qwizdom) in large lecture courses. With thousands of responses to the survey over several semesters, the study results helped generate a set of pedagogical guidelines for using clickers effectively in teaching (Zhu, 2007).

Faculty members are also researching new ways of teaching with technology and investigating the impact of new teaching structures on student learning. One faculty member, for instance, is experimenting with wikis and tracking their impact on student learning, especially on learning scientific and creative ways of thinking, which new technology supports and fosters well. Many institutions, such as Indiana University (http://citl.indiana.edu/programs/sotl/index.php) and Vanderbilt University, provide support in research design and methods, as well as other resources and grants for faculty who engage in scholarly research on teaching and learning.

As you think about conducting research on the impact of technology on your teaching and your students' learning, it is important that you consider the full range of changes technology may bring to the entire process of teaching and learning. The following questions are designed to help you start thinking about how you might evaluate the impact of technology on teaching and student learning in a course, curriculum, or a program.

- How did the use of technology help students achieve learning goals? Examples could include:
  - Demonstration of changes in student knowledge, skills, and attitudes (e.g., pre- and post-test results and comparison of student attitudes and learning outcomes before and after technology was integrated)
  - Demonstration of increased learning among subsets of students (e.g., students historically underrepresented in the discipline, non-majors, or those who did poorly in pre-requisite courses)
- How did the use of technology help change students' engagement in learning inside and outside of class?
  - Documentation of students' engagement during lecture (e.g., questions and answers) and outside of class (e.g., discussion or blog postings, quality of student postings and projects, tracking which subsets of students accessed lecture recordings most frequently)
  - Feedback or self-report of engagement in and outside of class

- How did the use of technology change teaching behaviors and practices? Examples of changes could include:
  - Amount of interaction between the instructor and students and among students themselves
  - Ways of addressing diverse learning styles
  - Lecture style (interactive or non-interactive)
  - Nature of student learning activities and assignments
  - Linkage of course content to real world
  - Amount and frequency of feedback to and from students
- How did the technology improve teaching effectiveness and efficiency? Examples could include:
  - Use of class time
  - Instructor's time on course preparation and management
  - Students' time on learning tasks
  - Access to course materials
  - Synchronous attendance and participation in class from off-site

IN CONCLUSION

The successful integration of technology entails careful consideration of course content, the capabilities of various technology tools, student access to and comfort with technology, and the instructor's view of his or her role in the teaching and learning process. The use of technology may change teaching methods and approaches to learning as well as attitudes, motivation, and interest in the subject. With careful thought and planning, faculty can take advantage of developments in instructional technology to enhance their courses, re-examine their own ideas about teaching, and promote greater student academic achievement.

Supplementary Readings

PowerPoint

- B. Brown, "PowerPoint-Induced Sleep," *Syllabus*, 2001, *14*(6), 17.
- T. Creed, *PowerPoint, No! Cyberspace, Yes*, 1999, available at http://www.ntlf.com/html/pi/9705/creed_1.htm.
- T. Rocklin, *PowerPoint Is Not Evil*, 1999, available at http://www.ntlf.com/html/sf/notevil.htm.
- E. R. Tufte, *The Cognitive Style of PowerPoint* (Cheshire, CT: Graphics Press, 2003).

- D. D. DuFrene and C. M. Lehman, "Concept, Content, Construction, and Contingencies: Getting the Horse Before the PowerPoint Cart," *Business Communication Quarterly*, 2004, *67*(1), 84–88.
- Y. Gabriel, "Against the Tyranny of PowerPoint: Technology-in-Use and Technology Abuse," *Organization Studies*, 2008, *29*(2), 255–276.

E-mail and Online Discussion

- T. Bender, *Discussion-Based Online Teaching to Enhance Student Learning: Theory, Practice, and Assessment* (Sterling, VA: Stylus, 2003).
- C. J. Bonk and K. S. King (eds.), *Electronic Collaborators: Learner-Centered Technologies for Literacy, Apprenticeship, and Discourse* (Mahwah, NJ: Erlbaum, 1998).
- D. Hanna, M. Glowacki-Dudka, and S. Conceicao-Runlee, *147 Practical Tips for Teaching Online Groups: Essentials of Web-Based Education* (Madison, WI: Atwood Publishing, 2000).
- S. Kleinman, "Strategies for Encouraging Active Learning, Interaction, and Academic Integrity in Online Courses," *Communication Teacher*, 2005, *19*(1), 13–18.
- C. MacKnight, "Teaching Critical Thinking through Online Discussions," available at http://net.educause.edu/ir/library/pdf/EQM0048.pdf.
- A. P. Rovai, "Strategies for Grading Online Discussions: Effects on Discussions and Classroom Community in Internet-Based University Courses," *Journal of Computing in Higher Education*, 2003, *15*(1), 89–107.
- G. Salmon, *E-Tivities: The Key to Active Online Learning* (London: Kogan Page, 2002).

Teaching with the Web

- S. Horton, *Web Teaching Guide: A Practical Approach to Creating Course Web Sites* (New Haven, CT: Yale University Press, 2000).
- B. H. Khan (ed.), *Web-Based Instruction* (Englewood Cliffs, NJ: Educational Technology Publications, 1997).
- G. R. Morrison, S. M. Ross, and J. E. Kemp, *Designing Effective Instruction* (New York: Wiley, 2001).
- EDUCAUSE Learning Initiative. 7 Things You Should Know About, 2005–2009. Available at http://www.educause.edu/ELI/ELIResources/7ThingsYouShouldKnowAbout/7495?bhcp=1.

Part 5

Skills for Use in Other Teaching Situations

Chapter 18

Teaching Large Classes (You Can Still Get Active Learning!)

In the middle of the 20th century, most first- and second-year courses were taught by lecture in large classrooms or auditoriums. Over the next decades, research demonstrated that better learning occurred if students had an opportunity to discuss the material. Thus, many large courses now supplement lectures with one or two hours of small-group discussion. However, with decreasing government support and increasing enrollments, more and more universities all over the world feel pressure to revert to large classes, without support from small discussion groups or tutorials.

Most of this chapter deals with skills and strategies useful in large groups, whether or not they are supplemented by discussion groups. Before concluding, I discuss aspects of the teacher's role involved in supervising teaching assistants who lead discussion or laboratory groups. Teaching assistants facilitate the smooth functioning of a large course. As they are the next generation of faculty, they should be included in this learning experience.

If you are assigned to teach a large course, you are likely to assume that you must lecture and use multiple-choice or other easily scorable tests, but large classes need not constrain you. You don't need to lecture—at least not all the time.

BLENDED LEARNING AS AN ALTERNATIVE STRATEGY

The advent of technology and its rapidly expanding capabilities are offering many institutions and faculty an alternative to only large lectures and multiple-choice testing. The alternative is not for everyone yet, but it's moving along quickly. This emerging concept is known as "blended learning," which describes courses that combine both face-to-face teaching and online learning. Some teachers implement this strategy by incorporating online discussions as part of a course that also includes in-person class discussions, but the concept is really bigger than that. Those who promote blended learning see it as matching the learning environment (e.g., tech based or not) with the learning goals (e.g., level of objectives) and the needs of the learner (e.g., preference or access). In a blended course, learners might have a choice of ways to take in information (e.g., via a textbook, a website, a lecture, a podcast) and have their learning evaluated (e.g., in-person test, remote site test, interview, written paper, podcast). This model goes beyond distance education or online learning in that it offers multiple alternatives and allows the learner to have some say in which is chosen. An interesting side observation on this point: As I was researching the literature to find some good ideas on this topic, I noticed that the bulk of the writing I found was from the international community, particularly from New Zealand and the Pacific Rim countries. I think this idea of blended learning is going to be a future direction that we all need to pay attention to, because it meets a lot of needs that education has right now, including cost, students served, public pressure, and optimal use of facilities. But it also might be able to allow us to match the instruction to the specifics of the learner more than we can now. Two of the most interesting pieces I read on this topic were De George-Walker and Keeffe (2010) from Australia who did a case study of blended learning course development that was aiming to make a course more learner centered; and Norberg, Dziuban, and Moskal (2011) from Sweden who proposed a model for instructional design that included all the dimensions of a blended course that others had mentioned, but added in the variable of time and synchronicity. However, right now most of us aren't there yet, so we'll move on to things we *can* do.

FACILITATING ACTIVE LEARNING

The most commonly used method of stimulating active learning in large courses is questioning and encouraging student questioning, as discussed in chapter 5, "Facilitating Discussion" and chapter 6, "How to Make Lectures More Effective." But many other tools in your active learning kit are usable in large classes. In chapter 14 "Active Learning: Group-Based Learning," I reported the research showing that students learn more in student-led discussions, or in learning cells, than they learn in traditional lectures. Thus, you can get the advantages of a multisection course by organizing students to meet in class or out of class for discussion. Active learning does not need to be restricted to in-class activity. You can organize study groups. You can use e-mail or online discussion boards. The chapter "Technology and Teaching" describes ways in which technology can facilitate learning both in and out of class.

Techniques such as think-pair-share, question posting, and the two-column method of large-group discussions were also described earlier. Small groups (described in the chapter "Facilitating Discussion") can be formed and asked to discuss how the material might be used or applied. Simply pausing occasionally to give students a couple of minutes to compare their notes can activate thinking (Ruhl, Hughes, and Schloss, 1987).

It is still possible, even using these techniques, for students to hold back in large classes, but technology may be coming to your rescue. Recent advances in wireless technology make it possible to have every student in the class actively respond to questions and problems using the personal response systems (clickers), as discussed in the chapters on technology and on lecturing. This procedure can also be done in groups, with each group's response rather than an individual's response entered on the keypad. The system can be used to take roll or simply to give the students an active learning opportunity. One of the most thorough and rigorous studies of clickers was done by Richard Mayer (2009). The study compared clicker-based questioning with just questions handed out on paper, answered by the students, collected and then discussed, and no questioning at all. Students in the clicker group showed a higher gain in understanding than the others. Those results were also found by Shaffer and Collura (2009); and Stowell (2007) found that students using clickers had a better emotional reaction to the situation as well. There are many other variables that need to be systematically studied before we know what really produces the better result, but I think you can use them without fear of adverse results, and with confidence you'll very likely achieve positive results. Of course, you can go low tech and just have students raise their hands or hold up a colored card to vote for an option, but it's not nearly as effective and there's no permanent record or visual summary available. But in a pinch, it still gets students responding.

Encouraging Student Writing in Large Classes

One of the most important drawbacks of large classes is the lack of student writing as active learning. Because grading essays is so time consuming, most faculty members reduce or eliminate writing assignments in a large class. Take heart! You can get some of the educational advantages of writing, and at the same time improve attention to the lecture, without being submerged by papers to grade.

The minute paper, described earlier, or the half sheet response described by Weaver and Cotrell (1985) are both useful tools for getting more writing as a way to learn. At an appropriate point in the lecture, announce the paper and the topic or question you want students to address; for example, you might ask the students to summarize the major point or points made so far in the lecture. Or you might give the students a choice of formats, such as writing a summary, a question, an application, or an example. When the time is up, you collect the papers or break the class into pairs or subgroups to review and discuss one another's papers.

Although I don't have a lot of research on this yet, social media are starting to be used as learning tools. One that might be particularly useful in large classes is instant messaging or tweeting. Of the reports I've seen to this point, Rockinson-Szapkiw and Szapkiw (2011) gave some good examples of how this could be done. One was similar to clickers, but with less restriction on the type of questions you can ask. They suggest using social media for in-class and out-of-class discussion. I've actually seen a video of this being done by a history professor in a large class. As she was discussing a topic, she invited students to tweet "reasonable" reactions to the ideas she posed. Those tweets were posted to the screen where everyone could see them, and she could make an immediate summary of what students were thinking or correct misconceptions. One advantage this has is that you can track who said what, in case you want to offer points for particularly good posts.

If you wish, you can evaluate and comment on any of these types of contributions as you would any other student work. Students can be motivated to think and write without the threat of grades, and this technique not only gets students thinking actively during the lecture, but also gives you feedback about what students are learning from the lecture.

The problem with evaluating these contributions in a large class is the huge amount of work that it causes for the instructor. However, I find that after reading a sample of answers, I can give generic feedback to the whole class in the form of general comments posted on the class website or brought up at the next class period. Students can then compare their efforts to these general comments.

If you are having students write brief papers, another alternative is the calibrated peer review system, first discussed by Robinson (2001) as a way to increase writing in large biology classes. In this computer-based system, students review one another's papers online in a grand randomized sequencing scheme. Each student is assigned to review three other students' written work, and receives three reviews of his or her own work in return. Each student's review of other students is weighted according to a calibration system and his or her contribution to the papers is figured accordingly. One advantage to this system is that the act of reviewing someone else's work can help the reviewer learn about his or her own writing.

STUDENT ANONYMITY

A major problem of teaching a large class is that students not only *feel* anonymous, they usually *are* anonymous. And as social psychological research has shown, people who are anonymous feel less personal responsibility—a consequence not only damaging to morale and order but also unlikely to facilitate learning. Moreover, the sense of distance from the instructor, and the loss of interpersonal bonds with the instructor and with other students often diminish motivation for learning.

The larger the group, the less likely that a given student will feel free to volunteer a contribution or question. Yet the students who prefer anonymity may be the very ones who most need to find that others respect their ideas.

What can we do? With increasing class size it becomes less and less possible to know students as individuals, and this fact is likely to make us feel that it is not worth trying to do anything. I think this is a mistake. In my experience, the students appreciate whatever efforts you make, even if they do not take advantage of them. The "Reducing Students' Feelings of Anonymity" box shows some things I've tried.

As we've seen in other contexts, you can use technology to your advantage in this aspect of teaching as well. For example, if you have students in your large class do minute papers and turn them in, you can send emails to students who write something that really strikes you as insightful or hitting the mark or that you want to acknowledge (Lucas, 2010). These don't have to be long, but it makes a connection to that student. Isbell and Cote (2009) actually did a study comparing subsequent performance of students who had done poorly on an early assignment and received a personal email expressing concern, compared to those not receiving one. The former group did better on subsequent assignments. Remember that you don't have to do every person every time, but some outreach sometime during the semester might make a huge difference in a large class, especially for students who are feeling lost.

If you don't want to (or can't) reduce student anonymity during the class period itself, you might consider encouraging students to form study groups outside of class. At least they will have a small number of classmates who they know and who know them. Some large-class instructors try to help students with this group formation by using technology to create a sort of mass calendar. Students who want to study at a particular time can consult the calendar and sign up to be available for studying at that time. Others who consult the calendar can see who is available when or where and get together with those other students at a time that fits their schedule.

ORGANIZATION IS THE KEY

The biggest challenges of teaching a large class are related to being organized. With a large class you can't do things very spontaneously; things have to be planned or they will flounder. What follows are some of the areas in which organization can make or break a class.

Giving Tests in Large Classes

In classes of 200 students or more, unwary instructors are likely to run into problems they would never dream of in teaching classes with an enrollment of twenty to thirty. Most of these problems are administrative. For example, course planning almost inevitably becomes more rigid in a large class because almost anything involving the participation of the students requires more preparation time.

Perhaps you're used to making up your tests the day before you administer them. With a large class this is almost impossible. Essay and short-answer tests that take relatively little time to construct take a long time to score for 200 students; so you may spend long hours trying to devise thought-provoking objective questions for a part of the test. But once you've made up the questions your troubles are not over, for office staff or your teaching assistant (TA) may require a good deal of time to make several hundred copies of a test. Thus, spur-of-the-moment tests are almost an impossibility, and by virtue of the necessity of planning ahead for tests, other aspects of the course also become more rigid.

Communicating with Large Classes

Of course, the most important aspect of teaching a large class is being able to maintain up-to-date communication with such a large number of people. Being certain that every student has the latest word on class or assignment changes, deadlines, and exams can be challenging. I can't stress enough the value of having a class website or class management system like Blackboard for a large class. Operating as information and communication central for the class, the website is available to students 24/7, so you don't have to be. In addition, most course management

Reducing Students' Feelings of Anonymity

1. Announce that you'll meet any students who are free for coffee after class. (You won't be swamped.)
2. Pass out invitations to several students to join you for coffee and to get acquainted after class.
3. Pass out brief student observation forms to several students at the beginning of class and ask them to meet with you to discuss their observations.
4. Circulate among early-arriving students to get acquainted before class starts.
5. Use a seating chart so that you can call students by name when they participate. If the room is set up with continuous desktop seating rather than tablet style seats, give each student a name tent and have them put it in front of them each class period. I make these tents do double duty by printing suggestions for active learning on the side facing the student. Of course, you have to be able to see and read the tents for this to work.
6. During your lecture, move out into the aisles to solicit comments.
7. If you can't use regularly scheduled discussion sections, set up an occasional afternoon or evening session for more informal discussion of an interesting question or for review before an examination.
8. Have students fill out an autobiographical sketch with name, hometown, year in college, and what they hope to get out of the course (Benjamin, 1991).
9. Create a set of flash cards with students' names on one side and their pictures on the other. Study them during odd moments, like when standing in lines or when on hold on the phone. Many institutions have started providing a photo roster of the class for the instructor. This saves a lot of time, but there is one caveat. You'd be surprised how often the live student looks nothing like his or her photo!
10. When students are working in groups regularly, you can learn the names of all the students in the group as a set. Then remembering any one student's name may trigger recall of all of them. I create group cards with the students' pictures on one side and their names on the other.

software systems have group e-mail functions that allow you to send out a single notice to the entire class in a single e-mail without it getting blocked by spam-blocking programs. Course websites will always have the latest word on course organization and the latest versions of any course handouts, so you will not need to constantly re-announce changes during class time. As students start asking questions via e-mail or on a class discussion board, you can gather all the similar questions together and post answers to them on the website, where students can be encouraged to look first for answers to their questions before coming to you. My own university made it a policy that e-mail and class websites are now considered official communication formats of the university.

Technology also helps you with managing office hours. For example, you can have an electronic appointment scheduler for students who want to visit you during office hours. A student checks the calendar, finds an open spot that matches his or her schedule, and registers for that time slot. Or you can hold "virtual office hours" by being available online at announced times. Any student who wants to "chat" can log in and ask questions from a distance. You have the advantage of being able to continue working from anywhere your computer is because it will announce that someone is online and wants to chat.

COORDINATING MULTISECTION COURSES

In any multisection course taught by several different instructors or TAs, the problem of coordination inevitably arises. The first approach to coordination is enforced uniformity of course content, sequence of topics, testing, grading, and even examples. Such a procedure has the advantage that students who later elect more advanced courses can be presumed to have a certain uniform amount of background experience. It is also efficient in that only one final examination must be constructed, only one course outline devised, and students can transfer from section to section with no difficulty in catching up. It also circumvents problems that arise when students complain about unequal treatment.

The disadvantage of this approach is that such uniformity often makes for dull, uninteresting teaching. If the instructors or teaching assistants are unenthusiastic about the course outline, they are likely to communicate this attitude to the students. If the course can be jointly planned, this may make for greater acceptance, but may also take a great deal of time.

A second approach to this problem is to set up completely autonomous sections, with all the instructors or TAs organizing and conducting their sections as they wish. The effectiveness of giving TAs that much autonomy depends on how well you train and supervise them.

TRAINING AND SUPERVISING TEACHING ASSISTANTS

Your responsibility begins well before the first class meetings, for your teaching assistants need to know what you are expecting in terms of attendance at lectures, participation in weekly planning and training sessions, testing and grading, office hours, and such. At my institution we have a checklist of possible TA responsibilities. At the beginning of the semester the TA and the supervising professor sit down together and work through their expectations and work assignments. Both sign and get a copy of the checklist so that there is no confusion later about what was expected and when.

Even more important than the formal requirements are the aspects of preparing the teaching assistants for meeting their first classes, establishing a good working relationship with their students, and developing the skills needed for leading discussions, answering questions, and carrying out other teaching responsibilities. Here are some suggestions for assisting teaching assistants:

1. Hold weekly meetings to discuss teaching problems and plans.
2. Collect feedback from students early in the term.
3. Observe classes and discuss your observations with the TA.

To get student feedback, you can use simple open-ended questions, such as:

"What have you liked about the class so far?"

"What suggestions do you have for improvement?"

Visiting classes or videotaping can provide useful information about nonverbal characteristics of the teacher and reactions of the students. But observation or videotaping takes time. If you have time, visit classes, but if you are short of time, there is little evidence that videotaping or observation results in significantly greater improvement in teaching than consultation on student ratings collected early in the term (and perhaps repeated a little later). So if you're short on time, invest it in consultation.

IN CONCLUSION

Class size is important.

When taught appropriately, small classes are likely to be better than large classes for achieving long-term goals, such as retention and use of knowledge, thinking, and attitude change.

Nonetheless, when dealing with large classes, you can come closer to the outcomes of small classes by:

1. Providing discussion sections taught by trained teaching assistants
2. Using teaching methods that facilitate active, meaningful learning

The fact that in a large class you will probably spend some of the time lecturing does not mean that students can now slip into passivity. What is important in active learning is active *thinking*. The techniques discussed in this and preceding chapters can produce active thinking and learning even in large lecture halls.

Supplementary Reading

Because almost every large university now has a program for training teaching assistants, there was a biennial meeting on training, and the papers from the meeting were typically published. The first volume is still one of the best:

- J. D. Nyquist, R. D. Abbott, D. H. Wulff, and J. Sprague (eds.), *Preparing the Professoriate of Tomorrow to Teach: Selected Readings in TA Training* (Dubuque, IA: Kendall/Hunt, 1991).

For teaching large classes:

- Jean MacGregor, James L. Cooper, Karl A. Smith, and Pamela Robinson (eds.), "Strategies for Energizing Large Classes: From Small Groups to Learning Communities," *New Directions for Learning and Teaching*, no. 81, May 2000.
- T. Gray and L. Madson (2007) "Ten ways to engage your students." *College Teaching*, 55(2), 83–87.
- C. Stanly and M. E. Porter (eds.), *Engaging Large Classes: Strategies and Techniques for College Faculty* (Bolton, MA: Onker Publishing, 2002).
- R. J. Sternberg (ed.), *Teaching Introductory Psychology: Survival Tips from the Experts* (Washington, DC: American Psychological Association, 1997).

For technology use:

- R. Mayer, et al. (2009) "Clickers in College Classrooms: Fostering Learning with Questioning Methods in Large Lecture Classes." *Contemporary Educational Psychology*, 34(1), 52–57.
- A. Norberg, C. Dzuiban, and P. Moskal (2011) "A Time-Based Blended Learning Model." *On the Horizon*, 19(3), 207–216.

Chapter 19

Laboratory Instruction: Ensuring an Active Learning Experience

Laboratory instruction permits learners to experience phenomena directly as well as understand how new knowledge is constructed. Although laboratory instruction derives from the revered apprenticeship model for learning practical arts, it is certainly not limited to the traditional "wet laboratories" of the physical and natural sciences. From practicum experiences in psychology and education, to studios in the fine and performance arts, instructors create learning environments where students can ask questions and seek answers modeled on the way in which professionals do their work. Historically, the latter performance-based disciplines do an intrinsically better job of engaging beginning students in authentic work (drawing, writing, acting) than the sciences do in getting students to do scientific inquiry and investigation.

Laboratory teaching assumes that firsthand experience is superior to other methods of developing the same skills. Laboratory instruction also presumes that the next generation of practitioners will be motivated by an opportunity to participate in practice. The prevailing rhetoric of "learning by doing" characterizes the passionate attachment that faculty have to this form of teaching.

Laboratory instruction presents a common dilemma about instructional design, namely, the balance between convergent and divergent assignments. Convergent laboratory design, where developing careful

---

This chapter was written by Brian Coppola of the University of Michigan.

manipulative skills can only be evaluated by comparison with robust, well-tested standards (i.e., the right answer) is criticized for simply validating results that are repeated year in and year out all over the world by students using rote, locked-step, or "cookbook" procedures. In an art class, this might be the faithful reproduction of an existing work, while in an engineering class it might be the duplication of a particularly challenging construct. Divergent design, by contrast, leaves open the interpretation of both questions and answers, and features the attributes of authentic research, such as hands-on, "mind's-on" work, individualized experimental design or decision making combined with collaborative tasks, and should all theoretically contribute positively to learning about the process of constructing knowledge and solving new problems.

Authentic, research-based information is hard earned, emerges over extended periods of time, and would appear to be inefficiently gained in comparison with abstractions presented in more traditional instruction. Thus, one would not expect laboratory instruction to have an advantage over teaching methods whose strength is in rapidly transmitting large amounts of factual information. Rather, one might expect the difference to be revealed in retention, in ability to apply learning, or in actual skill in experimental design, observation, or manipulation of materials and equipment.

Laboratory instruction also raises an opportunity to incorporate issues that are naturally aligned with practice, such as procedural safety, which ranges from the manipulation and proper handling of concentrated chemical substances to ethical human-subjects issues. Increasingly, formal discussion of research ethics concerning practices such as data handling, laboratory management, authorship, and peer review is being encouraged for beginning and advanced students alike (Arkright-Keeler and Stapleton, 2007; Coppola, 2000; Kovac, 1999; Sweeting, 1999), particularly as federal policies are increasingly raising the bar for informed practice.

STYLES OF LABORATORY INSTRUCTION

In an attempt to define different instructional goals and their corresponding methodologies, Domin (1999) created a taxonomy of laboratory instruction styles which, though originally based in chemistry, holds up well across many disciplines. Explicit analogies with other areas are not provided here, for they are beyond the scope of this chapter. However, it is important to note that these methods are not simple, neutral choices. Students' early laboratory experiences, which are strongly influenced by instructional design, are often the critical gateway for the level of experience or self-confidence that influences their decisions to persist (or not) in the sciences, particularly in the cases of women and underrepresented minorities (Seymour and Hewitt, 1997; Eccles, 1994). Instructional designs that favor cooperative environments with individual accountability, opportunities for creative design and expression, and chances for reflection and analysis all contribute to positive, motivating experiences which, in turn, favor persistence and continuation.

Domin's categories are expository instruction, inquiry instruction, discovery instruction, and problem-based learning.

Expository Instruction

The most popular and most criticized expository instruction features verification of pre-ordained results and an emphasis on manipulation skills, and it asks students to follow exactly prescribed directions (or "cookbook" procedures). A pre-laboratory session sets out what is to be observed and how to do it. Post-laboratory sessions review and recapitulate the information. In general, the goal for this kind of instruction is for students to develop manipulative or kinesthetic skills. In a typical activity used both in high school and in college, students might all receive a block of aluminum and be asked to follow an exact procedure for determining its density, the value of which is provided. Students follow precise directions, often filling in a worksheet with numerical values according to a prescribed script. The presumption is that a student who has successfully followed the procedure and arrived at the expected answer has also learned something about measurement and how it is done.

Expository instruction can be done on a large scale with minimal engagement by the instructor, it is largely impervious to variation in who does it, and it minimizes cost, space, and equipment. Unfortunately, it also may be true that almost no meaningful learning takes place (Hofstein and Lunetta, 1982), despite the manipulative or technical skills that might be gained.

Inquiry Instruction

In inquiry instruction, without a predetermined outcome, students are asked to formulate their own problem from the information at hand; in doing so, they mimic the process of constructing knowledge. The density activity might begin with a question posed to the students who have been given different-sized samples of the same metal: "What is the relationship between mass and volume in this material?" Different procedures for measuring volume are provided, and the results derived from these different methods are compared. Students have more choice in design and more responsibility in making sense of their results, and they must generally face more directly the importance of reproducibility in making measurements. Follow-up questions are either posed by the teacher ("Is density an intrinsic or extrinsic property?") or elicited from the students ("Is the density of all metals the same?").

Inquiry instruction is a compromise between closed- and open-ended instruction favored by national recommendations (National Research Council, 2000). In a practical sense, it is difficult to keep inquiry laboratories vital because it is difficult to conceal the details of the solutions to these problems from one generation of students to the next without a great deal of effort. Also, the drive to make the teaching process easier can slowly turn these inquiries into exposition.

Discovery Instruction

In discovery instruction, also called "guided inquiry," the teacher constructs an instructional setting with a prescribed outcome in mind and directs students toward that outcome. Discovery instruction seeks to make knowledge more personal for students and thereby more highly owned. Adapting the density experiment to discovery mode might begin with a pre-laboratory discussion in which the exercise is introduced by a question: "What measurements can be made to determine the physical properties of materials?" The students are encouraged to make predictions, formulate hypotheses, and then design experiments. All the while, the instructor controls the discussion, steering students toward the information from prior classes, including different mass-to-volume relationships as potentially useful quantities. The instructor also uses these opportunities to evaluate the experimental designs suggested by the students, motivating them with the sense of ownership and curiosity about the undetermined result, and inevitably guides the discussion toward the preplanned experiment. Students work individually or in groups, with enough variation in their activities for the class to pool their results. Afterward, the discussion led by the instructor moves the class to the intended lesson. Discovery-based instruction can invest the student in his or her own learning and can result in deeper understanding (Horowitz, 2003).

Problem-Based Learning

Problem-based learning (PBL) creates a context for students to generate their own questions, but it does so with strong foregrounding by the instructor (Albanese and Mitchell, 1993). PBL is popular across many disciplines. An instructor crafts and selects evidence and then presents the case study to the students, who in turn uncover what the faculty member has in mind as the root lessons.

Meta-lessons about doing research can be abstracted and returned as a PBL framework for collaborative, open-ended exercises (Coppola, 1995).

The density activity would begin with black enamel paint concealing the color of a group of differently shaped metal pieces. Wenzel's (1995, 1998) analytical chemistry program is noteworthy for its emphasis on framing a term-long investigation, often addressing a problem of high community interest (such as air quality) as the context for students to develop authentic investigative, procedural, and communications skills. The significant aspects of PBL include the following:

1. They are then expected to design experiments to solve the question. In this case, each student gets a different piece of metal; instead of asking students to identify the metal, which is far outside of their experience to design, the instructor asks them to determine who else in class has the same metal as they do.

2. It requires the class to make group decisions about the experiments they carry out, how they are going to share the information, and what the standards of reasonable comparison need to be. The class might select density as the property to measure. Students will need to decide on units of measurement, how many trials must be done, and what will constitute "the same" and "different" (Mills et al., 2000).

3. The students might request to do chemical tests on other samples of the metals in order to collect data. They might choose hardness, malleability, color (after scraping), or some combination of these after initial groups have been made.

4. Exposition and inquiry both have roles in carrying out an individual's work. Procedures for carrying out a known process should be able to be followed. Yet the purpose for collecting information (density) remains focused squarely on the goal (who has the same?) rather than on the measurement for its own sake.

5. Students need to decide how to share their data and how they will make their conclusions. Samples may be exchanged and tested independently if there are outlying data points or if some students have a hard time reproducing their experiments.

6. Inquiry inevitably leads to new questions. Once the relative identification is made and the students have grouped themselves according to the convergence of measured properties, new questions can be posed or elicited: "What are the identities of these metals?" "Is this information enough, or is other information needed?"

Relative identification is a widely applicable strategy for making problems. In chemistry, one might ask who has the same solid, liquid, mixture, or concentration of acid. In mathematics, one might ask who has numbers in the same type of series. In psychology, one might ask who has the same personality type; in the history of art, who has a painting from the same period; and in English, who has a paragraph with the same structure.

Some formal heuristics developed for learners in laboratory settings have demonstrated success. One of these is POE (Predict-Observe-Explain) (Champagne, Klofper, and Anderson, 1980); another is the MORE (Model-Observe-Reflect-Explain) (Tien, Rickey, and Stacy, 1999) method, which was developed for formal laboratory modules. Case studies are a kind of PBL that begin by posing questions based on a news headline ("Two would-be chemists die in explosion while attempting to make methamphetamine") and turning the case into a structured activity (Bieron and Dinan, 2000).

STUDIO INSTRUCTION BRINGS TOGETHER THE ARTS AND SCIENCES

Studio instruction is a ubiquitous method in art, architecture, and design (Zehner et al., 2010). Theory and practice combine when students can seamlessly move between instruction, design, questioning, testing, generating, and revising. Positive benchmarks from The Studio Teaching Project (www.studioteaching.org) include quality projects, positive community, high student engagement, commitment and interaction, and connections with industry and the profession. In Australia, there has been a significant growth in community-based project organized around the studio concept (Higgins, 2009).

The studio concept has emerged as a more generalized method, and provides a way to think about integrating the traditionally separated modes of lecture and laboratory (practicum) teaching in other disciplines. St. Edwards University (Austin, Texas) set aside the traditional class structure and uses two four-hour lab periods so that students are able to "act as scientists and learn as a scientist learns" (Altmiller, 1973). The University of North Carolina at Charlotte's inquiry-based "intimately meshed" lecture and lab (DiBiase and Wagner, 2002) and North Carolina State University's cAcL2 (concept Advancement through chemistry Lab-Lecture) active learning environment (Oliver-Hoyo et al., 2004) are other examples. A group of four chemistry departments—at California Polytechnic Institute (Bailey et al., 2000), Rensselaer Polytechnic Institute (Apple and Cutler, 1999), California State University at Fullerton (Gonzalez et al., 1999), and the State University of West Georgia (Khan et al., 2003)—adopted the studio teaching method, inspired in part by the studio in the RPI physics department (Wilson, 1994). The engineering disciplines, in general, have embraced studio instruction as a standard option (Crawley et al., 2007) in an overall design structure characterized as CDIO (Conceive, Design, Implement, and Operate). The benefits of studio instruction include increased student engagement (Fiford et al., 2011).

In general, adopting studio instruction has also involved remodeling the physical space in order to accommodate these pedagogical changes. The University of Michigan has experimented with the question of bringing this nontraditional instructional style into a traditional setting in order to lower the barrier for others who might not wish (or be able) to make the capital investment (Gottfried et al., 2003). In one intriguing large-scale study, the Michigan team observed that the benefits from their studio class, which were substantial for retaining at-risk students in particular, were more or less the same as for those students who were concurrently registered in the traditional (unlinked) lecture and laboratory classes; these results raised a significant cost-benefit question for the implementation of the studio option (Matz et al., 2010).

In a studio, learning and practice are intimately integrated and take place in the same space, so that transitions between theory and practice are unhindered (Perkins, 2005). Programs that seek to integrate the lecture and laboratory components of classes are constantly being developed (Gruenbacher, Natarajan, and Kuhn, 2006; Dunnivant et al., 2000), which speaks to the strong belief for the importance for combining the theoretical with the practical, or combining the knowledge with the ways in which knowledge is constructed. In the sciences, a studio implies an environment where students have access to concepts, problem solving, and experiments in the same space—and practice and theory are inseparable; interactive, hands-on experiences deliver fast results; and students use the results from one inquiry to pose questions, then design and carry out the next investigation. As in an art class, studio instruction in the sciences focuses on the artifacts created by students as the basis for discussion and further work. The studio teaching method is especially appealing because it does not limit itself to a single type of best practice. Instead, it allows mixing and matching of proven ways of teaching concepts.

The breaking of the tradition of centralized authority in teaching and learning coincides with society's demands for increasing the diversity of people who are prepared to do (or understand) science and technology. This is fortunate, because many believe that this increase can be accomplished by designing classrooms that foster success both broadly and inclusively. Seymour and Hewitt (1997) showed that "the most effective way to improve retention among women and students of color, and to build their numbers over the longer term, is to improve the quality of the learning experience for all students—including non-science majors who wish to study science and mathematics as part of their overall education." They also found that while almost all students value collaborative learning, students from underrepresented groups "appreciate it more and miss it when [it is] unavailable."

TURNING NOVICE RESEARCHERS INTO PRACTICING SCIENTISTS

The goals for upper-level laboratories may be quite different from those for lower-level laboratories, where professional development for a specialized workforce makes sense. Upper-level students who have access to better instrumentation or other resources can be asked to generate a more open-ended question derived from their entire undergraduate program. Not only can they prepare a proposal, but class members can also be asked to peer review and critique each other's work. After the work is completed (or attempted), the results can be made public via web publication or poster sessions to which other students and faculty respond (Henderson and Buising, 2000).

As illustrated previously, traditional verification laboratories can be adapted to more inquiry and open-ended activities. More than that, in recent years, there has been a strong movement to integrate more authentic research activities into the undergraduate program, not only in the form of undergraduate research projects, but also these to occur within the formal classroom structure of laboratory classes (National Science Foundation, 2003). Examples can be found throughout the sciences, including, for example, in chemistry (Center for Authentic Science Practice in Education, 2009), Geological Sciences (O'Reilly, 2002), Information Sciences (Becker, 2005), and the Biological Sciences (Eves et al., 2007).

Within the disciplines, undergraduate participation in research is probably as old as the integration of laboratory instruction into U.S. universities (Miller, 2008). Starting in the 1990s, there has been a growth of overarching institutional structures to recruit and support students in undergraduate research, which makes it easier for faculty members and students (particularly first- and second-year students) to connect with each other.

Miller (2008) points to the American Chemical Society's Committee on Professional Training, which described the following pedagogical goals for undergraduate research: a clearly communicated purpose and potential outcomes, well-defined objectives and methods (substantial in scope instead of a collection of small projects), reasonable chance of completion in the available time, contact with the professional literature, avoiding repetitive work, requiring use of advanced concepts, requiring a variety of techniques, culminating in a comprehensive report, introducing students to the standards of normative practice (including research ethics) in the discipline. The Council on Undergraduate Research (CUR, 2009) provides excellent guidelines, advice, and communication on this topic.

WET, DRY, AND *IN SILICO*

Experimental scientists, in general, believe that there is something fundamentally important about students getting first-hand experience in the way laboratory experiments are carried out, and that this is an indispensable, core understanding about the nature of science. Interestingly, there is no solid research base that supports this view, and the pressure to move away from traditional "wet" science laboratories is growing because they are timing consuming and costly in an era when enrollments are up and budgets are down. And as the diversity of experimental techniques continues to grow, it becomes increasingly more difficult to provide a comprehensive view of any area at all. The pressure to explore options is high.

"Dry" laboratories are environments where the raw experimental data are provided, and students need to work through the analyses but not the data collection. These are an attractive alternative, particularly for those students in the introductory program who are not intending to go on in the field. Because this approach saves time, it is argued that the students can have access to a far larger pool of data than they ever would if they were required to obtain it firsthand, and thus they benefit from increased analytical skills (Baker and Verran, 2004). Another growing area is the development of computer-based laboratory simulators, where students can practice planning and carrying out activities—often with highly sophisticated results. Students can work in cyber-environments that require them to doing everything from gathering and assembling their laboratory equipment, to dealing with the consequences of making mistakes, which would otherwise be dangerous in an actual lab setting. There is simply not enough known about the effects of these different approaches on the array of items that might be examined, such as experimental design, understanding the nature of science, and developing manipulative laboratory skills.

WHAT RESEARCH SAYS

The theoretical context for laboratory instruction is called situated learning (Lave and Wegner, 1991), which argues that the context in which learning takes place matters, so that learning about a laboratory science is more meaningful in a laboratory setting, and that research settings—because they are the most authentic context—provide the best environments for learning.

Individual studies make differential claims about the efficacy of one kind of laboratory instruction over another (Arce and Betancourt, 1997; Higginbotham, Pike, and Rice, 1998), but there is no general consensus about how one design gains advantage over another. Gains have been observed when students process information in the manner of experts in a laboratory that has an authentic design (Coppola, Ege, and Lawton, 1997). Such students are more intrinsically motivated by the course, and they develop better strategies for meaningful learning. Gains in both student learning and attitudes toward science have been reported from using the studio format in a high school setting (Faro and Swan, 2006).

Studies on the effects of undergraduate research are helping to motivate more research-based work in standard class settings. Students who participate in research gain concrete skills (such as using the primary literature, interpreting data, and communicating results) (Bauer and Bennett, 2003; Kardash, 2000), as well as benefits to their cognitive, personal, and professional development (Hunter, Laursen, and Seymour, 2007). These students show greater persistence in science (Hathaway, Nagda, and Gregerman, 2002; Kremer and Bringle, 1990), and particularly there is a greater chance for retaining students from historically underrepresented populations (Nagda et al., 1998).

Finally, despite positive findings that support the use of inquiry to teach concepts, changing methodology alone is not a panacea. Without carefully planning to integrate the entire student population, and without serious commitment from instructors and institutions, reform-based efforts can backfire, favoring the students who are more immune to deficiencies of their instructional environment, and may actually increase achievement gaps—typically disadvantaging exactly those students whom we wish to interest and motivate (Von Secker and Lissitz, 1999; Von Secker, 2002).

IN CONCLUSION

Laboratory instruction is a complex activity that needs to be examined closely and systematically. However, perhaps because expository instruction is so poor at promoting engaged and deeper learning, nearly any strategy that promotes more active learning and decision making by students is observed to produce learning gains. As is so often true, not only should the goals that one has for an instructional intervention be stated explicitly, but their alignment with the instructional methodology must be carefully managed.

Supplementary Reading

N. A. Glasgow's *New Curriculum for New Times: A Guide to Student-Centered, Problem-Based Learning* (Thousand Oaks, CA: Corwin Press, 1998) is an easily read and adaptable introduction.

V. L. Lechtanski's *Inquiry-Based Experiments for Chemistry* (New York: Oxford University Press, 2000) provides useful, explicit translations of standard experiments to inquiry-based methods.

L. C. McDermott and the Physics Education Group at the University of Washington, *Physics by Inquiry*, vol. 1 and vol. 2 (New York: Wiley, 1996) provide the best examples of instructional laboratory design based on disciple-centered educational research.

Student-Active Science (http://helios.hampshire.edu/~apmNS/sas_book.html) is a rich and multidisciplinary resource written by leaders in the field.

A. Hofstein, V. N. Lunetta, "The Laboratory in Science Education: Foundations for the Twenty-first Century" *Science Education* 2004, *88*(1), 28–54, is an update to the critical review of the research on the school science laboratory that they did in the early 1980s.

Part 6

Teaching for Higher-Level Goals

Teaching Students How to Become More Strategic and Self-Regulated Learners

Chapter 20

For many years, the study of student learning was divorced from the study of teaching. Good teaching practices were assumed to be universals that did not depend on individual differences among students or on teaching students how to study, learn, and think about course content. But these are exciting times for college instructors and students! Findings in educational and cognitive psychology have changed our views of the teaching/learning process and provide both conceptual and practical information about the ways that students learn and how instructors can use this information to inform their teaching practices. We now know that it is the interaction of good instructional practices with students' tactical use of learning strategies and skills, motivational processes, and self-regulation that results in positive learning outcomes (Weinstein, Acee, and Jung, 2011; Weinstein, Husman, and Dierking, 2000).

However, many college students do not know how to learn the content in the different domain areas they study. All instructors have some implicit or explicit conceptions or theories about what it means to learn

---

This chapter was written by Claire Ellen Weinstein of the University of Texas at Austin, Taylor W. Acee of Texas State University–San Marcos, Nancy Stano of the University of Texas at Austin, Debra K. Meyer of Elmhurst College, Jenefer Husman of Arizona State University, Wilbert J. McKeachie of the University of Michigan, and Cynthia A. King of Professional Research Consultants.

and think in their own discipline. Helping students become aware of these conceptions is an important aspect of teaching. As students learn subject matter, they also need to learn something about the skills involved in learning that subject matter. For example, students need to know how to reason through problems in engineering, how to read math texts, and how to identify important information about a particular literary work. Therefore, it is important that you use effective instructional practices for presenting content information as well as effective instructional practices for fostering the development and use of both general learning strategies (such as previewing a textbook chapter) and content-specific learning strategies (such as how to learn, understand and use mathematical formulas).

In the following sections, we discuss strategic learning and address several ways you can help develop students' learning-to-learn strategies and skills in the college classroom by increasing students' self-awareness, teaching domain-specific strategies, connecting new ideas with existing knowledge, modeling and teaching learning strategies, and providing feedback on students' use of learning strategies. We also highlight the instructor's role in helping students become more strategic and self-regulated in technology-rich instructional environments.

WHAT ARE THE CHARACTERISTICS OF STRATEGIC LEARNERS?

Most college instructors can easily recall strategic learners they have seen in their own courses. These learners approach instructional activities and tasks with a high degree of confidence that they can succeed, as well as a good idea of how to try to complete them. Strategic learners are diligent and resourceful in pursuit of a learning goal and do not give up easily, even in the face of difficulty. They understand that learning and studying are active processes largely under their own control. Strategic learners know when they understand new information and, perhaps even more important, when they do not. When they do encounter problems studying or learning, they use help-seeking strategies such as getting help from the instructor or teaching assistant, their classmates, or a student learning center. They also understand that studying and learning are systematic processes, again, largely under their own control (Paris, Lipson, and Wixson, 1983; Pintrich and De Groot, 1990; Schunk and Zimmerman, 1998, 2007; Weinstein, 1994; Weinstein and Acee, 2008; Weinstein, Acee, and Jung, 2010; Zimmerman, 1989, 1990, 1994, 1998, 2001, 2011; Zimmerman and Moylan, 2009; Zimmerman and Schunk, 2011).

Although we are all familiar with students who are strategic learners, it is still helpful to take a systematic look at some of the characteristics of these students. Understanding these characteristics is essential for deriving instructional strategies to help students be more strategic and self-regulated in pursuing their academic goals in your course and throughout their academic careers.

THE IMPORTANCE OF GOALS AND SELF-REFLECTION

How can you help students to become more effective learners? We know that strategic learners need to be able to set and use meaningful goals to help them learn and to help them generate and maintain their motivation for studying (Schunk, Pintrich, and Meece, 2008; Zimmerman, 2011). We can help students become clearer about their goals by encouraging them to set useful goals for our classes. Unfortunately, many students are not clear about their educational goals in general or about their goals for specific courses. Not every course holds the same interest value for every student, but usually there are at least some aspects of the course that each of them can perceive as useful. Providing your students with opportunities to identify how the material presented in your courses might be useful to them, now or in the future, as they strive to reach their own educational, personal, social, or occupational goals can enhance motivation as well as cognitive effort (Acee and Weinstein, 2010; Husman et al., 2004). Even a brief class discussion about upcoming topics and how these topics might relate to students' present or future interests can help. Asking students to write a brief paragraph or two about a topic and why it might be relevant to them now or in the future is another way to establish perceived relevance.

It is important to remember that we cannot give students goals—they must own their goals. However, with goal ownership comes responsibility. Students need to learn how to set, analyze, and use goals and how to respond to goal achievement and failure. Students also should learn how to implement strategies that will help them negotiate emotional responses to achieving or not achieving their goals (Boekaerts, 2011; Boekaerts and Niemivirta, 2000; Schutz and Pekrun, 2007). It is also important to assist students in establishing process rather than product goals. Even simply reminding students that the goal of the exercises or projects you assign to them is to gain mastery of the content will help support effective self-evaluation. Students are more likely to evaluate their success on the pieces of a project if they have goals for each of those pieces and if they know how to create goals that are realistic, specific and measureable, and have a stated start and completion date (Schunk, Pintrich, and Meece, 2008).

INCREASING STUDENTS' SELF-AWARENESS

Students who are aware of their learning goals tend to reflect on what it takes to learn. Thinking about thinking, or knowing about knowing, has come to be known as *metacognition* (Flavell, 1979; Pintrich, 2002; Zimmerman and Moylan, 2009). Metacognitive processes include knowledge about oneself as a learner, knowledge about academic tasks, and knowledge about strategies to use in order to accomplish academic tasks. Awareness about oneself as a learner helps students to allocate their personal resources, or the resources that are available in their academic institution such as group study sessions, tutoring programs, and learning centers. If students do not anticipate needing help with a potentially difficult course, or if they do not monitor their own comprehension closely, it is unlikely that they will take advantage of available resources. It will also be difficult for them to judge the personal resources they will need, such as extra study time or more opportunities for review and consolidation of the material before a test (Entwistle, 1992; Winne, 1996).

Increasing student self-awareness is imperative for effective strategy instruction. If students attribute their successes or failures to luck, an easy test, or innate ability, then there is no need for effort, time management, or learning strategies. Therefore, college instructors should provide opportunities for students to reflect on the general characteristics of their approaches to, and on their specific actions toward, academic tasks. This also helps students to benefit from their mistakes and not keep repeating them. As college faculty, we should increase student self-awareness of their learning strategies and teach students when and how to use strategies (Svinicki, Hagen, and Meyer, 1995; Weinstein, Acee, and Jung, 2010).

You also may want to survey students to promote self-awareness of strategies by asking them questions such as: How many hours do you spend a week studying for this course? Are you up-to-date on course assignments and readings? How do you take notes or study while reading the textbook? How do you take notes in class? Do you review your notes? When? How? Do you stop periodically and check to see if you understand the material?

USING EXISTING KNOWLEDGE TO HELP LEARN NEW THINGS

College professors have long known that teaching an introductory course is often more difficult than teaching an advanced course in the same area. Although many explanations for this finding have been offered, most of them involve students' lack of prior knowledge. It is all but impossible to think analytically or solve problems in an area without relevant knowledge. In addition, thinking about relevant knowledge also strengthens new learning by generating meaningful relations, or bridges, to new information. For example, if students think about what they already know concerning the economic causes of World War I, this can help them understand the economic causes of the Second World War. Strategic learners understand the role of relevant prior knowledge and can use this knowledge to help themselves learn new things (Alexander and Judy, 1988; Maggioni and Alexander, 2010).

We tend to use prior knowledge in one of two main ways: to create direct relations and to create analogical relations. When we create direct relations, we directly relate our prior knowledge to what we are trying to learn. For example, comparing and contrasting the causes of the two world wars involves direct relations. However, there are times when we do not have directly applicable prior knowledge, but we do have knowledge in an area that is somehow similar and may help us to understand the new information, ideas, or skills we are trying to learn. For example, we use analogies to help us relate familiar and new things that share some key characteristics but are very different in other ways. Using a post office to explain aspects of computer storage, referring to social disagreements as a way to explain conflicts in organizations, and using the structure of a bird to explain design elements of an airplane are all ways we use analogies to help students build meaning for new concepts that may, at first, seem dissimilar.

TEACHING DOMAIN-SPECIFIC AND COURSE-SPECIFIC STRATEGIES

College faculty teach students not only content but also modes of thought, and strategies for learning and thinking about the content in their courses (Donald, 1995, 2006). Different instructional means may result in students having the same amount of knowledge but not the same organization and understanding needed for different applications using this new knowledge. Comparisons of college teaching methods typically find few significant differences in tests of knowledge. There are, however, differences between teaching methods in retention, application, and transfer.

Besides developing methods to provide students with instruction concerning the ways of thinking within your content domains, you should also provide direct instruction concerning strategic learning approaches for the tasks that are specific to your content area. You can impact your students' strategic learning by helping them understand the nature and requirements of academic tasks in your course. As you assign a variety of academic tasks throughout the course, you need to define clearly how each assignment relates to course learning goals so students can approach tasks strategically. There are two levels at which we should address strategies: the domain of the course (e.g., how to think and write like a psychologist) and the course-specific materials and pedagogy (e.g., how lectures and labs are organized, how collaborative problem solving is structured).

Many college students approach all their courses in the same way; therefore, we must explicitly teach learning strategies that are domain-specific to our courses. For example, different disciplines have different discourse structures, different forms of argument, and different ways of approaching and solving problems. The domain differences between our course and our students' other courses should be clearly established. College faculty have found that cognitive modeling, thinking out loud, and demonstrating the use of texts in a self-regulated manner are ways to provide opportunities for students to learn about domain-specific strategies (Coppola, 1995; Zusho, Pintrich, and Coppola, 2003). Most students cannot write like a scientist unless they are taught scientific writing. Domain-specific approaches to learning are especially critical in introductory courses. Therefore, you should consider incorporating activities into your instruction such as the following:

1. Previewing the textbook and its text structure.
2. Providing anonymous examples of student work to illustrate both dos and don'ts.
3. Giving sample items from previous tests as practice.
4. Being clear about terminology that has domain-specific meaning.

In addition to learning strategies that are applicable to the domain of the course, students must learn strategies that are effective with the instructor's methodological, material, and assessment choices. When modeling the use of the course textbook as a domain-specific strategy, the instructor also can explicitly outline how the text complements or supplements the lecture or lab materials. As we introduce students to new approaches (e.g., problem-based learning or writing-across-the-curriculum techniques), it is important to also introduce them to the skills needed to successfully participate in our methods and enhance their confidence in applying these skills. Therefore, faculty should help students approach their courses strategically by outlining their individual instructional approaches and materials. For example:

1. As you deliver your first couple of lectures, take notes on an overhead or connected computer to emphasize what you consider to be the important points.

2. Before you begin a specific pedagogical approach, such as the case study method, take time to explain the method and the skills necessary to use it successfully.

3. Use some simple everyday examples of the approach you will be using so students can focus on the process rather than having to focus on both the content and the process.

4. Ask questions and provide example problems at the level of understanding that will be measured by tests or other assessments and point this out to the students.

We must remember that as faculty we can be models of self-regulated learning (Pintrich, 1995). Therefore, we should strive to model discipline-specific thinking processes and course-specific strategies for learning in our classrooms. If an instructor models self-regulation and provides feedback and guidance concerning their students' self-regulation, the instructor can have a significant effect on students' self-regulation (Schunk and Zimmerman, 2007; Zimmerman and Schunk, 2011).

We have said that strategic learners can take much of the responsibility for helping themselves study effectively and reach their learning goals. For these students, a core component of strategic learning is their repertoire of cognitive learning strategies (Weinstein, Acee, and Jung, 2011; Weinstein, Husman, and Dierking, 2000; Weinstein and Mayer, 1986). Cognitive learning strategies are goal-directed approaches and methods of thought that help students to build bridges between what they already know or have experienced and what they are trying to learn. These strategies are used to help build meaning in such a way that new information becomes part of an organized knowledge base that can be accessed in the future for recall, application, or problem solving. Research has shown that one of the hallmarks of expertise in an area is an organized knowledge base and a set of strategies for acquiring and integrating new knowledge (Alexander, Murphy, and Kulikowich, 2009; Chi et al., 1988).

The simplest forms of learning strategies involve repetition or review, such as reading over a difficult section of text or repeating an equation or rule. A bit more complexity is added when we try to paraphrase or summarize in our own words the material we are studying. Other strategies focus on organizing the information we are trying to learn by creating some type of scheme for the material. For example, creating an outline of the main events and characters in a story, making a timeline for historical occurrences, classifying scientific phenomena, and separating foreign vocabulary into parts of speech are all organizational strategies. Some learning strategies involve elaborating on, or analyzing, what we are trying to learn to make it more meaningful and memorable. For example, using analogies to access relevant prior knowledge, comparing and contrasting the explanations offered by two competing scientific theories, and thinking about the implications of a policy proposal are examples of elaboration strategies.

As instructors, we can all have a tremendous impact on helping students to develop a useful repertoire of learning strategies. One of the most powerful ways for teaching these strategies is through modeling. By using different types of strategies in our teaching, we can expose students to a wide variety of strategies in different content areas. However, it is not enough to simply use strategies in our teaching. It is also necessary to teach students how to do this on their own when they are studying. For example, after paraphrasing a discussion in class, point out what you did and why you did it. Briefly explain to the students what paraphrasing is and why it helps us to learn. You also could explain that it helps us to identify areas that we might not understand. If we have trouble paraphrasing something we are studying, it probably means we have not yet really learned it.

Finally, you should provide students with opportunities over time to practice and reflect on their uses of different learning strategies. As Pintrich (1995) noted, modeling the ways in which to learn strategically in our courses is necessary but not sufficient. We must structure opportunities for students to practice using these strategies. We also need to ask students not only *what* they think, but *how* they think, and *if* this was the most effective process for them. Guided practice with feedback is a powerful way to teach students how to learn because it provides students with opportunities to practice strategies and evaluate them to see which ones are or are not useful.

Testing practices also influence students' use of learning strategies. Rote memory questions such as, "According to the author, the shortage of teachers depends on three factors. Which three?" produce surface-level processing, whereas deep-level processing can be induced by questions such as "Explain the meaning of the following quotation—'Too many poor teachers will drive good ones out of the market.'" According to Pressley and McCormick (1995), one of the most powerful ways to influence the degree to which students use deep rather than surface strategies is through test demands. Students are more willing to learn to use deep processing strategies when it is evident to them that these types of strategies help them to meet the demands of the test or other evaluative procedures.

METHODS FOR CHECKING UNDERSTANDING

Strategic learners must be skillful self-regulators who periodically check on the usefulness of their learning methods by monitoring their progress toward learning goals and sub-goals (Zimmerman and Schunk, 2011). Without checking actively on their progress, many students may think that they understand, when in fact they do not. Often students do not realize there are holes in their understanding until they receive their grade on a test. This is because the test is the first time they were asked to check on their new knowledge in a way that would identify gaps or misunderstandings. Strategic learners know that the time to check understanding is before taking a test or other formal assessment measure. Checking on understanding and looking for gaps or mistakes in knowledge integration should be an ongoing activity present in every studying and learning context.

Checking our understanding can be as simple as trying to paraphrase or apply what we have been trying to learn. Many of the learning strategies we discussed earlier also can be used to test understanding. For example, trying to paraphrase in our own words what we are reading in a textbook is a good way to help build meaning, but it also helps us to identify gaps or errors in our understanding. If we try to apply our knowledge and have difficulty using it, or if we try to explain it to someone else and cannot do it, we would also know that we have some comprehension problems. Monitoring our comprehension is an important part of strategic learning that fosters self-regulation. Only if we know we have a problem in our understanding or a gap in our knowledge can we do something about it.

A very useful method for checking understanding and helping to teach a variety of learning strategies is the use of cooperative learning. Cooperative learning is a method that builds on peer tutoring. We have long known that in many traditional tutoring situations the tutor, not the student receiving the tutoring, benefits the most. While processing the content for presentation, the tutor is consolidating and integrating his or her content knowledge. At the same time, the tutor is also learning a great deal about how to learn. The tutor needs to diagnose the tutee's learning problem, or knowledge gap, in order to help the tutee overcome it. Refer to chapter 14 on group learning for a more complete discussion of the benefits of these methods.

KNOWING HOW TO LEARN IS NOT ENOUGH—STUDENTS MUST ALSO WANT TO LEARN

Strategic learners know a lot about learning and the types of strategies that will help them meet their learning goals. However, knowing what to do is not enough. Knowing how to do it is still not enough. Students must *want* to learn if they are to use the knowledge, strategies, and skills we have addressed so far. It is the interaction of what Scott Paris and his colleagues have called *skill* and *will* that results in self-regulated learning (Hofer, Yu, and Pintrich, 1998; Paris and Paris, 2001; Paris, Lipson, and Wixson, 1983; Pintrich and De Groot, 1990; Zimmerman, 2011). Many students know much more about effective study practices than what they actually use. Just as in the case of an overweight person who is an expert in weight loss techniques, knowledge is not always sufficient for action. We all have many different potential goals and actions competing for our attention and resources at any point in time. Which goals we select and how much effort we put toward those goals are at least partially determined by our motivations. Strategic learners know how to learn, but they also want to be effective learners. It is the interaction of skill and will that gives direction to their actions and helps them to persist at tasks even in the face of obstacles.

One way to enhance students' perceptions of their competence is by giving performance feedback that focuses on strategic effort and skill development. Simply telling students that they did well does not really focus on their role in the performance. Telling a student, "This is great! I can really see the effort you put into this," says a lot more. Talking directly about students' strategic efforts and the skills they are developing helps them to focus on their role in the learning process. Remember, a key component of strategic learning is believing that you can play an active role. If students do not believe they can make a difference, they will not use many of the effective strategies we have been discussing. See chapter 11 for a more complete discussion of the effects of motivation on learning.

PUTTING IT ALL TOGETHER—EXECUTIVE CONTROL PROCESSES IN STRATEGIC LEARNING

We have discussed both skill and will as important components of strategic learning. A third essential component is the use of executive control processes, or self-regulation (see Weinstein, Acee, and Jung, 2011; Weinstein, Husman, and Dierking, 2000; Zimmerman and Schunk, 2011). These control processes are used to manage the learning process from the beginning (setting the learning goal) to the end result. Strategic learners use executive control processes to (1) organize and manage their approach to reaching a learning goal, (2) keep them on target and warn them if they are not making sufficient progress toward meeting the goal in a timely and effective manner, and (3) build up a repertoire of effective strategies that they can call on in the future to complete similar tasks, thereby increasing their learning efficiency and productivity (Paris and Paris, 2001; Weinstein and Acee, 2008; Weinstein, Acee, and Jung, 2011). When students are facing new and unfamiliar tasks, they must do a lot of planning to help identify potentially effective methods to achieve their goals for task performance. Unfortunately, many students simply adopt a trial-and-error approach to learning, or they try to adapt other familiar strategies they have used for different tasks to the current one. The time invested in generating, following, monitoring, and perhaps modifying a learning plan is a good investment for reaching learning goals now and in the future. As we develop expertise, we do not need to dwell on developing a plan for each task we face. Generating and evaluating plans for reaching learning goals helps build up an effective repertoire that we can call on in the future when similar learning needs arise.

Several instructional approaches emphasize how college instructors can help students generate, maintain, and evaluate their learning methods—that is, self-regulate their learning within college coursework (Schunk and Zimmerman, 2007; Zimmerman and Schunk, 2011). When self-monitoring is successful, the student not only learns more, but also develops better strategies. In addition, students' successes increase their self-efficacy in the course and their motivation to learn. In addition to learning how to learn course content and how to control motivation, other researchers have emphasized that students must also learn "emotion control"—the management of emotions and levels of arousal while learning (Boekaerts, 2011; Boekaerts and Niemivirta, 2000; Schutz and Pekrun, 2007).

College faculty can help facilitate self-regulated learning by encouraging students to share examples of successful approaches to learning with each other. Guided discussions about what is and is not working help students refine their own methods and get ideas for other potential approaches.

We have discussed many ways to help students become more strategic, self-regulated learners in classroom learning contexts. Now we turn our attention to some of the special strategies and skills students need in online or technology-rich learning contexts.

WHAT INSTRUCTORS CAN DO TO HELP THEIR STUDENTS SUCCEED IN ONLINE OR BLENDED INSTRUCTIONAL ENVIRONMENTS

The online revolution has begun in earnest, and we all have much to be excited about. However, we cannot let our euphoria over this new instructional medium and the exciting educational possibilities it offers cloud our perceptions of the challenges inherent in online instruction from a student's perspective and the low success rates experienced by many students (see Mooney, 2011). E-learning offers tremendous control to the learner of both the instructional resources and the technical tools provided in these learning environments. In the hands of a student who is prepared to take responsibility for using these tools to enhance learning, they can indeed be powerful tools. But in the hands of students who have difficulty with strategic and self-regulated learning—such as problems with managing time, meeting commitments, and maintaining motivation—online learning can offer many challenges. Although some of the problem may be attributable to poorly designed materials, or novelty, or computer phobias, it is also becoming apparent that many students simply do not know enough about how to learn and, perhaps even more important, how to manage their learning in online instructional settings. Many studies have found that strategic and self-regulated learning variables are often the mediators between success and failure in online or blended learning contexts. (See Winters, Greene, and Costich, 2008, for an analysis of studies examining self-regulation and learning in computer-based learning environments.) With the rapid and exponentially expanding growth of online courses, it is imperative that instructors and course designers help students develop the self-regulation and skills needed to intelligently exercise learner control. The following suggestions are derived from research and applied literatures examining these issues. (See Clark and Mayer, 2008, and Mayer, 2009, for numerous guidelines for the design, instructional methods, and implementation models that can be used to enhance learning in online environments.)

1. Teach students about and how to use the special instructional features of programs, such as glossaries, self-tests, multimedia material, and supplementary information.

2. Teach students about and how to use the special technical tools available, such as chat rooms, contacting the instructor, synchronous and asynchronous discussions, and getting help.

3. Provide instruction in critical self-regulation areas, including:

   a. *Time management:* The flexibility of time and location is a distinguishing characteristic between most online courses and traditional classroom-based courses. This flexibility gives online learners much more choice and autonomy than traditional classroom learners. However, if they have problems with time management, they may be much more likely to put off their work more than they should and fall behind in their studies.

b. *Generating and maintaining motivation:* Online learners have a greater responsibility for generating and maintaining their motivation over time. The absence of direct instructor and peer pressure, and a study environment often full of competing tasks, such as spending more time with friends and family or at work, often make it difficult for students to commit to completing their coursework.

c. *Self-testing:* In online courses, it is critical that students monitor their own understanding and progress through the material.

d. *Managing anxiety:* If learners in online courses are uncertain about what they are supposed to do in a course or experience an unexpected problem, they may feel frustrated about online learning. In addition, learners with insufficient computer skills often feel anxious about online learning. Finally, the text-based nature of online communication requires students to communicate through writing and this might be distressing for those students who do not have the ability to express themselves effectively in writing.

4. Help students create a management plan for successfully completing an online lesson or course. This plan should be checked frequently and revised when necessary. The critical steps in the plan include:

a. Setting one or more goals.
b. Reflecting on the personal resources they will need to reach each goal.
c. Brainstorming and creating a plan of attack to reach each goal.
d. Selecting the methods they will use to accomplish their plan.
e. Implementing their plan.
f. Monitoring (on an ongoing basis) the success and timeliness of their plan.
g. Formatively evaluating their progress.
h. Modifying, if necessary, their methods or even their goals.
i. Summatively evaluating the outcomes to see whether they want to use this plan again in the future or whether they need to modify or discard it

5. Teach them help-seeking techniques like e-mailing or chatting with the instructor, teaching assistant, or other students in the class when they are having trouble.

6. Include high-level question prompting embedded within the online course so they can check their understanding of the material as they navigate through each lesson.

7. Create online graphic organizers.

IN CONCLUSION

Teaching strategic learning is more than an investment in your students' future learning; it also is an investment in the present. Strategic learners are better able to take advantage of your instruction and their studying activities. The time you invest will come back to you in enhanced student understanding and performance, as well as increased motivation. It is also important to remember that all of us have goals for what we hope the students in our classes will learn. In today's rapidly changing world, the ability to acquire or use knowledge and skills is more important than compiling a static knowledge base. There is an old Talmudic expression that loosely translates as: "If you feed a person a fish, you have fed them for a day, but if you teach them how to fish, you have fed them for a lifetime!" As college instructors, our task is to provide edible fish (content knowledge), but our task is also to teach our students how to fish (learning how to become strategic, self-regulated learners in our field).

Supplementary Reading

P. R. Pintrich (ed.), "Understanding Self-Regulated Learning," *New Directions for Teaching and Learning*, no. 63, June 1995, has chapters on the theories underlying self-regulation as well as practical applications to a variety of settings, disciplines, and students.

C. E. Weinstein, T. W. Acee, and J. H. Jung, "Self-Regulation and Learning Strategies," *New Directions for Teaching & Learning*, no. 126, Summer 2011, p. 45–53. doi: 10.1002/tl.443, overviews Weinstein's theoretical Model of Strategic Learning and a variety of learning strategies instructors can teach to their students.

B. J. Zimmerman and D. H. Schunk, *Handbook of Self-Regulation of Learning and Performance* (New York: Taylor & Francis, 2011), includes chapters on theory, research, and both domain-general (cut across all subject matters like time management) and domain-specific (particular to a content area such as math) educational applications by influential scholars in the field of educational psychology focusing on strategic and self-regulated learning.

Chapter 21

Teaching Thinking

History credits Plutarch with the observation that "the mind is not a vessel to be filled but a fire to be kindled." This statement elegantly captures distinctly different attitudes of educators about their overarching objectives in higher education. "Filling vessels," primarily through lecture, has been the dominant teaching strategy that most students experience in the college classroom. However, in the last few decades, widespread dissatisfaction with the performance of college graduates has generated new pressures for college educators to embrace Plutarch's ideal vision.

Barr and Tagg (1995) described and promoted this paradigm shift with their differentiation of *content-centered instruction* vs. *learner-centered instruction*.

Content-centered teachers transmit important facts and concepts with students and show limited attention to the process. Many content-centered teachers assume that exposing students to the ideas of the discipline will facilitate changes in students' thinking over time. Content-centered teachers often credit students' innate intelligence as responsible for their academic success. Consequently, it doesn't make much sense to invest valuable class time concentrating on process rather than using available time to explore the important concepts, theories, or

This chapter was written by Jane S. Halonen, University of West Florida.

frameworks of the discipline. For content-centered teachers, the goal is to fill vessels; vessel-fillers presume high-quality thinking will follow.

In contrast, learning-centered teachers are fire-starters. They embrace the responsibility for fostering changes in students' thinking skills. They believe that students grappling with ideas will lead to more meaningful and enduring learning. Factual knowledge rapidly deteriorates unless the ideas can be meaningfully encoded or practiced with some regularity (Eriksen, 1983). Consequently, learner-centered teachers regularly turn to active learning strategies to engage students in process. Cognitive scientists report that when students think about material in more meaningful ways, underlying brain structures will change to promote more enduring learning (Leamnson, 2000).

In this chapter, I explore the challenges associated with teaching thinking skills in college. First, we will start by examining the various motivational obstacles that deter students from engaging at a level that genuinely reflects thinking. Second, I will explore the challenges of defining terms in the promotion of thinking skills. Third, I will describe some of the popular pedagogical frameworks that promote thinking and discuss their implications for thinking pedagogy. Finally, the chapter concludes with some practical recommendations that can support and sustain fire-starting strategies.

WHAT ARE WE UP AGAINST?

Critics suggest that higher education has a disappointing track record in helping students develop strong thinking skills. They cite chronic complaints from employers that their new hires cannot think critically or solve problems. A recent, often cited study (*Academically Adrift: Limited Learning on College Campuses,* Arum and Roksa, 2011), documented that general education produced virtually no gains in their ability to think. Although many educators resist the sweeping negative conclusions drawn by Arum and Roksa, the popularity of the *Academically Adrift* reflects how accurately (and sadly) the work resonates with popular opinion that college may be a waste of time and resources.

Most universities have responded to increasing demands for accountability by crafting carefully constructed curricula in which thoughtful sequencing of thinking and learning experiences can maximize student gains (Maki, 2004). Students should be supported as they move from simpler learning challenges, such as getting introduced to basic concepts in the discipline, through the complex performance demands that might be required in a capstone course. As such, students progress from novice to baccalaureate-level expertise. Programs can capture the quality of their instruction through a well-tailored assessment plan that reflects the journey. Consequently, most colleges and universities now routinely promise the improvement of students' thinking as an explicit goal of the mission. However, students may be reluctant to engage with even the most competent educational objectives to improve thinking.

Why do so many students struggle to take advantage of the opportunities that college provides to hone their thinking skills? Several explanations pertain:

1. *They have limited practice.* Students may have had little exposure in their prior educational settings to engage with material in a demanding way. The majority of their experiences have probably focused on recording lecture notes and reciting information that has been transmitted to them, vessel-style. This process involves thinking at its least demanding levels.

2. *They have limited time.* Like most humans, students are inclined to take the most efficient/least effort path to completing their work. Unless instructors officially build in activities that require thinking with commensurate rewards for engaging at that level, students are likely to see thinking demands as a distraction with diminishing payoffs.

3. *They have limited patience.* Memorizing facts tends to produce a predictable sequence of activity and plan of attack; thinking activities are not as tidy. Thinking activities may seem rather open-ended and ambiguous. If students have not developed tolerance for activities that challenge them, then thinking exercises can be especially taxing, especially if the content triggers emotional responses that may be potentially unpleasant.

4. *They have limited direction.* Instructors typically are experts in their fields. They may not always articulate the steps needed to help novices in the field come to terms with what thinking will entail. Although students may be willing to engage at a deeper level with the course content, they may be unable to discern how to get started and how to refine and sustain their thinking practices.

5. *They have limited expectations.* Students don't always appreciate the scope of personal change that applying themselves in college will produce. If their endgames merely involve getting a requisite number of courses completed as passports to professional lives, then they can construe spending time refining their thinking skills as just an unwelcome and unnecessary detour.

THINKING PEDAGOGY AS A CONFUSED LANDSCAPE

Early in my teaching career I was very impressed by an exchange I had during class with a student. She made a wonderful connection between a principle I was trying to teach in my psychology course and a concept she was learning about in humanities. The connection was compelling, original, and subtle. I commented to the class, "That is excellent critical thinking." Wide-eyed, the student responded, "That is what critical thinking is? I hear teachers talk about critical thinking all the time but I didn't know that what you guys meant." In my course, her comment definitely constituted engaging with the material in a different, richer, and more personal manner. She knew critical thinking was a good and desirable activity, but had been struggling with what it truly meant in the context of her courses. Labeling her "output" as an example of critical thinking clarified something that had been fairly fuzzy up to that point, at least in the context of my class.

The pedagogy of thinking contains a dizzying array of terminology. Students are likely to hear about the desirability of various terms that express facets of thinking without necessarily getting the "how to" manual to perform according to teacher expectations within a specific discipline. The thinking landscape in higher education contains the following processes (and their close cousins):

- Critical thinking (analysis; evaluation; synthesis)
- Creative thinking (divergent thinking; analogical thinking; metaphorical thinking)
- Problem solving (convergent thinking; inquiry; synthesis; application)
- Reasoning (syllogistic thinking; induction; deduction; inference-making)
- Decision making (ethical decision-making; moral reasoning)

Disciplines differ on the emphases and value their practitioners place on the types of thinking. For example, a lab class in chemistry might focus primarily on the development of problem-solving skills whereas our colleagues in philosophy might zero in on logical principles. Both course experiences might facilitate creative thinking as secondary goals.

Although there are commonalities across disciplines in the act of critical thinking across fields, disciplines also promote distinctive features as well (Halonen, 1986). For example, critical thinking in the humanities has a decidedly different character than critical thinking in accounting. Disciplines sometimes tend to make this journey more complicated by having different definitions for the same terminology.

Building curricula based on student learning outcomes has helped to establish a national language and some common expectations about the most valued thinking skills. For example, the American Association of Colleges and Universities (AAC&U) identified "Essential Learning Outcomes" (2009) in their Liberal Education and America's Promise (LEAP) program. Among their essential outcomes, they proposed the following explicit thinking skills:

Intellectual and Practical Skills

- Inquiry and analysis
- Critical and critical thinking
- Quantitative and information literacy
- Teamwork and problem solving

Personal and Social Responsibility

- Ethical reasoning and action

Integrative and Applied Learning

- Synthesis and application

The articulation of the LEAP outcomes, followed by growing national acceptance, reinforces that the goals of college extend far beyond memorizing concepts and promote inter-faculty collaboration to ensure that such transformational goals for students' thinking skills can be achieved.

FRAMEWORKS THAT SUPPORT TEACHING THINKING

Any given course can provide a context in which students can learn to think more effectively and can make a contribution to the students' cognitive evolution, particularly when their faculty set explicit expectations and provide guidance on how students should think within the discipline. Many educators rely on systematic frameworks or specific theories to help them design learning experiences that can be pitched to achieve their preferred learning and thinking outcomes. In this section I explore specific dimensions of thinking that can influence successful design citing both classic and emerging perspectives. I also suggest how the perspectives can make a practical difference in the classroom.

How Do Thinking Skills Vary in Complexity?

Bloom's taxonomy (Bloom, 1956) is perhaps the most enduring thinking framework that influences American higher education pedagogy.

Bloom and his colleagues differentiated categories of thinking skills and sequenced them according to their complexity. The original taxonomy distinguished *lower order skills* (e.g., knowledge, comprehension, and application) from *higher order skills* (e.g., analysis, synthesis, and evaluation). Bloom's work became widely used to promote the development of both lower order and higher order thinking skills in college classrooms by encouraging faculty to identify explicitly for students what kinds of thinking would satisfy their class objectives (Luechauer and Shulman, 1996).

Anderson and Krathwohl (2001) revised Bloom's taxonomy to improve its pedagogical utility and accuracy. For example, Anderson's team recognized that "knowledge" was not really a process comparable to other terms in the original taxonomy. Consequently, they changed the first level of skill to "remember." Throughout the revised taxonomy, they incorporated language that worked more effectively to help educators develop workable and measurable objectives, consistent with the growing assessment demands. They changed "evaluation" to "evaluate" to stress outcomes as verbs rather than nouns. As in the original taxonomy, the new version retained a hierarchical design, but reorganized the sequence of higher order skills. As shown in Figure 21.1, Anderson and his team positioned "create" (formerly "synthesis") as the most complex cognitive skill in place of "evaluation" in the original scheme.

Educators who rely on Bloom's insights don't tend to be satisfied with lower level thinking achievements in their students. They actively deploy strategies that push students out of their memorizing comfort zones. They invite students to move beyond recall and recognition in their testing strategies testing. Ironically, students who complain that their instructors craft "tricky" multiple-choice test questions may be reacting to teachers who are attempting to push students into higher levels of engagement with the material. As students progress in their majors, they should face more complex thinking demands. Research papers, structured class discussions, and original presentations give students the appropriate opportunity to grapple with increasing thinking demands when instructors frame their directions properly.

How Do Thinking Characteristics Change Over Time in College?

Perry's (1970) scheme provided a framework that addresses how students' thinking changes during their journey through college. As such, the Perry scheme is more *metacognitive*, meaning that it promotes greater awareness and understanding of one's own thought processes. In Perry's model, beginning students demonstrate a strong preference for a simplistic world, a characteristic he referred to as *dualism*. As students begin to grapple with the complexities of disciplines, they will inevitably

The revision retains the hierarchical nature of thinking skills, but offers a new sequence in the hierarchy and emphasizes action verbs to promote more effective design of test questions and assignments.

Higher-Order Skills

Create
Reorganize elements into a new pattern, structure, or purpose (*generate, plan, produce*)

Evaluate
Come to a conclusion about something based on standards/criteria (*checking, critiquing, judging*)

Analyze
Subdivide content into meaningful parts and relate the parts (*differentiating, organizing, attributing*)

Apply
Use procedures to solve problems or complete tasks (*execute, implement*)

Understand
Construct new meaning by mixing new material with existing ideas (*interpret, exemplify, classify, summarize, infer, compare, explain*)

Lower-Order Skills

Remember
Retrieve pertinent facts from long-term memory (*recognize, recall*)

FIGURE 21.1 Anderson, Krathwohl, and Colleagues' (2001) Revision of Bloom's Taxonomy

Source: Anderson, L. W. and Krathwohl, D. R. (Eds.). (2001). *A Taxonomy for Learning, Teaching, and Assessing: A Revision of Bloom's Taxonomy of Educational Objectives.* New York: Longman.

begin to accept that there are multiple perspectives that can be brought to bear on any particular problem, which Perry dubbed *multiplism*; yet the multiplistic student still shows greater comfort with simplistic viewpoints. In the next stage, called *relativism*, students experience greater comfort with multiple explanations. Finally, at the stage of *commitment*, students experience greater comfort with multiple explanations. They forge reasoned positions despite the ambiguity inherent in complex situations and problems.

Educators who understand cognitive complexity as a developmental phenomenon tend to approach course design purposefully to reflect a classroom community comprised of learners at different stages of cognitive complexity. They understand that novice students will express disappointment when easy answers elude them. They design assignments that pay close attention to realistic capacity. They also concentrate on sequencing skill development to honor developmental progression.

How Does Motivation Influence Thinking Success?

Biggs and Collis (1982) developed the Structure of Observed Learning Outcomes (SOLO) taxonomy, a popular approach for many Australian and European educators, which differentiated *deep* versus *shallow learning strategies* to describe conscious choices that students make about their thinking involvement during their learning. Shallow learners invest minimal activity to get by; deep learners develop more fully by engaging in thinking and have longer lasting effects from their investment.

Similar to Perry's stages of development, the SOLO model also emphasized metacognitive changes that transpire in students as they develop more complex cognitive skills. For example, Biggs and Collis characterized unsophisticated students as *prestructural* in that they collect facts in isolation, favoring shallow learning strategies. At the next stage, which the authors described as *unistructural*, students can grasp central ideas but don't tend to make independent connections between concepts. At the *multistructural phase*, students make more connections but still may not grasp larger purposes involved in their learning. At the *relational* stage, students can readily see how the component pieces of their learning fit together to produce a meaningful whole. Finally, at the *extended abstract* stage, students can generalize beyond the immediate details of learning to extract optimal meaning from their learning; in this stage, students more routinely pursue deep learning strategies.

Educators should expect that students will make conscious choices about their level of commitment to any particular course. In some classes, students will be satisfied with shallow learning and lower order thinking accomplishments. Large classes that promote the use of assessment strategies relying solely on memorization skills will compound student tendencies not to delve deeply in contexts where they are not required to do so. On the other hand, targeting the enhancement of thinking skills typically means that assessment strategies will concentrate on the development of higher order thinking skills and deep involvement in the discipline.

How Does Intelligence Influence Thinking Capacity?

By the time most students enter college, they have developed some notions about their intellectual capacity, even in the absence of a formal evaluation of "IQ." Board scores and grade point averages, as well as success patterns in their college acceptances, further reinforce these self-impressions. Although students may have well-formed impressions about how "smart" they are—whether these are accurate or not—it is less likely that students will have comparable and definitive impressions about the overall quality of their thinking.

Contemporary psychologists have criticized traditional IQ measures in favor of models that differentiate intellectual strengths and weaknesses in different contexts. Sternberg (1985) developed the Triarchic Model of Intelligence to highlight different facets of adaptation. He hypothesized that *analytic thinking* most closely corresponds to traditional measures of intelligence. Analytical intelligence involves a stronger natural capacity to engage in abstraction, to compare and contrast, and to evaluate and analyze information. As experts in acquiring knowledge, students with strong analytic abilities tend to find academic expectations easier to manage than those whose analytic capacity is lower. *Creative intelligence* reflects the ability to find new connections, invent, and discover. This dimension entails how effectively individuals manage novelty. *Practical intelligence* manifests as the capacity to transfer learning readily to new situations. This element of Sternberg's theory addresses human capacity for being successful in the demands of everyday life.

Sternberg emphasizes that these "gifts" will be present in different proportions among classmates and those variations have implications for classroom design. Some students, those with analytic intelligence, will engage much more easily in the traditional demands of academic work supported by their intellectual profile and preferences. Being able to see students as capable in diverse kinds of thinking can produce richer assignment designs. For example, instructors might incorporate more opportunity for creative activity or concentrate on practical applications of academic concepts to engage students more broadly to develop their thinking skills.

How Does Learning Style Influence Thinking Development?

A pioneer in the concept of learning style, Kolb (1984) explored learning strengths and weaknesses as a function of experiential preferences. According to Kolb, successful learning involves a four-stage cycle with different kinds of thinking skills attendant to each cycle. Kolb hypothesized that students display greater comfort in different parts of the cycle and developed an inventory to identify their preferences.

Individuals with a preference for *concrete experience* are most likely to learn from direct involvement and practical examples. They prefer case studies to theory. Their thinking may be most strongly influenced by emotions and empathy. Students who prefer *reflective observation* relish learning tasks that involve careful observation and objective judgment. Their thinking is characterized by impartiality, attention to detail, and appreciation of performance criteria to guide fair judgment. *Active experimentation* represents students who learn best through projects that allow them to form hypotheses, investigate, and draw conclusions on their own. They tend to be bored by traditional lectures that rely on one-way transmission of information. Students who prefer *abstract conceptualization* enjoy theory, systematic analysis, and logic. They tend to be dispassionate but can be easily frustrated by unstructured activities that may seem time-wasting to them.

Perhaps more than any other theoretical approach, Kolb's work points to the importance of appealing to different kinds of learning and thinking styles in designing class experience for broad appeal. A straightforward lecture will engage only a small portion of learners, the abstract conceptualizers, who have already had a history of thinking success. Respecting the specialized kinds of thinking that happen throughout the Kolb cycle can encourage richer approaches to teaching thinking.

What Role Does Emotion Play in Thinking Success?

The doctrine of Cartesian dualism originally formulated by Rene Descartes proposed a powerful argument for the separation of mind and body. Cartesian dualism has had a far-reaching legacy that extends to the tendency to treat thinking and emotion and disconnected activities. In fact, stereotypes of those engaged in deep thought characterize the activity as either devoid of emotion or depict emotion as an unwelcome distraction. However, more recent critics have argued that the dualistic perspective is incomplete and misleading.

Damasio (1995) argued that rationality and emotionality are conjoined in a book pugnaciously entitled *Descartes Error: Emotion, Reason, and the Human Brain.* Damasio suggests that humans navigate their cognitive processing with a great deal of reliance on somatic markers or "gut instinct," driven by emotion. In some cases, emotions provide triggers during rational processes for deeper consideration. Emotions provide a backdrop against which we determine how long to persist at a task. Emotions contribute in positive and negative ways to deriving satisfying solutions. Damasio concluded that emotions and rationality are adaptively intertwined and inseparable.

Damasio's work encourages instructors to recognize the ways in which emotional reactions to the content and skills being presented can play an important role in thinking success. Rather than being divorced from emotion, thinking experiences are awash in affect. Lack of confidence can sabotage new thinkers before they have much chance to explore possibilities. Because thinking and learning are not typically easy, instructors need to provide some support when classroom experiences invoke strong emotional responses. Positive emotions also have an important role. The joy of a new insight or an episode of high-quality thinking can be acknowledged and celebrated and may usher in new options for majors. Not only does positive emotion build confidence as a thinker, it can reinforce the rewards of being a scholar. Skilled instructors don't eschew emotion; they monitor class affect to help them strike the right balance between rationality and emotions.

How Does Content Complexity Influence Thinking Success?

A pair of researchers from the United Kingdom (Meyer and Land, 2006) provided another pedagogical perspective that encourages instructors to look at the content in distinctive ways that can influence thinking development. Meyer and Land noted that disciplines contain concepts or principles that appear to be especially hard to grasp. They dubbed particularly challenging ideas within disciplines as "troublesome knowledge." However, they proposed that disciplines also feature "threshold concepts," ideas that have potential to create a portal into the confusion. Once students successfully grapple with a threshold concept, they can gain access to the discipline in transformative ways. They may look at the discipline, the world, and even themselves in dramatically different, enlightened ways. Meyer and Land's model casts the instructor as the expert who not only shares the content of their course but models the skills of the discipline in the process.

From the vaunted vantage point of the expert, instructors can sometimes lose touch with how mystifying a new discipline can be from the point of view of the novice. Expert understanding can be so second nature and automatically accessible to the expert that instructors may struggle to stay connected to just how hard the job of the learner can be, especially if the discipline itself is not intrinsically appealing to the learner.

An additional implication of the threshold concepts approach is an argument for reconfiguring curricular strategies to focus on the ideas and concepts that have the greatest transformational potential rather than enacting the traditional instructor obligation of "covering the field." Although individual learners may resonate with different concepts in the discipline as transformative, Meyer and Land argue that all disciplines provide a variety of portals that can move students from confusion into comprehension. However, that journey across the threshold can only take place through thinking.

IMPROVING THINKING QUALITY

What strategies are most useful in facilitating students learning how to think more effectively in college?

1. Be explicit in your syllabus that your goal will be to help them improve their thinking, especially learning to think "like a ___ (historian, psychologist, biologist)." Describe what constitutes successful thinking in the discipline at both lower and higher levels as explicitly as you can.

2. If you adopt any formal pedagogical framework that shapes your instructional design, explain the framework to your students in sufficient detail so they can more easily understand what you expect to see in their work. For example, describe the Bloom model with students during the orientation to the course to clarify your goals for their cognitive development. This strategy can reduce complaints that you are trying to be "tricky" when your test items are tapping higher order skills.

3. Provide ample opportunities to practice thinking during class. The results of grappling with ideas will have a more enduring impact than mere exposure to the thinking of others. Show excitement about all aspects of thinking: good questions, odd questions, partial answers, and unsolvable problems.

4. Welcome student questions that give you an opportunity to think out loud to demonstrate a discipline in action. Don't answer every student question yourself. Turn student questions into opportunities for all of the students to think their way to a satisfying answer and experience a satisfying process.

5. Acknowledge examples of good student thinking. Students often may not appreciate what constitutes a good example until you officially label it as such. When an example is off target or poorly developed, ask the class to collaborate to improve the response.

6. Require students to judge the quality of their own contributions. Encouraging self-assessment can promote greater autonomy in thinking by improving self-reflection and self-regulation skills (Dunn, McEntarffer, and Halonen, 2004).

7. Design challenges that will appeal to diverse learning styles (Jarvis, 2005). Some students will require more reflection time before they can express their thinking confidently, but incorporating diverse thinking challenges will enhance student engagement.

8. Guard against settling for appealing only to students whose learning profile matches your own. If you are only getting approving smiles and nods from students who look like future professor material, then consider ways to broaden appeal and adapt what you do for different styles and learning capacities.

9. Give yourself permission not to cover all of the content. Select from the relevant content to promote the thinking goals you have in mind. The trade-off involved in making this choice means a greater investment in skill development that is likely to have a more long-lasting impact than shallowly learned concepts with a fragile life-expectancy.

10. Be patient when students express greater comfort with shallower learning challenges. At the outset of a college education, it is developmentally normal to resist thinking in complex ways. The art of effective college teaching involves strategizing about ways to lower this resistance and increase the excitement of making bigger cognitive investments.

11. Put your own negative emotions in check when you conclude students are being lazy in response to your demands. Compare their strategies to your own "economy of effort" decisions. Try not to take what appears to be a rebuff of your best efforts so seriously.

12. Identify prospective threshold concepts in your discipline and structure course time to allow deep consideration of those transformative ideas. Abandon content that you deem to have reduced value from the standpoint of transformation.

13. Ask students to declare what level of commitment they intend to make in the course. Overt identifications of their intentions to be a deep versus a shallow learner in the class can help instructors zero in on students who will be more receptive to feedback and offers of assistance.

14. Acknowledge emotions that reinforce or interfere with learning. Attempt to normalize what is appropriate (e.g., performance anxiety when giving a public talk) and celebrate openly when students succeed in meeting expectations.

15. Regardless of your discipline, ask, "What do you think and why do you think so?" (Nessel and Graham, 2007). This strategy will work across disciplines to develop their specific cognitive abilities and their metacognitive appreciation of how college is helping them change.

IN CONCLUSION

Learning how to think more effectively is not easy, but students are unlikely to make systematic progress in their thinking skills without specific practice through well-designed pedagogy. Along with discipline based-strategies to sharpen their thinking, students need to develop habits of reflection about their experiences, their successes and failures, their plans and purposes, and their choices and consequences.

Teaching thinking skills also is not the easiest path, but it is likely to be more gratifying than a straight lecture mode. Building thinking into course design, making expectations explicit, providing significant practice opportunities, and delivering accurate feedback facilitates the achievement of desired thinking outcomes.

Supplementary Reading

Jeffery Howard provides helpful guidance for anyone planning a new experiential course in his *Service-Learning Course Design Workbook,* issued in Summer 2001 as a companion volume to the *Michigan Journal of Service Learning.*

A thoughtful discussion of what kinds of learning and development emerge from this form of education is found in Morris Keeton's *Experiential Learning* (San Francisco: Jossey-Bass, 1976).

Adams, J. L. *Conceptual Blockbusting: A Guide to Better Ideas* (Cambridge, MA: Perseus Publishing, 2001).

Halpern, Diane F. *Thought and Knowledge: An Introduction to Critical Thinking (2nd ed.)* (Mahwah, NJ: Lawrence Erlbaum Associates, Inc., 1989).

This volume provides a comprehensive view of critical thinking skills and dispositions using frameworks that apply across disciplines.

Chapter 22

The Ethics of Teaching

Imagine you're teaching a course at the introductory level, one that is required of all students who want to major in your department. And let's suppose that after the first exam a student whose performance was much below standard approaches you and offers you a considerable sum of money if you'll change a grade on the exam so the student can pass. What is the ethical thing to do in this situation?

Now imagine the same situation, but instead of offering you money, the student pleads for an opportunity to retake the exam because of extenuating circumstances during the first test administration. Now what is the ethical choice?

Next, imagine the same situation, but this time you are the one who notices that a student who has been working hard in your class, and whom you expected to do very well, has instead failed the exam miserably. How does this situation compare with the others from an ethical standpoint?

The first scenario seems fairly straightforward, a definite violation of ethics if you were to accept the money to change the grade. The second example is not as straightforward. To what extent should the student be allowed an opportunity that is not available to all the other students? Does providing that opportunity constitute unethical behavior? Or is it just unfair? Or is there a difference? In the third instance, to what extent should your assessment of a student's abilities counter actual performance? Where do you draw the line in helping students?

The most difficult questions that teachers face often have nothing to do with the content of the course or the way it is presented. They focus instead on the ethical issues of teaching, and how we relate to our students, to our institution, to our discipline, and to society at large. What are our responsibilities to each constituency, and what do we do when responsibilities conflict? Unfortunately, there are no easy answers to these questions. I raise them here as food for thought because you *will* face them sometime in your teaching career.

This chapter addresses the issue of ethics in teaching. What do we mean by "ethics in teaching"? In recent years, more and more has been written about the topic as the teaching mission of the university comes under increasing scrutiny (Cahn, 1994; Fisch, 1996; Lewis, 1997; Matthews, 1991; Strike, 1988). It seems only proper that those who currently teach and those who aspire to a faculty career be introduced to the concept.

What is an ethical question in teaching? Ethical questions are sometimes defined in terms of right and wrong (Strike, 1988); in terms of cultural norms such as honesty and promise keeping (Smith, 1996); or as "general guidelines, ideals, or expectations that need to be taken into account, along with other relevant conditions and circumstances, in the design and analysis of teaching" (Murray et al., 1996, p. 57).

In general, *ethical standards are intended to guide us in carrying out the responsibilities we have to the different groups with whom we interact.* Ethics violations can occur when we are tempted to act contrary to those standards. Ethical dilemmas occur when multiple responsibilities conflict or have more than one right answer (Strike, 1988).

In a 1991 research study of psychologists teaching at academic institutions, Tabachnick and colleagues reported reactions to various ethical questions involved in teaching at the college level. Respondents were asked to report how frequently they engaged in a wide range of various activities and the extent to which those activities were ethical or unethical. The activities included things as drastic as sexual harassment and mundane as teaching materials that the instructor had not yet fully mastered.

The behavior *most often* engaged in was teaching when not adequately prepared, although it was not a consistent pattern for most people. The authors attributed this behavior more to heavy workloads and rapid advances in the field than to the shirking of responsibilities.

The rarest of behaviors were those related to sexual harassment. Whether this study is an accurate reflection of behavior or of reluctance to report such behavior is impossible to tell. Also rare were actual sexual encounters with students.

Perhaps the most interesting sources of ethical conflicts from the Tabachnick study were a result of the conflicting roles of mentor/sponsor and evaluator. For example, over two-thirds of the respondents believed that allowing a student's likability to influence a grade was unethical, but over two-thirds reported doing it at some point anyway. The same sort of dilemma is seen when instructors interact socially with students. On the one hand, the interaction with faculty is reported as vital to student growth by Pascarella and Terenzini (1991, 2005); on the other, it raises the possibility of conflict.

In another study (Braxton and Bayer, 1999), a national sample of faculty in higher education was asked to rate the acceptability of a range of violations of teaching standards, such as "The instructor insists that the student take one particular perspective on course content" or "The instructor does not introduce new teaching methods or procedures." The researchers identified 126 different behaviors that a teacher might engage in and asked the participants to rate how strong a sanction each behavior should bring. The authors then identified two levels of sanctions that they felt were present in the data. The most serious sanctions were for those norms they labeled as inviolable. These included seven clusters: condescending negativism, inattentive planning, moral turpitude, particularistic grading, personal disregard, uncommunicated course details, and uncooperative cynicism.

The second set of clusters was labeled "admonitory norms"—behaviors that, though inappropriate, didn't evoke as strong a reaction from the participants. These included advisement negligence, authoritarian classrooms, inadequate communication, inadequate course design, inconvenience avoidance, insufficient syllabus, teaching secrecy, and undermining colleagues. The final conclusion by the authors was that there were four values that seemed to undergird the judgments of the participants: respect for students as individuals, equal consideration for all students, an obligation to prepare for teaching, and an obligation to participate in the governance and life of the institution.

Values like these are becoming more and more common in discussions about teaching in higher education (Carr, 2000; Markie, 1994). In fact, the American Association of University Professors provided a statement of professional ethics dealing with the responsibilities of faculty members that highlights what AAUP considers to be the special responsibilities of individuals in an academic position (AAUP, 1987). A similar set of principles was developed by the Society for Teaching and Learning in Higher Education (STLHE) and distributed to faculty in Canadian institutions (Murray et al., 1996). Perhaps these standards can help highlight what a faculty member should consider when making personal choices.

RESPONSIBILITIES TO STUDENTS

Both the AAUP guidelines and the STLHE guidelines recognize that one of a faculty member's first responsibilities is to the students. The specifics that follow illustrate the broad range of impact that faculty can have on student lives.

To Encourage the Free Pursuit of Learning

The primary purpose of teaching is to encourage learning; therefore, the first ethical responsibility an instructor has is to that goal. All that we do to prepare and conduct well-designed instruction is part of that responsibility. The ethical instructor knows the content to be learned, the students who will do the learning, and the methods that could be used to foster the learning. The STLHE guidelines state this explicitly in its first and second principles: content competence and pedagogical competence (Murray et al., 1996). In a discussion of the ethics of teaching psychology, Matthews (1991) interprets the American Psychological Association's professional standards as they apply to teaching. In her interpretation, faculty members are responsible for remaining current and presenting accurate and balanced views of the field.

There are many ways an instructor might violate these standards. Here are two examples:

- Most obvious is to fail in our duties in class preparation. One can't always be in top form, but just as we expect students to come to class prepared, we must make the same effort. This is one of the most commonly occurring violations reported by the sample (Tabachnick, Keith-Spiegel, and Pope, 1991) and was identified as a key admonitory norm by Braxton and Bayer (1999).
- A second, less obvious way is failing to remain current both in the content area and in instructional methods that foster learning. Although it is unlikely that faculty would not be current in the content, it is very likely that faculty will not have kept up with research into better instructional methods.

A second part of this responsibility is to protect and encourage the autonomy of our students so that eventually they no longer need our constant guidance. The STLHE guidelines list this as the fourth of its eight principles: "to contribute to the intellectual development of the student" (Murray et al., 1996). If students are to develop into thinking individuals, we must structure our interactions with them in such a way as to both model and support independent thinking, even when this means they might end up disagreeing with us.

To Demonstrate Respect for Students

Ethical instructors also respect the "otherness of students" (Churchill, 1982)—that is, the individual and independent nature of the students and the fact that students are at different stages of their lives than are the instructors. For example, instructors need to be aware of the special needs of their students, whether those be cultural, physical, or based on background (Matthews, 1991). This also means respecting students' goals, their choices, and their value as individuals (Strike, 1988), another key value listed by Braxton and Bayer (1999).

The most obvious venue for this particular principle is in the interactions we have with students in and out of class. During class, the way we respond to students' questions and comments should convey the idea that everyone's participation is welcome and respected. And outside of class, the way we greet students who come to office hours or see us in the halls speaks volumes about the level of respect we have for them. We show respect by being available when we say we will be, by keeping promised appointments, by being willing to listen to students' concerns, by giving as much thought and preparation to our interactions with undergraduates as we do to those with graduate students and colleagues.

An example of a not-so-obvious need to respect students as individuals is discussed in an article by Grauerholz and Copenhaver (1994) about the use of experiential teaching methods, especially those that involve a great deal of self-disclosure by students. The choice of instructional strategies such as journaling and small-group problem sharing may violate your students' rights and be harmful as well as unethical unless done with a great deal of care and concern for the students' well-being. Use of such teaching methods raises the issue of trust because when students trust an instructor, they are more willing to engage in self-examination. Making self-examination safe for students is reason enough to be sure that your relationship with students is one of trust and respect.

Similar issues of trust arise during the discussion of sensitive topics such as race, sexual preference, and religion. When faced with a potentially sensitive situation, you can:

- Provide early disclosure of the potentially sensitive nature of the topics.
- Make sure that students understand what is being presented as fact and what as opinion.
- Offer extra time outside of class to those students who need to discuss the topics and their reactions to them (Koocher and Keith-Spiegel, 1998).

I have advised faculty to draw up a set of "rules of engagement" for sensitive topics that could spark heated debate in class. These rules would specify how these debates would be conducted and would include things such as cooling-down activities, the obligation to be able to state the other person's position before attacking it, and the avoidance of personalizing arguments. If such guidelines are provided early in the course, students can feel more comfortable when sensitive topics are raised.

This does not mean that the topics will be avoided, because that would be a violation of the first of our guidelines: open inquiry. One can see how this conflict would raise ethical dilemmas for teachers, especially in disciplines where sensitive topics are the norm rather than the exception.

To Respect Confidentiality

The issue of self-disclosure leads to another large component of respect: the belief that students have a right to privacy in their dealings with us. Not only does this principle have the weight of ethics behind it, but in many cases it also carries the weight of law. For example, it is against the law to disclose personally identifying information along with student performance information. That means no posting of grades in a way that a student can be identified. Technology has now made it possible to communicate grades quickly to individual students without unauthorized disclosure. Here, however, we are speaking of less egregious violations of privacy, such as discussing a single student's situation with someone who does not have a legitimate interest in that student's case. Practices such as leaving student papers out so that they can be retrieved at the students' convenience might be a violation of this principle because that means students have access to their peers' work (Murray et al., 1996).

To Model the Best Scholarly and Ethical Standards

A teacher, whether by accident or by design, is more to students than a content expert. The teacher is a model of all that it means to be a scholar, a thinking person. We teach not only what we know but also what we are. Part of the ethics of teaching is to realize this responsibility and to become the best models we can be, which requires some serious self-reflection on our personal standards of scholarship and living. Clark Kerr (1994), in a discussion of ethics in the academic culture, supports this struggle when he says that we are obliged to present a variety of perspectives, our own as well as others', so that the facts can be judged for themselves. This does not imply that you must always take a dispassionate stance; but even, or perhaps especially, when you feel strongly about an issue, it is necessary to demonstrate by your actions that intelligent people can disagree and still remain rational. Giving students the ability to differentiate emotion from reason is an especially important responsibility of instructors, according to Hanson (1996). As she says, "Teachers who can nimbly convey the strengths of a position they in fact oppose, who can clearly display the weaknesses in a position they in fact embrace, are *modeling* a critical engagement from which students may learn their most important lessons" (p. 35).

To Foster Honest Academic Conduct and to Ensure Fair Evaluation

Perhaps the most obvious ethical problems arise in the area of evaluation of student learning, a point echoed in both the AAUP guidelines and those from the STLHE. Instructors are the arbiters of entrance into the profession and are therefore responsible for seeing to it that standards are upheld. However, we are also responsible for guaranteeing that all are given a fair chance of demonstrating their abilities. When we allow academic dishonesty to go unheeded, we violate the rights of all the students who are abiding by the rules. If we fail to establish an evaluation system that accurately assesses the students' progress, we are abdicating our responsibilities to both the students and the profession.

The most important type of fairness for students is interactional fairness (how individuals are treated), followed by procedural fairness (the degree to which there is impartiality in how grades are determined and performance is evaluated), and finally outcome fairness (the degree to which grades and other outcomes reflect performance) (Rodabaugh, 1996).

The conflicts most often occur when this standard of fairness is pitted against the first responsibility of respecting the individual and fostering independence. The examples that opened this chapter speak to this issue. How important is it that all students be evaluated in the same way? Are we being fairer if we maintain standards and vary conditions of evaluation or if we use individual standards according to the special situation of each student? Which factors are legitimate considerations? There is no agreement on these issues. The best we can do is to continue to discuss and deliberate, alone and in groups, because the conditions under which we operate today will not be the same as those in the future.

To Avoid Exploitation, Harassment, or Discrimination

One of the variables that should be at the forefront of our thinking about the ethics of teaching is the great power discrepancy between teacher and students. Whether we like it or not, whether we seek it or not, by virtue of our position alone we are invested with a great deal of power over the lives of our students. To make matters worse, many students invest us with even more power than we are entitled to. For this reason, both the AAUP and the STLHE guidelines list one or more principles concerning harassment, exploitation, and discrimination.

Abuse of this power is at the base of many of the ethical traps that lie strewn across our paths as teachers. The very special nature of the relationship between teacher and student is all too easy to abuse (Smith, 1996). The most blatant examples of unethical behavior, those most frequently mentioned in written codes of ethics, deal with exploitation or harassment of various types: sexual, racial, religious, even intellectual. The most egregious of these (and possibly the most debated) is sexual harassment in the form of improper relationships between instructors and students. Braxton and Bayer (1999) list this as the one inviolable norm that retained its importance regardless of type of institution surveyed or discipline represented by the respondent. It could be held forth as the most important norm they identified. The area of the proper relationships between teachers and students is particularly difficult for graduate students, who are both teachers and students. Because of their age they occupy a place between their own students and their own professors. Thus, they can be either harasser or harassed. Intimate relationships between teachers and students are generally considered inappropriate at least. The best decision for an instructor or a student is to keep the relationship on a professional level as long as the power imbalance exists.

But there are plenty of other forms of exploitation that occur in academia. For example, requiring students to engage in class activities that are unrelated to the educational purposes of the course but that serve our personal ends is an abuse of power. Making derogatory comments about population subgroups is an obvious example of harassment.

Another area of ethical problems involves receiving special considerations or benefits as a result of being in a position of authority. For example, is it a violation of ethics to adopt a less-than-adequate book simply because of an incentive made available by the publisher? How legitimate is it to accept an invitation to a party or other event as the guest of a student in your class? Does it matter if that student is no longer in your class? Does it matter if the event is somehow connected with the student's academic program—for example, a dinner honoring that student's work? We must be aware that by our position alone we will sometimes be put in a compromised situation in all innocence on our part or the student's.

MAKING ETHICAL CHOICES

The array of possibilities for ethical decisions seems endless. How, then, can we avoid stumbling somewhere along the line? Although there are no easy answers, there may be some ways of thinking about our actions as professionals that will maximize the possibility of acting ethically.

Some very interesting strategies are suggested by several authors in a book on ethical dimensions of teaching edited by Fisch (1996), and the reader is pointed in that direction. Here, however, I draw the following principles for evaluating one's actions from two sources, the first five from Brown and Krager (1985) and the last from Schön (1983). They are being offered "not to impose a set of rules for decision making and behavior, but as guidelines for continuous reflection on the nature of ethicality" (Reybold, 2008, p. 293).

1. *Autonomy*. Am I acting in ways that respect freedom and treat others as autonomous?

2. *Nonmalfeasance*. Am I causing harm through either commission or omission?

3. *Beneficence*. Do my actions benefit the other person rather than myself?

4. *Justice*. Do I treat those for whom I am responsible equitably?

5. *Fidelity*. Do I uphold my part of any relationship?

6. *Acting consciously*. What are the assumptions on which I base my actions and are they valid?

IN CONCLUSION

It is a great privilege to be a teacher. But all great privileges carry great responsibilities as well. Many of those responsibilities are subtle, thrust on us by the expectations of others rather than sought by us. Keeping those six principles in mind won't solve all the ethical dilemmas you face as a teacher, but they might give you a way to reflect on them alone and with other teachers. Teach your students to reflect both in and out of class. That reflection should never stop, because conscious reflection on values is perhaps the cornerstone of the ethics of teaching.

Supplementary Reading

- American Association of University Professors, "Statement on Professional Ethics," *Academe*, 1987, *73*(4), 49.
- S. M. Cahn, *Saints and Scamps: Ethics in Academia*, 2nd ed. (Totowa, NJ: Rowman & Littlefield, 1994).
- D. Carr, *Professionalism and Ethics in Teaching* (New York: Routledge, 2000).

- L. Fisch (ed.), "Ethical Dimensions of College and University Teaching: Understanding and Honoring the Special Relationship Between Teachers and Students," *New Directions for Teaching and Learning*, no. 66, 1996.
- W. L. Humphreys, "Values in Teaching and the Teaching of Values," *Teaching-Learning Issues*, no. 58 (Knoxville: Learning Research Center, University of Tennessee, 1986).
- C. Kerr, "Knowledge Ethics and the New Academic Culture," *Change*, 1994, *26*(1), 8–16.
- M. Lewis, *Poisoning the Ivy: The Seven Deadly Sins and Other Vices of Higher Education in America* (Armonk, NY: M. E. Sharpe, 1997).
- P. Markie, *A Professor's Duties: Ethical Issues in College Teaching* (Totowa, NJ: Rowman & Littlefield, 1994).
- D. Schön, *The Reflective Practitioner* (San Francisco: Jossey-Bass, 1983).

Part 7

Lifelong Learning as a Teacher

Chapter 23

Vitality and Growth Throughout Your Teaching Career

Bill and I have both been teaching for a long time (he for 60-plus years, I for 30-plus). Neither of us is as effective as we could be because we don't know today's student culture well enough to build good bridges between them and the course content. But both of us continue to be exhilarated going to class. And we continue to pick up new ideas to try out in next class. One of Bill's students commented on the student rating form, "Dr. McKeachie comes to class everyday as if there were no place on earth he'd rather be." What can be done to foster continued development and enjoyment for all teachers?

Part of the answer lies in motivation research. Human beings have survived as a species because we are learners. We enjoy learning; we become curious when we confront something more complex than we are accustomed to; we like to confront and master challenges; we take pleasure in becoming and feeling competent.

Human beings are also a social species. We are stimulated by interaction with other human beings; in times of stress, we rely on social support; we learn from one another. We also derive pleasure from helping others.

Teaching is thus an ideal career. There is infinite complexity and challenge. New developments in our discipline, new research and theory about learning and teaching, new technology, and creative new ideas for teaching continually emerge. Our roles often shift as changes in curriculum occur. There are never-ending opportunities to grow in competence and understanding.

Teaching is both an intellectual and a social activity. Each term, students come up with new questions, stimulate new insights. Classes offer ever-changing interpersonal dynamics. Getting to know and like each new group provides a continuing source of satisfaction and stimulation. And it is particularly rewarding when former students speak warmly of how we have made a difference in their lives.

The human interactions also offer challenges. There are always some students who seem to be uninterested, some who are confrontational, some who seldom appear. Trying to find out more about the reasons for their behavior, getting to know them better, finding their interests and trying to relate the course material to their interests and goals, involving them in teamwork with other students, demonstrating that you are committed to their learning—all of these may fail, but when something works, what satisfaction!

From the standpoint of motivation theory, it is thus clear that teaching offers great potential for continued vitality, growth, and satisfaction. But these do not come automatically. In fact, developing as a teacher is an ongoing activity. As you develop some skills and strategies that work, they generate positive reactions; this in turn increases your confidence; and that in turn generates more reflection and thinking about teaching as well as interest in developing additional skills.

HOW CAN YOU DEVELOP EFFECTIVE SKILLS AND STRATEGIES?

The easy answer is "Practice, practice, practice." Practice is important, but just as in sports or music, if one is practicing the wrong technique, one is not likely to improve. Psychologists would add to the "practice" maxim: "Practice with feedback—knowledge of results." But how can you get good feedback on what works and what doesn't?

Looking for New Ideas, Methods, and Strategies

There are three possibilities: reading, hearing, and seeing.

Reading We mention this first because you have been reading this book, which was written on the premise that most faculty members have learned how to learn from reading. At the end of each chapter are suggestions for other books or sources that can provide additional insights or suggestions. In addition to the more general resources to which we have referred, there are journals in each discipline dealing with teaching and education in that discipline.

Discussing Peers are among the best sources of ideas. Talking about teaching with colleagues can be an invaluable source of ideas as well as provide emotional support when a class hasn't gone well. The colleagues need not be in your own discipline. You will often get interesting ideas from teachers in other disciplines. Most professionals in teaching improvement will tell you that the typical comment on feedback sheets is: "The best thing about the workshop was getting ideas from faculty members in other fields who have similar interests and problems."

Seeing, Experiencing One of the best ways to learn a new skill is to see it performed. As you talk to your colleagues about teaching, ask if they would mind if you observed a class to see how they actually use a particular method. Faculty development centers frequently sponsor workshops in which you can see and experience particular methods of teaching or uses of technology. Videotapes demonstrating various methods of teaching are also available online.

How Can You Get Feedback to Help You Continue to Improve?

Feedback from Student Performance. We haven't taught well if students haven't learned; so the ultimate test of our teaching is evidence of learning. Unfortunately, just as students blame the instructor if they fail to learn, we blame the students for not learning.

But everyone can learn. Our task is to facilitate learning, and if our students are not learning, we have not motivated them, presented material at an appropriate level, arranged activities that would promote effective learning, or taught the students how to learn more effectively.

All too often we pay attention to mistakes, poor papers, and items that were missed on examinations as the basis for assigning grades but fail to think about how we might have better taught the material that was missed. Asking a colleague to look over a few student papers will not only help determine whether your expectations were unreasonable but also result in suggestions for ways of presenting the particular area in which students are not performing well. In every discipline there are some concepts or skills that seem to be particularly difficult to teach. Meyer and Land (2006) called them "threshold concepts" because they have to be gotten over to proceed. Often, experienced teachers have strategies for overcoming these difficulties. I've also found that disciplinary journals that have sections on teaching often have articles on just these concepts.

Feedback from Peers Probably the most common form of peer feedback is based on classroom visits. As Centra (1975) demonstrated, classroom observation by peers is a very unreliable source of evidence for decisions about promotion or merit pay. Even when the observer is not there to obtain evidence for our personnel files, we are likely to be concerned about what kind of impression we will make. Clearly we want an observer who will be helpful and whom we can trust. Bob Wilson at Berkeley found that retired faculty members were particularly helpful, not only because of their experience in teaching the discipline, but also because they were not involved in personnel decisions. Campbell Crockett, former dean at the University of Cincinnati, formed "helping pairs" among new teachers. Here the partners are in the same boat—both learning, presumably helping and being helped by each other—a symmetrical arrangement that reduced the threat.

The usefulness of peer observation depends partly on what you want to find out. If there is a particular aspect of your teaching that you are concerned about, be sure that the observer knows what to look for. Knowing what to look for is in fact a general principle applying to observations. Meeting with the observer to tell him or her before the observation what your goals are and what you are planning to do will increase the helpfulness of the observation. Centra (1993) gives some sample forms used for colleague observations, and you may work out your own observation form using items from these forms. But the major usefulness of colleague observation comes from your discussion after the observation. Here you have a chance to question, probe for examples, and ask for suggestions.

Feedback from Faculty Development Specialists Most colleges and universities now have faculty or staff members who are assigned the task of improving instruction. Often they are available to videotape or observe classes. Videotaping would seem on the face of it to be especially helpful. However, research has shown that only when the videotape is viewed with a consultant who calls our attention to the more important items is seeing the videotape likely to result in improvement.

One method used by many faculty developers is small-group instructional diagnosis (SGID), originated by Dr. Joseph Clark at the

University of Washington. This combines observation with feedback from students.

Typically a consultant using SGID meets before the class with the instructor who desires feedback; the purpose of this meeting is to learn about the class and the instructor's goals and needs, as well as to establish the procedures. The instructor explains the procedure to the class, assuring the class that comments will be confidential and used only to help him or her learn how the course is going. After teaching for about half the class period, the instructor turns the class over to the observer and leaves the room. The observer then asks the students to form small groups to discuss their learning experiences in the group. Often the observer asks the groups to answer such questions as "What aspects of the class have helped you learn? What aspects have been unhelpful? What suggestions do you have?"

After about ten minutes, a member previously designated as reporter gives each group's answers to the questions. The consultant summarizes the reports and asks for student comments. After the class, the consultant discusses the reports with the teacher and offers encouragement, suggestions if the instructor is unsure about what alternatives might help, and clarification if the instructor finds some comments confusing or contradictory. At the next class meeting, the instructor discusses the feedback, indicating what changes will be made or why certain things cannot be changed.

Feedback from Students Probably the most familiar form of feedback from students is student ratings of teaching. Student ratings are now administered in almost all colleges and universities in the United States and are becoming common in other countries. However, their primary purpose is often to collect data for personnel evaluation, and this complicates and sometimes conflicts with their usefulness for improving teaching. One problem is that those who use student ratings for personnel purposes often feel (unjustifiably) that they need to use a standard form that can be used to compare teachers, across disciplines, in a variety of types of classes, in required as well as elective courses, in large and small classes, and in a variety of contexts. The result is that the questions on the form are so general that they may be irrelevant to a particular class and, even if relevant, are worded so generally that they offer little guidance for improvement. Moreover, they are typically given at the end of the semester, when it is too late to make much improvement for the class from which the feedback comes. So how can we use student ratings for continued growth in teaching effectiveness?

Keys to Improvement with Feedback from Students

1. *Get the feedback early enough to make a difference for the students who give it.* A good time to collect feedback from students is after the third or fourth week of the term. The important thing is that you have time to adjust to this particular class. (Remember that each class is different. What works well in one class may not in the next.) As was mentioned with respect to SGID, you should review the feedback with the class, indicating which suggestions you intend to implement, and discussing differences of opinion among students.

2. *Don't feel that you need to use the standard form.* If you want ratings, choose items that will be useful to you. The advantage of ratings is that you can cover a number of aspects of teaching relatively quickly. But open-ended questions are often equally or more useful. Usually you can simply ask students to write on two questions:

- "What have you liked about the course so far?" or "What aspects of the course have been valuable for your learning so far?"
- "What suggestions do you have for improvement?"

Sometimes you can use questions such as:

- "What have you done that has helped you learn effectively in this course?"
- "What has the teacher done that has helped you learn?"

You can even ask students for comments on a particular class session in the last five minutes of class.

3. *Supplement end-of-course ratings.* All faculty members in our college are required to collect student ratings at the end of the term. Five items are mandatory, and the rest of the items may be chosen by the department and instructor from a large list of possible items, including some open-ended items. We suggest choosing two types of items—those having to do with goals of education and those dealing with specific behaviors.

Some scaled items with respect to goals are usually something like:

- "I became more interested in the subject matter of this course."
- "My intellectual curiosity has been stimulated by this course."
- "I am learning to think more clearly about the area of this course."

Behavioral items could include:

- "The instructor knew students' names."
- "The instructor gives multiple examples."
- "The instructor points out practical applications."

Open-ended items would be something like the ones listed earlier.

IN CONCLUSION

The great thing about teaching is that there is always more to learn. The various sources of ideas and feedback that we have described help us to improve. As we improve, our students respond more positively, and their increased interest and enthusiasm sparks us to even more effort and enjoyment. Obviously, the course is not always onward and upward. There are moments of frustration and despair, but there are enough good times to help us through those that are not so good.

Most of this book has dealt teaching in the classroom, but research has shown that those faculty members who have the most impact on students spend time with students outside the classroom. This is not only important for the students' development, but it also contributes to your continuing vitality as a teacher.

Over the years, both Bill and I have visited hundreds of colleges and universities, both in this country and in others. What most impresses us is that, no matter how difficult the circumstances, there are always some vital, effective teachers. They come in no one personality, no one discipline, no one institution. Somehow teachers find a way to cope and are able to stimulate effective learning.

This chapter has discussed at length ways to grow. However much you are intrigued by new possibilities, it is important not to forget what you enjoy doing. Our final advice is, "*Have fun!*"

Supplementary Reading

The many books recommended as supplementary reading in previous chapters are relevant to your lifelong learning, but to save you the trouble of looking back, we will mention here once again several books that nicely cover the major areas of teaching:

- S. Ambrose, M. Bridges, M. DiPietro, M. Lovett, and M. Norman, *How Learning Works: 7 Research-Based Principles for Smart Teaching*. (San Francisco: Jossey-Bass Publishers, 2010). This is a very approachable base for understanding many of the principles of learning and motivation.
- T. Angelo and K.P. Cross, *Classroom Assessment Techniques: A Handbook for College Teachers* (San Francisco: Jossey-Bass Publishers, 1993). The CATs, as they are called in this book, are a wonderful selection of active strategies that can be used to track student learning.
- W. Buskist and J. Groccia (eds.), "Evidence-Based Teaching". *New Directions for Teaching and Learning* no. 128 (San Francisco: Jossey-Bass Publishers, 2011).

- P. Cooper and C. Simonds, *Communication for the Classroom Teacher*, 8th edition (Boston: Pearson/Allyn and Bacon, 2007).
- B. G. Davis, *Tools for Teaching*, 2nd edition (San Francisco: Jossey-Bass, 2009).
- D. Duffy and J. Jones, *Teaching within the Rhythms of the Semester.* (San Francisco: Jossey-Bass Publisher, 1995). This book approaches the semester as an organizing timeline since classes ebb and flow during the semester.
- K. Eble, *The Craft of Teaching*, 2nd edition (San Francisco: Jossey-Bass, 1988). Don't think that a 1988 book must be out of date by now. This is a good book to read when you've lost your initial anxiety and want to think about teaching as a craft and a calling.
- L. Dee Fink, *Creating Significant Learning Experiences* (San Francisco: Jossey-Bass, 2003). Fink focuses on ways of structuring instruction to maximize goals.
- Linc Fisch, *The Chalk Dust Collection: Thoughts and Reflections on Teaching in Colleges and Universities* (Stillwater, OK: New Forums Press, 1996). A thoughtful, often amusing collection of essays with much good sense.
- Diane F. Halpern and Milton D. Hakel (eds.), "Applying the Science of Learning to University Teaching and Beyond," *New Directions for Teaching and Learning*, no. 89 (San Francisco: Jossey-Bass, 2002).
- R. Prieto and S. A. Meyers, *The Teaching Assistant Handbook* (Stillwater, OK: New Forums Press, 2001).
- Parker Palmer's book, *The Courage to Teach: Exploring the Inner Landscape of a Teacher's Life* (San Francisco: Jossey-Bass, 1998). This book will inspire you.
- Beth M. Schwartz and Regan Gurung (2012) *Evidence-based Teaching for Higher Education.* Washington, DC: American Psychological Association. This is a compilation of research on teaching. Each chapter covers an area of teaching that has been studied, such as building rapport, using technology, teaching online and many more.
- M. Weimer *Learner-Centered Teaching: Five Key Changes to Practice* (San Francisco: Jossey-Bass, 2002). Maryellen Weimer was the long time editor of *The Teaching Professor* and has many excellent books on a range of topics for college teachers.
- G. Wiggins and J. McTighe *Understanding by Design* (Upper Saddle River, NJ: ASCD-Merrill Prentice Hall, 1998). This is an enlightening how-to book on designing instruction backwards – starting with understanding.

The following five books come from authors writing from the perspective of experience in other countries. Their contents are relevant to university teachers in all countries.

- J. Biggs, *Teaching for Quality Learning at University* (Buckingham, UK, and Philadelphia: Society for Research into Higher Education and Open University Press, 1999).
- Nira Hativa, *Teaching for Effective Learning in Higher Education* (Dordrecht: Kluwer, 2000).
- John Hattie (2009) *Visible Learning: A Synthesis of over 800 Meta-analyses Relating to Achievement*. London: Routledge. The title says it all. The author compiled the results of meta-analyses into a pretty comprehensive list of what works and what doesn't, and how much each aspect of education contributes to student achievement.
- Daphne Pan, *Learning to Teach, Learning to Learn* (Singapore: National University of Singapore, 2001).
- P. Ramsden, *Learning to Teach in Higher Education* (London and New York: Routledge, 1992).

Many university faculty development centers publish newsletters for their own faculties. In addition there are two national publications on college teaching: *The National Teaching and Learning Forum* and *The Teaching Professor*. Both have helpful articles.

Websites that might be of interest:

- National Teaching Learning Forum—www.ntlf.com/html/lib/bib/bib.htm
- Professional and Organizational Development Network in Higher Education—www.podnetwork.org/resources/periodicals.htm and www.podnetwork.org/resources/facultydev.htm
- The Carnegie Foundation for the Advancement of Teaching—www.carnegiefoundation.org

REFERENCES

ABCNEWS.com. (2004, April 29). Full-service fakery: Inside the life of a professional essay writer and test taker [Online]. Available at: http://abcnews.go.com/Primetime/story?id=132377&page=1.

Acee, T. W., and Weinstein, C. E. (2010). Effects of a value reappraisal intervention on statistics students' motivation and performance. *Journal of Experimental Education, 78*, 487–512. doi:10.1080/00220970903352753.

Achacoso, M., and Svinicki, M. (eds.). (2005, Spring). New testing alternatives. *New Directions for Teaching and Learning* (no. 100). San Francisco, CA: Jossey-Bass.

Adams, J. (2005). What makes the grade? Faculty and student perceptions. *Teaching of Psychology, 32*(1), 21–24.

Aguayo, D., Herman, K., Ojeda, L., and Flores, L. (2011). Culture predicts Mexican Americans' college self-efficacy and college performance. *Journal of Diversity in Higher Education, 4*, 79–89.

Albanese, M. A., and Mitchell, S. (1993). Problem-based learning: A review of literature on its outcomes and implementation issues. *Academic Medicine, 68*, 52–81.

Alexander, P. A., and Judy, J. E. (1988). The interaction of domain-specific and strategic knowledge in academic performance. *Review of Educational Research, 58*(4), 375–404.

Alexander, P. A., Murphy, P. K., and Kulikowich, J. M. (2009). Expertise and the adult learner: A historical, psychological, and methodological exploration. In M. C. Smith and N. DeFrates-Densch (eds.), *Handbook of Research on Adult Learning and Development* (pp. 484–523). New York: Taylor & Francis.

Altman, H., and Cashin, W. (1992). Writing a syllabus. IDEA Paper # 27. Available at: www.theideacenter.org/IDEAPaper27.

Altmiller, H. (1973). Another approach to freshman chemistry. *Journal of Chemical Education, 50*, 249.

Alverno College Faculty. (1994). *Student Assessment Learning at Alverno College*. Milwaukee, WI: Alverno Publications.

American Association of Colleges and Universities (AAC&U). (2009). *The LEAP Vision for Learning: Outcomes, Practices, and Impact and Employers' views*. Washington, DC: AAC&U.

American Association of University Professors (AAUP). (1987). Statement on professional ethics. *Academe, 73*(4), 49.

American Psychological Association (APA). (2010). *APAGS Resource Guide for Ethnic Minority Graduate Students.* Available at: http://apa.org/pubs/books/ethnic-minority-guide.aspx.

Ames, C. (1992). Classrooms: Goals, structures, and student motivation. *Journal of Educational Psychology, 84,* 261–271.

Anderson, L. W., and Krathwohl, D. R. (eds.). (2001). *A Taxonomy for Learning, Teaching, and Assessing: A Revision of Bloom's Taxonomy of Educational Objectives.* New York: Longman.

Andre, T. (1987). Questions and learning from reading. *Questioning Exchange, 1*(1), 47–86.

Angelo, T. A., and Cross, K. P. (1993). *Classroom Assessment Techniques: A Handbook for College Faculty* (2nd ed.). San Francisco, CA: Jossey-Bass.

Annis, L. F. (1981). Effect of preference for assigned lecture notes on student achievement. *Journal of Educational Research, 74,* 179–181.

———. (1983). The processes and effects of peer tutoring. *Human Learning, 2,* 39–47.

Apfelthaler, G., Hansen, K., Keuchel, S., Mueller, C., Neubauer, M., Ong, S., and Tapachai, N. (2007). Cross-cultural differences in learning and education. In D. Palfreyman and D. McBride (eds.), *Learning and Teaching Across Cultures in Higher Education.* New York: Palgrave Macmillan.

Apple, T., and Cutler, A. (1999). The Rensselaer studio General Chemistry course. *Journal of Chemical Education, 76,* 462–463.

Arce, J., and Betancourt, R. (1997). Student-designed experiments in scientific lab instruction. *Journal of College Science Teaching, 27,* 114–118.

Arkright-Keeler, D. L., and Stapleton, S. (2007). Education resources for guiding discussions on ethics in science. *Biochemistry and Molecular Biology Education, 35,* 24–47.

Arnold, S. M., Bender, J., Cytrynbaum, S., Newman, B. M., Ringwald, B., Ringwald, J., and Rosenwein, R. (1970). The natural history of the classroom. In R. Mann (ed.), *The College Classroom.* New York: Wiley.

Aronson, E. (1978). *The Jigsaw Classroom.* Oxford, England: Sage.

Aronson, J., Lustina, M., Good, C., Keogh, K., Steele, C., and Brown, J. (1999). When White men can't do math: Necessary and sufficient factors in stereotype threat. *Journal of Experimental Social Psychology, 35,* 29–46.

Arredondo, P. (1991). Counseling Latinas. In C. Lee and B. Richardson (eds.), *Multicultural Issues in Counseling: New Approaches to Diversity* (pp. 143–156). Alexandria, VA: American Counseling Association.

Arum, R., and Roksa, J. (2011). *Academically Adrift: Limited Learning on College Campuses.* Chicago, IL: University of Chicago.

Attneave, C. (1982). American Indian and Alaskan native families: Emigrants in their own homeland. In M. McGoldrick, J. Pearce, and J. Giordano (eds.), *Ethnicity and Family Therapy* (pp. 55–83). New York: Guilford Press.

Babb, K., and Ross, C. (2009). The timing of online lecture slide availability and its effect on attendance, participation, and exam performance. *Computers & Education*, *52*, 868–881.

Bailey, C. A., Kingsbury, K., Kulinowski, K., Paradis, J., and Schoonover, R. (2000). An integrated lecture-laboratory environment of General Chemistry. *Journal of Chemical Education*, *77*, 195–199.

Baker, L., and Lombardi, B. (1985). Students' lecture notes and their relation to test performance. *Teaching of Psychology*, *12*(1), 28–32.

Baker, N., and Verran, J. (2004). The future of microbiology laboratory classes—wet, dry or in combination? *Nature Reviews Microbiology*, *2*, 338–342.

Bargh, J. A., and Schul, Y. (1980). On the cognitive benefits of teaching. *Journal of Educational Psychology*, *72*(5), 593–604.

Barr, R. B., and Tagg, J. (1995). From teaching to learning—A new paradigm for undergraduate education. *Change*, *27*, 12–25.

Baruth, L., and Manning, M. (1991). *Multicultural Counseling and Psychotherapy*. New York: Merrill.

Basol, G., and Johanson, G. (2009). Effectiveness of frequent testing over achievement: A meta-analysis. *International Journal of Human Sciences*, *6*(2), 99–121.

Bauer, K. W., and Bennett, J. S. (2003). Alumni perceptions used to assess undergraduate research experience. *The Journal of Higher Education*, *74*, 210–230.

Baxter-Magolda, M., King, P., and Drobney, K. (2010). Practices that provide effective academic challenge for first-year students. *Journal of Excellence in College Teaching*, *21*(2), 45–65.

Becker, J. (2005). Cutting edge research by undergraduates on a shoestring? *Journal of Computing Sciences*, *21*, 160–168.

Benjamin, L. (1991). Personalization and active learning in the large introductory psychology class. *Teaching of Psychology*, *18*(2), 68–74.

———. (2005). Setting course goals: Privileges and responsibilities in a world of ideas. *Teaching of Psychology*, *32*(3), 146–149.

Berge, Z. (2000). Components of the online classroom. In R. E. Weiss, D. S. Knowlton, B. W. Speck (eds.), Principles of effective teaching in the online classroom. *New Directions for Teaching and Learning* (no. 84, pp. 23–28). San Francisco, CA: Jossey-Bass.

Berlyne, D. E. (1954a). An experimental study of human curiosity. *British Journal of Psychology*, *45*, 256–265.

———. (1954b). A theory of human curiosity. *British Journal of Psychology*, *45*, 180–181.

Bernstein, D., and Bass, R. (2005). The scholarship of teaching and learning. *Academe*, *91*(4), 37–43.

Berry, T., Cook, L., Hill, N., and Stevens, K. (2011). An exploratory analysis of textbook usage and study habit: Misperceptions and barriers to success. *College Teaching*, *59*(1), 31–39.

Bieron, J. F., and Dinan, F. J. (2000). Not your ordinary lab day. *Journal of College Science Teaching, 30*(1), 44–47.

Biggs, J. (1999). *Teaching for Quality Learning at University*. Buckingham, UK: SRHE, and Philadelphia, PA: Open University Press.

Biggs, J. B., and Collis, K. (1982). *Evaluating the Quality of Learning: The SOLO Taxonomy*. New York: Academic Press.

Bjorklund, W., and Rehling, D. (2010). Student perceptions of classroom incivility. *College Teaching, 58,* 15–18.

Black, P., and Wiliam, D. (1998). Assessment and classroom learning. *Assessment in Education, 5*(1), 7–74.

Bligh, D. (2000). *What's the Use of Lectures?* San Francisco, CA: Jossey-Bass.

Block, C. (1981). Black Americans and the cross-cultural counseling and psychotherapy experience. In A. Marsella and P. Pedersen (eds.), *Cross-Cultural Counseling and Psychotherapy* (pp. 177–194). New York: Pergamon Press.

Bloom, B. S. (ed.). (1956). *Taxonomy of Educational Objectives: The Classification of Educational Goals*. New York: Longman.

Bloxham, S., and Campbell, L. (September 1–3, 2008). *Creating a Feedback Dialogue: Exploring the Use of Interactive Coversheets*. Paper presented at the Improving Student Learning Symposium, University of Durham.

Blumberg, P. (2009). Maximizing learning through course alignment and experience with different types of knowledge. *Innovative Higher Education, 34*(2), 93–103.

Boekaerts, M. (2011). Emotions, emotion regulation, and self-regulation of learning. In B. J. Zimmerman and D. H. Schunk (eds.), *Handbook of Self-Regulation of Learning and Performance* (pp. 408–425). New York, NY: Taylor & Francis.

Boekaerts, M., and Niemivirta, M. (2000). Self-regulation in learning: Finding a balance between learning- and ego-protective goals. In M. Boekaerts, P. R. Pintrich, and M. Zeidner (eds.), *Handbook of Self-Regulation* (pp. 417–450). San Diego, CA: Academic Press.

Boekaerts, M., Pintrich, P. R., and Zeidner, M. (eds.). (2000). *Handbook of Self-Regulation*. San Diego, CA: Academic Press.

Bolin, A., Khramtsova, I., and Saarnio, D., (2005). Using student journals to stimulate authentic learning: Balancing Bloom's cognitive and affective domains. *Teaching of Psychology, 32*(3), 154–159.

Bonk, C. J., and Cunningham, D. J. (1998). Searching for learner-centered, constructivist, and sociocultural components of collaborative educational learning tools. In C. J. Bonk and S. K. King (eds.), *Electronic Collaborators: Learner-Centered Technologies for Literacy, Apprenticeship, and Discourse* (pp. 25–50). Mahwah, NJ: Erlbaum.

Boud, D., Cohen, R., and Sampson, J. (2001). *Peer Learning in Higher Education: Learning from and with Each Other*. Sterling, VA: Kogan Page.

Bowser, B., Young, G., and Jones, T. (1993). *Confronting Diversity Issues on Campus*. Newbury Park, CA: Sage.

Braxton, J. M., and Bayer, A. (1999). *Faculty Misconduct in Collegiate Teaching*. Baltimore, MD: Johns Hopkins Press.

———. (2004). Addressing faculty and student classroom improprieties. *New Directions for Teaching and Learning* (no 99). San Francisco, CA: Jossey-Bass Publisher.

Bray, M., and Kehle, T. (eds.), (2011). *The Oxford Handbook of School Psychology. Oxford Library of Psychology*. New York: Oxford University Press.

Brown, J. S. (2000). Growing up digital: How the Web changes work, education, and the ways people learn. *Change*, *32*(2), 11–20.

Brown, R. D., and Krager, L. (1985). Ethical issues in graduate education: Faculty and student responsibilities. *Journal of Higher Education*, *56*, 403–418.

Brown, S., and Kysilka, M. (2002). *Applying Multicultural and Global Concepts in the Classroom and Beyond*. Boston, MA: Allyn and Bacon.

Bruff, D. (2009). *Teaching with Classroom Response Systems: Creating Active Learning Environments*. San Francisco, CA: John Wiley and Sons.

Cahn, S. (1994). *Saints and Scamps: Ethics in Academia*. Lanham, MD: Rowan and Littlefield Publishers, Inc.

Calzada, E. (2010). Bringing culture into parent training with Latinos. *Cognitive and Behavioral Practice*, *17*, 167–175.

Campbell, R. (1999). Mouths, machines, and minds. *The Psychologist*, *12*, 446–449.

Canada, M., and Speck, B. (2001). Developing and implementing service learning programs. *New Directions for Higher Education* (no. 114). San Francisco, CA: Jossey-Bass.

Cano, M., and Castilo, L. (2010). The role of enculturation and acculturation on Latina college student distress. *Journal of Hispanic Higher Education*, *9*, 221–231.

Carney, A., Fry, S., Gabriele, R., and Ballard, M. (2008). Reeling in the big fish: Changing pedagogy to encourage the completion of reading assignments. *College Teaching*, *56*(4), 195–200.

Caron, M. D., Whitbourne, S. K., and Halgin, R. P. (1992). Fraudulent excuse making among college students. *Teaching of Psychology*, *19*(2), 90–93.

Carr, D. (2000). *Professionalism and Ethics in Teaching*. New York: Routledge.

Case, K., Bartsch, R., McEnery, L., Hall, S., Humann, A., and Foster, D. (2008). Establishing a comfortable classroom from day one: Student perceptions of the reciprocal interview. *College Teaching*, *56*(4), 210–214.

Casteel, M. A., and Bridges, K. R. (2007). Goodbye lecture: A student-led seminar approach for teaching upper division courses. *Teaching of Psychology*, *34*(2), 107–110.

Caverly, D., Mandeville, S., and Nicholson, S. (1995). Plan: A study-reading strategy for informational text. *Journal of Adolescent and Adult Literacy*, *39*(3), 190–121.

Center for Authentic Science Practice in Education. (2009). [Online]. Available at: http://www.purdue.edu/dp/caspie.

Centra, J. A. (1975). Colleagues as raters of classroom instruction. *Journal of Higher Education*, *46*, 327–337.

———. (1993). *Reflective Faculty Evaluation: Enhancing Teaching and Determining Faculty Effectiveness*. San Francisco, CA: Jossey-Bass.

Cervantes, R., and Cordova, D. (2011). Life experiences of Hispanic adolescents: Developmental and language considerations in acculturation stress. *Journal of Community Psychology*, *39*, 336–352.

Champagne, A. B., Klofper, L. E., and Anderson, J. H. (1980). Factors influencing the learning of classical mechanics. *American Journal of Physics*, *48*, 1074–1079.

Chang, T. M., Crombag, H. F., van der Drift, K. D. J. M., and Moonen, J. M. (1983). *Distance Learning: On the Design of an Open University*. Boston, MA: Kluwer-Nijhoff.

Chi, M. T. H., Glaser, R., and Farr, M. J. (eds.). (1988). *The Nature of Expertise*. Hillsdale, NJ: Erlbaum.

Chickering, A. W., and Gamson, Z. F. (1987). Seven principles for good practice in undergraduate education. *Wingspread Journal*, *9*(2), special insert.

Churchill, L. R. (1982). The teaching of ethics and moral values in teaching. *Journal of Higher Education*, *53*(3), 296–306.

Clague, M. (Summer, 2004). Personal communication.

Clapp, W. C., Rubens, M. T., Sabharwal, J., and Gazzaley, A. (2011). Deficit in switching between functional brain networks underlies the impact of multitasking on working memory in older adults. *Publications of the National Academy of Sciences*, *108*, 7212–7217.

Clark, J. (2008). PowerPoint and pedagogy: Maintaining student interest in university lectures. *College Teaching*, *56*(1), 39–44.

Clark, R., and Mayer, R. E. (2008). *E-Learning and the Science of Instruction* (2nd ed.). San Francisco, CA: Jossey-Bass.

Clark, R. E. (1994a). Media and method. *Educational Technology Research and Development*, *42*(3), 7–10.

———. (1994b). Media will never influence learning. *Educational Technology, Research and Development*, *42*(2), 21–29.

Coghlan, E., Futey, D., Little, J., Lomas, C., Oblinger, D., and Windham, C. (2007). ELI discovery tool: Guide to podcasting [Online]. Retrieved February 12, 2009. Available at: http://www.educause.edu/GuideToPodcasting/12830.

Cohen, P., Kulik, J., and Kulik, C. L. (1982). Educational outcomes of tutoring: A meta-analysis of findings. *American Educational Research Journal*, *19*(2), 237–248.

Cokley, K., McClain, S., Enciso, A., Jones, B., and Martinez, M. (2010, August). Ethnic minority differences in imposter phenomenon and minority-status stress. Poster session presented at the meeting of the American Psychological Association, San Diego, CA.

Coldren, J., and Hively, J. (2009). Interpersonal teaching style and student impression formation. *College Teaching, 57*(2), 93–98.

Connor-Greene, P. A. (2006). Interdisciplinary critical inquiry: Teaching about the social construction of madness. *Teaching of Psychology, 33,* 6–13.

Cooper, J. L., Robinson, P., and Ball, D. (eds.). (2003). *Small group instruction in higher education: Lessons from the past, visions of the future.* Stillwater, OK: New Forums Press.

Coppola, B. P. (1995, Summer). Progress in practice: Using concepts from motivation and self-regulated learning research to improve chemistry instruction. In P. R. Pintrich (ed.), Understanding self-regulated learning. *New Directions for Teaching and Learning* (no. 63, pp. 87–96). San Francisco, CA: Jossey-Bass.

———. (2000). Targeting entry points for ethics in chemistry teaching and learning. *Journal of Chemical Education, 77,* 1506–1511.

Coppola, B. P., Ege, S. N., and Lawton, R. G. (1997). The University of Michigan undergraduate chemistry curriculum: 2. Instructional strategies and assessment. *Journal of Chemical Education, 74,* 84–94.

Costin, F. (1972). Three-choice versus four-choice items: Implications for reliability and validity of objective achievement tests. *Educational and Psychological Measurement, 32,* 1035–1038.

Covington, M. V. (1999). Caring about learning: The nature and nurture of subject-matter appreciation. *Educational Psychologist, 34,* 127–136.

Crawley, E., Malmqvist, J., Östlund, S., and Brodeur, D. (2007). *Rethinking Engineering Education: The CDIO Approach.* New York: Springer.

Creed, T. (1997). PowerPoint, No! Cyberspace, Yes. *National Teaching and Learning Forum, 6*(4), 5–7.

Cronbach, L. J., and Snow, R. E. (1977). *Aptitudes and Instructional Methods: A Handbook for Research on Interaction.* New York: Irvington.

Cross, K. P., and Steadman, M. H. (1996). *Classroom Research: Implementing the Scholarship of Teaching.* San Francisco, CA: Jossey-Bass.

Culver, T., and Morse, L. (2008). Helping students use their textbooks more effectively. *Teaching Professor, 22*(4), 5.

CUR. (2009). Council on undergraduate research [Online]. Available at: http://www.cur.org.

Damasio, A. (1994). *Descartes' Error: Emotion, Reason, and the Human Brain.* New York: Putnam Publishing.

Damasio, A. (1994). *Descartes' Error: Emotion, Reason, and the Human Brain.* New York: The Hearst Company.

Davies, P. (2000, November). Computerized peer assessment. *Innovation in Education and Training International, 37*(4), 346–355.

Day, R. S. (1980). Teaching from notes: Some cognitive consequences. *New Directions for Teaching and Learning* (no. 2, pp. 95–112). San Francisco, CA: Jossey-Bass.

Deci, E., and Ryan, R. (2000). The "what" and "why" of goal pursuits: Human needs and the self-determination of behavior. *Psychological Inquiry, 11,* 227–268.

De George-Walker, L., and Keeffe, M. (2010). Self-determined blended learning: A case study of blended learning design. *Higher Education Research & Development, 29*(1), 1–13.

de Simone, C. (2007). Application of concept mapping. *College Teaching, 55*(1), 33–36.

Dever, B., and Karabenick, S. (2011). Is authoritative teaching beneficial for all students? A multi-level model of the effects of teaching style on interest and achievement. *School Psychology Quarterly, 26,* 131–144.

DeVries, M., Golon, A., and Castellano, J. (2011). Making education relevant for gifted Native Americans: Teaching to their learning style. In J. Castellano and A. Frazier (eds.), *Special Populations in Gifted Education: Understanding Our Most Able Students from Diverse Backgrounds* (pp. 47–72). Waco, TX: Prufrock Press.

Dewey, R. (1995, March). Finding the right introductory psychology textbook. *APS Observer,* 32–35.

DeZure, D., Kaplan, M., and Deerman, M. (2001). Research on student notetaking: Implications for faculty and graduate student instructors. CRLT Occasional Paper, No. 16. Ann Arbor, MI: University of Michigan Center for Research on Learning and Teaching. Available at: http://www.crlt.umich.edu/publinks/CRLT_no16.pdf.

DiBiase, W. J., and Wagner, E. P. (2002). Aligning General Chemistry laboratory with lecture at a large university. *School of Science and Mathematics, 102,* 158–171.

Dillon, J. T. (1982). The effect of questions in education and other enterprises. *Journal of Curriculum Studies, 14,* 127–152.

Dixon, D., and Portman, T. (2010). The beauty of being native. In J. Ponterotto, J. Casas, L. Suzuki, and C. Alexander (eds.), *Handbook of Multicultural Counseling* (3rd ed., pp. 215–225). Thousand Oaks, CA: Sage.

Dolbin-MacNab, M. (2009). Becoming a parent again: An exploration of transformation among grandparents raising grandchildren. In J. Mancini and K. Roberto (eds.), *Pathways of Human Development: Explorations of Change* (pp. 207–226). Lanham, MD: Lexington Books/ Rowman and Littlefield.

Domin, D. S. (1999). A review of laboratory instruction styles. *Journal of Chemical Education, 76,* 543–547.

Donald, J. G. (1995). Disciplinary differences in knowledge validation. *New Directions for Teaching and Learning* (no. 63, pp. 7–17). San Francisco, CA: Jossey-Bass.

———. (2006). Enhancing the quality of teaching in Canada. *New Directions for Higher Education, 133,* 23–31. doi: 10.1002/he.

Dovidio, J., Hebl, M., Richeson J., and Shelton, J. (2006). Nonverbal communication, race, and intergroup interaction. In V. Manusov and

M. Patterson (eds.), *The Sage Handbook of Nonverbal Communication* (pp. 219–235). Thousand Oaks, CA: Sage.

Drake, R. (2011). Why should faculty be involved in supplemental instruction? *College Teaching, 59*(4), 135–141.

Dunn, D. S., McEntarffer, R., and Halonen, J. S. (2004). Empowering psychology students through self-assessment. In D. S. Dunn, C. M. Mehrotra, and J. S. Halonen (eds.), *Measuring Up: Educational Assessment Challenges and Practices for Psychology*. Washington, DC: American Psychological Association.

Dunnivant, F. M., Moore, A., Alfano, M. J., Brzenk, R., Buckley, P. T., Newman, M. E. (2000). Understanding the Greenhouse Effect: Is global warming real? *Journal of Chemical Education, 77*, 1602–1603.

Dweck, C. S. (1986). Motivational processes affecting learning. *American Psychologist, 41*, 1040–1048.

Dweck, C. S. (2006). *Mindset: The New Psychology of Success*. New York: Random House.

D'Ydewalle, G., Swerts, A., and de Corte, E. (1983). Study time and test performance as a function of test expectations. *Contemporary Educational Psychology, 8*(1), 55–67.

Dyment, J., and O'Connell, T. (2010). The quality of reflection in student journals: A review of limiting and enabling factors. *Innovative Higher Education, 35*(4), 233–244.

Eccles, J. (1994). Understanding women's educational and occupational choices. *Psychology of Women Quarterly, 18*, 585–609.

The Economist Intelligence Unit. (2008). The future of higher education: How technology will shape learning. Available at: http://www.nmc.org/pdf/Future-of-Higher-Ed-(NMC).pdf.

The Educated Nation. Available at: http://www.educatednation.com/.

The EDUCAUSE Learning Initiative. (2006) 7 things you should know about mapping mashups [Online]. Available at: http://www.educause.edu/ELI/7ThingsYouShouldKnowAboutMappi/156819.

Ehrmann, S. C. (1995, March/April). Asking the right questions: What does research tell us about technology and higher learning? *Change, 27*(2), 20–27.

Elam, C., Stratton, T., and Gibson, D. (2007, Spring). Welcoming a new generation to college: The millennial students. *Journal of College Admission*, 20–25.

Elbow, P. (1994). Freewriting. In Alan Purves (ed.), *Encyclopedia of English Studies and Language Arts* (pp. 509–510). Urbana, IL: National Council of Teachers of English.

———(ed.). (2000a). Using the collage for collaborative writing. In *Everyone Can Write: Essays Toward a Hopeful Theory of Writing and Teaching Writing* (pp. 372–378). New York: Oxford University Press.

———(ed.). (2000b). Your cheatin' art: A collage. In *Everyone Can Write: Essays Toward a Hopeful Theory of Writing and Teaching Writing* (pp. 300–313). New York: Oxford University Press.

Elbow, P., and Belanoff, P. (2003). *Sharing and Responding*. New York: McGraw-Hill.

Ellis, Y., Daniels, B., and Jauregui, A. (2010). The Effect of multitasking on the grade performance of business students. *Research in Higher Education, 8*(1), 1–11.

Elmendorf, H., and Ottenhoff, J. (2009). The importance of conversation in learning and the value of web-based discussion tools. Academic Commons [Online]. Available at: http://www.academiccommons.org/commons/essay/importance-conversation-learning.

Entwistle, N. J. (1992). Student learning and study strategies. In B. R. Clark and G. Neave (eds.), *Encyclopedia of higher education*. Oxford: Pergamon.

Erdur-Baker, O., Aberson, C., Barrow, J., and Draper, M. (2006). Nature and severity of college students' psychological concerns: A comparison of clinical and non-clinical samples. *Professional Psychology: Research and Practice, 37*(3), 317–323.

Eriksen, S. C. (1983). Private measures of good teaching. *Teaching of Psychology, 10*, 133–136.

Eves, R. L., Davis, L. E., Brown, D. G., and Lamberts, W. L. (2007). Integration of field studies and undergraduate research into an interdisciplinary course: Natural history of tropical carbonate ecosystems. *Journal of College Science Teaching, 36*, 22–27.

Eyler, J., Giles, Jr., D. E., and Astin, A. (1999). *Where's the Learning in Service-Learning?* San Francisco, CA: Jossey-Bass.

Ezzedeen, S. (2008). Facilitating class discussions around current and controversial issues: Ten recommendations for teachers. *College Teaching, 56*(4), 230–236.

Faro, S., and Swan, K. (2006). An investigation into the efficacy of the studio model at the high school level. *Journal of Educational Computing Research, 35*, 45–59.

Felder, R. M. (2001, August). Technology-based instruction and cooperative learning. *The Interface: IEEE Education Society*, 2–3. Available at http://www4.ncsu.edu/unity/lockers/users/f/felder/public/Papers/Interface_Response_Letter.html.

Feldman, S., and Rosenthal, D. (1990). The acculturation of autonomy expectations in Chinese high schoolers residing in two western nations. *International Journal of Psychology, 25*, 259–281.

Fernald, P. (2004). The Monte Carlo Quiz. *College Teaching, 52*(3), 95–99.

Fiford, R., Tomitsch, M., Dunstan, C. R., Plumbe, R. (2011). Exploring how elements of studio teaching can improve student engagement. *Synergy, 31*, 46–52.

Fink, L. Dee (2003). *Creating Significant Learning Experiences.* San Francisco, CA: Joseph Wiley & Sons, Inc.

Fisch, L. (ed.). (1996). Ethical dimensions of college and university teaching: Understanding and honoring the special relationship between teachers and students. *New Directions for Teaching and Learning* (no. 66). San Francisco, CA: Jossey-Bass.

———. (2001). The devil's advocate strikes again. *Journal of Staff, Program, and Organizational Development, 18*(1), 49–51.

Fischer, M., and Massey, D. (2007). The effects of affirmative action in higher education. *Social Science Research, 36*(2), 531–549.

Flavell, J. H. (1979). Metacognition and cognitive mentoring: A new area of cognitive-developmental inquiry. *American Psychologist, 34*, 906–911.

Fleming, V. (2001). Helping students to learn to learn by using a checklist, modified rubrics, and e-mail. *Journal on Excellence in College Teaching, 12*(1), 5–22.

Fluckiger, J., Vigil, Y., Pasco, R., and Danielson, K. (2010). Formative feedback: Involving students as partners in assessment to enhance learning. *College Teaching, 58*(4), 136–140.

Fonseca, B., and Chi, M. T. H. (2011). Instruction based on self-explanation. In P. Alexander and R. Mayer (eds.), *Handbook of Research on Learning and Instruction* (pp. 296–321). New York: Routledge.

Foos, P. W., and Fisher, R. P. (1988). Using tests as learning opportunities. *Journal of Educational Psychology, 88*(2), 179–183.

Foster, D., and Herman, A. (2011). Linking the first week of class to end-of-semester satisfaction: Using a reciprocal interview activity to create an active and comfortable classroom. *College Teaching, 59*(3), 111–116.

Fox, S. (2011). Americans Living with Disabilities and Their Technology Profile. *Pew Internet and the American Life Project.* Available at: http://www.pewinternet.org/Reports/2011/Disability.aspx.

Fox, S., and Vitak, J. (2008). Degrees of Access (May 2008 data). *Pew Internet and American life project* [Online]. Available at: http://www.pewinternet.org/Presentations/2008/Degrees-of-Access-(May-2008-data).aspx.

Freyberg, S., and Markus, H. (2007). Cultural models of education in American Indian, Asian American and European American contexts. *Social Psychology of Education, 10*, 213–246.

Fry, R. (2003). *Hispanic youth dropping out of U. S. schools: Measuring the challenge.* Washington, DC: Pew Hispanic Center.

Fuentes, M., Kiyana, A., and Rosario, E. (2003). *Keeping Latinos in High School: The Role of Context.* Paper presented at the annual meeting of the American Psychological Association, Toronto, Canada.

Furco, A. (1996). Service-learning: A balanced approach to experiential education. *In Expanding Boundaries: Service and Learning* (pp. 2–6). Washington, DC: Corporation for National Service.

Gabelnick, F., MacGregor, J., Matthews, R., and Smith, R. (1990). Learning communities: Creating connections among students, faculty and disciplines. *New Directions for Teaching and Learning* (no. 11). San Francisco, CA: Jossey-Bass.

Gamson, W. A. (1966). *SIMSOC: A Manual for Participants*. Ann Arbor, MI: Campus Publishers.

Garcia-Sheets, M. (2008). Perception of campus climate by university students of color: Implications for practice. *Dissertation Abstracts: Section A: Humanities and Social Sciences, 69*(4A), 1231.

Gardner, S., and Holley, K. (2011). "Those invisible barriers are real": The progression of first-generation students through doctoral education. *Equity and Excellence in Education,* 44, 77–92.

Garwick, A., and Auger, S. (2000). What do providers need to know about American Indian culture? Recommendations from urban Indian family caregivers. *Families, Systems and Health, 18*, 177–190.

Gay, G. (2010). *Culturally Responsive Teaching: Theory, Research and Practice* (2nd ed.). New York: Teachers College, Columbia University.

Gerdeman, R. (2000). Academic dishonesty and the community college. *ERIC Digest*. ERIC Clearinghouse for Community Colleges (ED447840).

Gerretson, H., and Golson, E. (2005). Synopsis of the use of course-embedded assessment in a medium-sized public university's general education program. *The Journal of General Education, 54*(2), 130–146.

Gibbs, G. (1999). Using assessment strategically to change the way students learn. In S. Brown and A. Glassner (eds.), *Assessment Matters in Higher Education: Choosing and Using Diverse Approaches* (pp. 41–54). Buckingham, UK: Society for Research in Higher Education/Open University Press.

Giers, V., and Kreiner, D. (2009). Incorporating active learning with PowerPoint-based lectures using content-based questions. *Teaching of Psychology, 36*(2), 134–139.

Gifford, R. (2011). The role of nonverbal communication in interpersonal relations. In L. Horowitz and S. Strack (eds.), *Handbook of Interpersonal Psychology: Theory, Research, Assessment, and Therapeutic Interventions* (pp. 171–190). Hoboken, NJ: John Wiley & Sons.

Gilovich, T. (1991). *How We Know What Isn't So*. New York: The Free Press.

Glaser, R., and Chi, M. T. H. (1988). Overview. In M. T. H. Chi, R. Glaser, and M. Farr (eds.), *The Nature of Expertise* (pp. xv-xxviii). Hillsdale, NJ: Erlbaum.

Goldschmid, M. L. (1971). The learning cell: An instructional innovation. *Learning and Development*, 2(5), 1–6.

———. (1975, May). *When Students Teach Students*. Paper presented at the International Conference on Improving University Teaching, Heidelberg, Germany.

Goldschmid, M. L., and Shore, B. M. (1974). The learning cell: A field test of an educational innovation. In W. A. Verreck (ed.), *Methodological Problems in Research and Development in Higher Education* (pp. 218–236). Amsterdam, Netherlands: Swets and Zeitlinger.

Goldstein, G. (2007). Using classroom assessment techniques in an introductory statistics class. *College Teaching, 55*(2), 77–82.

Gone, J. (2008). 'So I can be like a Whiteman': The cultural psychology of space and place in American Indian mental health. *Culture & Psychology, 14*, 369–399.

Gonzalez, B. L., Wegner, P. A., Foley, B., and Thadani, V. (1999). Studio classroom and conceptual learning in chemistry. *Abstracts of Papers of the American Chemical Society*, 217th ACS National Meeting, Anaheim, CA, March 21–25, 1999; American Chemical Society: Washington, DC, 1999; CHED 071.

Gordon, M., and Fay, C. (2010). The effects of grading and teaching practices on students' perceptions of grading fairness. *College Teaching, 58*(3), 93–98.

Gottfried, A. C., Hessler, J. A., Sweeder, R. D., Bartolin, J. M., Coppola, B. P., Banaszak Holl, M. M., Reynolds, B. P., and Stewart, I. C. (2003). Studio 130: Design, testing, and implementation. *Abstracts of Papers of the American Chemical Society, 225*, 647.

Gould, J. (2008, July–August). Get real: Feel like an imposter? You're not alone. *Monitor on Psychology, 39*(7).

Grauerholz, E., and Copenhaver, S. (1994). When the personal becomes problematic: The ethics of using experiential teaching methods. *Teaching Sociology, 22*(4), 319–327.

Gray, T., and Madson, L. (2007). Ten easy ways to engage your students. *College Teaching, 55*(2), 83–87.

Green, M. C. (2004). Storytelling in teaching. *APS Observer, 17*(4), 37–39.

Gruber, H. E., and Weitman, M. (1962, April). Self-directed study: Experiments in higher education. Report No. 19. Boulder, CO: University of Colorado, Behavior Research Laboratory.

Gruenbacher, D., Natarajan, B., and Kuhn, W. B. (2006, October 28–31). Work in progress: An integrated laboratory experience—A new environment for teaching communications. *Frontiers in Education Conference. FIE 2006, 36th Annual, 1*, 7–8.

Gudykunst, W. (2004). *Bridging Differences: Effective Intergroup Communication* (4th ed.). Thousand Oaks, CA: Sage.

Gudykunst, W., Ting-Toomey, S., and Nishida, T. (eds.). (1996). *Communication in Personal Relationships Across Cultures*. Thousand Oaks, CA: Sage.

Gurung, R. (2003). Pedagogical aids and student performance. *Teaching of Psychology, 30*(2), 92–95.

Haines, D. B., and McKeachie, W. J. (1967). Cooperative vs. competitive discussion methods in teaching introductory psychology. *Journal of Educational Psychology, 58*, 386–390.

Halonen, J. S. (1986). *Teaching critical thinking in psychology.* Milwaukee, WI: Alverno Productions.

Halpern, D. F., and Hakel, M. D. (2003). Applying the science of learning to the university and beyond. *Change, 35*(4), 36–41.

Hanson, K. (1996). Between apathy and advocacy: Teaching and modeling ethical reflection. *New Directions for Teaching and Learning* (no. 66, pp. 33–36). San Francisco, CA: Jossey-Bass.

Harackiewicz, J., Barron, K. E., and Elliott, A. J. (1998). Rethinking achievement goals: When are they adaptive for college students and why? *Educational Psychologist, 33*, 1–21.

Harp, S., and Maslich, A. (2005). The consequences of including seductive details during lecture. *Teaching of Psychology, 32*(2), 100–103.

Harrigan, J. (2005). Proxemics, kinesics, and gaze. In J. Harrigan, R. Rosenthal and K. Scherer (eds.), *The New Handbook of Methods in Nonverbal Behavior Research, Series in Affective Science* (pp. 137–198). New York: Wiley and Sons.

Harter, S. (1978). Effective motivation reconsidered: Toward a developmental model. *Human Development, 21*, 34–64.

Hartley, J. (2002). Studying for the future. *Journal of Further and Higher Education, 26*(3), 207–227.

Hartley, J., and Davies, I. K. (1978). Note-taking: A critical review. *Programmed Learning and Educational Technology, 15*, 207–224.

Hartman, F. R. (1961). Recognition learning under multiple channel presentation and testing conditions. *Audio-Visual Communication Review, 9*, 24–43.

Hartman, H. J. (1990). Factors affecting the tutoring process. *Journal of Developmental Education, 14*(2), 2–6.

Hathaway, R. S., Nagda, B. A., and Gregerman, S. R. (2002). The relationship of undergraduate research participation to graduate and professional education pursuit: An empirical study. *Journal of College Student Development, 43*, 614–631.

Hattie, J., and Timperley, H. (2007). The power of feedback. *Review of Educational Research, 77*, 81–112.

Head, S. (2003). *The New Ruthless Economy: Work and Power in the Digital Age.* New York: Oxford University Press.

Hembrooke, H., and Gay, G. (2003). The laptop and the lecture: The effects of multitasking in learning environments. *Journal of Computing in Higher Education, 15*(1), 46–65.

Henderson, L., and Buising, C. (2000). A research-based molecular biology laboratory. *Journal of College Science Teaching, 30*(5), 322–327.

Henning, J. (2005). Leading discussions: Opening up the conversation. *College Teaching, 53*(3), 90–94.

Higginbotham, C., Pike, C. F., and Rice, J. K. (1998). Spectroscopy in sol-gel matrices: An open-ended laboratory experience for upper-level undergraduates. *Journal of Chemical Education, 75*, 461.

Higgins, M., Aitken-Rose, E., Dixon, J. (2009). The pedagogy of the planning studio: A view from down under. *Journal for Education in the Built Environment, 4*(1), 8–30.

Hodges, E. (1994, Summer). Some realities of revision: What students don't or won't understand. *English in Texas, 25*(4), 13–16.

Hofer, B. (1997). *The Development of Personal Epistemology: Dimensions, Disciplinary Differences, and Instructional Practices*. Unpublished doctoral thesis, University of Michigan.

Hofer, B. K., Yu, S. L., and Pintrich, P. R. (1998). Teaching college students to be self-regulated learners. In D. H. Schunk and B. J. Zimmerman (eds.), *Self-Regulated Learning: From Teaching to Self-Reflective Practice* (pp. 57–85). New York: Guilford.

Hofstein, A., and Lunetta, V. N. (1982). The role of the laboratory in science teaching: Neglected aspects of research. *Review of Educational Research, 52*(2), 201–217.

Holman, L. (2011). Millennial students' mental models of search: Implications for academic librarians and database developers. *The Journal of Academic Librarianship, 37*(1), 19–27.

Hoover, E. (2007). Researchers challenge view of "millennial" students. *Chronicle of Higher Education, 54*(11), 44.

———. (2009, October 11). The Millennial Muddle: How stereotyping students became a thriving industry and a bundle of contradictions. *Chronicle of Higher Education*.

Hoover, J., Klingner, J., Baca, L., and Patton, J. (2008). *Methods for Teaching Culturally and Linguistically Diverse Exceptional Learners*. Upper Saddle River, NJ: Pearson/Merrill Prentice Hall.

Horowitz, G. (2003). A discovery approach to three organic laboratory techniques: Extraction, recrystallization, and distillation. *Journal of Chemical Education, 80*, 1039–1043.

Houston, J. P. (1983). Alternate test forms as a means of reducing multiple-choice answer copying in the classroom. *Journal of Educational Psychology, 75*(4), 572–575.

Howe, N., and Strauss, W. (2000). *Millennials Rising: The Next Great Generation*. New York: Vintage Books.

Hunter, A. B., Laursen, S. L., and Seymour, E. (2007). Becoming a scientist: The role of undergraduate research in students' cognitive, personal, and professional development. *Science Education, 91(1)*, 36–74.

Husman, J., Derryberry, W. P., Crowson, H. M., and Lomax, R. (2004). Instrumentality, task value, and intrinsic motivation: Making sense of their independent interdependence. *Contemporary Educational Psychology, 29*, 63–76.

Isbell, L., and Cote, N. (2009). Connecting with struggling students to improve performance in large classes. *Teaching of Psychology, 36*(3), 185–188.

Jansen, J. (2010). Use of Internet in Higher Income Households. *Pew Internet and the American Life Project.* Available at http://www.pewinternet.org/Reports/2010/Better-off-households/Overview.aspx.

Jarvis, M. (2005). *The Psychology of Effective Learning and Teaching.* Cheltenham, UK: Nelson Thornes.

Jensen, J. (1985). Perspective on nonverbal intercultural communication. In L. Samovar and R. Porter (eds.), *Intercultural Communication: A Reader* (pp. 256–272). Belmont, CA: Wadsworth.

Johnson, B., and Kiviniemi, M. (2009). The effect of online chapter quizzes on exam performance in an undergraduate social psychology course. *Teaching of Psychology, 36*(1), 33–37.

Johnson, D. M. (1975). Increasing originality on essay examinations in psychology. *Teaching of Psychology, 2*, 99–102.

Johnson, D. W., and Johnson, R. T. (1995). *Creative Controversy: Intellectual Challenge in the Classroom.* Edina, MN: Interaction Book Company.

Johnson, D. W., Johnson, R. L, and Smith, K. A. (2000 January/February). Constructive controversy: The educative power of intellectual conflict. *Change Magazine*, 28–37.

Johnson, D. W., Maruyama, G., Johnson, R., Nelson, D., and Skon, L. (1981). The effects of cooperative, competitive, and individualistic goal structures on achievement: A meta-analysis. *Psychological Bulletin, 89*, 47–62.

Jordan, A. E. (2001). College student cheating: The role of motivation, perceived norms, attitudes, and knowledge of institutional policy. *Ethics and Behavior, 11*, 233–247.

Khan, F. A., Leavitt, A. J., Garmon, L. B., Harper, W. D. (2003). *Abstracts of Papers of the American Chemical Society*, 226th ACS National Meeting, New York, September 7–11; American Chemical Society: Washington, DC; CHED 262.

Kardash, C. M. (2000). Evaluation of an undergraduate research experience: Perceptions of undergraduate interns and their faculty mentors. *Journal of Educational Psychology, 92*, 191–201.

Katz, D. (1950). *Gestalt psychology*. New York: Ronald Press.

Keller, F. S. (1968). Goodbye teacher,... *Journal of Applied Behavior Analysis, 10*, 165–167.

Kennedy, L. M., Smith, A., Wells, A. T., and Wellman, B. (2008). Networked Families. *Pew Internet and American Life Project*. Available at: http://www.pewinternet.org/Reports/2008/Networked-Families.aspx.

Kerr, C. (1994). Knowledge and ethics and the new academic culture. *Change, 26*(1), 8–16.

Khan, F. A., Leavitt, A. J., Garmon, L. B., and Harper, W. D. (2003). An integrated chemistry environment using studio, workshop, and labworks: Systematically changing the teaching of General Chemistry. *Abstracts of Papers of the American Chemical Society*, 226th ACS National Meeting, New York, September 7–11, 2003; American Chemical Society: Washington, DC, 2003; CHED 262.

Kiewra, K. A. (1989). A review of notetaking: The encoding storage paradigm and beyond. *Educational Psychology Review*, *1*(2), 147–172.

Kim, B., Wong, Y., and Maffini, C. (2010). Annual review of Asian American psychology, 2009. *Asian American Journal of Psychology*, *1*(4), 227–260.

King, A. (1990). Enhancing peer interaction and learning in the classroom. *American Educational Research Journal*, *27*, 664–687.

———. (1997). Ask to think—Tell why: A model of transactive peer tutoring for scaffolding higher-level complex learning. *Educational Psychologist*, *32*, 221–235.

King, R. B., and Watkins, D. A. (in press). "Socializing" achievement goal theory: The need for social goals. *Psychological Studies*.

Kinzie, J. (2010). Perspectives from campus leaders on the current state of student learning outcomes assessment. *Assessment Update*, *22*(5), 1–15.

Kluger, A. N., and DeNisi, A. (1996). The effects of feedback intervention on performance: A historical review, a meta-analysis, and a preliminary feedback intervention theory. *Psychological Bulletin*, *119*, 254–284.

Knight, P. (2006). The local practices of assessment. *Assessment and Evaluation in Higher Education*, *31*(4), 435–452.

Ko, S., and Rossen. S. (2001). *Teaching Online: A Practical Guide*. Boston, MA: Houghton Mifflin.

Kolb, D. A. (1984). *Experiential Learning*. Englewood Cliffs, NJ: Prentice Hall.

Kolb, L. (2008). *Toys to Tools: Connecting Student Cell Phones to Education*. Washington, DC: International Society for Technology in Education.

Koocher, G., and Keith-Spiegel, P. (1998). *Ethics in Psychology: Professional Standards and Cases*. Mahwah, NJ: Erlbaum.

Kovac, J. (1999). Professional ethics in the college and university science curriculum. *Science and Education*, *8*, 309–319.

Kozma, R. (1994). Will media influence learning? Reframing the debate. *Educational Technology, Research and Development*, *42*(2), 7–19.

Krathwohl, D., Bloom, B. S., and Masia, B. (eds.). (1964). *Taxonomy of Educational Objectives, Handbook II: Affective Domain*. New York: David McKay.

Kremer, J. F., and Bringle, R. G. (1990). The effects of an intensive research experience on the careers of talented undergraduates. *Journal of Research and Development in Education*, *24*, 1–5.

Kuh, G., and Ewell, P. (2010). The state of learning outcomes assessment in the United States. Etat de L'evaluation des resultats de l'enseignement aux Etats-Unis. *Organisation for Economic Cooperation & Development, 22*(1), 9–28.

Kulik, J. (2003). Effects of using instructional technology in colleges and universities: What controlled evaluation studies say [Online]. Available at: http://sri.com/policy/csted/reports/sandt/it/.

Kuo, T., and Simon, A. (2009) How many tests to we really need? *College Teaching, 57*(3), 156–160.

LaFromboise, T., Coleman, H., and Gerton, J. (1998). Psychological impact of biculturalism. In P. Organista, K. Chun, and G. Marin (eds.), *Readings in Ethnic Psychology* (pp. 123–155). New York: Routledge.

Langer, E. (1997). *The Power of Mindful Learning*. Reading, MA: Addison Wesley Publishers.

Latus, M. (2007). Stressors among first-generation college students: A retrospective inquiry. *Dissertation Abstracts: Section A: Humanities and Social Sciences, 68*(1-B), 626.

Lave, J., and Wegner, E. (1991). *Situated Learning: Legitimate Peripheral Participation*. Cambridge, UK: Cambridge University Press.

Leamnson, R. (2000). Learning as biological brain change. *Change, 32*, 34–40.

Lee, J., Donjan, W., and Brown, E. (2010). American Indian/Alaskan Native undergraduate retention at predominantly White institutions: An elaboration of Tinto's theory of college student departure. *Journal of College Student Retention: Research, Theory and Practice, 12*, 257–276.

Lee, P. (2008). Cross-cultural differences between European Americans and Chinese Americans with respect to the concepts of self and communication. *Dissertation Abstracts: Section A: Humanities and Social Sciences; 69*(4-B), 2672.

Lee, W. (1999). *An Introduction to Multicultural Counseling*. Bristol, PA: Accelerated Development.

Lei, S., Bartlett, K., Gorney, S., and Herschbach, T. (2010). Resistance to reading compliance among college students: Instructors' perspectives. *College Student Journal, 44*(2), 219–229.

Leith, G. O. M. (1977). Implications of cognitive psychology for the improvement of teaching and learning in universities. In B. Massey (ed.), *Proceedings of the Third International Conference, Improving University Teaching* (pp. 111–138). College Park: University of Maryland.

Leong, F., Ebreo, A., Kinoshita, L., Inman, A., and Yang, L. (eds.) (2007). *Handbook of Asian American psychology* (2nd ed.). Thousand Oaks, CA: Sage.

Lepper, M. R., and Hodell, M. (1989). Intrinsic motivation in the classroom. In C. Ames and R. Ames (eds.), *Research on Motivation in Education* (Vol. 3, pp. 73–105). San Diego, CA: Academic Press.

Lepper, M. R., and Malone, T. W. (1985). Intrinsic motivation and instructional effectiveness in computer-based education. In R. E. Snow and M. J. Farr (eds.), *Aptitude, Learning and Instruction: III. Conative and Affective Process Analyses*. Hillsdale, NJ: Erlbaum.

Lewis, M. (1997). *Poisoning the Ivy: The Seven Deadly Sins and Other Vices of Higher Education in America*. Armonk, NY: Sharpe.

Lidren, D. M., Meier, S. E., and Brigham, T. A. (1991). The effects of minimal and maximal peer tutoring systems on the academic performance of college students. *Psychological Record, 41*, 69–77.

Lin, Y. G., McKeachie, W. J., and Kim, Y. C. (2003). College student intrinsic and/or extrinsic motivation and learning. *Learning and Individual Differences, 13*, 251–258.

Liu, L., and Maddux, C. D. (2005). Influences of course design on student evaluations: An initial logistic prediction model. *Journal of Excellence in College Teaching, 16*(1), 125–147.

Lineweaver, T. (2010). Online discussion assignments improve students' class preparation. *Teaching of Psychology, 37*(3), 204–209.

Lone-Knapp, F. (2000). Rez talk: How reservation residents describe themselves. *American Indian Quarterly, 24*, 635–640.

Lloyd, J. M., Dean, L. A., and Cooper, D. L. (2007). Students' technology use and its effects on peer relationships, academic involvement, and healthy lifestyles. *NASPA Journal, 44*(3), 481–495.

Lucas, G. (2010). Initiating student-teacher contact via personalized responses to one minute papers. *College Teaching, 58*(2), 39–42.

Luechauer, D. L., and Shulman, G. M. (1996, June) Training transformational leaders: A call for practicing empowerment in the classroom. *International Journal of Public Administration,*: 827–848. Retrieved August 14, 2012 from *Academic OneFile* Website.

Lunsford, R. (1997). When less is more: Principles for responding in the disciplines. In M. Sorcinelli and P. Elbow (eds.), *Writing to Learn: Strategies for Assigning and Responding to Writing Across the Disciplines*. (pp. 91–104) San Francisco, CA: Jossey-Bass.

Lyman, F. (2008, October 20). Students enjoy lower costs, lighter backpacks as e-textbook availability expands dramatically. *Community College Week*, 8.

MacGregor, J. (ed.). (1993, Spring). Student self-evaluation: Fostering reflective learning. *New Directions for Teaching and Learning* (no. 56). San Francisco, CA: Jossey-Bass.

Maehr, M. L., and Midgley, C. (1991, Summer–Fall). Enhancing student motivation—A schoolwide approach. *Educational Psychologist, 26*(3–4), 399–427.

Maehr, M. L., and Zusho, A. (2009). Achievement goal theory: The past, present, and future. In K. Wentzel and A. Wigfield (eds.), *Handbook of Motivation in School* (pp. 77–104). New York: Routledge.

Maggioni, L., and Alexander, P. A. (in press). Knowledge domains and domain learning. In B. McGaw, P. L. Peterson, and E. Baker (eds.), *International Encyclopedia of Education* (3rd ed.). Amsterdam, Netherlands: Elsevier.

Maier, N. R. F. (1952). *Principles of Human Relations*. New York: Wiley.

———. (1963). *Problem-Solving Discussions and Conferences*. New York: McGraw-Hill.

Maier, N. R. F., and Maier, L. A. (1957). An experimental test of the effects of "developmental" vs. "free" discussion on the quality of group decisions. *Journal of Applied Psychology, 41*, 320–323.

Maki, P. (2004). *Assessing for Learning: Building a Sustainable Commitment Across the Institution*. Sterling, VA: Stylus.

Mann, R. et al. (1970). *The college classroom: Conflict, change and learning*. New York: Wiley.

Manusov, V., and Patterson, Miles L. (eds.). (2006). *The Sage Handbook of Nonverbal Communication*. Thousand Oaks, CA: Sage.

Marbach-Ad, G., and Sokolove, P. (2000). Can undergraduate biology students learn to ask higher level questions? *Journal of Research in Science Teaching, 37*(8), 854–870.

Marcinkiewicz, H. R., and Clariana, R. B. (1997). The performance effects of headings within multiple-choice tests. *British Journal of Educational Psychology, 67*, 111–117.

Markie, P. (1994). *A Professor's Duties: Ethical Issues in College Teaching*. Totowa, NJ: Rowman & Littlefield.

Martin, D., and Hurley, M. (2005). Supplemental instruction. In D. Martin and M. Hurley (eds.), *Challenging and Supporting the First Year Student* (pp. 308–319). San Francisco, CA: Jossey-Bass Publisher.

Marton, F., and Säljö, R. (1976a). On qualitative differences in learning: I—Outcome and process. *British Journal of Educational Psychology, 46*, 4–11.

———. (1976b). On qualitative differences in learning: II—Outcome as a function of the learner's conception of the task. *British Journal of Educational Psychology, 46*, 115–127.

Maruyama, M. (1982). Yellow youth's psychological struggle. *AAPA Journal, 7*(1), 21–29.

Maton, K., Wimms, H., Grant, S., Wittig, M., Rogers, M., and Vasquez, M. (2011). Experiences and perspectives of African American, Latina/o, Asian American, and European American psychology graduate students: A national study. *Cultural Diversity and Ethnic Minority Psychology*, 17, 68–78.

Matsumoto, D. (2006). Culture and Nonverbal Behavior. In V. Manusov and M Patterson (eds.), *The Sage Handbook of Nonverbal Communication* (pp. 219–235). Thousand Oaks, CA: Sage.

Matthews, J. (1991). The teaching of ethics and the ethics of teaching. *Teaching of Psychology, 18*(2), 80–85.

Matz, R. L., Rothman, E. D., Krajcik, J. S., Banaszak Holl, M. M. (2010, March). *Concurrent Enrollment in General Chemistry Lecture and Laboratory Decreases Withdrawal Rates and Increases Final Grades in the Lecture.* Paper presented at the National Association of Research in Science Teaching Annual Conference, Strand of College Science Teaching and Learning (Grades 13–20), Philadelphia, PA.

Mayer, R. (1997). Multimedia learning: Are we asking the right questions? *Educational Psychologist, 31*, 1–19.

———. (2003). The promise of multimedia learning: Using the same instructional design methods across different media. *Learning and Instruction, 13*, 125–139.

———. (2008). *Learning and Instruction* (2nd ed.). Upper Saddle River, NJ: Pearson Merrill Prentice Hall.

———. (2009). *Multimedia Learning*. New York: Cambridge University Press.

Mayer, R., Stull, A., DeLeeuw, K., Almeroth, K., Bimber, B., Chun, D., Bulger, M., Campbell, J., Knight, A., and Zhang, H. (2009). Clickers in college classrooms: Fostering learning with questioning methods in large lecture classes. *Contemporary Educational Psychology, 34*, 51–57.

Mazur, E. (1997). *Peer Instruction: A User's Manual*. Upper Saddle River, NJ: Prentice Hall.

Mazzie, L. (2008, October 27). Is a laptop–free zone the answer to the laptop debate [Web log post]? Available at: http://law.marquette.edu/facultyblog/2008/10/27/is-a-laptop-free-zone-the-answer-to-the-laptop-debate/.

McAdoo, H. (ed.). (1999). *Family Ethnicity: Strength in Diversity* (2nd ed.). Thousand Oaks, CA: Sage.

McCabe, D. L., and Trevino, L. K. (1996). What we know about cheating in college: Longitudinal trends and recent developments. *Change, 28*(1), 29–33.

McCabe, D. L., Trevino, L., and Butterfield, K. (2001, January–February). Dishonesty in academic environments: The influence of peer reporting requirements. *Journal of Higher Education, 72*(1), 29–45.

McClelland, D., Atkinson, J. W., Clark, R. A., and Lowell, E. L. (1953). *The Achievement Motive*. New York: Appleton-Century-Crofts.

McCluskey, H. Y. (1934). An experimental comparison of two methods of correcting the outcomes of examination. *School and Society, 40*, 566–568.

McElwee, R. (2009). Facilitating students' preparation for class: Discussion of and evidence for effective participation preparation assignments. *Journal of Excellence in College Teaching, 20*(4), 105–120.

McGregor, L. (2006). Teaching and mentoring racially and ethnically diverse students. In W. Buskist and S. Davis (eds.), *Handbook of the Teaching of Psychology*. (pp. 164–169) Malden, MA: Blackwell.

McKeachie, W. J., Pintrich, P. R., and Lin, Y. G. (1985). Teaching learning strategies. *Educational Psychologist, 20*(3), 153–160.

McKeachie, W. J., Pintrich, P. R., Lin, Y. G., Smith, D. A. F., and Sharma, R. (1990). *Teaching and Learning in the College Classroom: A Review of the Research Literature* (2nd ed.). Ann Arbor: NCRIPTAL, University of Michigan.

McKeachie, W. J., Pollie, D., and Speisman, J. (1955). Relieving anxiety in classroom examinations. *Journal of Abnormal and Social Psychology, 50*, 93–98.

McKinney, J., McKinney, K., Franluk, R., and Schweitzer, J. (2006). The college classroom as community. *College Teaching, 54*(3), 281–284.

McKinnon, M. (1999). PBL in Hong Kong. *PBL Insight, 2*(1), 1–6.

McLeod, S. H. (1992). Responding to plagiarism: The role of the WPA. *WPA: Writing Program Administration, 15*(3), 7–16.

McMurtry, K. (2001, November). E-cheating: Combating a 21st century challenge. *T. H. E. Journal Online* [Online]. Available at: http://www.thejournal.com/magazine/vault/A3724.cfm.

Meece, J. L., Anderman, E. M., and Anderman, L. H. (2006). Classroom goal structure, student motivation, and academic achievement. *Annual Review of Psychology*, 57, 487–503.

Mentkowski, M., and Loacker, G. (1985). Assessing and validating the outcomes of college. *New Directions for Institutional Research*, September, 47–64.

Mentkowski et al., (2000) Learning that Lasts. San Francisco, CA: Jossey-Bass.

Metzger, R. L., Boschee, P. F., Haugen, T., and Schnobrich, B. L. (1979). The classroom as learning context: Changing rooms affects performance. *Journal of Educational Psychology, 71*(4), 440–442.

Meyer, J. H. F., and Land, R. (2006). *Overcoming barriers to student understanding: Threshold concepts and troublesome knowledge.* London: Routledge.

Michaelsen, L. K., Knight, A. B., and Fink, L. D. (eds.). (2004). *Team-Based Learning: A Transformative Use of Small Groups*. Sterling, VA: Stylus Publications.

Michaelsen, L. K., Sweet, M., and Parmelee, D. (eds.). (2008). Team-based learning: Small-group learning's next big step. *New Directions for Teaching and Learning* (no. 116). San Francisco, CA: Jossey-Bass.

Miller, H. (1998). Assessment with a purpose. *Innovation Journal*, 35–37.

Miller, J. E., and Groccia, J. E. (1997). Are four heads better than one? A comparison of cooperative and traditional teaching formats in an introductory biology course. *Innovative Higher Education, 21*, 253–273.

Miller, R. L. (2008). Introduction and a brief history of undergraduate research in psychology. In R. L. Miller, R. F. Rycek, E. Balcetis,

S. T. Barney, B. C. Beins, S. R. Burns, R. Smith, and M. E. Ware (eds.), *Developing, Promoting, & Sustaining the Undergraduate Research Experience in Psychology* [Online]. Retrieved June 01, 2009 from the *Society for the Teaching of Psychology* Website. Available at: http://teachpsych.org/resources/e-books/ur2008/ur2008.php.

Mills, P., Sweeney, W. V., Marino, R., and Clarkson, S. A. (2000). New approach to teaching introductory science: The gas module. *Journal of Chemical Education, 77*, 1161–1165.

Mindess, A. (1999). *Reading between the signs*. Yarmouth, ME: Intercultural Press.

Monaco, G. E. (1977). *Inferences as a Function of Test-Expectancy in the Classroom*. Kansas State University Psychology Series, KSU-HIPI Report 73–3.

Mooney, C. (ed.). (2011). Online learning: How effective is the virtual classroom? [Special section]. *The Chronicle of Higher Education*.

Moran, C. (2003). What we have hoped for. *Computers and Composition, 20*(4), 343–358.

Moreno, R., Reisslein, M., and Ozogul, G. (2009). Optimizing worked-example instruction in Electrical Engineering: The role of fading and feedback during problem-solving practice. *Journal of Engineering Education, 98*(1), 83–92.

Mousavi, S., Low, R., and Sweller, J. (1995). Reducing cognitive load by mixing auditory and visual presentation modes. *Journal of Psychology, 87*, 319–334.

Mueller, D. J., and Wasser, V. (1977). Implications of changing answers on objective test items. *Journal of Educational Measurement, 14*(1), 9–13.

Murray, H., Gillese, W., Lennon, M., Mercer, P., and Robinson, M. (1996). Ethical principles for college and university teaching. *New Directions for Teaching and Learning* (no. 66, pp. 57–64). San Francisco, CA: Jossey-Bass.

Murray, H. G. (1997). Effective teaching behaviors in the college classroom. In R. P. Perry and J. C. Smart (eds.), *Effective Teaching in Higher Education: Research and Practice* (pp. 171–204). New York: Agathon.

Myers, C., and Myers, S. (2007). Assessing assessment: The effects of two exam formats on course achievement and evaluation. *Innovative Higher Education, 31*(4), 227–236.

Nagata, D., Cheng, W., and Tsai-Chae, A. (2010). Chinese American grandmothering: A qualitative exploration. *Asian American Journal of Psychology, 1*, 151–161.

Nagda, B. A., Gregerman, S. R., Jonides, J., von Hippel, W., and Lerner, J. S. (1998). Undergraduate student-faculty research partnerships affect student retention. *The Review of Higher Education, 22*, 55–72.

National Research Council. (2000). *Inquiry and the National Science Education Standards: A Guide for Teaching and Learning*. Washington, DC: National Academy Press.

National Science Foundation. (2003). Exploring the concept of undergraduate research centers [Online]. Available at: http://urc.arizona.edu.

Naveh-Benjamin, M., and Lin, Y. G. (1991). *Assessing Students' Organization of Concepts: A Manual of Measuring Course-Specific Knowledge Structures*. Ann Arbor, MI: NCRIPTAL, University of Michigan.

Naveh-Benjamin, M., Lin, Y. G., and McKeachie, W. J. (1989). Development of cognitive structures in three academic disciplines and their relations to students' study skills, anxiety and motivation: Further use of the ordered-tree technique. *Journal of Higher Education Studies*, *4*, 10–15.

Naveh-Benjamin, M., McKeachie, W. J., Lin, Y. G., and Tucker, D. G. (1986). Inferring students' cognitive structures and their development using the "ordered tree" technique. *Journal of Educational Psychology*, *78*, 130–140.

Nessel, D. D., and Graham, J. M. (2007). *Thinking Strategies for Student Achievement: Improving Learning Across the Curriculum, K–12* (2nd ed.). Thousand Oaks, CA: Corwin Press.

Nevid, J., and Mahon, K. (2009). Mastery quizzing as a signaling device to cue attention to lecture material. *Teaching of Psychology*, *36*, 29–32.

Nicol, D. (2009). Assessment for learner self-regulation: Enhancing achievement in the first year using learning technologies. *Assessment and Evaluation in Higher Education*, *34*(3), 335–352.

Nicol, D. J., and Macfarlane-Dick, D. (2006). Formative assessment and self-regulated learning: A model and seven principles of good feedback practice. *Studies in Higher Education*, *31*(2), 199–218.

Nilson, L. (2007). *The Graphic Syllabus and Outcomes Map: Communicating Your Course*. San Francisco, CA: Jossey-Bass.

Nishida, T. (1996). Communication in personal relationships in Japan. In W. Gudykunst, S. Ting-Toomey, and T. Nishida (eds.), *Communication in Personal Relationships Across Cultures* (pp. 102–121). Thousand Oaks, CA: Sage.

Norberg, A., Dziuban, C., and Moskal, P. (2011). A time-based blended learning model. *On the Horizon*, *19*(3), 207–216.

Northern Michigan University. (2010). Suggestions for laptop use in class. *Available at:* http://idt.nmu.edu/laptopuse.php.

Northrop, D. (2011). ZOOM: Teaching time, space, and approaches to knowledge. Available at: http://www.crlt.umich.edu/TIP/2011.php.

O'Donnell, A. (2006). The role of peers and group learning. In P. Alexander and P. Winne (eds.), *Handbook of Educational Psychology* (2nd ed., pp. 781–802). Mahwah, NJ: Lawrence Earlbaum.

Ojeda, L., Navarro, R., and Morales, A. (2011). The role of la familia on Mexican American men's college persistence intentions. *Psychology of Men & Masculinity*, *12*, 216–229.

Oliver-Hoyo, M. T., Allen, D. A., Hunt, W. F., Hutson, J., and Pitts, A. (2004). Effects of an active learning environment: Teaching innovations at a Research I institution. *Journal of Chemical Education*, *81*, 441–448.

O'Reilly, R. (2002). You can lead a student to water, but can you make them think? An evaluation of a situated learning environment: An Ocean in the Classroom. *Australian Journal of Educational Technology, 18*, 169–186.

Padilla-Walker, L. (2006). The impact of daily extra credit quizzes on exam performance. *Teaching of Psychology, 33*(4), 236–239.

Palomba, C., and Banta, T. (1999). *Assessment Essentials: Planning, Implementing, and Improving Assessment in Higher Education*. San Francisco, CA: Jossey-Bass.

Patrick, H., Hicks, L., and Ryan, A. M. (1997). Relations of perceived social efficacy and social goal pursuit to self-efficacy for academic work. *Journal of Early Adolescence, 17*(2), 109–128.

Paris, S. G., Lipson, M. Y., and Wixson, K. K. (1983). Becoming a strategic reader. *Contemporary Educational Psychology, 8*, 293–316.

Paris, S. G., and Paris, A. H. (2001). Classroom applications of research on self-regulated learning. *Educational Psychologist, 36*, 89–101.

Park, Y., and Kim, B. (2008). Asian and European American cultural values and communication styles among Asian American and European American college students. *Cultural Diversity and Ethnic Minority Psychology, 13*, 47–56.

Parkes, J., Fix, T., and Harris, M. (2003). What syllabi communicate about assessment in college classrooms. *Journal of Excellence in College Teaching. 14*(1), 61–83.

Pascarella, E. T., and Terenzini, F. (1991, 2005). *How College Affects Students* (Vol. 1 and 2). San Francisco, CA: Jossey-Bass.

Peckham, G., and Sutherland, L. (2000). The role of self-assessment in moderating students' expectations. *South African Journal of Higher Education, 14*, 75–78.

Peper, R. J., and Mayer, R. E. (1978). Note taking as a generative activity. *Journal of Educational Psychology, 70*(4), 514–522.

Perkins, D. (2005). The case for a cooperative studio classroom: Teaching petrology in a different way. *Journal of Geoscience Education, 53*, 101–109.

Perry, R. P., Stupinsky, R. H., Hall, N. C., Chipperfield, J. G., and Weiner, B. (2010). Bad starts and better finishes: Attributional retraining and initial performance in competitive achievement settings. *Journal of Social and Clinical Psychology, 29*, 668–700.

Perry, W. G., Jr. (1970). *Forms of Intellectual and Ethical Development in the College Years: A Scheme*. New York: Holt, Rinehart, and Winston.

———. (1981). Cognitive and ethical growth: The making of meaning. In A. W. Chickering (ed.), *The Modern American College* (pp. 76–116). San Francisco, CA: Jossey-Bass.

Phillips, H. J., and Powers, R. B. (1979). The college seminar: Participation under instructor-led and student-led discussion groups. *Teaching of Psychology*, 6(2), 67–70.

Pike, G., and Kuh, G. (2005). First- and second-generation college students: A comparison of their engagement and intellectual development. *Journal of Higher Education*, 76, 276–300.

Pintrich, P. R. (ed.). (1995, Summer). Understanding self-regulated learning. *New Directions for Teaching and Learning* (no. 63). San Francisco, CA: Jossey-Bass.

———. (2002). The role of metacognitive knowledge in learning, teaching and assessing. *Theory into Practice*, *41*(4), 219–225.

———. (2003). Motivation and classroom learning. In W. M. Reynolds and G. E. Miller (eds.), *Handbook of Psychology: Educational Psychology* (Vol. 7, pp. 103–122). New York: Wiley.

Pintrich, P. R., and De Groot, E. V. (1990). Motivational and self-regulated learning components of classroom academic performance. *Journal of Educational Psychology*, *82*, 33–40.

Pintrich, P. R., and Garcia, T. (1991). Student goal orientation and self-regulation in the college classroom. In M. Maehr and P. R. Pintrich (eds.), *Advances in Motivation and Achievement: Goals and Self-Regulatory Processes* (vol. 7, pp. 371–402). Greenwich, CT: JAI Press.

Pintrich, P., and Schunk, D. (2002). *Motivation in Education: Theory, Research and Applications* (2nd ed.). Upper Saddle River, NJ: Merrill/Prentice Hall.

Pressley, M., and McCormick, C. B. (1995). *Cognition, Teaching and Assessment*. New York: HarperCollins.

Pressley, M., Wood, E., Woloshyn, V. E., Martin, V., King, A., and Menke, D. (1992). Encouraging mindful use of prior knowledge: Attempting to construct explanatory answers facilitates learning. *Educational Psychologist*, *27*(1), 91–109.

Prieger, J. E., and Hu, W. (2008). The broadband digital divide and the nexus of race, competition, and quality. *Information Economics and Policy*, *20*, 150–167.

Prince, M. (2004). Does active learning work? A review of the research. *Journal of Engineering Education*, *93*(3), 223–231.

Pulvers, K., and Diekhoff, G. (1999). The relationship between academic dishonesty and college classroom environment. *Research in Higher Education*, *40*(4), 487–498.

Rae, T. (2011, January 14). As Wikipedia turns 10, It focuses on ways to improve student learning. *Chronicle of Higher Education: Wired Campus*. Available at: http://chronicle.com/blogs/wiredcampus/as-wikipedia-turns-10-it-focuses-on-ways-to-improve-student-learning/29067.

Reybold, L. (2008). The social and political structuring of faculty ethicality in education. *Innovative Higher Education*, *32*(5), 279–295.

Reyes, P., Scribner, J., and Scribner, A. (eds.). (1999). *Lessons from High Performing Hispanic Schools*. New York: Teachers College Press.

Rhoads, R., and Howard, J. (eds.) (1998, Winter). Academic service learning: A pedagogy of action and reflection. In *New directions for teaching and learning* (no. 73). San Francisco, CA: Jossey-Bass.

Robin, B. (2011). The educational uses of digital storytelling. Available at: http://digitalstorytelling.coe.uh.edu.

Robinson, F. P. (1961). *Effective Study.* New York: Harper-Row Publishers.

Robinson, R. (2001, September). Calibrated peer review: An application to increase student reading and writing skills. *American Biology Teacher, 63*(7), 478–480.

Rockinson-Szapkiw, A., and Szapkiw, M. (2011). Engaging higher education students through tweeting. In S. Barton et al. (eds.), *Proceedings of Global Learn Asia Pacific 2011* (pp. 360–364). Chesapeake, VA: AACE Publications.

Rodabaugh, R. (1996). Institutional commitment to fairness in teaching. *New Directions for Teaching and Learning* (no. 66, pp. 37–46). San Francisco, CA: Jossey-Bass.

Roehling, P., Kooi, T., Dykema, S., Quisenberry, B., and Vandlen, C. (2010). Engaging the millennial generation in class discussion. *College Teaching, 59*(1), 1–6.

Roig, M. (2008). The relationship between learning style preference and achievement in the adult student in a multicultural college. *Dissertation Abstracts: Section A: Humanities and Social Sciences, 69*(3-A), 853.

Romiszowski, A., and Mason, R. (2004). Computer-mediated communication. In D. H. Jonassen (ed.), *Handbook for Research in Educational Communications and Technology* (2nd ed., pp. 397–432). Mahwah, NJ: Lawrence Erlbaum.

Roselli, R., and Brophy, S. (2006). Experiences with formative assessments in engineering classrooms. *Journal of Engineering Education, 95*(4), 325–333.

Roser, C. (2008). Encouraging students to read the texts: The jigsaw method. *Teaching History: A Journal of Methods, 33*, 1, 20–28.

Rovai, A. (2007). Facilitating online discussions effectively. *Internet and Higher Education, 10*, 77–88.

Royer, P. N. (1977). Effects of specificity and position of written instructional objectives on learning from a lecture. *Journal of Educational Psychology, 69*, 40–45.

Ruhl, K. L., Hughes, C. A., and Schloss, P. J. (1987). Using the pause procedure to enhance lecture recall. *Teacher Education and Special Education, 10*, 14–18.

Ruiz, P. (1995). Assessing, diagnosing and treating culturally diverse individuals: A Hispanic perspective. *Psychiatric Quarterly, 66*, 329–341.

Ruiz, R., and Padilla, A. (1977). Counseling Latinos. *Personnel and Guidance Journal, 55*, 401–408.

Ryan, R., and Deci, E. (2000). When rewards compete with nature: The undermining of intrinsic motivation and self-regulation. In C. Sansone and J. Harackiewicz (eds.), *Intrinsic and Extrinsic Motivation: The Search for Optimal Motivation and Performance*. (pp. 14–48) San Diego, CA: Academic Press.

Sadler, D. R. (1989). Formative assessment and the design of instructional systems. *Instructional Science, 18*, 119–144.

Sage, G. (1991). Counseling American Indian adults. In C. Lee and B. Richardson (eds.), *Multicultural Issues in Counseling: New Approaches to Diversity* (pp. 23–35). Alexandria, VA: American Counseling Association.

Sanchez, A., and Atkinson, D. (1983). Mexican American cultural commitment, preference for counselor ethnicity, and willingness to use counseling. *Journal of Counseling Psychology, 30*, 215–220.

Saville, B., Zinn, T., Brown, A., and Marchuk, K. (2010). Syllabus detail and students' perceptions of teacher effectiveness. *Teaching of Psychology, 37*(3), 186–189.

Schofield, T., Parke, R., Castaneda, E., and Coltrane, S. (2008). Patterns of gaze between parents and children in European American and Mexican American families. *Journal of Nonverbal Behavior, 32*, 171–186.

Schomberg, S. F. (1986, April). *Involving High Ability Students in Learning Groups*. Paper presented at AERA in San Francisco, CA.

Schön, D. (1983). *The Reflective Practitioner*. San Francisco, CA: Jossey-Bass.

Schrader-Kniffki, M. (2007). Silence and politeness in Spanish and Zapotec interactions (Oaxaca, Mexico). In M. Placencia and C. Garcia (eds.), *Research on Politeness in the Spanish-Speaking World* (pp. 305–335). Mahwah, NJ: Lawrence Erlbaum.

Schunk, D. H., Pintrich, P. R., and Meece, J. L. (2008). *Motivation in Education: Theory, Research, and Applications* (3rd ed.). Upper Saddle River, NJ: Prentice Hall.

Schunk, D. H., and Zimmerman, B. J. (eds.). (1998). *Self-Regulated Learning: From Teaching to Self-Reflective Practice*. New York: Guilford.

———. (2003). Self-regulation and learning. In W. M. Reynolds and G. E. Miller (eds.), *Handbook of Psychology: Educational Psychology* (Vol. 7, pp. 59–78). New York: John Wiley.

———. (2007). *Motivation and Self-Regulated Learning: Theory, Research and Applications*. Mahwah, NJ: Erlbaum.

Schutz, P. A., and Pekrun, R. (2007). *Emotion in Education*. San Diego, CA: Academic Press.

Schwartz, B. (2004) The Paradox of Choice: Why More is Less. New York: ECCO.

Seymour, E., and Hewitt, N. (1997). *Talking About Leaving: Why Undergraduates Leave the Sciences*. Boulder, CO: Westview Press.

Shaffer, D., and Collura, M. (2009). Evaluating the effectiveness of a personal response system in the classroom. *Teaching of Psychology, 36*(4), 273–277.

Shelfstad, J. (2011). How Flat World Knowledge is transforming college textbook publishing. *Publishers' Research Quarterly, 27,* 254–258.

Shulman, G. M., Luechauer, D. L., and Shulman, C. (1996). Assessment for learner empowerment: The meta-cognitive map. In T. W. Banta, J. P. Lund, K. E. Black, and F. W. Oblander (eds.), *Assessment in Practice: Putting Principles to Work on Colleges Campuses.* (pp. 281–284) San Francisco, CA. Jossey-Bass.

Shulman, L. (2002). Fostering a scholarship of teaching and learning. Louise McBee Lecture series, Institute of Higher Education, University of Georgia, Athens, GA.

Siemens, G. (2004). A learning theory for the digital age. *Available at:* http://www.elearnspace.org/Articles/connectivism.htm.

Silverman, R., Welty, W. M., and Lyon, S. (1994). *Educational Psychology Cases for Teacher Problem Solving*. New York: McGraw-Hill.

Singham, M. (2009, October 11). More than 'millennials': Colleges must look beyond generational stereotypes. *Chronicle of Higher Education.* Retrieved August 29, 2012. Available at: http://chronicle.com/article/More-Than-Millennials-/48751/.

Slattery, J., and Carlson, J. (2005). Preparing an effective syllabus. *College Teaching, 53*(4), 159–164.

Smith, D. (1996). The ethics of teaching. In *New Directions for Teaching and Learning* (no. 66, pp. 5–14). San Francisco, CA: Jossey-Bass.

Smith, K., Sheppard, S., Johnson, D., and Johnson, R. (2005). Pedagogies of engagement: Classroom-based practices. *Journal of Engineering Education, 9*(1), 87–101.

Smith, M. K., Wood, W. B., Adams, W. K., Wieman, J. K., Knight, J. N., Guild, N., and Su, T. T. (2009). Why peer discussion improves student performance on in-class concept questions. *Science, 323* (5910), 122–124.

Smith, T., and Silva, L. (2011). Ethnic identity and personal well-being of people of color: A meta-analysis.. *Journal of Counseling Psychology, 58,* 42–60.

Smith, W. F., and Rockett, F. C. (1958). Test performance as a function of anxiety, instructor, and instructions. *Journal of Educational Research, 52,* 138–141.

Snow, R. E., and Peterson, P. L. (1980). Recognizing differences in student attitudes. *New Directions for Teaching and Learning* (no. 2). San Francisco, CA: Jossey-Bass.

Solomon, D., Rosenberg, L., and Bezdek, W. E. (1964). Teacher behavior and student learning. *Journal of Educational Psychology, 55,* 23–30.

Sorcinelli, M., and Elbow, P. (1997). Writing to learn: Strategies for assigning and responding to writing across the disciplines. In *New directions for teaching and learning.* San Francisco, CA: Jossey-Bass.

Spence-Brown, R. (2001). The eye of the beholder: Authenticity in an embedded assessment task. *Language Testing, 18*(4), 463–481.

Stanton, H. (1992). *The University Teacher,* 13(1). A newsletter of The University of Tasmania.

Steele, C., and Aronson, J. (1995). Stereotype threat and the intellectual test performance of African Americans. *Journal of Personality and Social Psychology, 69,* 797–811.

Sternberg, R. J. (1985). *Beyond IQ: A Triarchic Theory of Intelligence.* Cambridge, UK: Cambridge University Press.

Sternberg, R. J. (2003). *The Rainbow Project: What's wrong with college admissions and how psychology can fix it.* Invited address at the annual convention of the American Psychological Association, Toronto, Canada.

Sternberg, R. J., and Grigorenko, E. L. (2008). In L. A. Suzuki and J. G. Ponterotte (eds.), *Handbook of Multicultural Assessment: Clinical, Psychological, and Educational Applications.* (pp. 449–470) San Francisco, CA: Jossey-Bass.

Sternberg, R. J., and Kaufman, S. (eds.). (2011). *The Cambridge Handbook of Intelligence. Cambridge Handbooks in Psychology.* New York: Cambridge University Press.

Stickney, J. (2010). Reconciling forms of Asian humility with assessment practices and character education programs in North America. *Ethics and Education, 5,* 67–80.

Stowell, J., and Nelson, J. (2007). Benefits of electronic audience response systems on student participation, learning and emotion. *Teaching of Psychology, 34*(4), 253–258.

Strike, K. (1988). The ethics of teaching. *Phi Delta Kappan, 70*(2), 156–158.

Stuart, R. (2004). Twelve practical suggestions for achieving multicultural competence. *Professional Psychology, 35,* 3–9.

Sue, D. (2006). The invisible Whiteness of being: Whiteness, White supremacy, White privilege, and racism. In M. Constantine and D. Sue (eds.), *Addressing racism: Facilitating cultural competence in mental health and educational settings* (pp. 15–30). Boston, MA: Ebooks Corporation Limited.

Sue, D. W., and Sue, D. (2007). *Counseling the Culturally Diverse: Theory and Practice* (5th ed.). New York: Wiley.

Suinn, R. (2007). "Welcome" spells the route to a better climate. *gradPSYCH, 5,* 40.

Suinn, R. (2010). Reviewing acculturation: A factor affecting health, adjustment, school achievement, and counseling. *Asian American Journal of Psychology, 1,* 5–17.

Sutton, C., and Broken Nose, M. (1996). American Indian families: An overview. In M. McGoldrick, J. Giordano, and J. Pearce (eds.), *Ethnicity and Family Therapy* (2nd ed., pp. 31–44). New York: Guilford Press.

Svinicki, M. (2004). *Learning and Motivation in the Postsecondary Classroom.* San Francisco, CA: Jossey-Bass.

Svinicki, M. D. (2008). The scout's motto: Be prepared. *National Teaching Learning Forum, 17*(5), 12.

Svinicki, M. D., Hagen, A. S., and Meyer, D. K. (1995). Research on learning: A means to enhance instructional methods. In R. Menges and M. Weimer (eds.), *Better Teaching and Learning in College: Toward More Scholarly Practice* (pp. 257–296). San Francisco, CA: Jossey-Bass.

Sweeting, L. (1999). Ethics in science for undergraduate students. *Journal of Chemical Education, 76,* 369–372.

Swinomish Tribal Mental Health Project. (1991). *A Gathering of Wisdoms.* LaConner, WA: Swinomish Tribal Community.

Tabachnick, B., Keith-Spiegel, P., and Pope, K. (1991). Ethics of teaching: Beliefs and behaviors of psychologists as educators. *American Psychologist, 46*(5), 506–515.

Tatum, B. (1993). Coming of age: Black youth in White Communities. *Focus, 7*(2), 15–16.

Tchudi, S. (ed.). (1997). *Alternatives to Grading Student Writing*. Urbana, IL: NCTE.

Tewari, N., and Alvarez, A. (2009). *Asian American Psychology: Current Perspectives.* New York: Routledge/Taylor and Francis Group.

Thompson, V., Bazile, A., and Akbar, M. (2004). African Americans' perceptions of psychotherapy and psychotherapists. *Professional Psychology: Research and Practice, 35,* 19–26.

Tien, L. T., Rickey, D., and Stacy, A. M. (1999). The MORE thinking frame: Guiding students' thinking in the laboratory. *Journal of College Science Teaching, 28*(5), 318–324.

Tileston, D. (2005). *10 Best teaching practices* (3rd ed). Thousand Oaks, CA: Corwin.

Ting-Toomey, S., and Chung, L. (2005). *Understanding Intercultural Communication.* Los Angeles, CA: Roxbury.

Todd, N., and Abrams, E. (2011). White dialectics: A new framework for theory, research, and practice with White students. *The Counseling Psychologist, 39,* 353–395.

Topping, K. (1998, Fall). Peer assessment between students in colleges and universities. *Review of Educational Research, 68*(3), 249–276.

Toppino, T. C., and Brochin, H. A. (1989). Learning from tests: The case of true-false examinations. *Journal of Educational Research, 83,* 119–124.

Travers, R. (1950). *How To Make Achievement Tests.* New York: Odyssey Press.

Trend Data. (2009). Demographics of Internet Users. *Pew Internet and American Life Project* [Online]. Available at: http://www.pewinternet.org/Data-Tools/Download-Data/Trend-Data.aspx.

Trimble, J. (2010). The virtues of cultural resonance, competence, and relational collaboration with Native American Indian communities: A synthesis of the counseling and psychotherapy literature. *The Counseling Psychologist, 38,* 243–256.

Tufte, E. (2003). *The Cognitive Style of PowerPoint*. Cheshire, CT: Graphics Press.

Uchida, D., Cetron, M., and McKenzie, F. (1996). *Preparing Students for the 21st Century*. Arlington, VA: American Association of School Administrators.

Van Overwalle, F., Segebarth, K., and Goldchstein, M. (1989). Improving performance of freshmen through attributional testimonies from fellow students. *British Journal of Educational Psychology, 59,* 75–85.

Vea, B. (2008). The college experiences of Filipina/o Americans and other AAPI subgroups disaggregating the data. *Dissertation Abstracts: Section A: Humanities and Social Sciences; 69*(3-A0), 908.

Veenstra, M. V. J., and Elshout, J. J. (1995). Differential effects of instructional support on learning in simulation environments. *Instructional Science, 22,* 363–383.

Verbos, A., Kennedy, D., and Gladstone, J. (2011). "Coyote was walking. . .": Management education in Indian Time. *Journal of Management Education, 35,* 51–65.

Von Secker, C. (2002). Effects of inquiry-based teacher practices on science excellence and equity. *Journal of Educational Research, 95,* 151–160.

Von Secker, C., and Lissitz, R. W. (1999). Estimating the impact of instructional practices on student achievement in science. *Journal of Research in Science Teaching, 36,* 110–112.

Vontress, C., and Epp, L. (1997). Historical hostility in the African American client: Implications for counseling. *Journal of Multicultural Counseling and Development, 25,* 170–184.

Wales, C. E., and Nardi, A. (1982, November). *Teaching decision making with guided design*. Idea paper, No. 9. Kansas State University, Center for Faculty Evaluation and Development, Manhattan, KS.

Walker, A., and MacPhee, D. (2011). How home gets to school: Parental control strategies predict children's school readiness. *Early Childhood Research Quarterly*, 26, 355–364.

Walker, M. (2006). An investigation into written comments on assignments: Do students find them usable? *Assessment and Evaluation in Higher Education, 34*(1), 67–78.

Walvoord, B., and Anderson, V. (1998). *Effective Grading: A Tool for Learning and Assessment*. San Francisco, CA: Jossey-Bass.

Weaver, M. R. (2006). Do students value feedback? Students' perceptions of tutors' written responses. *Assessment and Evaluation in Higher Education, 31*(3), 379–394.

Weaver, R. L., II, and Cotrell, H. W. (1985). Mental aerobics: The half-sheet response. *Innovative Higher Education, 10*, 23–31.

Weiner, B. (2001). Intrapersonal and interpersonal theories of motivation from an attribution perspective. In F. Salili, C. Chiu, and Y. Hong (eds.), *Student Motivation: The Culture and Context of Learning* (pp. 17–30). New York: Kluwer.

Weinstein, C. E. (1994). Strategic learning/strategic teaching: Flip sides of a coin. In P. R. Pintrich, D. R. Brown, and C. E. Weinstein (eds.), *Student Motivation, Cognition, and Learning: Essays in Honor of Wilbert J. McKeachie*. (pp. 257–274) Hillsdale, NJ: Erlbaum.

Weinstein, C. E., and Acee, T. W. (2008). Cognitive view of learning. In N. J. Salkind (ed.), *Encyclopedia of Educational Psychology*. (pp. 164–165) Thousand Oaks, CA: Sage Publications, Inc.

Weinstein, C. E., Acee, T. W., and Jung, J. H. (2010). Learning strategies. In B. McGaw, P. L. Peterson, and E. Baker (eds.), *International encyclopedia of education* (3rd ed., pp. 323–329). New York, NY: Elsevier.

Weinstein, C. E., Husman, J., and Dierking, D. R. (2000). Self-regulation interventions with a focus on learning strategies. In M. Boekaerts, P. Pintrich, and M. Zeidner (eds.), *Handbook of Self-Regulation*. San Diego, CA: Academic Press.

Weinstein, C. E., and Mayer, R. E. (1986). The teaching of learning strategies. In M. Wittrock (ed.), *Handbook of Research on Teaching* (3rd ed., pp. 315–327). New York: Macmillan.

Wenzel, T. J. (1995). A new approach to undergraduate analytical chemistry. *Analytical Chemistry, 67*, 470A–475A.

———. (1998). Cooperative group learning in undergraduate analytical chemistry. *Analytical Chemistry, 70*(23), 790A–795A.

Wentzel, K., and Wigfield, A. (1998). Academic and social motivational influences on students' academic performance. *Educational Psychology Review, 10*, 155–175.

Werth, E., and Werth, L. (2011). Effective training for millennial students. *Adult Learning, 22*(3), 12–19.

Wheeler, S. (2010). Digital literacy 1: What digital literacies? Available at: http://steve-wheeler.blogspot.com/2010/11/what-digital-literacies.html.

Whitley, B. (1998). Factors associated with cheating among college students: A review. *Research in Higher Education, 39*(3), 235–274.

Wigfield, A., and Eccles, J. S. (2000). Expectancy-value theory of achievement motivation. *Contemporary Educational Psychology, 25*, 68–81.

Wiggins, G., and McTighe, J. (2001). *Understanding by Design*. Columbus, OH: Merrill Education/ASCD College Textbook Series.

Wilhite, S. C. (1983). Prepassage questions: The influence of structural importance. *Journal of Educational Psychology, 75*(2), 234–244.

Williams, S. (2005). Guiding students through the jungle of research-based literature. *College Teaching, 53*(4), 137–139.

Wilson, J. M. (1994). The CUPLE physics studio. *Physics Teacher, 32,* 518–523.

Wilson, K., and Korn, J. H. (2007). Attention during lectures: Beyond ten minutes. *Teaching of Psychology, 34*(2), 85–89.

Wilson, M., and Sloane, K. (2000). From principles to practice: An embedded assessment system. *Applied Measurement in Education, 12*(2), 181–208.

Wilson, M. E. (2004). Teaching, learning, and millennial students. *New Directions for Student Services* (no. 106, pp. 59–71). San Francisco, CA: Jossey-Bass Publisher.

Wilson, R. C. (1986). Improving faculty teaching: Effective use of student evaluations and consultation. *Journal of Higher Education, 57,* 196–211.

Wilson, T. D., and Linville, P. W. (1982). Improving the academic performance of college freshmen: Attribution therapy revisited. *Journal of Personality and Social Psychology, 42,* 367–376.

Winne, P. (1996). A metacognitive view of individual differences in self-regulated learning. *Learning and Individual Differences, 8,* 327–353.

Winters, F. I., Greene, J. A., and Costich, C. M. (2008). Self-regulation of learning within computer-based learning environments: A critical analysis. *Educational Psychology Review, 20,* 429–444.

Wood, D., Wood, H., and Middleton, D. (1978). An experimental evaluation of four face-to-face teaching strategies. *International Journal of Behavioural Development, 1,*131–147.

Yamauchi, L., and Tharp, R. (1995). Culturally compatible conversations in Native American classrooms. *Linguistics and Education, 74,* 349–367.

Yan, L., and Kember, D. (2004). Avoider and engager approaches by out-of-class groups: The group equivalent to individual learning approaches. *Learning and Instruction, 14,* 27–49.

Yoder, J., and Hochevar, C. (2005). Encouraging active learning can improve students' performance on examinations. *Teaching of Psychology, 32*(2), 91–95.

Young, A. (1997, Winter). Mentoring, modeling, monitoring, motivating: Response to students' ungraded writing as academic conversation. In M. D. Sorcinelli and P. Elbow (eds.), Writing to learn: Strategies for assigning and responding to writing across the disciplines. *New Directions for Teaching and Learning* (no. 69). (pp. 27–40) San Francisco, CA: Jossey-Bass.

Zabrucky, K., and Bays, R. (2011). Helping students know what they know. *College Teaching, 59*(3), 123–123.

Zehner, R., Forsyth, G., de la Harpe, B., Peterson, F., Musgrave, E., Neale, D., Frankham, N., Wilson, S., Watson, K. (2010, July). *Optimising Student Outcomes: Guidelines for Curriculum Development from the*

Australian Studio Teaching Project. Paper presented at ConnectED 2010, 2nd International Conference on Design Education, Sydney.

Zhu, E. (2007). Teaching with Clickers. CRLT Occasional Paper, No. 22. Ann Arbor, MI: University of Michigan Center for Research on Learning and Teaching [Online]. Available at: http://www.crlt.umich.edu/publinks/CRLT_no22.pdf.

Zimmerman, B. J. (1989). Models of self-regulated learning and academic achievement. In B. J. Zimmerman and D. H. Schunk (eds.), *Self-Regulated Learning and Academic Achievement: Theory, Research, and Practice* (pp. 1–25). New York: Springer-Verlag.

———. (1990). Self-regulated learning and academic achievement [Special issue]. *Educational Psychologist, 25*(1).

———. (1994). Dimensions of academic self-regulation: A conceptual framework for education. In D. H. Schunk and B. J. Zimmerman (eds.), *Self-Regulation of Learning and Performance: Issues and Educational Applications* (pp. 3–19). Hillsdale, NJ: Erlbaum.

———. (1998). Developing self-fulfilling cycles of academic regulation: An analysis of exemplary instructional models. In D. H. Schunk and B. J. Zimmerman (eds.), *Self-Regulated Learning: From Teaching to Self-Reflective Practice* (pp. 1–19). New York: Guilford.

———. (2001). Theories of self-regulated learning and academic achievement: An overview and analysis. In B. J. Zimmerman and D. H. Schunk (eds.), *Self-Regulated Learning and Academic Achievement: Theoretical Perspectives* (2nd ed., pp. 1–37). Mahwah, NJ: Erlbaum.

———. (2011). Motivational sources and outcomes of self-regulated learning and performance. In B. J. Zimmerman and D. H. Schunk (eds.), *Handbook of Self-Regulation of Learning and Performance* (pp. 408–425). New York: Taylor & Francis.

Zimmerman, B. J., and Moylan, A. R. (2009). Self-regulation: Where metacognition and motivation intersect. In D. J. Hacker, J. Dunlosky, and A. C. Graesser (eds.), *Handbook of Metacognition in Education.* Boca Raton, FL: Lawrence Erlbaum Associates/Taylor & Francis Group.

Zimmerman, B. J., and Schunk, D. H. (2011) *Handbook of Self-regulation of Learning and Performance.* New York: Taylor & Francis.

Zusho, A., and Clayton, K. (2011). Culturalizing achievement goal theory and research. *Educational Psychologist, 46,* 239–260.

Zusho, A., Karabenick, S., Sims, B. C., and Rhee, C. K. (2007). Learning and motivation in college classrooms. In R. Perry and J. Smart (eds.), *Handbook on Teaching and Learning in Higher Education* (pp. 611–659). Dordrecht: Springer.

Zusho, A., Pintrich, P. R., and Coppola, B. (2003). Skill and will: The role of motivation and cognition in the learning of college chemistry. *International Journal of Science Education, 25*(9), 1081–1094.

INDEX

Note: Notes are indicated by the letter *n*.

A

B

C

D

E

F

G

H

I

J

K

L

M

N

O

P

Q

R

S

T

U

W

Y

Z